Japan at Nature's Edge

Japan at Nature's Edge

The Environmental Context of a Global Power

edited by
IAN JARED MILLER
JULIA ADENEY THOMAS
and BRETT L. WALKER

UNIVERSITY OF HAWAI'I PRESS
HONOLULU

18 17 16 15 14 13   6 5 4 3 2 1

Library of Congress Cataloging-in-Publication Data

Japan at nature's edge : the environmental context of a global power /
edited by Ian Jared Miller, Julia Adeney Thomas, and Brett L. Walker.
    pages   cm
Papers from a conference held in the fall of 2008 near Big Sky, Montana.
Includes bibliographical references and index.
ISBN 978-0-8248-3692-4 (cloth : alk. paper) —
ISBN 978-0-8248-3876-8 (pbk. : alk. paper)
    1. Human ecology—Japan—Congresses. 2. Nature and civilization—Japan—
Congresses. I. Miller, Ian Jared, [date–] editor of compilation. II. Thomas,
Julia Adeney, [date–] editor of compilation. III. Walker, Brett L., [date–]
editor of compilation.
    GF666.J36 2013
    304.20952—dc23
                    2013008411

Designed by Mardee Melton
Printed by Sheridan Books, Inc.

PUBLICATION OF THIS BOOK
IS SUPPORTED BY A GRANT FROM

Figure Foundation

FOR

JAMES R. BARTHOLOMEW
pioneer, friend, and teacher

CONTENTS

PREFACE
BRETT L. WALKER

At 2:46 p.m. on March 11, 2011, a massive earthquake devastated northeastern Japan and caused Earth's most threatening nuclear crisis since Chernobyl. The quake was 9.0 on the Richter scale, the most powerful to ever strike the often-hit country, and it unleashed a tsunami that swept away entire communities. As of July 2011, the death toll and missing had exceeded twenty-four thousand, with thousands of others housed in makeshift shelters. The Japanese archipelago sits precariously on a subduction zone between the Philippine Sea Plate and the Pacific Plate, a tectonic reality that the Japanese are reminded of some fifteen hundred times annually. The March 11 shaker, however, was different than most of these minor ones.

The quake and accompanying tsunami crippled the cooling system at the sprawling Fukushima Daiichi Nuclear Power Plant, eventually causing three of the reactors in the complex to suffer fuel meltdowns. In a desperate effort to cool the plants after the disaster, the Japanese government and Tokyo Electric Power Company (TEPCO) pumped and dumped thousands of gallons of water onto the plants, buying important time but also creating a pollution problem on a colossal scale. In June, when TEPCO installed filters to siphon oil, cesium, and salt from the radioactive water pooled at the plant, the system broke down within hours because high levels of cesium depleted the filtration system. The siphoning system was deployed by TEPCO because the company was quickly running out of space to store the radioactive water from the plant. As of the writing of this preface, Japan was still struggling to come to terms with its new nuclear reality, one that will likely destroy miles of coastline, render hundreds of square miles uninhabitable, expose people and animal life to dangerous levels of radiation, leave tens of thousands of lives in concrete rubble, and spark renewed global concern about the safety of nuclear power. By September 2011, morphological abnormalities had occurred in such insect life as lycaenid butterflies, suggesting that the fictional world portrayed in the film *Godzilla* (1954), one rooted in the anxieties of the atomic age, has become a biological reality, if on a different horizon.

The earthquake and tsunami highlight many of the themes discussed in this volume. Indeed, on March 11 it was hard to discern where Japan's natural disaster ended and where its manmade one began. When the thirty-foot wall of water careened onto Japan's northeastern coastline, moving at the speed of a jetliner, it flooded a highly engineered space, one constructed of cement retaining walls, coastal fishing ports and loading docks, airports and department store parking lots, carefully tended farmlands and plastic greenhouses, and other man-made landscapes. The wall of water washed away people and their pets and farm animals, cutting across the striations of species, social class, ethnicity, gender, and occupation. When the wall of water entered Japan's social and engineered landscape, it was channeled, directed, and twisted by this man-made space, making it not a natural disaster at all. The Japanese ideas of engineering and controlling nature, of inhabiting coastal floodplains and utilizing harbor areas, and of redirecting and dispersing water all determined the direction of this tsunami wave. The natural and the man-made blurred in the churning swell, becoming essentially useless categories. The wall of water was never shown flooding natural landscapes, because there were none. Rather, the wave flooded man-made landscapes. It is the making of this and other engineered landscapes, the exploitation and control of marine and terrestrial environments, and the high environmental toll of these and other practices that are the subjects of this volume. This volume is about the environmental context of a global power.

From its inception, I have viewed *Japan at Nature's Edge: The Environmental Context of a Global Power* as potentially having the same intellectual importance as the five books published for the Conference on Modern Japan (1958) by Princeton University Press (which started with the *Changing Japanese Attitudes toward Modernization* volume), or the *Japan in Transition from Tokugawa to Meiji* project (1986), which featured conferences at the Lake Wilderness Conference Center at the University of Washington (1981), the Quail Roost Conference Center at the University of North Carolina (1981), and White Sulphur Springs, West Virginia (1982). These volumes, which focused on themes surrounding modernization, set the tone for scholarship on Japan for a generation. *Japan at Nature's Edge* expands this previous focus on Japanese modernization to explore Japan's role in global environmental transformation. It is about how Japanese ideas have shaped bodies and landscapes over the centuries. Its premise is that Japan's physical environment and the broader global realm of its ecological footprint are artifacts of its history and culture. If we are to understand the complex problems of a human-fashioned environment, then we must endeavor to understand humans, their cultures, economies, sciences, and societies, because these realms drive their interaction with the natural world.

Considering the global and immediate nature of Earth's environmental crisis, a predicament highlighted by Japan's March 2011 disaster, *Japan at Nature's Edge* brings a sense of urgency to the study of Japan and its global connections. For a nation once defined by its "exquisite harmony" with nature, Japan appears more involved in a total, unharmonious war to transcend nature through overengineering, overfishing, whaling, a popular culture that seeks to transcend all connections to nature, and constructing endless industrial landscapes. Whether *Animal Planet* programming of Japan's whaling fleet trying to evade the made-for-television crew of the *Steve Irwin*, the flagship of the Sea Shepherd Conservation Society's antiwhaling endeavors in the Southern Ocean, or photographs of the Sendai Airport being washed away by the March 2011 tsunami, Japan has become a nation defined less by its economic prowess, clever electronic gadgets, and natural harmony than by its bruising war with the environment. Japan teeters on nature's edge, a country trying to transcend—through engineering, industry, and culture—its earthbound roots. Its popular culture seems to colonize ground in a netherworld, having forsaken its original one. Pikachu of Pokémon fame, for example, or any of the other round-eyed robots, hermaphroditic monsters, or cutesy characters that have so captured the scholarly imagination of Japan specialists in recent years, are symptomatic of a serial alienation from the natural world. Japan may invent new taxonomies of bright-yellow fantastic creatures to fill the void left on an increasingly ecologically barren archipelago, but nature always wrenches humans back to reality. The March 11 tsunami did precisely that. Scholars of Japan can no longer be content to ruminate on Japan's unique cultural contributions to scent judging or trendy animated heroes without asking about the demands that culture makes on nature resources. They must instead bring their considerable talents to bear in order to explain how Japan has contributed to global environmental trends, including regional ecological collapse and global climate change. Like the menacing "black ships" of the mid-nineteenth century, Earth's environmental crisis has forced Japan studies to open up to global concerns and connections, not simply mull over internal, specialized debates. Our future depends on it.

It is hard to deny that the environmental turn has been a latecomer to Japan studies, particularly historical studies. The diffident embrace of the environmental turn stems in part from the perception of Japan as a unique community where culture and nature are in harmony. In this view, the Japanese have crafted an exceptional relationship with their natural world, one that is carefully sculpted like bonsai trees in a temple garden. Consequently, many scholars of Japan explore the country's cultural heritage exclusively without concern for physical and biological legacies. Undeniably, the last two decades of scholarship on Japan prove this point, though, of course, there have been a handful of important exceptions. Scholars have examined far-reaching aspects of Japan's meteoric modernization in the nineteenth and early twentieth centuries, but only a few have begun to explore the deep environmental consequences of modernization. This is changing, of course, but it is doing so slowly. In the current paradigm, the natural world affects the development of culture, but culture rarely affects the development of the natural world. It is important to remember that the Japanese archipelago is a physical manifestation of Japanese culture, not the other way around. This was one of the lessons of March 11, 2011.

The purpose of *Japan at Nature's Edge* is to assert the importance of the environment in understanding Japan's history and to propose a new balance between nature and culture, one weighted much more heavily on the side of natural legacies. Ideas and culture do shape the natural world, because it, like the poetry of Heian aristocrats, has become a relic of history. This approach does not discount culture. Instead, it suggests that the Japanese experience of nature, like that of all human beings, is a complex and intimate negotiation between the physical and cultural worlds. Neither the Japanese islands and their surrounding seas, with their particular biota and chemical makeup, nor Japanese culture, with its manifold forms of economic, social, political, and aesthetic expression, are stable elements in this transaction. Indeed, bodies (human and otherwise) and landscapes (urban and rural) are constituted and reconstituted continually in the transaction.

In the fall of 2008, the contributors to *Japan at Nature's Edge* gathered at the 320 Guest Ranch near Big Sky, Montana, to hold panels and lively discussions on a variety of topics related to Japan's environmental experiences during a Michael P. Malone Memorial Conference. Paula Lutz, dean of the College of Letters and Science, and Thomas McCoy, vice-president for Research, Creativity, and Technology Transfer at Montana State University, generously funded this conference, as did the Institute for Scholarship in the Liberal Arts at the University of Notre Dame, the Reischauer Institute for Japanese Studies at Harvard University, and the Harvard University Center for the Environment. Julia Adeney Thomas and Ian Miller proved generous and smart collaborators, as did Susan Pharr and Ted Gilman. My colleagues at Montana State proved to be their usual boisterous selves and strengthened this volume in a number of ways. I value their insights and suggestions, not to mention their warm hospitality during the conference.

Over the course of four days, the debates proved passionate, and the final written product demonstrates a real shift in ways of thinking about Japan, ones not necessarily fixated on eclipsing the natural orb with a cultural one. I am hopeful that *Japan at Nature's Edge* will spark more interest in Japan studies, particularly in Japan's place in the current global ecological reality.

Writing
Japan at Nature's Edge
The Promises and Perils of Environmental History

IAN JARED MILLER

If that double-bolted land, Japan, is ever to become hospitable, it is the whale-ship to whom the credit will be due; for already she is on the threshold.

—MELVILLE, *MOBY DICK*

Two episodes come to mind whenever I think about *Japan at Nature's Edge*—the promises and perils of a book about Japan's environmental history. Given the association between the Japanese and whaling in the international environmental imagination, it is perhaps appropriate that whales figure in each episode. The first event, the arrival of Commodore Matthew C. Perry of the US Navy, the man credited with "opening" Japan to the West, in the waters of Edo Bay (present-day Tokyo Bay) in 1853 illustrates the capacity of environmental themes to help us rethink even the grandest historical events. The second, the 2009 release of the Academy Award–winning documentary *The Cove*, is far more humble but perhaps no less telling. Hugely controversial in Japan, this disturbing film about a dying dolphin fishery carries many of the issues at stake in Perry's day into our own, illuminating some of the ways that "nature"—abstract and at times even sentimental as an idea but often deadly serious in actual fact—continues to define Japan's place in the world. This introduction uses these two episodes to frame the work of our volume and to show how Japan, in turn, is framed as an environmental subject in the act of writing history.

The Dawn of the Anthropocene

Cetaceans have always been a problem in US–Japan relations. It was the pursuit of large whales that first brought American ships into the seas near Japan in significant numbers, and when Perry steamed into Edo Bay at the head of an intimidating squadron of warships that included two state-of-the-art, coal-burning "black ships," he carried a letter from President Millard Fillmore demanding that shipwrecked American sailors and whalers be returned unmolested, their property intact. Perry's arrival in Japan is commonly thought to signal the country's "dawn to the West," the spark that ignited the nation's emergence as the first non-Western industrial and imperial power, but it might also be seen as marking the opening of a new chapter in the country's long environmental history. After all, it was the pursuit of coal, natural resources, and profit—more than any driving notion of civilization or enlightenment, for example—that brought Perry to Japan's doorstep.[1]

Whale oil was the petroleum of Perry's age, and like petroleum today the pursuit of this diminishing natural resource shaped America's place in the world. Then, as now, the natural environment—then embodied in the blubber of whales, now condensed in the organic compounds of crude oil—influenced even those areas of everyday life that, on the surface at least, appear most purely artificial and "unnatural." Whale products were ubiquitous in manufacturing in both the United States and Japan. Flexible and durable, baleen was the plastic of its day, appearing in everything from the latest women's fashions to early typewriter mechanisms; oil rendered from blubber or spermaceti lit middle-class homes, provided a fixative for cosmetics and a common pharmacological component, and lubricated the gears of modern machinery. Whale oil even became a prominent (if often unrecognized) part of the processed food industry in both places. Margarine, ice cream, and other "creamy" products used it until the 1960s. In these and other ways, the material history of whale products—much like that of petroleum—illuminates otherwise hidden linkages between consumer behavior and ecological change.[2]

By the early 1800s, as America embarked on its extended industrial ascendency, big whales were so valuable that once-vast Atlantic whale populations were quickly hunted into collapse. And so, at the dawn of the industrial age, New England whalers turned their eyes to the distant horizons of the North Pacific, where the American pursuit of profitable natural resources was cloaked in appeals to the moral rectitude of free trade. It was a formative moment. For, as William Tsutsui's chapter on the development of Japan's "pelagic empire" demonstrates, it instituted connections between ocean resources and empire that went on to shape Japan's own emergence as an imperial and naval power.

The natural world, some might say, set the stage for Japan's modernization. Nature and climate have long played this role in histories written about Japan. Harvard professor and former US ambassador to Japan Edwin O. Reischauer opened his classic 1977 textbook *The Japanese* by introducing the land and climate in which his subjects lived out their lives. "The Japanese, like all peoples," he began, "have been shaped in large part by the land in which they live. Its location, climate, and natural endowments are unchangeable facts that have set limits to their development and helped give it specific direction." Today, only thirty-some years later, those facts and limits mean something very different than they did for Reischauer, who tended to see history developing along an ascending path of progress. As we recognize that human impacts on the natural environment are on a scale that was previously unthinkable, the notion that land, climate, and resources are somehow "unchangeable" appears as either a quaint reminder of a simpler time or a willful disavowal of the costs of industrialization. Many of the indices of modernization cited by Reischauer and others of his generation—rates of consumption and the use of inanimate energy sources, for example—are now read as registers of environmental cost.[3]

One of the chief aims of this volume is to account for that change, to reintroduce the natural world to the study of Japan in a manner that neither aestheticizes nature as a repository of national essence (an assumption that is embedded in Reischauer's work) nor treats it as a mere collection of unchanging physical facts. The natural environment, each of the chapters collected here argues in a different way, is never an inert stage.

This complexity is evident in the circumstances of Perry's arrival in Japan. The commodore may not have been taken by the leviathan, as was Ahab, the antihero of Herman Melville's classic *Moby Dick* (published just two years before Perry arrived in Japan), but the sailors shipwrecked on the shores of "that double-bolted land, Japan" were most certainly put there by the power of wind, tide, and perhaps even their cetaceous quarry. Nineteenth-century whalers understood that whales—icons of pristine nature in today's world—are not just spectacular giants to be seen at one's leisure in visits to the theme park or the movie theater; they can also be the stuff of work, the source of wealth, and, in some rare cases, the agents of one's demise.[4] If we follow the whaler's gaze and look beneath the ocean's surface, as the chapters collected in our opening section on Japan's "Oceans and Empires" do, we see dynamic and at times threatening ecosystems shaped by natural and anthropogenic forces. A powerful sense of contingency is added to one of the epochal moments of modern Japanese history when Reischauer's unchangeable facts become fugitive resources, as they do in Micah Muscolino's chapter on the contested history of Sino-Japanese fisheries management. This contingency is further amplified when we learn to see human beings as ecological coactors whose choices, relationships, and actions are in part determined by plants, soils, currents, climates, and even thinking animals—whales, for example.[5]

All that is solid melts into air when modernization and climate change become synonymous. We live, the Nobel Prize–winning climate specialist Paul J. Crutzen argues, in the "Anthropocene," a time when anthropogenic change is so pervasive that it has overtaken geophysical factors as the dominant impact on the earth's climate and ecology, and the pace of that change is accelerating. Human beings have altered the global climate down to the molecular level, Crutzen and others tell us, and the scope of those changes has become so prevalent that the author Bill McKibben and others have begun to argue that we are fast approaching "the end of nature."[6] Not all of the results of this situation have been material, as Christine Marran points out in her chapter. The denatured landscapes of suburban Japan, she argues, have yielded a sense of alienation from animals and the natural world so widespread that the arrival of a single wayward seal in the city's ecologically barren canal system inspired a mass media frenzy in 2002.

We have entered a historical moment defined by a new sense of ecological and environmental limits. Climate change and resource depletion have become part of a shared global environmental vernacular. Nowhere, as shown by our set of chapters on the triple-disaster (earthquake, tsunami, nuclear crisis) of March 11, 2011, is this more the case than in Japan, a country long framed as a "small island nation, poor in natural resources" that is now at the center of a compound disaster with global implications. It is a disaster, Sara Pritchard's chapter demonstrates, born as much of a modernist faith in technology as of anything purely "natural," and it has forced Japanese to reconsider the desirability of nuclear power in a country whose history is punctuated by earthquakes and tsunamis.

Postwar Japan's nuclear-driven energy regime, as Daniel Aldrich explains in his chapter on postdisaster nuclear policy, emerged out of the same Cold War culture that yielded Reischauer's faith in the possibilities of modernization. And, much as Japanese policy makers and consumers are now forced to reassess those choices, this volume argues that environmental issues must be allowed to take a place alongside the central concerns that drive humanistic and social scientific research on Japan. The question of who (or what) the subject of this "environmental turn" should be and to whom (or what) it has a relation are topics of substantial disagreement in these pages, much as they are in the broader field of environmental history. Some authors find agency in the plant or animal worlds, for example, while others limit their scope of inquiry to policy circles or intellectual elites. Underlying this diversity, however, is the shared conviction that environmental problems are, by their very nature, historical. The opposite holds true as well: in different ways and with different implications, each of our chapters demonstrates that historical problems are always environmental in nature. Take our whales, for example. Crutzen argues that it was James Watt's coal-burning steam engine, the progenitor of the engines that drove Perry's flagship, the USS *Mississippi*—lubricated in part by spermaceti harvested from the heads of sperm whales—that ignited the Anthropocene.

Mechanisms such as the steam engine have a social and ecological role that is neglected in many histories of Japan. Technology mediates and blurs our relationship with nature. This idea is at the center of our chapters on "Changing Landscapes," which explore the sometimes unsettling ways in which human technologies have reshaped Japan's terrestrial landscape. Technologies, these chapters suggest, are more than mere systems of machines; they are part of social and ecological worlds. As such, they are not merely "things" that come from outside of society and have an "impact"; rather, they are social products that emerge out of complex economic and environmental contexts, much as Japanese modernity emerged around the moment of Commodore Perry's arrival rather than because of it.[7] Those contexts, as the Perry example serves to illustrate, can be at once local and global. Our interaction with the environment, chapters such as Timothy George's haunting piece on the development of arsenic mining in the small village of Toroku, is often given form by different technologies. Similarly, David Howell, in his chapter on the history of night soil, shows that even human excrement could blur the lines between commodities, technologies, and waste when agriculturalists rendered it as "fertilizer" rather than "shit." From rice paddies to mining sites, environments are often defined by technology, straddling the line between what is "natural" and what is "artificial."

In this sense, *Japan at Nature's Edge* asks us to do more than simply recognize the importance of natural resources in the master narratives of human history. Taken as a whole, the volume shows that careful attention to the role of natural phenomena in human events has the capacity to unsettle the epistemological and physical grounds that prefigure so much academic writing.[8] The book seeks not only to reintroduce the study of the natural environment to the study of Japan but also to resituate Japan *in* the changing global environment. The preposition suggests a double meaning, signaling both the international dimensions of environmental questions and an ecological embeddedness that humanists and social scientists are trained to discount, a struthious habit, Harriet Ritvo has argued elsewhere, that only weakens our work.[9] It is a disciplinary logic that is built into the landscapes of our professional lives, dividing our campuses between the sciences on the one hand and the social sciences and humanities on the other. By locating historical events in the natural environment, the chapters here call this dichotomy into question. The ramifications of this epistemological earthquake are, as my coeditor Julia Adeney Thomas argues in her epilogue, as yet uncertain, but returning our heads to the disciplinary sand is not an option.[10] We argue for a methodology situated at the edge of the traditional disciplines, open to two-way traffic between the sciences and the humanities.

As the evocation of Crutzen's Anthropocene serves to underscore, time itself becomes a problem when we begin to think differently about questions of space and agency. Historians of Japan are accustomed to thinking critically about time, of course. The monopolization of the calendar was one of the most striking accomplishments of the imperial system put in place in the middle of the nineteenth century. Then, as the leaders of the 1868 coup d'etat known as the Meiji Restoration struggled to unite the country following the collapse of the early modern Tokugawa regime (1600–1868), the calendar was reconfigured in the service of the emperor and the state. Where heterogeneous timescales had previously coexisted, the government sought to institute a homogenous system tied to the reign of each emperor. Several of our authors have chosen to frame their chapters within this reign-name system, offering comments on the Meiji (1868–1912), Taishō (1912–1926), Shōwa (1926–1989), and Heisei (1989–present) periods—and often for good reason, since historical actors commonly reckoned their own lives according to the imperial calendar.[11] But, as Phillip Brown's chapter on riparian management in the Echigo Plain makes clear, we are still left asking how the chronology of human social change, measured in years, decades, and centuries, can be reconciled with the diverse timescales at work in the natural world, which range from the rapid life cycles of bacteria, insects, and so on to the *longue durée* of Brown's work or the geologic time of Crutzen's analysis.

Environmental history carries particular risks when focused on areas outside of the developed West. As the evocation of Perry and Melville serves to underscore, the ties that bind empire and environment are thick and tight, and they extend beyond considerations of the material environment into the world of ideology. Writing about the so-called non-West carries a heavy historical burden. Federico Marcon's chapter on the remarkable effort by early modern Japan's Tokugawa rulers to catalog the natural bounty of the archipelago tells us that environmental writing and policy are little different. Appeals to nature and science are powerful political tools, as our chapters on "Vistas and Vantage Points" illustrate in vivid detail. In the age of empire, local populations were often either incorporated into the realm of nature as animal-like figures at the very margins of human civilization or exiled from an idealized nonhuman "wilderness" as irrational actors ill suited to the "proper" stewardship of land and resources. In the first instance, the results ranged from enslavement and genocide to bigotry and the condescension of the "civilizing mission." The second, far less carefully considered until quite recently, has been central to the development of modern conservationism. Nature preserves were often carved from land already in use by indigenous communities. When an area was deemed worthy of protection, those communities were typically excluded from ecosystems that they had in fact helped to create in the first place. In such cases, the pristine nature of the environmental imagination became a tool of exclusion as well as preservation.[12]

This dynamic might be called "environmental orientalism," since it functions along much the same axes as Edward Said's classic analysis of colonial and postcolonial discourse, and it continues to shape environmental ideas and policy in

Japan and elsewhere to this day.[13] Environmentalism can cloak power in the moralizing, rights-based, or objective language of environmental protection, animal rights, or science, especially—as Takehiro Watanabe's chapter on attempts by villagers to win compensation for corporate pollution caused by the powerful multinational Sumitomo Corporation shows—when "people" are excluded from "nature."

Japan's history tells us that the pursuit of apparently salutary environmental goals—the "zeroing out" of fish-catch quotas in the face of overfishing, for example, or the sequestering of forest areas in order to protect certain animal species—can have disastrous social consequences.[14] Artisanal fisheries were a crucial source of protein in early modern Japan. Income from and access to forest resources were often all that stood between a particular community and famine. One of the enduring lessons of environmental history is the law of unintended consequences. When environmentalists (or environmental historians, for that matter) fail to pay heed to the ideological dynamics surrounding their work, they enter dangerous waters indeed.[15] Even as they demonstrate the value of histories of fisheries and small-scale factory labor, for example, the chapters here tell us that we cannot properly understand the growth of the Japanese Empire or the development of modern conglomerates such as Sumitomo without close attention to the ecological factors that enabled both of those developments.

The Twilight of *The Cove*

Nowhere are these dynamics more evident than in the turbulent politics surrounding my second episode: the 2009 release of the American documentary film *The Cove*. Directed by Louie Psihoyos and featuring Richard O'Barry, who became famous in the 1960s as the man responsible for the capture and training of the dolphins used in the iconic American television series *Flipper*, the film's significance resides in the most intimate aspects of the human engagement with the environment and the strange intersection between our innate human curiosity about animals and mass consumer capitalism. An exposé of a Japanese dolphin fishery, *The Cove* was a great success outside of Japan. It won the 2010 Oscar for Best Documentary Feature and numerous other awards. The film received a considerably cooler reception in Japan, however. Japanese officials and fishermen depicted in the movie warned that they might sue the filmmakers if it was shown in their country, and members of the film's staff reported being physically assaulted by individuals opposed to the movie. "These people would kill me if they could," O'Barry, who has become a dolphin "abolitionist" in the years since leaving *Flipper*, remarks ominously at the beginning of the film.

Homicide seems an unlikely outcome—Japan is the safest large industrial society on the planet—but there is no question that the movie has brought emotions to the boiling point on both sides of the Pacific. What kind of story (and about *dolphins*, of all things) could spark such widespread anger? An "eco-thriller," it turns out, and a consummate example of "environmental orientalism." "The Cove tells the amazing true story of how an elite team of activists, filmmakers and freedivers embarked on a covert mission to penetrate a hidden cove in Japan," according to the film's promotional Web site, "shining light on a dark and deadly secret."[16] It is a tale of animal rights and environmental activism cloaked in the narrative trappings of a spy adventure and informed by the durable tropes of American-style civilization and enlightenment, a distant derivation of the imperial sentiments that informed Perry's "opening" of Japan.

The cove in question is located in the small Japanese town of Taiji, the self-described "cradle of traditional whaling," located along the Pacific coast of Wakayama Prefecture, and it is the center of the town's once-thriving dolphin and whale fishery. Determined to breach this "natural fortress," the well-financed, mostly American team of activists and filmmakers join together with the special effects wizards at George Lucas' Industrial Light and Magic and electronic surveillance gurus to infiltrate the inlet. Daring nighttime raids, camouflaged infrared cameras, and even an elaborate surveillance post hidden inside a moving man-made island finally bring filmmakers and viewers alike into Taiji's carefully guarded waters.

When we enter the bay, we are confronted with a stomach-churning bloodbath. Hemmed in by multiple net lines, the inlet is a watery abattoir, the butchery for a dolphin fishery that slaughtered thousands of animals per year at its peak. Psihoyos takes us right into the heart of the killing, showing dozens of Japanese fisherman riding in small boats above a foaming red sea churning with flailing bodies. Military-grade underwater microphones register the panicked wails of dolphins in distress as silent Japanese fisherman thrust their long-handled knives into the water again and again. Many of these animals will end up cut into crimson cubes under clear plastic-wrap in the refrigerated section of the nation's supermarkets, labeled as "whale" meat, or *kujira,* the reification of an imagined Japanese culinary tradition formulated in the context of late modern economic malaise.

Not all of the animals herded into the cove are killed, however. Much as it was in Perry's day, a complicated international economics is at work in the Taiji fishery, a dynamic that owes a debt to the desires of middle-class American families as well as to the tastes of Japanese consumers. A select few Taiji dolphins and whales are inspected, measured, and removed from the watery corral, destined for careers performing in aquaria and dolphin shows throughout Japan and around the world, including places such as the hugely popular American Sea World attractions owned by Anheuser-Busch. Dolphin and whale shows are a multibillion-dollar industry in the United States alone, and Taiji is a center in the global exotic marine animal trade, providing bottlenose dolphins and false killer whales, among other species, to programs like Sea World, where they become anthropomorphized mascots for the world's oceans. It is a cruel irony of late modern consumer capitalism that these "smiling" environmental icons are harvested along Taiji's bloody coast. "This is all because of Flipper," O'Barry remarks despairingly at one point, arguing that it is the mass fascination with dolphins, which he helped create, that drives the Taiji fishery. A whale sold to one of these shows can fetch as much as $150,000.[17]

The global fascination with dolphins and whales means big profits in the small town of Taiji, and (like workers at most any meatpacking plant in the United States) local fishermen and politicians are understandably eager to protect the industry. Like so many other small towns and cities across rural Japan, Taiji's economy is depressed, and as other sources of income have drained away, together with Japan's global economic reach, the dolphin fishery has become an increasingly important source of jobs and income. It is also, perhaps as a result, a cornerstone of local politics, part of a conservative political strategy aimed at hardening voting blocs in national elections. In this sense, the sponsorship of whaling as a national tradition in Japan shares a basic political logic with the efforts of lobbying groups in the United States such as the National Rifle Association to make gun ownership into a sign of authentic American identity. Both whaling and the gun lobby are tied to significant commercial interests (fishing cooperatives and weapons manufacturers), and public support for each speaks to key political constituencies in their respective countries.

The town has created a marine animal training facility in order to extract maximum value from these charismatic mammals. The training facility is located next to the lavish Taiji Whaling Museum, which also helps manage whaling and fishing activities in the town. Visitors to Taiji, which is marketed nationally as "Whale Town Taiji," can stroll a short distance from the museum to see the town's own extensive performing dolphin and whale shows, housed in an elaborate "Marinarium," a series of "natural seawater pools" in a sealed-off cove (separate from *the* cove). After the show, one can "shake hands with the performing dolphins" for a fee before taking a short walk (past the go-cart track) over to the *Kyōmaru*, a dry-docked decommissioned 208-foot whaling ship. After strolling the decks and sighting down the 75-millimeter harpoon gun, a typical visitor might retire to the White Whale Public Hostel (a nod to Ahab's nemesis) for a full-course whale dinner costing slightly more than $50 per person.[18] Claims of "secret missions" and the covert actions of "'*Oceans Eleven*'–style teams" notwithstanding, whaling isn't a secret here. It is a source of municipal pride, an integral part of the local economy, and a local (as opposed to national) delicacy.

Let us take a moment to linger over the sumptuous menu at the hostel, for it is in these dishes that the horizons of *The Cove* most clearly coincide with those of our book. The full-course dinner is an extravagant meal, including no fewer than six whale-meat courses. Whale bacon and whale carpaccio follow whale sashimi and such regional specialties as *harihari nabe* (whale meat and mizuna greens simmered in broth). The full set includes all of the house specialties, but it is also the most expensive meal on the menu. More economically minded guests might choose the whale sashimi set, and it is easy to imagine that children staying at the hostel from out of town might prefer whale *tonkatsu* (breaded, deep-fried whale cutlets) to the meatier flavors of whale sashimi, since despite efforts to claim whale eating as a national tradition, it is only in recent decades that it has ceased to be either an unusual delicacy or, for many older Japanese, a distasteful reminder of national defeat. Under the US-led Allied occupation of Japan (1945–1952), authorities added whale meat to school lunches nationwide as a source of protein for undernourished postwar kids. Local children, the kids of the same fishermen who work in the cove, might prove less likely to turn away from raw whale, however, since Psihoyos tells us that until quite recently dolphin was a regular part of lunches at the Taiji public schools.

These meals are interesting for any number of reasons, but one stands out as particularly chilling: the meat on the menu is toxic. When visitors sit down to a meal of whale bacon or Taiji's grade-schoolers serve themselves lunch, to the extent that it is bottlenose dolphin on their plates, they are exposing themselves to dangerous levels of methyl mercury, the same toxic compound that devastated the small Japanese city of Minamata in the middle of the twentieth century. There, tainted wastewater was drained into Minamata Bay from a factory owned by the Chisso Corporation, a multinational chemical manufacturer. Highly toxic methyl mercury from the industrial waste bioaccumulated in shellfish and fish that were part of Minamata's thriving local fishery. As tainted marine products made their way onto residents' plates and into their bodies, the men, women, and children of Minamata became predators in a food web that transported lethal toxins along with vital nutrition.[19]

These citizens were not the apex predators in this particular food chain, however. That position, my coeditor Brett L. Walker has argued, was held by a considerably smaller and far more fragile organism: the human fetus. As the mercury pumped into Minamata's waters by Chisso wound its way upward through various food chains, the concentrations of the chemical biomagnified at each step, reaching peak concentrations when they crossed the placental barrier into the developing fetus, several times more sensitive to the neurotoxin than adults. There, together with other toxins such as dioxins and polychlorinated biphenyl (PCB), which also bioaccumulate in the body and warp fetal development, they wreaked a genetic and developmental havoc that left many families bereft and caused many others unaccountable suffering as their children were born disabled, deformed, and in pain.[20] "Minamata disease," now the common international term for extreme methyl mercury poisoning, may be among Japan's grimmest contributions to world civilization.

"This is going to be another Minamata," O'Barry remarks in *The Cove,* illustrating the ways in which environmental history itself can become a tool in contemporary environmental contests. The real effects of dolphin poisoning remain to be investigated, but there is no question that the flesh of Taiji's dolphins is corrupted. The concentrations of mercury found in Taiji's dolphins, according to Professor Endō Tetsuya, a toxicologist at the Health Sciences University of Hokkaido who appears in the film, were two thousand parts per million (ppm), or five thousand times higher than the 0.4 ppm total level of mercury recommended in Japan.

What are we to make of this revelation? Who (or what) is the subject of this story and to whom (or what) is it addressed? The filmmakers clearly seek to channel our outrage and shock toward the liberation of Taiji's dolphins. The slaughter, Psihoyos says, is "just the tip of the iceberg," but the film's core concern remains with the dolphins in the cove. The fact of mercury contamination mainly lends the weight of a human health crisis to the filmmakers' struggle to stop the killing. As an environmental historian, I would direct our attention elsewhere while remaining sympathetic to the plight of Taiji's dolphins: intelligent, highly emotional creatures with rich social instincts.

To the historian's eye, the slaughter in the cove is interesting mainly for what it says about the filmmakers and their audience. For Japanese and American viewers alike, the idea that people eat dolphins may be shocking, but it is hardly a secret. The images from the cove are most important for their visual impact. They give the lie to official assertions that the killings in Taiji are somehow "humane" and "instant," and they play on one of the deep ironies of modern life. Residents of developed economies—Japanese, American, or otherwise—rarely see our food die anymore. Even as worldwide meat consumption has skyrocketed—as of 2006, meat surpassed fish as the largest source of animal protein in even the Japanese diet—the act of slaughter has been increasingly hidden from view. Our meat (and much of our fish) arrives in sanitized shapes that bear no obvious resemblance to the morphology of the animal itself. We crave flesh, but we are allergic to blood and death, and this places us in a unique historical moment.[21] We have become alienated from the source of our food.

Minamata and Taiji are significant in this regard, and they illustrate a crucial aspect of this book: namely, the ways in which bodies, human and otherwise, are woven into the modern industrialized world. This notion of environmental embodiment is at the center of the group of chapters entitled "Between Bodies," a label meant to signal our shared recognition that the human body is itself an ecologically embedded thing. When we focus on the acts of hunting and eating—certainly among the most intimate human encounters with animals and the natural environment—we are forced to recognize the peculiar doubled nature of the human condition. We are not, to borrow a turn of phrase from the environmental historian Linda Nash, "simply agents of environmental change but also objects of that change."[22] In cases of environmental pollution and public health emergencies, this reminder is particularly startling, but as Andrew Bernstein shows in his chapter on the embodied (and deeply gendered) history of weather observation atop Mt. Fuji, the same argument holds true throughout the myriad realms of human practice and experience. Whether we are eating rations atop the Fuji snowpack or snacking on dolphin meat while watching the Taiji dolphin show, we are participating in a food web that can reach, in the latter case, deep into the fecund eddies of the North Pacific, where the cold waters of the northerly Oyashio Current meet the warm southerly flow of the Kuroshio, the hunting grounds for Taiji's bottlenose dolphins, highly efficient social hunters and victims of mercury poisoning much like their killers in Taiji.

As we engineer the environment, as both episodes show and several of the chapters in the present volume demonstrate, we are ourselves engineered in turn, and our reach is often greater than we suspect. The methylated mercury in Taiji's dolphins may be the result of Japanese corporate malfeasance, as it was in Minamata, but it is probably also the product of broader economic and cultural dynamics that reflect the choices of, say, North American consumers as well as the actions of Taiji's residents. Atmospheric mercury circulates and recirculates over vast distances, and it comes from the basic stuff of modern life, billowing out of the coal-burning power plants that supply much of our electricity, settling out of car emissions, and leaching out of cell phones, compact fluorescent light bulbs, and even LCD screens such as the one in front of me right now.

The winner of an Academy Award, *The Cove* is one of the most compelling examples of environmental storytelling in recent years, and it deserves our attention as such. In the space of ninety-six minutes, Psihoyos and his team convert the passive act of watching a movie into an entertaining form of witness. Absent are the slow, careful tones of *An Inconvenient Truth*. The exposition and contextualization of history writing or even a Ken Burns–style documentary are almost entirely lacking. From start to finish, viewers are swept along by a driving narrative that combines a sense of humor with a sense of purpose. When David Bowie's anthem "Heroes" erupts over the closing credits—"I, I wish you could swim/Like the dolphins/Like dolphins can swim/Though nothing, nothing will keep us together/We can beat them, forever and ever/Oh, we can be heroes just for one day"—you cannot help but feel that you are a part of something important. "Audiences laugh, they cry and then they leave the theater saying 'what can I do?'" O'Barry observed in an interview after the film's release.[23]

But stories are never neutral, as Karen Thornber's chapter on ambivalence and ambiguity in Japanese fiction writing on the natural world shows. They are an expression of power, argues the environmental historian William Cronon. "By writing stories about environmental change," Cronon writes, pulling literary theory into environmental history to good effect, "we divide the causal relationships of an ecosystem with a rhetorical razor that defines included and excluded, relevant and irrelevant, empowered and disempowered." In the act of separating story from nonstory, he continues, "we wield the most powerful yet dangerous tool of the narrative form." [24] Psihoyos' film encapsulates both the promise of such stories and the peril that comes when "nature" is allowed to overshadow other less charismatic (in the case of dolphins and their hunters) constituencies, and as such it is important to a book such as ours.

I began this introduction with an evocation of the promises and the perils of environmental history, and I have chosen to talk about *The Cove* because it so clearly encapsulates both of these aspects. Nowhere is this tension more evident than in what is, for me, the most poignant scene in the film, a moment that may mark the twilight of the historical period in some sense initiated by Perry's arrival. It is (quite literally) a stolen moment, captured by cameras hidden by Psihoyos' team in their nighttime infiltration of the cove, and it records a private time of relaxed reverie around a campfire at the ocean's edge. There, a group of Taiji fishermen can be heard in affable conversation. It is the only time in the film we are allowed to hear their voices speaking in measured tones. "Between Midway and Hawai'i," says one, probably a veteran speaking to younger men, "I saw sperm whales from horizon to horizon." He continues somewhat wistfully: "Just like dolphins. There was a time when sperm whales were as plentiful as dolphins." Another man speaks up: "When I was in Chile," he says with evident nostalgia and perhaps a bit of awe, "I saw blue whales from horizon to horizon." He goes on: "Wherever you looked, the ocean was truly black. It was covered with blue whales; my arms were exhausted."

"From horizon to horizon": it is a moment that the filmmakers seem to have chosen as an indictment. The carnage of the slaughter, presumably carried out by these same men, immediately follows the quiet campfire scene. "They're doing it exactly like they did with the large whales," Psihoyos says after the bloody denouement. "They're slaughtering every one they can get." But who, the historians have to ask, are "they"? The fishermen's reverie signals something very different when embedded in a narrative that includes Perry's arrival in Edo Bay. Then, as we saw at the opening of this introduction, Japan marked a fresh horizon in the global history of industrial whaling. As Jakobina Arch argues in her chapter for this volume, the Americans not only brought with them a raft of ideas about civilization and empire when they arrived in Japan, they also sparked the emergence of Japanese pelagic (as opposed to shore-based) whaling, and it is likely that when the men of Taiji sailed into seas black with whales they were joined there by an international fleet. Seen in this light, "they" takes on a different countenance.

Dolphins are welcome companions for suntanned surfers from southern California or Kamakura, Japan. But they are also a source of income to working-class laborers in Taiji, men who in sociological terms may share more with Jurgis Rudkus and the other characters in Upton Sinclair's 1906 novel *The Jungle* or the whalers who inspired Herman Melville's *Moby Dick*—certainly in great measure responsible for the reduction of the world's whale populations—than they do with the voters of the American Academy of Motion Picture Arts and Sciences or shoppers on a trendy street in downtown Tokyo today. As Miyamoto Ken'ichi shows in his chapter on pollution protest and the troubled evolution of Japanese compensation law, "they" are from the social class most likely to experience the painful realities of industrial poisoning in Japan—the same class whose children became apex predators in Minamata.

By resorting to the nationalized logic of "us" and "them," the film not only elides the important role of class in this story, it also recapitulates the same national logic that allows Japanese politicians and Taiji fishermen alike to claim whaling as a sacrosanct aspect of "traditional" Japanese culture in the first place. The rhetorical razor cuts both ways. It is a classic problem of failed imagination, and it speaks to the central purpose of this book. As the men of Taiji know all too well, there are only so many whales in the sea, and when we shift our vision, the preservation of those animals becomes something other than an irreconcilable debate between "us" and "them" over "barbarism" and "tradition." It is not only whales that are disappearing in the Anthropocene but whalers as well, and it is not just dolphins who serve as harbingers of uncertain nature. We commonly associate Perry's arrival with the broader process of modernization that culminated in Japan's emergence as a modern nation-state, but the chapters gathered here suggest the need for a new kind of narrative: environmentally engaged stories that help us begin to reconsider not only who and what counts *in* history but also what counts *as* history.

Notes

I would like to thank my coeditors and the two anonymous readers from University of Hawai'i Press for their detailed comments on this chapter. Andrew Gordon, David Howell, and Crate Herbert also read and commented on the full essay. Our generous hosts and commentators from Montana State University—Susan Cohen, Kristen Intemann, Timothy LeCain, Michelle Maskiell, Mary Murphy, Michael Reidy, Billy Smith, Peter Tillack, and Tomomi Yamaguchi—also contributed to this chapter and to the volume as a whole.

1. Many of the gifts given by Perry to Japanese officials upon his return in 1854—meant as emblems of America's technological prowess and cutting-edge craftsmanship—used spermaceti harvested from the heads of sperm whales and, in the case of perfumes meant for the Japanese empress, ambergris. On Perry's arrival, see Peter Duus, *The Japanese Discovery of America: A Brief History with Documents* (New York: St. Martin's Press, 1997). See also John Dower, "Black Ships & Samurai: Commodore Perry and the Opening of Japan (1853–1854)," MIT Visualizing Cultures, accessed February 1, 2010: http://ocw.mit.edu/ans7870/21f/21f.027/black_ships_and_samurai/index.html. On whales and whaling in nineteenth-century America, see D. Graham Burnett, *Trying Leviathan: The Nineteenth-Century New York Court Case that Put the Whale on Trial and Challenged the Order of Nature* (Princeton, NJ: Princeton University Press, 2007).

2. On the uses of whales and the politics of whaling in Japan, see Hiroyuki Watanabe, *Hogei mondai no rekishi shakaigaku: Kin-gendai Nihon ni okeru kujira to ningen* (Tokyo: Tōshindō, 2006). See also Masami Iwasaki-Goodman, *Ningen to kankyō to bunka: Kujira o jiku ni shita ichi kōsatsu* (Tokyo: Shimizu Kōbundō Shobō, 2005).

3. Edwin O. Reischauer, *The Japanese* (Cambridge, MA: Belknap Press, 1977), 3. Robert E. Ward and Roy C. Macridis offered one of the most commonly cited rubrics of this kind in their edited volume, *Modern Political Systems: Asia* (Englewood Cliffs, NJ: Prentice-Hall, 1963). They placed high ratios of "inanimate to animate sources of energy" at the top of their list of characteristics of modernization. Similar debates shaped the 1960 Hakone Conference that led to the publication of editor Marius Jansen's influential *Changing Japanese Attitudes toward Modernization* (Princeton, NJ: Princeton University Press, 1965). On the conference, see Victor Koschmann, "Modernization and Democratic Values: The 'Japanese Model' in the 1960s," in *Staging Growth: Modernization Development and the Global Cold War*, ed. David C. Engerman, Nils Gilman, Mark H. Haefele, and Michael E. Latham (Amherst, MA: University of Massachusetts Press, 2003), 225–251.

4. On the exhibition of whales in theme parks, see Susan G. Davis, *Spectacular Nature: Corporate Culture and the Sea World Experience* (Berkeley: University of California Press, 1997). It is worth noting that Sea World, in addition to its role as a site of work, play, and profit, is also now one of the few environments in which North Americans still experience deadly encounters with large predators. Tim Desmond, "The Killer Whale Who Kills," *New York Times,* March 8, 2010.

5. William Cronon, "A Place for Stories: Nature, History, and Narrative," *Journal of American History* 78:4 (March 1992): 1347–1376.

6. On the Anthropocene, see Paul J. Crutzen and Eugene F. Stoermer, "The Anthropocene," *IGBP* [International Geosphere-Biosphere Programme] *Newsletter* 41 (2000): 17–18. See also Paul J. Crutzen, "Geology of Mankind," *Nature* 415:3 (January 3, 2002): 23, and Bill McKibben, *The End of Nature* (New York: Random House, 1989).

7. David Nye, *Electrifying America: Social Meanings of a New Technology* (Cambridge, MA: MIT Press, 1990), ix.

8. I am drawing here on Hayden White's notion of "metahistory," or the tropological modes and attendant linguistic protocols that prefigure nearly all history writing. The implications are quite different in this case, however, as we are asking not just for the reconsideration of the linguistic and poetic structures analyzed by White but also for another kind of reconsideration altogether, one grounded in the physical environment as much as it is in the cultural. It is important to note at the outset that these two approaches can be complimentary rather than oppositional. The old debates between advocates of particular

kinds of "theory" and those who would see us look elsewhere for our historical tools miss the mark. Environmental history, as William Cronon argued so convincingly more than a decade ago, must by its very nature address both sides of this equation. Nature and culture are both human creations, and both of them shape human societies, ideas, and bodies. See Cronon, "A Place for Stories," 1347–1376. See also Hayden White, *Metahistory: The Historical Imagination in Nineteenth-Century Europe* (Baltimore: Johns Hopkins University Press, 1975).

9. Harriet Ritvo, *The Platypus and the Mermaid, and Other Figments of the Classifying Imagination* (Cambridge, MA: Harvard University Press, 1997), xii.

10. See also Julia Adeney Thomas, "The Exquisite Corpses of Nature and History: The Case of the DMZ," *Asia-Pacific Journal: Japan Focus,* accessed July 15, 2010: http://www.japanfocus.org/-Julia_Adeney-Thomas/3242.

11. This question is not unique to the study of Japan. Dan Smail has convincingly argued that histories of Western civilization remain unconsciously beholden to another kind of "sacred history," tied to Judeo-Christian chronologies despite the increasingly secular nature of history writing in general. Such choices, he suggests, limit our historical vision in their failure to think carefully about when, precisely, we should begin our histories. Daniel Lord Smail, "In the Grip of Sacred History," *American Historical Review* (December 2005), accessed September 28, 2010: http://www.historycooperative.org/journals/ahr/110.5/smail.html. On the origins of modern historical time in Japan, see Stefan Tanaka, *New Times in Modern Japan* (Princeton, NJ: Princeton University Press, 2004).

12. For the classic analysis along these lines, see Ramachandra Guha, "Radical American Environmentalism and Wilderness Preservation: A Third World Critique," *Environmental Ethics* 11:1 (spring 1989): 71–83. See also Carolyn Merchant, *Reinventing Eden: The Fate of Nature in Western Culture* (New York: Routledge, 2003), and Roderick Neumann, *Imposing Wilderness: Struggles over Livelihood and Nature Preservation in Africa* (Berkeley: University of California Press, 1998). On the related history of parks and green space in modern Japan, see Thomas R. H. Havens, *Parkscapes: Green Spaces in Modern Japan* (Honolulu: University of Hawaiʻi Press, 2011).

13. See S. Sawyer and Arun Agrawai, "Environmental Orientalisms," *Cultural Critique* 45 (spring 2000): 71–108.

14. See Ramachandra Guha, *The Unquiet Woods: Ecological Change and Peasant Resistance in the Himalaya* (Berkeley: University of California Press, 1989). Conrad Totman has shown convincingly that state-led conservation initiatives could be quite effective in early modern and premodern Japan. See Totman, *The Green Archipelago: Forestry in Pre-Industrial Japan* (Berkeley: University of California Press, 1989).

15. Cronon, "A Place for Stories," 1349.

16. http://thecovemovie.com/academynominee.htm. Accessed February 16, 2010.

17. http://www.savejapandolphins.org/. Accessed July 15, 2010.

18. http://www.town.taiji.wakayama.jp/hakubutukan/sub_shuuhennosisetu.html. Accessed February 1, 2010. http://www.town.taiji.lg.jp/hakugei/sub02.html. Accessed February 1, 2010.

19. On Minamata, see Timothy George, *Minamata: Pollution and the Struggle for Democracy in Postwar Japan* (Cambridge, MA: Harvard University Asia Center, 2001).

20. Brett L. Walker, *Toxic Archipelago: A History of Industrial Disease in Japan* (Seattle: University of Washington Press, 2010).

21. Richard W. Bulliet, *Hunters, Herders, and Hamburgers: The Past and Future of Human-Animal Relationships* (New York: Columbia University Press, 2005).

22. Linda Nash, *Inescapable Ecologies: A History of Environment, Disease, and Knowledge* (Berkeley: University of California Press, 2006), 8.

23. "The Cove: Press Notes" (Los Angeles: Oceanic Preservation Society, 2009), 2.

24. Cronon, "A Place for Stories," 1349–1350.

OCEANS AND EMPIRES | I

1

The Pelagic Empire
Reconsidering Japanese Expansion

WILLIAM M. TSUTSUI

The Terrestrial Bias

This essay is based on the modest proposition that understanding imperialism requires us to consider oceans as well as land masses. Given the ongoing and global "fad in oceanic studies," encompassing historians, literary scholars, and social scientists, such a contention is hardly revolutionary.[1] Nevertheless, as W. Jeffrey Bolster has noted, environmental historians have long shared a common "blind spot" when it comes to "the 70 percent of the globe covered by salt water."[2] Following in the wake of Rachel Carson, who in her 1951 classic *The Sea Around Us* wrote naively (or perhaps just optimistically) that man "cannot control or change the ocean as, in his brief tenancy on Earth, he has subdued and plundered the continents," the field of environmental history has demonstrated what J. R. McNeill calls "a terrestrial bias."[3] Departing from such long-standing prejudices, I contend here that imperialism and the patterns of resource exploitation which it has connoted, at least in its twentieth-century incarnations, were not phenomena just of dry-land environments but very much left their marks on the seas as well. Using the case study of the Japanese Empire from the late nineteenth century through World War II, I argue for the importance of a marine perspective on the motivations, methods, and consequences of modern imperialism, as well as for the practice of environmental history.

Oceans and Empires

Historians have generally conceived Japanese expansionism as a purely terrestrial affair. The narrative of Japan's imperial ascent is almost invariably traced through chronologies of territorial acquisition, the annexation of islands, archipelagoes, and regions, along with their populations and natural resources. The milestones of Japanese imperialism are rooted, above all, in military exploits and the domination of land: the Ryukyu Islands in 1871, the Bonin Islands in 1875, the Kurils in the same year, Taiwan (booty of the Sino-Japanese War) in 1895, the southern half of Sakhalin Island and the Liaodong Peninsula (trophies of the Russo-Japanese War) in 1905, Korea in 1910, the islands of Micronesia (known to the Japanese as Nan'yō) obtained during World War I, the absorption of Manchuria after 1931, the drive into China after 1937, and the vast, rapid gains in Southeast Asia, the southwestern Pacific, and even the Aleutians after December 7, 1941. In short, the historiography of Japanese imperialism has to date been concerned almost exclusively with terra firma.

Such scholarly preoccupation with dry land as the basis of empire building has not been peculiar to the Japanese case. In the broader historical literature on imperialism, oceans are seen as conduits or cordons, avenues to empire rather than the sources of empire, paths along which goods, capital, settlers, and military hardware could flow between metropole and colony but not sites of colonization or imperial ambition per se. Alfred Mahan's impression of the oceans, first articulated in 1890, has been persistent: "The first and most obvious light in which the sea presents itself from the political and social point of view is that of a great highway; or better, perhaps, of a wide common, over which men may pass in all directions, but on which some well-worn paths show that controlling reasons have led them to choose certain lines of travel rather than others."[4] Even in more recent analyses, oceans figure only as "transnational contact zones" or "border worlds," liminal spaces never of an empire but eternally amidst them.[5] In the voluminous writings on the British Empire—a maritime imperium if there ever was one—the high seas are usually characterized as the stage for British naval power and the global passageway for British commerce, but they are seldom locations in and of themselves of imperial exploitation and dominion.[6] Thus, although Thomas Metcalf expansively claims that "the Raj comprehended the sea as well as the land" in his innovative study of Britain's "Indian Ocean–centered empire," he ends up falling back on hoary notions of oceanic space connecting the continental outposts of empire but not itself constituting empire.[7] Britannia may have ruled the waves, but, so historians tell us, she left little in the way of a mark upon them.

Much of the difficulty in trying to conceive empires in marine terms derives from the fundamentally terrestrial nature of most of the time-honored theories of imperialism. Hobson and Lenin were clearly not thinking oceanically when they proclaimed the motor of imperialism to be the capitalistic hunger for new outlets for surplus capital and new markets for surplus production, neither of which could apparently be satisfied at sea. Other interpretations of imperialism, premised on "prestige, trade, missionary zeal, strategic locale, comparative advantage," and lebensraum (the provision of new living space for bulging home populations) are only slightly more conducive to an oceanic perspective.[8] Only in theories that locate the imperial urge in the search for secure sources of raw materials—clearly a major motivation in modern Japanese expansionism—does the notion of the seas as sites for empire find easy accommodation with mainstream historical analysis. And while some scholars have proposed capacious definitions of "informal empire"—notably John Gallagher and Ronald Robinson, who famously declared, "The conventional interpretation of . . . empire continues to rest upon study of the formal empire alone, which is rather like judging the size and character of icebergs solely from the parts above the water-line"—no historian has posited how that submerged portion of the imperial iceberg could encompass dominion of the world's oceans.[9]

My assertion in this chapter is that Japanese imperialism cannot be understood adequately without consideration of Japan's incremental domination and exploitation of offshore fisheries in its surrounding seas and, eventually, of much of the western Pacific Ocean. Japan's economic exploitation of the seas paralleled the nation's economic and military advance on the Asian continent. Moreover, the growth of Japan's "pelagic empire," as I call it, was propelled by many of the same political and economic forces—and pursued under the same ideological aegis—as the nation's continental expansion. Perhaps most importantly, bringing the oceans and fisheries into the picture sheds new light on the nature of Japanese imperialism and its motivations. In this, I echo Bernard Klein and Gesa Mackenthun in arguing that "the ocean itself needs to be analyzed as a deeply historical location, . . . material and very real." Along with Klein and Mackenthun, I "take issue with the cultural myth that the ocean is outside and beyond history . . . that a fully historicized land stands somehow diametrically opposed to an atemporal, 'ahistorical' sea."[10] Only by exploring the historical sea can the profound complexities and contradictions of imperialism be fully appreciated, particularly in the case of the Japanese empire.

Fisheries and the Making of Maritime Empire

Japan has a long history of intensive coastal fishing and whaling. Nonetheless, significant offshore fisheries began to develop only in the late nineteenth century. From 1875, after the Treaty of St. Petersburg granted fishing rights in Russian territory to Japanese nationals, Japanese interests quickly established substantial fishing operations in Sakhalin and along Russia's Sea of Okhotsk littoral. In Sakhalin, for example, the number of Japanese fishermen grew from about three hundred in 1875 to over seven thousand in 1904; by way of comparison, Russian fishermen on the island at the time totaled less than two hundred.[11] After the Russo-Japanese War, similar fishing concessions were won off of Kamchatka, and

Japanese firms aggressively developed them. New fishing technologies introduced from the West also significantly expanded the ranges and ambitions of Japanese fishermen. The first modern otter trawler, imported from Britain, was commissioned in 1908, and within five years well over a hundred of them were working the seas around Japan.[12] The first motor-powered tuna boat was launched in 1906, and such vessels were soon pursuing skipjack as far afield as the Bonin Islands.[13] This initial drive to establish fisheries outside Japan's home waters, we should note, took place at the very time that Japan was making its first steps toward establishing a formal terrestrial empire, with the territorial gains won from the Sino-Japanese and Russo-Japanese Wars, as well as the 1910 annexation of Korea. In some of these cases (such as Taiwan), fishermen followed the flag, starting operations after the fact of colonization, but in others (such as Sakhalin and Korea), the fisheries came first, often preceding military and colonial occupation by decades.

In the first thirty years of the twentieth century, the Japanese fishing industry expanded briskly, whether measured in terms of the number of vessels, the employment of fishermen, the volume of catch, or the geographic range of fishing grounds. As the Ministry of Commerce and Agriculture reported, "With the steady increase of population . . . the demand for fishing products is showing a striking advance, a condition still further accelerated by the increasing demand from abroad. Under these circumstances the fishermen can no longer remain satisfied with coasting work alone, but are obliged to a greater extent than ever before to venture into the open sea and even to the distant coasts of Corea [sic] and the South Sea Islands."[14] While technological advances did contribute to the industry's growth, it was this venturing into the open sea and to those distant coasts that most buoyed Japanese fisheries.[15] In the single decade from 1908 to 1917, Japanese offshore catches increased fivefold. Japanese trawlers began plying the East China and Yellow Seas in 1921, systematically entered the South China Sea in 1927, and started hauling bream and croaker from the Gulf of Tonkin in 1928. From soon after Japan's acquisition of the mandated islands of Micronesia, Japanese boats eagerly chased tuna through much of the southwestern Pacific. From 1909, Japanese crabbers were active in the Kurils, and starting in 1922 small armadas of Japanese factory ships worked off the Russian maritime provinces and in the Sea of Okhotsk. In crabbing, as in Japan's other new fisheries, the results were staggering: in 1931, for example, Japan produced 407,542 cases of canned crab, more than eighty times as much as had been processed just a decade earlier.[16]

The drive to expand offshore fisheries was even more intense during the 1930s. After 1931 and the Manchurian Incident, Japanese imperialism entered a new phase: a more aggressive advance on the Asian continent was combined with an increasingly autonomous course in foreign policy and a new determination to create an autarkic economic sphere for the Japanese Empire. But somewhat surprisingly, the accelerated development of the fishing industry was not aimed primarily at food security, at providing ever more marine protein for the home population and the swelling ranks of imperial subjects. Instead, Japanese fisheries in the 1930s were oriented to an unprecedented degree toward exports, selling products to Europe and North America that would generate desperately needed foreign exchange, essential—in spite of the explicit goal of autarky—to keep the oil, iron ore, and rubber flowing into Japan. Thus Japanese crabbers and salmon fishers, their canned catches destined for Western kitchens, stepped up their operations and extended their fishing areas. Canned tuna was also a profitable export, especially to the US market, and Japanese tuna fleets combed virtually the entire Pacific Ocean in the 1930s. Trawlers and factory ships swept the Japan Sea, the Sea of Okhotsk, and the Bering Sea, producing large quantities of fishmeal and liver oil, most of it sold to German consumers. The Japan Pearl Company operated mother ships and more than 150 diesel-powered luggers extracting rich harvests of pearl shell, an ever-bankable export, from the waters north of Australia.[17] Even in the colonial states of Southeast Asia—Malaya, Singapore, the Dutch East Indies—Japanese interests exclusively controlled the supply and distribution of fresh fish.[18] Whaling was also stepped up: in the mid-1930s, for the first time, Japanese whalers ventured beyond their coastal waters and sent factory ships into the Antarctic, their whale oil destined primarily for European margarine and soap factories. In 1930, Japan accounted for only 1 percent of the world's whale catch; by 1938, Japan claimed 12 percent of the total and was the largest producer after England and Norway.[19]

As one booster noted in 1940,

> The fishing industry serves Japan as an important source of foreign exchange. Her exports of marine products amount annually in value to between ¥150,000,000 and ¥160,000,000 and thus rank third after raw silk, and cotton yarn and piece-goods exports. Also, the fish cost practically nothing, whereas raw cotton must be imported for the textile industry and vast mulberry plantations must be maintained by silk-growers. It should be noted, too, that about one-half of those engaged in the fishing industry are farmers and peasants who catch fish as a sideline.[20]

The final point was a significant one, at least to many Japanese policy makers, who recognized during the 1930s that part-time employment of agriculturalists in the fisheries was a crucial support for Japan's depressed rural economy. Seasonal demand just in the canneries of the Kurils provided between twenty and thirty thousand jobs for farmers from hard-hit northeastern Japan.[21]

The expansion of the Japanese offshore fishing industry was, since its inception in the late nineteenth century, nurtured, guided, and underwritten by the Japanese state. Japanese diplomats, for example, always bargained hard for fishing rights in treaty negotiations, especially when it came to guaranteeing Japanese fishers access to the rich grounds off the coast of the Russian Far East. The muscle of the Imperial Navy was also mobilized to safeguard Japanese fishing fleets while intimidating potential competitors from other nations.[22] The government was generous with subsidies for deep-sea operations, first granted in the Pelagic Fisheries Encouragement Law of 1897. In the following decades, Japanese fishermen could count on government aid to improve technology, increase the scale and range of operations, establish fisheries in newly won colonies, and (above all) to promote the production of export goods.[23] Furthermore, the state encouraged, funded, and occasionally even directly undertook elaborate reconnaissance expeditions, where small numbers of Japanese trawlers were sent into distant waters previously unexploited. Such exploratory missions in the 1920s paved the way for large-scale Japanese trawling in the South China Sea, off the Russian coast of the Sea of Japan, and in the Bering Sea; in the 1930s, expeditions were sent to the Mexican Pacific coast, to the Bay of La Plata in Argentina, to the Gulf of Siam, the Bay of Bengal, the Gulf of Carpentaria off of Australia, and even into the Arabian Sea. Had World War II not intervened, regular Japanese fishing operations would doubtless have commenced in many of these promising offshore locations.[24]

To conceive of the seas as a "wide common," as Alfred Mahan did at the close of the nineteenth century, is to ignore the ways in which imperial rivalries and the hierarchies of national power in the age of empire were enacted on—and in turn shaped—the world's oceans. In the case of the yellow croaker fishery in the East China Sea, for example, Japanese trawlers displaced local Chinese fishermen through diplomatic pressure, threats of military force, and technological superiority. As Micah Muscolino has concluded, "the unequal power relations that existed between Japan and China during the early twentieth century exerted a direct influence on patterns of marine resource exploitation."[25] When the differential in national power was unfavorable to Japan, as in the late-1930s dispute with the United States over salmon fishing in Bristol Bay, Tokyo was forced to back down and limit the catches taken by the Japanese fleet. In its maritime conflicts with Russia (and later the Soviet Union), Japan was able to advance its fisheries interests at moments of relative strength, such as in the wake of victory in the Russo-Japanese War, while negotiating diplomatically and posturing militarily during the periods of rough parity and intense imperial contention. The seas of East Asia were also a site for demonstrating international cooperation in the early twentieth century, notably through the 1911 Fur Seal Convention, a pioneering multinational wildlife conservation treaty, which mandated strict kill quotas among the major sealing nations (the United States, Russia, Britain, and Japan).[26]

If the oceans were thus more than mere empty spaces between empires, it is also clear that domination of the seas in the age of imperialism was based on more than just resource extraction. Although fisheries were central to Japan's advance as a pelagic empire, the expression of Japanese power on (and beneath) the waves of the world's oceans was multifaceted. Japanese merchant shipping, for instance, tracked the same trajectory of growth as Japan's deep-sea fisheries did from the Meiji period up to the start of World War II. By the late 1930s, Japan's merchant marine—bolstered by decades of government subsidies and sustained by the nation's active role in global trade—had grown to the third largest in the world, with a fast, modern fleet and a "commanding position in the Eastern seas."[27] Japan, one booster declared in 1909, "should spare no effort to make her Mercantile Marine second to none in the world. When maritime prosperity is achieved, the wealth and military strength of a nation follow immediately. To take part in amicable competition on the peaceful waters of the Pacific rather than to enter upon land contests is this empire's choice."[28] Or as Iwasaki Yatarō, the founder of the Mitsubishi enterprises, was fond of saying, "Encircle the globe with Japanese lines!"[29] Such lines included not just passenger and freighter routes but also undersea telegraph cables, which formed a hidden network on the world's ocean floors. These cables reached Japan in 1871, and by 1923 Japanese interests had laid more than fourteen thousand kilometers of cable under the Pacific and to the Asian continent.[30] After World War I, Japan also controlled the strategic Micronesian islands of Yap, an important junction for trans-Pacific cables and a persistent source of friction with the United States, which was concerned about the security of its submarine cable network.[31]

Japan also mobilized science to better understand the oceans and thus facilitate imperial dominion over them. The historians of science Michael Reidy and Helen Rozwadowski have demonstrated how, in the case of nineteenth-century Britain, scientific exploration of the seas and the advance of empire proceeded in tandem. The emerging field of oceanography "reflected the desire to tackle new frontiers, to extend the realm of imperialist expansion," while "leadership of the modern world required access to, understanding of, and control of the world's maritime frontier," what Reidy tagged a "liquid imperialism."[32] Japan was a latecomer to the scientific study of the oceans but rapidly built its research and training capacity in modern marine science starting in the 1880s. The Imperial Fisheries Institute, founded by private interests in 1889 and brought under the supervision of the Ministry of Agriculture and Commerce in 1897, provided central coordination for research and development programs. A network of government experiment stations, marine laboratories, and oceanographic observation posts (totaling eighty-seven in 1939) ringed the main islands of Japan, and they were seeded throughout the empire, including in Taiwan, Sakhalin, and the mandated territories of Nan'yō. A number of prefectures opened their own fisheries experiment stations, the central government operated numerous oceanographic research vessels, and marine science degree programs were offered at the imperial universities in Tokyo and Hokkaido.[33] Precocious Japanese fisheries oceanographers founded a scientific society as early as 1944 and advanced studies of fisheries hydrography were conducted by Japanese researchers (independent of similar work being done in Europe and America) well before World War II.[34]

Imagining a Pelagic Empire

Especially from the 1930s, the growth of Japanese fisheries and the advance of Japanese interests on the high seas were pursued under an ideological banner and described with a bombastic rhetoric fully consistent with the logic and language of Japanese imperialism. Japan was hailed as the "ocean empire" (*kaiyō teikoku* Nihon) and a "marine nation" (*kaikoku* Nihon); one author proclaimed that, "From the Age of the Gods, Japan has been a kingdom of fisheries (*suisan ōkoku*)."[35] A popular patriotic song from the late 1930s, Fuse Hajime's "Taiheiyō kōshinkyoku" (The Pacific March), stirringly evoked Japan's oceanic dreams:

> Our ambition is infinite
> We will show the world the resolve
> Of our ocean people.
> Looking up at the battleship flag
> We humbly take in the sight
> Of the chrysanthemum against the ship's bow
> The Pacific, our ocean
> The wind sparkling on this very morning
> Let's extend our imperial homeland's lifeline![36]

Japan's heady drive to world leadership in fishing production was explained as a natural process; as "a nation of born fishermen," surrounded on all four sides by the seas, Japan was environmentally, historically, and culturally conditioned to dominate regional and global fisheries, at least according to some commentators.[37] "Passing their lives on these waters," Baron Murata Tamotsu declared in 1909, "our ancestors were emboldened to venture further and further from land. . . . As they were 'children of the water,' so their descendants are born sailors. It is no wonder, then, that . . . thus accustomed to the deep seas, the Japanese [are] always at home upon them."[38] The pioneering folklorist Yanagita Kunio posited an even deeper cultural genealogy linking Japan to the ocean around it. As early as the 1920s, Yanagita suggested that the origins of Japanese culture lay in the South Pacific, with ocean currents having carried folk traditions along a "passage on the sea" (*kaijō no michi*) from Micronesia through the Ryukyus and to Japan's home islands.[39] Yanagita's theories both reflected and promoted a long-standing Japanese fascination with the South Seas that emerged in the late nineteenth century and intensified after Japan's naval glories in the Russo-Japanese War. Many commentators romanticized the marine frontier, investing the limitless waves of the Pacific with hopes for Japan's imperial future, just as other expansionist dreamers saw Japan's fate on the boundless plains of Manchuria. The journalist Hattori Tōru was not alone in insisting that Japan's destiny lay to the south rather than the north, not on the grasslands of the Asian continent but "in the vast reaches of the hazy ocean."[40]

Many analysts also explained Japan's dominance of Pacific fisheries with a clear ring of social Darwinism. Japan's fishing industry had expanded so rapidly not because of trickery, predatory practices, or unfair government assistance; the real reason, Japanese writers maintained, was that Japan's fishermen simply worked harder. Considering the case of Kamchatka, where Russian investment in fisheries had long been minimal, one analyst suggested, "The Japanese redoubled their efforts to explore and develop these resources and they naturally became the masters of those waters."[41] Another writer argued that the British and the Japanese had attained lasting maritime greatness not just because of their naval might but because of their canny utilization of the world's oceans—the British through commercial shipping, the Japanese in fisheries. The once-great empires that did not make such strategic use of the seas—the Spanish, Portuguese, and Dutch—lost their global clout and ended up languishing among history's also-rans.[42] When it came to fishing, one Japanese writer claimed, "we have acquired such skill that no other nation can compete with us."[43]

The height of Japan's ideological construction of an ocean empire may have come in 1941, just months before the attack on Pearl Harbor, with the proclamation of *umi no kinenbi* (Marine Memorial Day) as a national holiday. Pushed by shipping interests and shepherded through the bureaucracy by Communications Minister Murata Shōzō, *umi no kinenbi* was established to "give thanks for the blessings of the sea and pray for the prosperity of maritime Japan (*kaiyōkoku Nihon*)."[44] The connection between Japan's imperial destiny and dominion over the waves was made explicit by Murata, who wrote of the "vital importance," especially in a time of "thorough preparation for total war," of a national commitment to "deepening understanding of the oceans and endeavoring resolutely to advance upon the seas."[45] The date chosen for *umi no kinenbi*, July 20, was also freighted with imperial symbolism, as it commemorated the day in 1876 when the Meiji emperor returned to Yokohama on board the topsail schooner *Meiji Maru* from a triumphal tour around Hokkaido, then a frontier being claimed and colonized by the modernizing Japanese state.[46] With the creation of a marine holiday—and one apparently designed to "support the building of the Greater East Asian Co-Prosperity Sphere"[47]—the seas were comfortably integrated into Japan's national narrative of empire as well as its vision of future imperial expansion.

Even highly critical treatments of Japanese expansionism and the capitalist system that sustained deep-sea fisheries revealed the profound imaginative connections weaving together the oceans, national identity, and imperial dreams in mid-twentieth-century Japan. For example, Kobayashi Takiji's 1929 novella *Kanikōsen* (The Factory Ship), now considered a classic of Japanese proletarian literature, provided unusual insights into the intersection of fishing and empire in the Japanese popular consciousness. Kobayashi's didactic story follows the voyage of a Japanese crab-canning ship up the coast of Kamchatka, chronicling the brutality of management, the suffering of labor, the emergence of a revolutionary consciousness among the crew, and the mobilization of Japan's modern industrial fisheries in the capitalist quest for profits and the national quest for empire. As the ship makes its way toward Russian waters, the superintendent tries to motivate the workers with patriotic sentiments and imperial aspirations:

> We're involved in a serious international problem. It boils down to this: who's stronger—we, the people of the Japanese empire, or the Russkies? It's a crucial, man-to-man battle. If we lose—and I don't think it will ever happen—every one of you sons of Japan with balls swinging from your crotch must be prepared to slit open your belly and dump yourself in the Kamchatka Sea. We're small, but I'll be damned if we go down before those big stupid Russkies. Our Kamchatka operations involve canning sardines and salmon as well as crabs. From the international standpoint, we're way ahead of the other nations in this area. . . . I don't know if what I'm saying makes sense to you. Anyway, just remember that we are going to fight our way through the northern seas for this mission even at the risk of our lives.[48]

Although Kobayashi ends *Kanikōsen* with a hopeful postscript on the advance of socialism, his primary story is, as he puts it, "a page from the history of the infiltration of capitalism into new territories [*shokuminchi*]."[49] The invocation of imperialism here is clear. Less certain, however, is what Kobayashi means by those "new territories": Japan? The floating factories of industrial crabbing? Or, most provocatively of all, the oceans that were being stripped of their resources, becoming sites of class struggle, and undergoing "infiltration" as the possessions of empire?

Not surprisingly, the nations on the receiving end of Japan's marine expansionism also perceived Japan's relentless fisheries advances in imperialistic terms. After Japanese boats began harvesting salmon in Bristol Bay in 1937, the American protests—from Alaskan fishing interests, native peoples, and the halls of power in Washington—were deafening. One observer at the time described Japan's fishing sortie as a "damaging invasion"; the Alaska territory's delegate to the US House of Representatives labeled it an "attack"; and another vilified the Japanese for their "ruthless methods of exploitation and contempt for the rights and interests of others."[50] Later writers would describe 1937 as the beginning of the "great Japanese sea invasion" and the arrival in American waters of "the far-flung Fish Empire." One fisheries expert, warning of the "march of the Rising Sun," suggested that "fisheries have always been a part of the Japanese expansionist thinking."[51] Sentiments in Russia, where Japanese marine intrusions (like those dramatized in Kobayashi's *Kanikōsen*) were of longer standing and potentially of much greater economic impact, and in China, where the "yellow croaker war" in the East China Sea fueled patriotic passions during the 1920s and 1930s, were much the same.[52] Indeed, throughout the Pacific (and even beyond), Japanese fishermen were almost universally perceived as lawbreakers and predators, fearsome not just for their brashness in entering fishing grounds long monopolized by others but also for their chilling efficiency in finding and exploiting valuable fish stocks.[53]

On the eve of Pearl Harbor, Japan's pelagic empire stretched from the Bering Sea to the Antarctic and along the coastlines of virtually every Asian country, from the pearl beds off of Darwin, Australia, to the trawling grounds of the Gulf of California. Fleets of modern factory ships, state-of-the-art whaling catcher boats, onshore canning facilities, ice-making operations on Pacific atolls, and no fewer than 1.4 million fishermen, processors, and aquaculturalists kept Japan's sprawling fisheries realm humming and growing. Imperial Japan exploited the oceans with every bit as much thoroughness and efficiency as it exploited the ore veins of Manchuria, the rice paddies of Korea, or the forests of Taiwan. The irony, however, was that at the very time that Japan's terrestrial empire would reach its greatest heights—in those heady months after December 7, 1941—Japan's pelagic empire would decline and wither. Though some Japanese dreamed that total war would bring total oceanic dominance, in the wake of Pearl Harbor virtually all deep-sea fishing and whaling came abruptly to an end. The Imperial Navy drafted the vast majority of Japan's oceangoing fishing vessels—as well as most of its skilled seamen—into war service. All of Japan's large factory ships were destroyed during the war, as were 95 percent of the nation's otter trawlers. But even had the offshore fleets been preserved, there would not have been sufficient supplies to keep them operating during the hostilities. Indeed, even coastal fisheries were severely hampered after 1941 by mounting shortages of cotton yarn, ramie, manila hemp, and, most importantly, petroleum. And, of course, by 1943 an undersea profusion of American submarines meant that no Japanese ships—fishing vessels included—could venture from port unmolested.[54]

In any case, with Tokyo's decision in 1941 for an autonomous path and an autarkic future in East Asia, the primary motivation for the pelagic empire simply evaporated. With foreign trade obviated by war and the generation of foreign exchange thus irrelevant, distant-water fisheries lost their raison d'être. Developed since the 1930s as an export-oriented cash cow rather than as a primary supply of food for the home country, the offshore fishing industry was, strangely enough, a victim of Japan's wartime withdrawal from the international economy.

In the end, Japan's oceanic expansionism of the first half of the twentieth century, like its better-known project of terrestrial imperialism, was largely economic in motivation, opportunistic in its creation, ingenious and dynamic in its execution, and remarkably efficient in its exploitation of resources. The seas were a part of the Japanese Empire materially, ideologically, culturally, and in certain ways politically, technologically, and socially as well.

The history of Japanese imperialism reveals the seas as a space of national contestation between and of empires, shaped by the distinctive mode of production of modern fisheries and refracted through imaginative filters of patriotism, economic promise, and imperial destiny. Recognizing the ocean as a socially constructed space—the seas are "not merely a space used *by* society," as Philip Steinberg observes, but "one component of the space *of* society"—necessitates a rethinking of the existing theoretical frameworks for understanding imperialism. Not only does the case of Japan's pelagic empire challenge historians to conceive of imperialism in unaccustomed, spatial ways, but it encourages renewed attention to the environmental dimensions of empire—especially those that depart from time-honored anthropocentric and narrowly terrestrial presumptions. Above all, the experience of Japan's "far-flung Fish Empire" compels us to consider an amphibious approach to imperialism, one that can move freely between the landlocked historiography of the past and the broad expanses of future historical inquiry that an oceanic perspective affords.

The Legacies of Maritime Empire

Even today, more than sixty years after the end of World War II and the collapse of the Japanese Empire, the echoes and legacies of Japan's pelagic imperialism remain apparent and may be more divisive politically, more consequential economically, and charged ideologically more than ever before. Perhaps most obviously, competition for possession of the seas and for the ability to define them imaginatively continues for Japan and its maritime neighbors. The dispute over the four southernmost islands in the Kuril chain, known to the Japanese as the Northern Territories, has haunted Russian-Japanese relations and long precluded the negotiation of a peace treaty ending World War II between the two nations. Competing claims over the barren, uninhabited Senkaku (Diaoyu) Islands west of Okinawa, the largest of which measures just 1.7 square miles, have also proven a political flashpoint. Integrated into the Japanese Empire in 1895, the islands—with a highly strategic location in the East China Sea and supposedly surrounded by oil- and gas-rich waters—are a source of ongoing contention among China, Taiwan, and Japan. National pride and competition for marine and (potential) mineral resources have also fueled debates over Dokdo (called Takeshima by the Japanese), a jumble of thirty-seven islets and rocks between the Korean Peninsula and the western coast of Honshu. Similar tensions surround the use of the name "Sea of Japan," which the North and South Korean governments regard as an offensive remnant of Japanese imperialism, but which Tokyo asserts has longer historical roots in European cartography of Asia. Such impassioned debates are evidence that the seas today are no less a site of national ambitions, economic expectations, and popular aspirations than they were during the mid-twentieth-century high tide of Japan's oceanic empire building.

Even at the height of prewar imperialism, in the decades prior to 1945, little effort was made by Japan—or by the other colonial powers in Asia—to delimit and claim as sovereign space the world's oceans and seas. Indeed, Japan has historically been an outspoken advocate of the "freedom of the seas" (mare liberum) and minimal (three-nautical-mile) territorial waters.[55] The dominant liberal ocean regime served Japan well in expanding its fishing grounds prior to World War II as well as in reestablishing its position as the world's premier fishing nation (and a leader in merchant shipping) shortly after the war.[56] Japan's turn to "oceanic autarky" during the 1930s and war years, like its embrace of the goal of economic autarky at the same time, was thus only a temporary deviation, a detour from a long-term commitment to the open-oceans policy that had generally served Japanese interests so well. Japan's twentieth-century rise to the status of world economic power was thus premised not just on a liberal world trading order but also on a permissive international regime for accessing and extracting resources from the oceans. And although Japan was among the last major maritime nations to accept the "enclosure movement" of the seas after World War II, the global adoption of twelve-mile territorial waters and two hundred-mile exclusive economic zones (EEZs) could be seen as just the start of a new phase in Japan's oceanic adventurism. With the loss of many overseas fishing grounds starting in the 1970s, Japan's dominance in global fisheries waned and the nation rapidly moved from a net exporter to an aggressive importer of fishery products. Japanese firms sought to ensure supply to the hungry home market, one of the world's largest per capita consumers of fish, by aggressively pursuing joint ventures, especially in developing nations; these relationships, which have often proved exploitative of host country labor and marine resources, are justifiably characterized by some observers as a form of neocolonialism.[57] At the same time, with the establishment of its own EEZ, Japan suddenly found itself an oceanic superpower:

> With the coming into effect of the Law of the Sea Convention, Japan has come to administer an offshore area spanning 4.47 million square kilometers—12 times more than its total landmass of 380,000 km^2 and the sixth largest in the world. Thanks to its possession of scattered Pacific Ocean islands, Japan's total area (land and sea combined) now covers 4.85 million km^2, which is among the world's top 10. . . . Among the deep-sea areas under Japan's administration are the Japan Trench, Izu-Ogasawara Trench, Nankai Trough, and Ryukyu Trench, and in terms of cubic volume, Japan's EEZ is estimated to be the fourth largest in the world.[58]

So, it seems, in an age of creeping territorialization of the world's oceans, Japan's once grandiose visions of a pelagic imperium may yet be realized.

Notes

1. Eric Taliacozzo, "Review Essay: Underneath the Indian Ocean," *Journal of Asian Studies* 67:3 (August 2008): 1039.

2. W. Jeffrey Bolster, "Putting the Ocean in Atlantic History: Maritime Communities and Marine Ecology in the Northwest Atlantic, 1500–1800," *American Historical Review* 113:1 (February 2008): 23.

3. Rachel Carson, *The Sea Around Us* (New York: Oxford University Press, 1951), 15; J. R. McNeill, "Observations on the Nature and Culture of Environmental History," *History and Theory* 42 (December 2003): 42.

4. Alfred Mahan, *The Influence of Sea Power upon History 1660–1783* (Boston: Little Brown, 1918 [1890]), 25.

5. Bernhard Klein and Gesa Mackenthun, "The Sea Is History," in *Sea Changes: Historicizing the Ocean,* ed. Klein and Mackenthun (New York: Routledge, 2004). In a 1999 *Geographical Review* special issue, "Oceans Connect," guest editors Kären Wigen and Jessica Harland-Jacobs urged scholars to consider, "What if seas were shifted from the margins to the center of academic vision?" Wigen and Harland-Jacobs, "Guest Editors' Introduction," *Geographical Review* 89:2 (April 1999): ii. In their reconceptualization (and in the essays in the special issue), however, the focus was on redefining terrestrial regions (littorals, ocean basins) on a maritime basis rather than seeking a means of integrating historical and geographical understandings of "ocean space" with notions of the nation state, regions, and the land. Oceans thus emerged less as "places"—analogous in some way to terra firma—and more as open conduits for trade, cultural exchange, and social contact, what Wigen and Martin Lewis called "lively zones of contact (and

conflict)." Lewis and Wigen, "A Maritime Response to the Crisis in Area Studies," *Geographical Review* 89:2 (April 1999): 165.

6. See, for example, David Armitage, *The Ideological Origins of the British Empire* (Cambridge: Cambridge University Press, 2000). Elizabeth Mancke's work on European empire building and "oceanic dominance" suggests some of the pitfalls of bringing a pelagic perspective to the study of imperialism. Her article "Early Modern Expansion and the Politicization of Oceanic Space," *Geographical Review* 89:2 (April 1999): 225–236, sheds more light on the role of islands—rather than the oceans that surround them—in the process of imperial conquest. The essays in Jerry Bentley, Renate Bridenthal, and Kären Wigen, eds., *Seascapes: Maritime Histories, Littoral Cultures, and Transoceanic Exchanges* (Honolulu: University of Hawai'i Press, 2007), also reveal continued scholarly hesitation in viewing the oceans as sites of imperialism, emphasizing the projection of imperial power *across* the seas rather than *on* or *in* them. The only scholars to date to argue explicitly for an imperial history of the oceans are historians of science and particularly of oceanographic science. See Helen Rozwadowski, *Fathoming the Ocean: The Discovery and Exploration of the Deep Sea* (Cambridge, MA: Harvard University Press, 2005); Michael Reidy, *Tides of History: Ocean Science and Her Majesty's Navy* (Chicago: University of Chicago Press, 2008).

7. Thomas Metcalf, *Imperial Connections: India in the Indian Ocean Arena, 1860–1920* (Berkeley: University of California Press, 2007), 9, 15.

8. Mark Peattie, "Introduction," in *The Japanese Colonial Empire*, ed. Ramon Myers and Mark Peattie (Princeton, NJ: Princeton University Press, 1984), 4–5.

9. John Gallagher and Ronald Robinson, "The Imperialism of Free Trade," *Economic History Review,* second series 6:1 (1953): 1.

10. Klein and Mackenthun, "The Sea Is History," 2. Kate Barclay has posited connections between fisheries and Japanese nationalism and imperialism, although her focus is primarily on post–World War II developments. Barclay, "Ocean, Empire, and Nation: Japanese Fisheries Politics," in *Water, Sovereignty and Borders in Asia and Oceania*, ed. Devleena Ghosh, Heather Goodall, and Stephanie Hemelryk Donald (Abingdon, UK: Routledge, 2009), 38–49.

11. John Stephan, *Sakhalin: A History* (Oxford: Clarendon Press, 1971), 76. Japan had a long-term interest in the expansion of fisheries to its north, stretching back to Tokugawa period (1600–1868) efforts to tap the maritime resources of Hokkaido. Herring, salmon, sea cucumber, kelp, and a variety of other near-ocean and littoral fisheries were exploited for Japanese consumption well prior to the Meiji Restoration of 1868. See David Howell, *Capitalism from Within: Economy, Society, and the State in a Japanese Fishery* (Berkeley: University of California Press, 1995), and Brett Walker, *The Conquest of Ainu Lands: Ecology and Culture in Japanese Expansion, 1590–1800* (Berkeley: University of California Press, 2001).

12. *Japanese Offshore Trawling* (Tokyo: Supreme Commander for the Allied Powers, Natural Resources Section Report 138, 1950), 7.

13. *The Japanese Tuna Fisheries* (Tokyo: Supreme Commander for the Allied Powers, Natural Resources Section Report 104, 1948), 6.

14. Alfred Stead, ed., *Japan by the Japanese: A Survey by Its Highest Authorities* (New York: Dodd Mead, 1904), 428–429.

15. On the expansion of Japan's deep-sea fisheries, see *The Economic Development of the Japanese Fishing Industry* (Tokyo: Association for Liberty of Trading, 1933?), 5. Overexploitation of coastal fishing grounds was almost certainly a significant factor in Japan's expansion into offshore fisheries. As one Japanese fisheries expert wrote in the 1930s,

"At present we are often told of the devastation of the coastal fisheries or of the scarcity of fish along the coast. We are unable to prove the patent facts of these reports, due to the imperfection of statistics, but the decrease of fish and the deterioration of their breeding rate are felt everywhere" (quoted in *Economic Development*, 21). Despite such dire pronouncements, statistics indicate that the coastal catch actually increased gradually in the decades prior to World War II, although the rate of growth in the coastal fisheries lagged far behind that of Japan's rapidly expanding offshore operations. A concise introduction to Japanese offshore fisheries in the twentieth century is Roger Smith, "Japan's High Seas Fisheries in the North Pacific Ocean: Food Security and Foreign Policy," in *Japan at the Millennium: Joining Past and Future*, ed. David Edgington (Vancouver, Canada: UBC Press, 2003).

16. *Economic Development of the Japanese Fishing Industry*, 9.

17. Mark Peattie, *Nan'yō: The Rise and Fall of the Japanese in Micronesia, 1885–1945* (Honolulu: University of Hawai'i Press, 1988), 141.

18. Haraguchi Takejiro, "Japan's Contributions in the South Seas," *Contemporary Japan* 8:2 (April 1939): 261–262; Mark Peattie, "*Nanshin*: The Southern Advance, 1931–1942, as a Prelude to the Japanese Occupation of Southeast Asia," in *The Japanese Wartime Empire, 1931–1945*, ed. Peter Duus, Ramon Myers, and Mark Peattie (Princeton, NJ: Princeton University Press, 1996), 201.

19. *Japanese Whaling Industry Prior to 1946* (Tokyo: Supreme Commander for the Allied Powers, Natural Resources Section Report 126, 1950).

20. Shozui Sen'ichi, "Our Fishing Industry," *Contemporary Japan* 9:6 (June 1940): 701.

21. John Stephan, *The Kuril Islands* (Oxford: Oxford University Press, 1974), 122; *Economic Development of the Japanese Fishing Industry*, 13; Howell, *Capitalism from Within*, chapter 5.

22. Stephan, *Kuril Islands*, 130.

23. *Japan, Special Catalogue, Fisheries* (Tokyo: Imperial Fisheries Bureau, 1915), 101–104; Smith, "Japan's High Seas Fisheries," 69–70.

24. Georg Borgstrom, *Japan's World Success in Fishing* (London: Fishing News Books, 1964), 252–255.

25. Micah Muscolino, "The Yellow Croaker War: Fishery Disputes between China and Japan, 1925–1935," *Environmental History* 13:2 (April 2008): 320.

26. *Japanese Fur Sealing* (Tokyo: Supreme Commander for the Allied Powers, Natural Resources Section Report 129, 1950).

27. Kondō Rempei, "Japanese Communications: The Mercantile Marine," in *Fifty Years of New Japan*, vol. 1, ed. Ōkuma Shigenobu (London: Smith, Elder, 1909), 447.

28. Ibid., 464.

29. William Wray, *Mitsubishi and the N.Y.K., 1870–1914: Business Strategy in the Japanese Shipping Industry* (Cambridge, MA: Harvard Council on East Asian Studies, 1984), 1.

30. Daniel Headrick, *The Invisible Weapon: Telecommunications and International Politics 1851–1945* (New York: Oxford University Press, 1991), 44, 196–199.

31. Peattie, *Nan'yō*, 57–61.

32. Rozwadowski, *Fathoming the Ocean*, 215; Reidy, *Tides of History*, 294.

33. *Japan, Special Catalogue, Fisheries*, 105–139; Kasuga Nobuichi, "Fisheries Research Work," in *Japan's Fisheries Industry 1939* (Tokyo: Japan Times & Mail, 1939), 16–17. See also Micah Muscolino's chapter in this volume.

34. Helen Rozwadowski, *The Sea Knows No Boundaries: A Century of Marine Science under ICES* (Seattle: University of Washington Press, 2002), 141, 328–329.

35. Kuwata Tōichi, *Suisan Nihon* (Tokyo: Dai Nihon yūbenkai kōdansha, 1942), 1–2. Such phrases recall the slogans and buzzwords that surrounded Japan's terrestrial expansionism. See, for example, Louise Young, *Japan's Total Empire: Manchuria and the Culture of Wartime Imperialism* (Berkeley: University of California Press, 1998).

36. Quoted in Marcia Yonemoto, "Maps and Metaphors of the 'Small Eastern Sea' in Tokugawa Japan (1603–1868)," *Geographical Review* 89:2 (April 1999): 169.

37. Shindo Shintaro, "Fishing in Soviet Waters," *Contemporary Japan* 7:2 (September 1938): 245.

38. Murata Tamotsu, "Japanese Industries: Marine Products," in *Fifty Years of New Japan,* vol. 1, ed. Ōkuma, 594.

39. Oguma Eiji, *A Genealogy of "Japanese" Self-images,* trans. David Askew (Melbourne, Australia: Trans Pacific Press, 2002), chapter 12; Yoshikuni Igarashi, "Mothra's Gigantic Egg: Consuming the South Pacific in 1960s Japan," in *In Godzilla's Footsteps: Japanese Pop Culture Icons on the Global Stage,* ed. William Tsutsui and Michiko Ito (New York: Palgrave Macmillan, 2006), 84–86.

40. Quoted in Peattie, *Nan'yō,* 8.

41. Shindo, "Fishing in Soviet Waters," 243–244.

42. Kuwata, *Suisan Nihon,* 7ff.

43. *Economic Development of the Japanese Fishing Industry,* 1.

44. Kanō Mikiyo, "Tennōsei-garami no Nihon no shukujitsu," *Shūkan Kin'yōbi* 3:16 (April 28, 1995): 56. See also "Marine Day and the Basic Ocean Law," Nippon Foundation, Maritime Programs, In-Depth Articles (August 2007) http://www.nippon-foundation. or.jp/eng/current/20070808MarineDay.html. Accessed February 16, 2009.

45. Murata Shōzō, quoted by Hashimoto Atsushi, speaking to the Sangiin bunkyō iinkai (Japanese Diet, House of Councilors Education Committee), February 28, 1996, Dai-132-kai kokkai sangiin bunkyō iinkai kaigiroku dai-2-gō, 7. Kokkai kaigiroku kensa shisutemu, http://kokkai.ndl.go.jp/. Accessed February 18, 2009.

46. Donald Keene, *Emperor of Japan: Meiji and His World, 1852–1912* (New York: Columbia University Press, 2002), 253; *Meiji maru shi* (Tokyo: Tokyo Shōsen Daigaku, 1982), 12–14. Some controversy surrounded the revival of *umi no kinenbi* as a new national holiday, *umi no hi* (Marine Day), in 1996. Several commentators criticized the choice of date for the holiday, noting connections to the authoritarian "emperor system" (*tennōsei*) and raising "the painful history in which 'maritime Japan' (*kaiyōkoku* Nihon) was the prow of aggresive war throughout Asia." Suzuki Ikuko, "'Umi no hi' shukujitsuka ni 'tennōsei to sensō sanbi' to hantai no koe," *Tsukuru* 25:2 (Feburary 1995): 15. Even in 2007, an activist group in Osaka organized a program to protest "'Ocean Day' (*umi no hi*) and ATTACK the nation's ambition as an Oceanic Nation." http://japan.indymedia.org/newswire/display/ 3544. Accessed February 18, 2009.

47. Kanō, "Tennōsei-garami no Nihon no shukujitsu," 56.

48. Kobayashi Takiji, *"The Factory Ship" and "The Absentee Landlord,"* trans. Frank Motofuji (Seattle: University of Washington Press, 1973), 10.

49. Ibid., 83.

50. Joseph Bingham (1938), quoted in Julian Minghi, "The Conflict of Salmon Fishing Policies in the North Pacific," *Pacific Viewpoint* 2:1 (March 1961): 77; Anthony Dimond, quoted in Larry Leonard, *International Regulation of Fisheries* (Washington, DC: Carnegie Endowment for International Peace, 1944), 134; *Fisheries Programs in Japan, 1945–1951* (Tokyo: Supreme Commander for the Allied Powers, Natural Resources Section Report

152, 1951), 29. See Sayuri Guthrie-Shimizu, "Occupation Policy and the Japanese Fisheries Management Regime, 1945–1952," in *Democracy in Occupied Japan: The U.S. Occupation and Japanese Politics and Society,* ed. Mark Caprio and Yoneyuki Sugita (London: Routledge, 2007), 48–52.

51. Borgstrom, *Japan's World Success in Fishing,* 239, 274, 272.

52. Leonard, *International Regulation of Fisheries,* 27ff.; Muscolino, "The Yellow Croaker War," 305–324.

53. Guthrie-Shimizu, "Occupation Policy," 53.

54. William Tsutsui, "Landscapes in the Dark Valley: Toward an Environmental History of Wartime Japan," *Environmental History* 8:2 (April 2003): 294–311.

55. Smith, "Japan's High Seas Fisheries"; Tsuneo Akaha, *Japan in Global Ocean Politics* (Honolulu: University of Hawai'i Press, 1985).

56. *The Japanese Tuna Fishing Industry,* ed. and trans. Wilvan Van Campen (Washington, DC: US Department of the Interior, Fish and Wildlife Service, Special Scientific Report: Fisheries No. 79, 1952).

57. Yamaka Junko, "Fisheries in Asia and the Pacific—Japan's Involvement and Its Problems," *AMPO* 16:1–2 (1984): 82–105. In 2000, Japan could only claim third place in marine landings among the world's leading fishing nations, trailing China and Peru. Japan had, however, become the world's top importer of fish by the new millennium. Japanese per capita consumption of fish in 2001 was 69.1 kg/year, more than four times the world average of 16.0 kg/year. See Wilfram Ken Swartz, "Global Maps of the Growth of Japanese Marine Fisheries and Fish Consumption" (unpublished MS thesis, University of British Columbia, 2004), http://www.fisheries.ubc.ca/archive/grad/abstracts/wilfthesis.pdf. Accessed May 29, 2009.

58. Terashima Hiroshi, "On Becoming an Ocean State," *Japan Echo* 34:1 (February 2007): 37–39; Matsuzawa Takatoshi, "What Is the Volume of Japan's 200-nm Exclusive Economic Zone?" *Ocean Policy Research Foundation Newsletter* 123 (September 2005), http://www.sof.or.jp/en/news/101–150/123_2.php. Accessed February 16, 2009. In terms of cubic volume, Japan trails the United States, Australia, and Kiribati with 15.8 million cubic kilometers of sea water in its two hundred–mile EEZ.

2

From Meat to Machine Oil

*The Nineteenth-Century Development
of Whaling in Wakayama*

JAKOBINA ARCH

Casualties of Commerce

On December 24, 1878, a massive right whale (*Eubalaena japonica*) swam with her calf toward the Kumano coast of Wakayama Prefecture (fig. 2.1). The weather that afternoon was cold and rainy, with a northeasterly wind kicking up a dangerous chop on the water. Despite the bad weather, lookouts were stationed on a mountain near Taiji Harbor, peering through the rain for any sign of whales. At the same time, around three hundred whalers watched the mountain for a signal. It was late in the day by the time the nearly seventeen-meter whale and her four-meter calf came close enough for the lookouts to spot their backs rising out of the waves. Taiji whalers had not yet caught a single whale that season and were facing ruin, so despite the dangerous conditions, the signal flags went up and the men rowed out after the whales. This decision resulted in the deaths of over one hundred men: some from wounds sustained in the hunt, but most from exposure when their boats were dragged farther offshore by the entangled whales. The whales escaped, although they too almost certainly died later from their wounds.[1]

This hunt left the village of Taiji gutted, with mostly old men and children to carry on fishing. But it did not destroy the whaling industry in Wakayama Prefecture, or even in Taiji. Though this was approximately when the Japanese whaling industry shifted from traditional to modern industrial whaling, the Taiji disaster did not force the shift. Men from the three Kumano whaling villages of Taiji, Koza, and Miwasaki (see fig. 2.1) persisted in this dangerous occupation into the twentieth century, and to this day Japan remains one of the few countries that still hunts whales.[2]

At the end of the nineteenth century, the Japanese whaling industry transformed from a centuries-old native practice to a version of modern, industrial

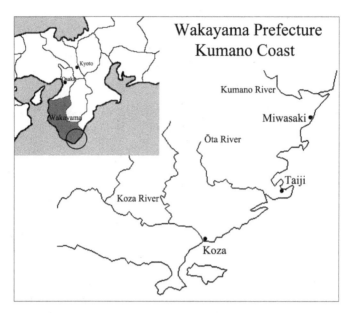

FIGURE 2.1 Wakayama Prefecture is gray in the inset map, with the Kumano coast circled. Taiji, Miwasaki, and Koza are the three whaling villages in this region.

whaling indistinguishable from that of America, Norway, or Germany. This was during a time of rapid economic change and strengthening of the Meiji state (1868–1912). The whaling industry in Wakayama was under state influence at this time. The relative influence of the Meiji state and Western technology in fostering the development of modern industries is a major question in modern Japanese history.[3] Did the Meiji-era state-sponsored adoption of new technologies provide the keys to promoting innovation in the whaling industry, or was it a more independent development?[4] This question speaks not only to our understanding of Meiji industrialization and modernization but also to the role of whaling in Japan. An understanding of the development of modern Japanese whaling is necessary to engage with the common arguments made in support of whaling today, arguments that rely on the assumption of a long tradition of continuous whaling culture from the premodern through the modern eras.[5] With a dramatic shift in techniques, it is difficult to postulate an ongoing tradition of whaling equally important in the premodern and modern eras.

Without the Western overexploitation of Pacific whale populations altering the character of the space of production in which Kumano whalers operated, the industry might have continued as it had for the previous two hundred years, regardless of state pressure to adopt foreign technology. In other words, even though the transition to modern whaling methods in Japan was at least partially tied to Meiji-era industrial development, to understand the process of change in Wakayama one must also consider the environmental conditions under which the whalers worked. Society is shaped by the interaction between people and the spaces they live in and—more importantly—that they produce, as Henri Lefebvre argues.[6] According to Marcia Yonemoto, early modern oceanic space in Japan was seen as coastal and focused more strongly on its interaction with the land next to it than its ties to the vast, open Pacific.[7] But as international Pacific whaling reduced the number of whales migrating along the Kuroshio Current near the shore, Kumano whalers were forced to change both their mode of production and the space in which they worked. Despite the effort to restrict most foreign trade during the Tokugawa period (1600–1868), the Japanese could not shut out foreign influences on the shared resource of Pacific whales.[8] Tokugawa officials and Taiji whalers found themselves part of a global economy centered around what environmental historians call "movable nature."[9]

Before the Meiji state ever came to power, the Western whaling industry dramatically reduced populations of easy-to-catch species in the Pacific, and the development of the modern whaling industry in Wakayama was dependent on this fact. The tendency to portray "Meiji industrialization" as a homogeneous process obscures the particular circumstances that governed each industry's development; even in Wakayama, where the Meiji state did play a role, this role only makes sense within the broader context of nineteenth-century whaling specific to this industry. The history of Western whaling is one of progressive exploitation of increasingly difficult-to-catch whales; as previously favored species were driven below sustainable levels, the necessity of finding new target species pushed the technological developments needed to catch more difficult species.[10] The process is particularly clear in the Pacific, which became a whaling ground for Western ships in the 1830s. By 1846, there were 735 American whaling ships in the Pacific, representing approximately 80 percent of the world's whaling fleet. They produced 4–5 million gallons of sperm whale oil per year and 6–10 million gallons from other species.[11] Right whales, with their extremely thick blubber, served as a prime target from 1835 to the 1850s. When European and American whalers began to use fast, coal-fueled ships and harpoon guns after 1860, it was because the only whales left worth hunting were rorquals—the streamlined members of the Balaenopteridae family, the largest group of baleen whales—because these were the whales previously too fast to catch.[12]

Japanese coastal whaling had a long history as a relatively speculative enterprise, one that continued to attract new investors and groups because whaling towns had few other options for support, even when declining whale populations provided diminishing returns. Whales were such a valuable resource that it was said that "if one whale is captured, seven villages prosper."[13] Although arguments today center on the consumption of whale meat, it was not just the meat that was valuable. Bones were boiled and crushed into fertilizer. Whale oil was used in lamps and as an insecticide on rice crops. New uses and expanding markets for whale products were welcomed: whale oil's effectiveness as an insecticide after the Kyōho famine (1732–1733) opened a market for whales with less palatable meat, such as sperm whales (*Physeter macrocephalus*) and orca (*Orcinus orca*).[14] Japanese ate some of the entrails, while others they boiled down for oil. The remaining pieces found their way into an assortment of products such as Bunraku puppets, document seals, and musical instruments. Furthermore, the Kumano coast has high mountains and very little good agricultural land. The villagers there historically relied upon fishing for their livelihood, depending on a littoral space centered on coastal waters rather than on the land surrounding the village, especially during whaling season, a time of year with no major fish populations to rely on.[15] In the early stages, large-scale whaling could be quite profitable, and it was often a popular enterprise for those attracted by get-rich-quick schemes. Soon after the development of net whaling in 1675, whalers in the village of Koza took eighty-five whales in a good year and forty in a bad year.[16] However, profits were not guaranteed, and the initial cost was quite large. Hamanaka Eikichi, a historian of the Taiji whaling industry, estimates between 270 and 470 people went out on the water in any given hunt, with 100 more on shore as lookouts and in the processing sheds. Their daily ration of rice contributed greatly to whalers' expenses.[17] Damaged and destroyed nets, boats, and harpoons also had to be replaced annually. Because of such large capital outlay and the uncertainty of the catch, whaling was an unstable enterprise: many groups folded after only a few years, replaced by others eager for a chance at high profits.[18]

When whaling groups collapsed, new groups made use of previous techniques and expertise. Western pelagic (offshore) whaling focused on processing whales for oil out at sea, whereas Japanese coastal whaling towed the whales back to shore to be rendered down for meat, oil, and other parts. Thus, there would seem to be little basis for comparison between Japanese and Western efforts, but by the end of the nineteenth century Japanese whalers began trying American techniques, particularly the use of explosive harpoons or bomb lances. When that proved unsuccessful, they turned to the Norwegian factory ship method, with a mounted harpoon gun on the bow of a fast, engine-driven ship. Kumano whalers attempted to adopt these new technologies because declining whale populations made it increasingly difficult to sustain their livelihood, but they tried to integrate the new technologies into traditional coastal whaling practices.

Jessamyn Abel has argued from an international relations perspective that the Meiji modernization drive and the concurrent need to join the ranks of the "civilized" whaling nations primarily influenced this change in Japanese whaling techniques.[19] However, international policy had only a minor influence on the Kumano whaling industry. Kalland and Moeran, in their work on Japanese whaling, have also argued for the central role of Taiji whalers' expertise in developing modern Japanese whaling. However, their argument rests on the movement of whalers out of their home village to become part of new whaling bases focused on pelagic whaling.[20] This movement occurred only after it had become clear that, as Pacific populations crashed, neither traditional methods nor adaptations of them were capable of catching enough whales in the usual hunting grounds.

Gradual changes could only go so far before it became clear that the traditional whaling grounds, linked to larger cetacean migration patterns, had changed too much, and whalers would have to shift to new areas or new species. The process of shifting from traditional coastal whaling to modern pelagic whaling was not a simple one. Whales in the nineteenth century were a shared resource geographically, if not always temporally. The change in environmental conditions caused by unregulated international competition for increasingly scarce resources was the most important factor driving new practices in the Japanese whaling industry.[21]

Whales as Resources

Three main species of whales came close enough to be targeted by Kumano's shore-based whaling industry. Whalers preferred right whales, but they also hunted gray whales (*Eschrictius robustus*) and humpback whales (*Megaptera novaeangliae*), all of which migrated along the Kuroshio Current (fig. 2.2). Due to intense over-fishing in the nineteenth and twentieth centuries, right whales became the rarest and most endangered large whales.[22] Even today, their breeding grounds are not known, which makes it difficult to determine exact migration patterns between breeding grounds and summer feeding grounds, either for today's population or historically.[23]

In fact, estimates are not available for historic population sizes of any of these species. Pacific right whale populations were decimated by American whalers beginning in 1835.[24] This effort was concentrated north of Japan, in the whales' summer feeding grounds. Between 1835 and 1849, American whalers brought back oil and baleen from somewhere between 10,985 and 11,455 right whales. This effort virtually eliminated the Pacific right whale population: between 1850 and 1854, the American whaling fleet was only able to take less than 10 percent of the previous catch.[25] A similar historical survey of Pacific humpback whale populations is not available.[26] It is even more difficult to determine the history of gray whales, which are no longer found in the vicinity of Japan. Whaling historian Omura Hideo estimates, based on catch data from as far back as 1656, that a small

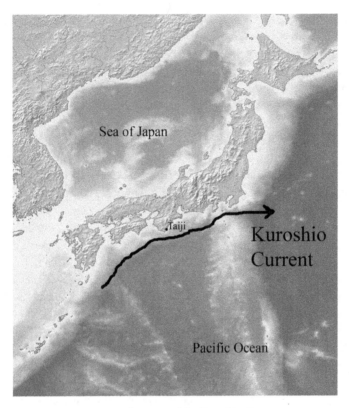

FIGURE 2.2 Approximate location of the Kuroshio Current.

population of gray whales migrated past the shores of Kōchi and Wakayama prefectures until the nineteenth century. An average take for a single group in Kōchi was four to six gray whales per year in 1800–1865, but it declined to three to four per year from 1874 to 1896. This was consistently lower than the average number of humpbacks taken (twelve to fourteen for the earlier period, six for the later). The crash in the right whale population after 1835 is also apparent in these data: on average, seven whales were caught per year in 1800–1835, but only one per year was caught during 1849–1896.[27]

Thus, overall numbers of whales migrating past the Kumano coast by the end of the nineteenth century declined sharply. This decline meant possible ruin for the whaling villages of Taiji, Koza, and Miwasaki, where whaling was central to the economy. But whaling did not have economic importance alone. Modern whaling apologists such as Komatsu Masayuki have made the argument that the variety and completeness of using all parts of the whale historically means that the Japanese had a more nuanced view of whales than more thoroughly exploitation-focused

Western whaling nations did, with their focus solely on the extraction of oil and baleen.[28] This is based not just on the idea of Japanese whale meat consumption and thorough usage of parts (which could be seen as simply another form of exploitation) but also on the fact that there were memorial services for dead whales. If dramatic differences existed between views of traditional Japanese whalers and whalers practicing modern techniques, then the transition to modern whaling in Japan could have required a similarly dramatic shift in their views of whales.[29] Yet my examination of the whaling industry in Wakayama revealed no such shift in attitude but rather a gradual adaptation by local whalers to the loss of a formerly abundant local resource.

One example supposedly distinguishing Japanese whalers' attitudes from westerners is their view of cow-calf pairs. Richard Ellis claimed Japanese whalers would not hunt cow-calf pairs "in order to preserve the species."[30] In support, he noted that mountain lookouts flew a special flag to indicate the sighting of prohibited cow-calf pairs. Kalland and Moeran also note that Japanese did not hunt cow-calf pairs due to a "long-observed taboo."[31] If this were true, then the decision to hunt a right whale cow and calf in the Taiji disaster of 1878 would indicate a shift in whaling customs. But there is no evidence of historical concern for preserving such pairs in Kumano. Mountain outlooks did have signals indicating which species of whale had been sighted, but such signals meant only that whalers liked to know the species they pursued in order to adjust their responses to the whale's behavior (some whales were known to be particularly vicious when attacked).[32] Japanese authors, including Taiji Gorōsaku, a whaler raised in Taiji, do indicate a particular interest in cow-calf pairs, especially right whales.[33] But while they note that whalers were sometimes cautious about hunting cow-calf pairs, it was not because of concern for preservation of species or population management. A concern for the value of animal species in and of themselves rather than as resources is a more modern view that Ellis and others are projecting back into historical whaling, with the assistance of the myth of Japanese oneness with nature, to support their presumption of a historical concern for balanced ecosystems and maintenance of biodiversity.

Taiji's explanation of why whalers in his family sometimes avoided hunting cow-calf pairs is that the bond between these whales produced fierce protective behavior, increasing the danger of the hunt beyond reasonable limits, especially with right whales. It was often better to simply avoid getting too close to such dangerous whales.[34] But historian Yamashita Shōto notes that in some circumstances they were specifically targeted: hunting whales with calves could be easier than hunting single whales, because one would stay by the other when attacked. He provides examples of the proper way to capture both mother and calf from manuscripts as old as 1689. Nowhere do they state that it was against custom to try to catch whales with calves. Both authors simply describe the particular care taken by whalers in these cases.[35] Just as in other whaling cultures, Japanese whalers took advantage of the bond between cows and calves, knowing that it was necessary to trap the calf (easier to entangle than the larger parent) but not to injure it fatally until the mother had been caught.

Adaptations to New Pressures

Over the nineteenth century, Japanese whalers had variable but declining success. From 1824 to 1867, the Koza whaling group had a steady profit only between 1852 and 1859, with particularly extreme variations in profits and losses in the years following.[36] Given the decline in the American take between 1850 and 1854, the profitable years for Koza may have been related to a shift in the normal ranges of whale populations in the Pacific, as they avoided areas of concentrated whaling in the open ocean.[37] Because most large whales do not have calves annually, such a short-term increase in coastal whale populations would have reflected a redistribution of whales, not an overall population growth. Japanese whalers taking advantage of the greater availability of coastal whales during this period would only have exacerbated the overall decline.

Economic pressures became severe enough by the early nineteenth century that the Taiji whaling group turned over management to the government of Kishū domain to secure a 2,000 *ryō* (a pre-Meiji monetary unit) loan to continue the business, although the domain left the local manager, Taiji Yoriyasu, in charge of daily operations.[38] Whalers in Miwasaki had similar difficulties, and management and funding of their group was taken over by Kishū domain in 1826 after village petitions.[39] In Koza, the operation had been owned half by the villagers and half by the domain since 1668. Joint efforts of the government and the villagers were needed to raise enough loans to revive whaling more than once in the nineteenth century.[40] With these continued financial troubles, changes were clearly necessary. Koza whalers sent letters describing the potential destruction of their whaling group due to hardship in 1866 and 1872.[41] In order to justify government support, one letter even claimed that "the case of whales is, of course, a part of the national interest."[42] The authors of the letter did not explain what kind of national interest (*kokueki*) whaling contributed to, but arguments for national interest were important in promoting merchants' political power before the Meiji Restoration, and afterward they were used in a similar fashion by nationalists or others who wanted to rationalize their efforts as benefiting the whole nation.[43] This reference might have suggested a way in which Japan could compete with Western nations, or they may have been indicating the potential for high tax payments. For example, in the unusually successful year of 1857 (twenty whales caught), the Koza whaling group had a net profit of 253 silver *kan*, over 420 times the amount an average farmer earned annually from cash crops.[44]

Even with such economic pressure, Kumano whalers' decision to abandon a two-hundred-year-old tradition in favor of new foreign techniques is difficult to understand if one assumes that the lineage of modern Japanese whaling owes more to long-standing tradition than to the new techniques and equipment adopted at the turn of the twentieth century.[45] The modern industry developed in response to changes in whale availability in the coastal hunting grounds. In some cases this involved relying on adaptation of new technologies to old techniques, but the most successful endeavors adopted Western pelagic whaling models. The 1878 disaster in Taiji demonstrates most clearly the conditions under which change was becoming necessary.[46] In better years, whalers would not have set out on such a hunt. But with no whales caught yet that season—and with many poor years before that—Taiji whalers had difficulty resisting the lure of a right whale whose size was unparalleled in village memory. The whalers managed to entangle the whale mother and calf in their nets late in the afternoon, but in the strengthening storm few boats were able to pull into shore before nightfall, even after cutting the whales free. The violent fight with the whales left many injured, and the storm scattered the boats overnight. In the end, somewhere between 111 and 135 people died. The disaster was great enough that it made national news in the *Yomiuri shinbun* (Yomiuri newspaper): first in a garbled secondhand report of the incident, then in a second article giving a more complete report on January 16, 1879. By that time, the death toll was 72, with 124 people still unaccounted for.[47] It was not until March 18, 1879, that the last four survivors returned home from an island where they had been stranded.

This disaster ended the local elite family's management of Taiji whaling, which had begun with the founding of the first whaling group there by Wada Yorimoto in 1603.[48] In 1882, a non-Wada whaling group based on Mukōjima (in Taiji Harbor) tried to take over. The long history of Wada and Taiji family managers made villagers reluctant to cede authority to outsiders. After the introduction of Mukōjima managers, the village split into supporters of the Mukōjima group and allies of Wada Yoroku, who scraped together his own group to compete with them. Intense conflict between the two factions was only resolved five years later with the help of outside mediation.[49] In this way, the 1878 disaster and the fierce arguments that followed provided an impetus for change in the Taiji whaling industry. Even so, the upheaval did not directly lead to improved techniques. Wada began to try foreign techniques only after the opposing factions came to an agreement.[50] At this time, Americans were developing their own new technologies, including the bomb lance.[51] Some Japanese had witnessed attempts at the bomb lance as early as 1857, so this was the first new technology they tried.[52]

An early example of the use of explosive harpoons appears in a *Yomiuri shinbun* article from 1878, where whalers in Koza tested three harpoons made by a watchmaker in Osaka.[53] Their tests were apparently unsuccessful. A man named Maeda Kenzō did better in 1892. After proving himself as a harpooner in Taiji hunting pilot whales (*Globicephala macrorhynchus*), he went to America and gained experience with firearms, adapting this knowledge to develop a repeating harpoon gun that would fire three (later five) small harpoons to kill pilot whales.[54] Although not a bomb lance, it did make successful use of American technology. This is in part because pilot whales are coastal animals, best hunted using inshore techniques like those used in traditional net whaling. Such small whales were rapidly becoming the only ones close enough to shore to be hunted in this fashion. Maeda's gun did not require any major changes to boats or crew but instead was successful because it shifted targets to a previously ignored species, just as international pelagic whaling was beginning to do for whales on the other end of the size spectrum.

Taiji whalers were thus reluctant to drastically restructure their methods. Just one year before bomb lances were tested in Kumano waters, a man named Moroki Sennosuke put together a whaling fleet to set up a traditional net whaling base in Pusan, Korea, using some Taiji boats, equipment, and men. On their way, they met up with engine-driven boats in Kobe Harbor. The crews of the Taiji beater boats challenged the modern boats to a race. To the surprise of the spectators, the beater boats won handily.[55] In other words, technology had not yet advanced to the point where mechanized boats could best a highly trained and motivated crew of rowers, and the reorganization of labor required to pursue a modernized industry was not cost effective when laborers could rely on traditional skills and organization.

In 1897, Wada's financier Hiramatsu Yoichirō tried to set up a base in Taiji for American-style whaling, using bomb lances and a system of catcher boats sent out from a main ship, where they would bring the whale after it was killed.[56] This technique involved an organization of boats and whalers very different from the traditional shore-based method, and it lasted only two or three years before shutting down without ever catching a whale. Kumano Whaling, Ltd. (Kumano Hogei KK), founded in Taiji in 1900, was the first to successfully use a bomb lance to capture a whale along the Kumano coast in 1902. But this corporation also could not remain solvent; shore-based companies simply could not find enough whales on which to use the supposedly more efficient American harpooning technique. Kumano Whaling ran through all its initial 15,000 yen without ever making a profit.[57]

Global Pressures, Local Changes

Modern whaling was not a shore-based operation, run by village elites, but rather a corporate one. These corporations used the expertise of village whalers but quickly moved away from the structure of locally based whaling groups. They also merged into increasingly national enterprises, so that by the 1910s there were only three whaling companies in Japan running all offshore operations.[58] (Local efforts, such as the pursuit of pilot whales in Taiji, were separate from these pelagic whalers.)

This corporate shift is important for two reasons. First, whalers from Kumano were heavily involved in such corporations. Oriental Whaling Ltd. (Tōyō Hogei KK), which continued under different names through World War II, had a base in Taiji.[59] However, the crews on the new pelagic whaling ships were no longer tied to their villages as they had been when bringing whales back to shore for processing. Thus, the adoption of foreign techniques resulted in a far less localized whaling industry.[60] Second, the most successful whaling corporations did not have their roots in Wakayama. This was not because whalers there were unwilling to attempt changes, as can be seen from efforts to adopt the bomb lance or from the development of pilot whaling.[61] The problem, rather, was one of economics and geography, influenced by the actions of other whaling nations in the Pacific.

The geography of the Kumano coast is harsh enough that the inhabitants of coastal villages do not have many options for making a living outside of fishing. At the end of the nineteenth century, the villagers' ability to make whaling profitable declined along with the number of whales coming inshore. As the case of Taiji shows, people living in a region with a strong tradition of whaling found it difficult to be at the center of a transformation to new methods and organization of the industry. But even though the transformation to a corporate, pelagic whaling system was difficult, it was still a better option than abandoning the industry that defined the villages. The transformation of whaling in Kumano did not happen because whalers suddenly realized the greater efficiency of foreign methods. Japanese could not adopt previously successful American techniques to take advantage of whale populations because these populations had already been driven nearly to extinction by these techniques. Whalers either had to redefine their work in terms of an entirely new space—the open Pacific—or they had to redefine that space to focus on new target species within familiar coastal waters, since the distribution of animals and thus the whaling environment were no longer the same.

Because whaling targeted animals moving throughout the Pacific, whalers were particularly vulnerable to outside influences. But the case of the whaling industry is representative of other maritime occupations: the portion of villagers' lives spent on land is far less important than time spent in maritime space, which defined them and made them vulnerable to pressures from across the ocean. Even in cases where more of the industry is land based, such as the salmon fisheries of the US Pacific Northwest, pressures on populations out at sea must be weighed just as carefully as pressures that are more visible to humans, such as the degradation of inland spawning sites from which the salmon are taken.[62] Without fully considering events in maritime space, drastic changes in coastal fishing industries can only be partially explained. This examination of the maritime environment on which Kumano whalers relied, in conjunction with government policies reacting to global politics, provides a more complete explanation of the ways Japanese whaling's modern transformation arose from responses to global impacts on whale populations.

Notes

1. The disaster is described in Taiji Gorōsaku, *Kumano Taijimura hogei no hanashi* (The story of Taiji village, Kumano's whaling, Osaka: Kishūjinsha, 1937), 74–92, including a copy of the diary of one of the managers, Kin'emon. This account is used by Takigawa Teizō in *Kumano Taiji no denshō: Takigawa Teizō ikō* (Taiji, Kumano's folklore: Taikgawa Teizō's posthumous manuscripts, Tokyo: Kōsakusha, 1982), 125–129. The Taiji Town Office also provides information about the disaster through the Taiji Whaling Museum on the main page at http://www.town.taiji.wakayama.jp/museum and on "Ōsemi nagare (Large right whale passing by)" http://www.town.taiji.wakayama.jp/kankou/seminagare.html. Kondō Isao translated the diary into modern Japanese in *Nihon engan hogei no kōbō* (The rise and fall of Japanese coastal whaling, Japan Kokubunji-shi: San'yōsha, 2001), 174–176.

2. The contemporary debate about Japanese whaling will not be discussed here, but it is important to note the persistence of whaling in Japan despite major changes in technique and organization and the objections of other countries.

3. For the role of the state in Japan's economic development, see Chalmers A. Johnson, *MITI and the Japanese Miracle: The Growth of Industrial Policy, 1925–1975* (Stanford, CA: Stanford University Press, 1982).

4. This question of the source of Japan's modernization and the contribution of traditional culture vs. imported technologies has been debated particularly by scholars explaining the Meiji transition as due to more than just extrinsic factors; for example, Kären Wigen, *The Making of a Japanese Periphery, 1750–1920* (Berkeley: University of California Press, 1995); David L. Howell, *Capitalism from Within: Economy, Society and the State in a Japanese Fishery* (Berkeley: University of California Press, 1995); and also David L. Howell, "Proto-Industrial Origins of Japanese Capitalism," *Journal of Asian Studies* 51 (1992): 269–286.

5. This argument is made by Komatsu Masayuki, a former Japanese Fisheries Agency officer, whaling commissioner, and supporter of Japanese whaling. See Komatsu, *Kujira sono rekishi to bunka* (Whales: Their history and culture, Tokyo: Goma Shobō, 2005), and Komatsu, *Yoku wakaru kujira ronsō: Hogei no mirai o hiraku* (Well-known whale controversy: Opening up whaling's future, Tokyo: Seizandō Shoten, 2005).

6. Henri Lefebvre, *The Production of Space,* trans. Donald Nicholson-Smith (Cambridge, MA: Blackwell, 1997). His notions of the ways that physical spaces shape social structures are instructive even though they focus on land-based systems rather than maritime space, with the exception of Venice.

7. Marcia Yonemoto, "Maps and Metaphors of the 'Small Eastern Sea' in Tokugawa Japan (1603–1868)," *Geographical Review* 89 (April 1999): 169–187.

8. To restrict foreign trade, the Tokugawa government did not allow the construction of any ships large enough to venture beyond Japanese coastal waters. Therefore, Japanese

whalers did not have ships that could pursue whales into deep offshore waters where Americans were whaling. Furthermore, Japanese whaling operations were shore based, while American whalers processed their catches at sea.

9. See, for example, Mark Fiege, "The Weedy West: Mobile Nature, Boundaries, and Common Space in the Montana Landscape," *Western Historical Quarterly* 36 (spring 2005): 22–47.

10. See the "Chronology of World Whaling" chapter in Daniel Francis, *A History of World Whaling* (Ottawa, Canada: Viking/Penguin, 1990), 9–14, for a rough timeline.

11. Francis, *History of World Whaling,* 79. Alexander Starbuck's estimate of the total number of whales taken from 1804–1878, cited in Morita Katsuaki, "American Whaling and His View on Whale Resources," in *The 3rd Summit of Japanese Traditional Whaling Communities: Muroto, Kochi: Report and Proceedings,* ed. Nihon kujirarui kenkyūjo/Japan Whaling Association, 97–106 (Muroto shi, Japan; Tokyo: Muroto City Office; Institute of Cetacean Research, 2005), 100, was 190,000 right whales and 220,000 sperm whales, or an average of approximately 2,500 right whales and 2,900 sperm whales every year for seventy-four years.

12. The Balaenopteridae family includes fin whales (*Balaenoptera physalus*), which can sustain speeds of 20 knots (37 kilometers/hour). For comparison, the record speed of clipper ships, the fastest sailing ships of the nineteenth century, was 22 knots (45 kilometers/hour), and the average was much less; Jane D. Lyon, *Clipper Ships and Captains* (New York: American Heritage Publishing, 1962).

13. Rendered as "*ittō toreru to, shichi ura nigiwau*" in Andō Seiichi, *Zusetsu Wakayama-ken no rekishi* (Illustrated history of Wakayama Prefecture, Tokyo: Kawade shobō shinsha, 1988), 209.

14. Andō, *Zusetsu Wakayama-ken no rekishi*. This shift in usage is indicative of the growth of a conception of whales as more than food. Although Japanese whaling was not on a scale equal to British or American efforts, it was beginning to share a view of whales as repositories of oil by the 1740s.

15. Yamashita Shōto, *Hogei I* (Whaling, vol. 1). *Mono to Ningen no Bunkashi,* vol. 120 (Tokyo: Hōsei Daigaku Shuppankyoku, 2004), 250.

16. Takigawa, *Kumano Taiji no denshō.*

17. Hamanaka Eikichi, *Taiji chōshi* (History of Taiji Village, Wakayama-ken Taiji-chō: Taijichō, 1979): 429. This appears comparable to whaling in other areas of Japan. Arne Kalland, in *Fishing Villages in Tokugawa Japan,* Nordic Institute of Asian Studies Recent Monographs no. 69 (Honolulu: University of Hawaiʻi Press, 1995), estimates that it was difficult to run a whaling group with fewer than three hundred people during the whaling season. Some groups had as many as a thousand.

18. Kalland, *Fishing Villages in Tokugawa Japan.*

19. Jessamyn Abel, "The Ambivalence of Whaling: Conflicting Cultures in Identity Formation," in *JAPANimals: History and Culture in Japan's Animal Life,* ed. Gregory M. Pflugfelder and Brett L. Walker (Ann Arbor: Center for Japanese Studies, University of Michigan, 2005).

20. Arne Kalland and Brian Moeran, *Japanese Whaling: End of an Era?* Nordic Institute of Asian Studies Monograph Series no. 61 (London: Curzon Press, 1992), 32.

21. The pattern here is just one example of the tragedy of the commons, where unregulated free access to a resource leads to overharvesting as every individual harvester maximizes his own profit; Garret Hardin, "The Tragedy of the Commons: The Population

Problem Has No Technical Solution; It Requires a Fundamental Extension of Morality," *Science* 162 (December 13, 1968): 1243–1248. This is also referred to as the "fisherman's problem" by Arthur McEvoy, *The Fisherman's Problem: Ecology and Law in the California Fisheries, 1850–1980* (Cambridge: Cambridge University Press, 1980), 10. The depletion of Pacific whale stocks was also felt by coastal fisheries for gray whales off California during the late nineteenth century, according to McEvoy (74–75, 80). For other studies that consider complex environmental as well as anthropogenic factors in the decline of resource animal populations, see Andrew Isenberg, *The Destruction of the Bison: An Environmental History, 1750–1920* (Cambridge: Cambridge University Press, 2001); McEvoy, *The Fisherman's Problem;* Joseph E. Taylor, *Making Salmon: An Environmental History of the Northwest Fisheries Crisis* (Seattle: University of Washington Press, 1999); and Richard White, *The Organic Machine: The Remaking of the Columbia River* (New York: Hill & Wang, 1995).

22. Before the North Pacific population of right whales became a target in the mid-nineteenth century, it contained at least ten thousand whales. The exact number remaining is unknown, but a rough estimate for the entire Pacific Ocean is around nine hundred whales, with less than three hundred in the western Pacific. See National Marine Fisheries Service, "Endangered and Threatened Species; Proposed Endangered Status for North Pacific Right Whale," *Federal Register* 71 (2006): 77694–77704.

23. J. E. Scarff, "Historic Distribution and Abundance of the Right Whale (*Eubalaena glacialis*) in the North Pacific, Bering Sea, Sea of Okhotsk and Sea of Japan from the Maury Whale Charts," *Annual Report International Whaling Commission* 41 (1991): 467–489.

24. This pressure on animal populations to extract resources for American industry was not unique to whaling. As industry developed ways to exploit resources on a larger scale, population crashes and near-extinction also followed for Pacific salmon (as described in McEvoy, *The Fisherman's Problem;* Taylor, *Making Salmon;* and White, *The Organic Machine*) and bison (Isenberg, *Destruction of the Bison*). Environmental changes such as the arrival of domestic farm animals and the restructuring of the landscape with dams in the Pacific Northwest and railroads in the American Midwest contributed to the downfall of these populations. In the case of Pacific whale populations, the equivalent of landscape changes could have been changes in the areas of the ocean used by whales as they moved to escape hunting pressure. Unfortunately, whaling records are our only source of population data, so it is not possible to investigate to what extent any shift of whale ranges into marginal habitats influenced survival rates.

25. Scarff, "Historic Distribution and Abundance," 489.

26. J. Calambokidis et al., "Movements and Population Structure of Humpback Whales in the North Pacific," *Marine Mammal Science* 17:4 (2001): 769. Details of contemporary humpback population movements are in Mori Kyoichi et al. "Distribution, Migration and Local Movements of Humpback Whale (*Megaptera novaeangliae*) in the Adjacent Waters of the Ogasawara (Bonin) Islands, Japan," *Journal of the School of Marine Science and Technology, Tokai University, Shimizu* 45 (1998): 197.

27. Hideo Omura, "History of Gray Whales in Japan," in *The Gray Whale Eschrischtius robustus,* ed. Mary Lou Jones, Steven L Swartz, and Stephen Leatherwood (New York: Academic Press, 1984): 57–77.

28. See, for example, Komatsu, *Kujira sono rekishi to bunka;* Komatsu, *Yoku wakaru kujira ronsō;* and Kalland, *Fishing Villages in Tokugawa Japan.* This statement also appears in the summary of Japanese whaling in Richard Ellis, *Men and Whales* (New York: Knopf, 1991).

29. This was the case for other animals, such as wolves, which were once worshipped but then exterminated because of the rise of capitalism, industrial agriculture, and other forces, as is pointed out in Brett L. Walker, *The Lost Wolves of Japan* (University of Washington Press, 2005). However, even when the structure of Japanese whaling became more industrial, there was no such dramatic shift in attitude toward whales, possibly because both traditional and industrial interactions with whales involved killing them and using them as a natural resource.

30. Ellis, *Men and Whales*, 84.

31. Kalland and Moeran, *Japanese Whaling: End of an Era?*, 31.

32. For example, Taiji Gorōsaku notes that whalers had to be particularly careful about right whale cows with calves because they were more vicious when provoked than other species; his book is reprinted as Taiji Gorōsaku, "Kumano Taijiura hogei no hanashi (The story of Taiji village, Kumano's whaling)" in *Kujira, iruka no minzoku* (Peoples/races of whales, dolphins), ed. Tanigawa Ken'ichi, Nihon minzoku bunka shiryō shūsei 18 (Collection of historical sources for Japanese people's culture, Tokyo: San'ichi shobō, 1997), 74.

33. Taiji, *Kumano Taijiura hogei no hanashi*, and also Yamashita, *Hogei I*.

34. Taiji, *Kumano Taijiura hogei no hanashi*, 74.

35. Yamashita discusses whales with calves in chapter 4, *Hogei I*, 194–205.

36. Kasahara Masao, *Kinsei gyoson no shiteki kenkyū: Kishū no gyoson o sozai to shite* (Early modern fishing villages historical research: On the subject of Kii Province's fishing villages, Tokyo: Meicho shuppan, 1993).

37. The decline in American catches is noted in Scarff, "Historic Distribution and Abundance," 489.

38. According to Susan Hanley's analysis in "A High Standard of Living in Nineteenth-Century Japan: Fact or Fantasy?" *Journal of Economic History* 43:1 (1983): 183–192, this would be more than twice the average annual household budget of a high-level samurai (about 850 *ryō*). The transfer of management is mentioned in both Takigawa, *Kumano Taiji no denshō*, and Kasahara, *Kinsei gyoson no shiteki kenkyū*.

39. Kasahara, *Kinsei gyoson no shiteki kenkyū*, 156.

40. Yamashita, *Hogei I*, 250.

41. The first set of petitions is in Wakayama kenshi hensan iinkai, *Wakayama kenshi: Kinsei shiryō* vol. 4, section 4, source 7, 732–739. The second letter is in Wakayama kenshi, *Wakayama kenshi: Kin-gendai shiryō* (Modern historical sources) vol. 5.5 (Wakayama-shi: Wakayama-ken, 1976), section 5, source 1, 670–671.

42. Rendered as "*geigyo no gi wa so yori gokokueki ittan ni aru*," Wakayama kenshi, *Wakayama kenshi: Kin-gendai shiryō* vol 5.5, section 5, source 2, 672.

43. Luke Roberts discusses the evolution of *kokueki* in *Mercantilism in a Japanese Domain: The Merchant Origins of Economic Nationalism in 18th-Century Tosa* (Cambridge: Cambridge University Press, 1998). The concept was a means for merchants to justify their value in a social structure that placed them at the bottom of the social scale. It later was co-opted by Meiji nationalists in their construction of a nationally organized political economy.

44. Kasahara, *Kinsei gyoson no shiteki kenkyū*, 216. Monetary conversion based on Hanley, "A High Standard of Living."

45. This assumption is especially prevalent among supporters of whaling today, arguing for whaling's importance in Japanese culture. For example, Komatsu, *Kujira sono rekishi to bunka*, and Kalland and Moeran, *Japanese Whaling*.

46. Taiji Gorōsaku, *Kumano Taijiura hogei no hanashi*, 74–92.

47. "Wakayamaken Kumano ni danshi seinen no sukunai gyoson ari (In Kumano, Wakayama Prefecture, there is a fishing village with few young men and adults)," *Yomiuri shinbun* (January 10, 1879, morning ed.): 2. The second article, "Wakayamaken Taijimura (Taijiura wo teisei) no hogeisen sōnan, shisha 46, fumei 124 (In Taiji village, Wakayama Prefecture [Revised from Taiji temple], whaleboat disaster, 46 dead, 124 unknown/missing)," *Yomiuri shinbun* (January 16, 1879): 2, was much closer to the information given by Gorōsaku.

48. The Wada family did not maintain a whaling group continuously from 1603 until the late nineteenth century, but whaling groups tended to be run by this family of village administrators throughout the Tokugawa period under the name of Wada or Taiji (from a cadet branch).

49. Hamanaka, *Taiji chōshi*, 441–442.

50. Ibid., 442.

51. People had experimented with harpoon guns since at least 1731, but they tended to explode in the gunner's hands. It was not until 1861 that American Thomas Roys developed the shoulder-mounted harpoon gun. Ellis, *Men and Whales*.

52. According to the description of Hogei Kikigaki on page 118 of *Nihon jōmin bunka kenkyūjo* (Research group on Japanese commoner's culture), Shakai keizai shiryō zassan (Socio-economics historical sources miscellaneous collection, Tokyo: Nihon jōmin bunka kenkyūjo: hatsubai Nihon shuppan haikyū, 1943), there was a strong interest in explosive harpoons from an American whaler who had arrived in Hakodate in 1857, when some Kumano whalers were opening whaling operations in Hokkaido.

53. "Kayaku wo shikonda kujiramori wo hatsumei, shisakuhin 3-pon ga kansei shi Wakayamaken de jikken e/Osaka" (Gunpowder-prepared whale lance developed, 3 prototypes completed, to be tested in Wakayama Prefecture/Osaka), *Yomiuri shinbun* (November 19, 1878): 3.

54. Fukumoto, *Nihon hogei shiwa*; also Hamanaka, *Taiji chōshi*.

55. The beater boats chased whales into nets held by other boats and thus were the boats most skilled at rowing quickly. Hamanaka, *Taiji chōshi*, 442–443.

56. Ibid., 443.

57. For the adoption of Western whaling techniques in Taiji, see Hamanaka, *Taiji chōshi*, chapter 2, section 3: "Yōshiki hogei no sōgyō" (Western whaling operations), 443–458.

58. For a detailed view of whaling corporations and mergers, see Watanabe Hiroyuki, *Hogei mondai no rekishi shakaigaku: Kin-gendai Nihon ni okeru kujira to ningen* (A historical sociology of the whaling issue: Relationships between whales and human beings in modern Japan, Tokyo: Tōshindō, 2006), especially table 1-1 on 22–23.

59. Hamanaka, *Taiji chōshi*, noted that Great Eastern Fishing Ltd. (Daitō Gyogyō KK) whaled off the Kumano coast, supplying whale meat to the merchants who had sold the meat from earlier whaling operations.

60. Kalland, *Fishing Villages in Tokugawa Japan*, cites Wada's whaling group based in Taiji as unusual in using the same whaling grounds for over one hundred years (189). They would thus be least likely to give up those whaling grounds and their traditional organization.

61. Watanabe, *Hogei mondai no rekishi shakaigaku*, provides a brief description of net whaling and then moves on to Norwegian-style whaling without mentioning American-style whaling.

62. Even in studies such as Taylor's *Making Salmon* and White's *Organic Machine*, focusing on environmental and anthropogenic factors in salmon population decline, the offshore portion of the salmon life cycle is barely considered. This is less true in McEvoy, *The Fisherman's Problem*, which includes an examination of pelagic California fisheries. Whales are not unique: it is simply more obvious that pressures out in the open ocean are more important for an animal living so far from human spaces.

3

Fisheries Build Up the Nation
Maritime Environmental Encounters
between Japan and China

MICAH MUSCOLINO

Oceans and China's Modernity

Between 1898 and 1906, China's political elites and thousands of Chinese students who spent time studying abroad enthusiastically appropriated intellectual currents originating from Japan. This chapter focuses on a lesser-known aspect of these international currents: the environmental dimensions of Japan's role in the formation of Chinese modernity. The influence of modern Japanese conceptions of the sea and its resources can be traced to Meiji times (1868–1912), when Chinese students in Japan gained exposure to the discipline of fisheries management. Whereas fear and ambiguity characterized premodern Japanese perceptions of the ocean, during the Meiji period, as William Tsutsui demonstrated in chapter 1, Western-educated Japanese writers reimagined the ocean as the foundation for Japan's drive to join the world's imperialist powers.[1] Beginning in the late nineteenth century, Japanese fisheries management discourse was inspired by a scientific and social Darwinian worldview pervasive in Meiji Japan, centered on the idea that national survival necessitated extending control over the ocean and exploiting it as efficiently as possible.[2] After returning to China following their studies in Japan, Japanese-trained Chinese fisheries experts applied this understanding of the marine environment to their own country's fisheries. Echoing their Japanese counterparts, Chinese reformers invoked fisheries management to uphold the nation's sovereignty against looming foreign threats.

Even if the nation was at the center of this environmental discourse, the scale of dissemination was transnational, encompassing Japan, China, and the wider world. Akira Iriye has shown that between 1868 and roughly 1919, Chinese and Japanese elites shared a determination to make their countries militarily strong.[3] These ambitions fit with a "power-centered" world dominated by European nations that became Great Powers by amassing armaments and colonies.[4] Since military strength came from powerful armed forces as well as overseas spheres of influence, this definition of geopolitical power was "interchangeable with imperialism."[5] In modern Japan and China, these geopolitical imperatives gave rise to a distinctive understanding of the marine environment.

Philip Steinberg proposes that in the age of industrial capitalism, the ocean was constructed as an "other" in opposition to the land. The ocean was cast as a "non-territory" that resisted rational planning and existed as an empty "force field" outside the territory of nation-states. In this formulation, the ocean was not a place in which social power was exerted, but a perpetually "empty" space across which power was projected.[6] However, Steinberg's view of the ocean as a space outside society fits poorly with representations of the marine environment in early twentieth-century Japan and China. In a power-centered world order, fisheries management became a tool with which the nation augmented wealth and power by exerting territorial control over parts of the ocean and rationally developing their resources. Rather than a void existing outside of society or the nation, the ocean appeared as a set of developable places that sovereign states could dominate and harness using modern science and technology. Fisheries management was a rational, modernist body of knowledge about the environment that enabled the nation to build up its geopolitical power at the expense of others. This radical simplification of nature in the name of rational control and management was not limited to oceans, but it also applied to mines, agriculture, and other environmental engineering projects.[7]

Even as Japan served as the principal conduit through which modern fisheries management entered China, it also constituted an alarming threat to China's marine fisheries, as Chinese experts discovered. To Chinese fisheries experts, the danger came from Japan's mechanized fishing fleet, which moved into waters off China's coast in the 1910s and 1920s. To block Japanese competition for marine resources off the China coast, reforms pursued in China during the Republican period (1911–1949) drew on techniques that facilitated modern Japan's fisheries expansion. Chinese nationalism, in short, appropriated environmental ideas from the Japanese Empire and redeployed them in opposition to it. These exchanges complicate any opposition between nationalist and imperialist modes of interaction with the environment. This competitive drive to exploit the marine environment and attain geopolitical power—whether in the name of empire or nation—had severe consequences.

Ocean and Nation in Meiji Japan

Throughout the Meiji period, Japanese elites regularly visited international exhibitions in Europe and America and eventually held such spectacles in Japan.[8]

To Japanese participants, such "self-indulgent celebrations of the triumph of industrial technology and the nation-state" presented an opportunity to study advanced foreign techniques and promote them in Japan.[9] This refashioning of foreign knowledge brought with it new ways of thinking about nature. Among the Japanese observers at the great exhibitions in Vienna (1873), Philadelphia (1875), and Paris (1878 and 1900) were fisheries experts sent to investigate European and American aquaculture, fish processing, and manufacturing enterprises. Inspired by these international spectacles, the Meiji government held its own national fisheries exhibitions to spread advances in fishing techniques made in certain regions of Japan all over the country. The first fisheries exhibition opened in Tokyo's Ueno Park in 1883, attracting over twenty-three thousand visitors.[10]

As Japan strove to foster Western-style modernity, Japanese elites recast fishing as an industry to be developed as part of the national economy. Emulating professional associations that existed in Western countries, Japanese fisheries experts formed the Fisheries Society of Japan in 1882.[11] To cultivate scientific and technological expertise, in 1889 the Fisheries Society organized one of Japan's earliest institutes of higher education dedicated to fisheries studies. In 1897 the school's administration transferred to the imperial government. Research and investigation were added to the school's scope, and its name was changed to the Tokyo Fisheries Institute (Suisan kōshūjo).[12]

Fisheries management in Meiji Japan—like scientific agriculture on the newly colonized island of Hokkaido—was framed as thoroughly modern and progressive.[13] The mission of the Tokyo Fisheries Institute was to teach the "scientific principles" (gakuri) of fisheries. In this definition, fisheries studies consisted of "studying techniques for utilizing animals, plants, and minerals as food, fertilizer, industrial applications, and medicinal ingredients in the three main areas of fishing, manufacturing, and aquaculture." While emphasizing practical techniques, the school's curriculum included related scientific disciplines such as zoology, botany, physics, chemistry, geography, oceanography, meteorology, economics, and fisheries law.[14] Ultimately, scientific knowledge would enable efficient exploitation of the marine environment and produce new goods for human consumption.

With the application of modern science and technology, fisheries management would strengthen the nation through rational development of nature. From the outset, the growth of Japan's fishing industry paralleled its industrialization efforts at home and imperial expansion abroad. As the Japan Fisheries Society put it, "The reason for expanding fisheries is to contribute to national wealth and power."[15] During the Chinese-Japanese War of 1894–1895, this link between nature and power crystallized in the slogan "Fisheries build up the nation" (Suisan rikkoku). The Japan Fisheries Society put the ideal into practice, provisioning canned fish as rations for troops stationed overseas.[16]

The correlation between the fishing industry, national strength, and imperial expansion in Meiji was evident in the field of fisheries education. A statement from 1884 announcing the Japan Fisheries Society's intention to set up a fisheries school explained the need for the institution as follows: "In the West it is said that England is celebrated throughout the world for commerce; America is celebrated throughout the world for agriculture. For our country to overtake England and America, gain a magnificent reputation all over, start to rival the other nations of the world, and reach a status that is not shameful, there is no other foundation apart from developing the fishing industry. . . . The way for our country to surpass the other nations of the world is to make our precious fishing industry success-ful."[17] This rhetorical stance placed fisheries at the center of Japan's national and—since every powerful nation had to have an empire—imperial identity. In a world of competing nation-states, fisheries development could take Japan to a position of prominence comparable to Great Britain and the United States. As a Japanese fish-eries textbook published in 1900 concluded, "Fisheries development is the basis of a rich nation, as well as the basis of a strong army."[18] Invoking the slogan "Rich Nation Strong Army," which drove Meiji economic and technological thinking, justified the importance of fisheries studies.[19] The modern Japanese state's scien-tifically informed interventions were to turn the sea into a place of empire. For this reason alone, fisheries education demanded attention.

The Japanese Origins of Modern Fisheries Management in China

During the first three decades of the twentieth century, Chinese reformers embarked on efforts to remake China's fishing industry according to environmen-tal understandings that traveled to China by way of Japan. From Japanese prede-cessors, China inherited a version of fisheries management that represented the sea as an arena for international competition for resources. This conception of marine space brought anxiety and urgency, since failure to harness resources jeop-ardized national sovereignty.

In the waning years of the Qing dynasty (1644–1911), the reformist entrepre-neur Zhang Jian launched the earliest call to modernize China's fisheries after a visit to Japan in 1903, where he observed advances made in the country's fishing industry during the late nineteenth century.[20] Zhang advocated opening a fishing company in the provinces of Zhejiang and Jiangsu, with branches in other coastal provinces. This company would introduce modern technology by purchasing a steam trawler from a German company in Shandong Province's port of Qing-dao, which could patrol fishing grounds and prevent foreign encroachments. The Jiangsu-Zhejiang Fishing Company (Jiang-Zhe yuye gongsi) opened in 1905 with

Zhang as its manager, but the company suffered heavy financial losses, and by the 1920s it closed down.[21]

Despite the business failure, this reform effort brought modern ideas about fisheries from Japan to China. Dissemination took place in Chinese fisheries education institutions modeled on those in Japan.[22] Zhang stressed the importance of fisheries studies by explaining that Europe, Australia, and Japan all held fisheries exhibitions that displayed domestic and foreign products. China also needed a system of fisheries schools like those in Meiji Japan. "The study of spawning, the principles of stock raising, enterprises for manufacturing, and regulations for protection are all matters of fisheries studies."[23] Japan originally learned such techniques from Western countries, but after Japanese students mastered these skills they no longer relied on foreigners. Zhang's proposal for the Jiangsu-Zhejiang Fishing Company contained plans for a fisheries school at the company's headquarters.[24]

With Zhang's support, in 1912 a Chinese graduate of the Tokyo Fisheries Institute set up the Jiangsu Provincial Fisheries School near Shanghai.[25] Over the next two decades, students who returned from Japan opened several other fisheries schools and research centers in China. Throughout the Republican period, nearly all the faculty at Chinese fisheries schools had studied or trained in Japan.[26] In the late 1920s, almost one-third of the Republic of China Fisheries Studies Association (Zhonghua minguo shuichan xuehui), including all of its "life members," had spent time studying in Japanese fisheries schools.[27]

A Japanese fisheries studies textbook translated into Chinese in 1911 as *Fisheries Studies: New Edition* (*Shuichanxue xinbian*) shows how discourses formed in Japan—which stressed scientific progress and the geopolitical significance of resource exploitation—were appropriated in China. The introduction explained that fisheries studies concerned techniques for utilizing animals and plants in aquatic environments. Although marine resources were abundant, as the text pointed out, they were not inexhaustible. Protective regulations ensured that existing species would not decline, while aquaculture made it possible to transplant species into waters where they did not currently exist. Even though people did not exploit all the ocean's resources, every one of them had potential uses. "If things are discarded, it is not because those things are useless. It is because research on techniques for utilizing them is not refined."[28] Perfecting the techniques and fully utilizing marine resources demanded knowledge of the usual array of scientific disciplines: zoology, botany, physics, chemistry, geography, oceanography, and economics. Applying principles from these fields would "promote benefits from the waters to enrich the nation."[29]

A later section of the textbook tied fisheries development to control of the marine environment and naval power. Fisheries expansion was cast as global competition for resources that encompassed Japan, China, and the rest of the world.

The sea was rendered as a geopolitical grid on which nations vied for exclusive influence:

> Nations divide the globe into territories, which all of them protect. Outsiders are not allowed to overstep these boundaries, and this is recognized by all nations. Coastal nations also possess sovereignty over their internal and adjacent seas. All fishing rights within these seas belong to the people of the nation, and foreigners cannot usurp them. But if profits exist everyone covets them, and the seas are vast and difficult to patrol everywhere, so violations of these rights inevitably occur. European and American fishermen previously only fished in the Atlantic Ocean, but since its marine resources have declined and catches are not as abundant as before, they have gradually moved east into the Pacific.[30]

Westerners already tried to hunt seals and whales in seas around Japan. Since the abundance of China's fishing grounds rivaled Japan's, the book's Chinese editor warned, it was only a matter of time before foreigners moved into waters off of China and threatened its fishing rights. But if China developed the fishing industry and strengthened its naval forces, foreigners would not intimidate China. Furthermore, Chinese boats would be able to profit from pelagic fishing grounds in international waters.[31] Even if fishing grounds were outside a nation's coastal waters, territorial control of ocean spaces secured and maintained national power. The ocean was an arena for national strength and imperial expansion.

Nation, Empire, and Environment

In the Republican period, Chinese fisheries experts did not realize their developmental ambitions. To disseminate improvements in gear and processing, the Chinese state replicated the research and education institutes that stimulated fisheries development in Meiji Japan.[32] In 1919, China's government deputed Wang Wentai, another Japanese-educated fisheries expert, to set up a fisheries training institute in the port of Haizhou in northern Jiangsu.[33] Inadequate funding stifled Wang's efforts, but reports written during his time as director of the Haizhou Fisheries Training Institute demonstrate the importance of Japanese models in the formation of Chinese fisheries management discourse. Japan's colonial possessions presented the example to follow. Before Japanese took control of Manchuria, Wang stated, the region's fisheries were woefully underdeveloped. Thereafter, Japanese investigations discovered numerous varieties of whale, bream, shark, and abalone. With this Japanese research, fisheries production in Manchuria had more than doubled over the preceding fifteen years.

Wang's explanation for the weakness of China's fishing industry and the solutions he proposed to remedy it reflected fisheries management concepts he learned in Japan. Wang urged the Chinese government to encourage fishing enterprises to make advances in aquaculture. "If only new fishing gear and methods are used, then fishermen will simply overfish even more and searching for profits will lead to losses instead, which is not a wise policy."[34]

As Takahashi Yoshitaka has argued, preoccupation with protecting the spawning of fish species entered Japan in the late nineteenth century when Japanese fisheries experts participated in international fisheries exhibitions. In fact, the stated mission of the Japan Fisheries Society was to "exchange experience and knowledge related to fisheries and improve spawning in fisheries."[35] Once they came to Japan, these techniques acquired distinctive meanings. Japanese fisheries experts saw presence or absence of efforts to promote the reproduction of marine resources as a yardstick for differentiating between civilized and uncivilized nations. Ensuring reproduction of marine resources required eliminating "harmful and severe fishing methods" that damaged fish stocks and promotion of aquaculture techniques to make resources more abundant.[36]

In Europe and North America, efforts to ensure abundance through stock raising and hatcheries generally failed due to lack of understanding of the physiology and biology of fish, release into unsuitable habitats, and inability of fish to survive predators or compete with other organisms. The idea that aquaculture could sustain fisheries production regardless of exploitative pressures grew out of "the Enlightenment worldview that nature itself could be made industrial and that the transformation of biological organisms into highly productive monocultures was a reasonable path to follow."[37] In Japan, as in Western countries, these assumptions proved ill founded.

Despite the invocation of seemingly conservationist principles by Japanese fisheries experts, growth of Japan's fishing industry required perpetual movement into more distant frontiers to sustain production. During the early Meiji period, Japan overcame stagnating output caused by concentration on overexploited nearshore stocks. To break out of this impasse, fisheries experts employed at schools like the Tokyo Fisheries Institute encouraged more efficient boats and gear capable of operating in more distant seas to expand the scope of fishing grounds.[38]

To further these goals, the Meiji government enacted legislation in 1898 that gave financial incentives to boats that fished in international waters.[39] One of the original motives behind this legislation was to drive foreign fishing vessels out of Japan's coastal seas.[40] Following Japan's example, Chinese fisheries experts urged their government to deal with declining returns from nearshore fishing grounds and keep foreigners out of the nation's coastal waters. However, China never actually gave this financial support to its fishing vessels.[41]

In addition, Chinese fisheries experts looked to Japanese models to spread knowledge about the effective use of marine resources. In Wang Wentai's estimation, China needed to form cooperative fishing associations (Chinese: *yuye zuhe,* Japanese: *gyogyō kumiai*) like the ones that the Japanese had founded in territories they occupied in Shandong and Manchuria. As Wang pointed out, all coastal areas in Japan had fishing cooperatives through which the government directed the fishing population to achieve their mutual benefits and develop the industry.[42]

Japan's military presence in China made setting up cooperative associations and fortifying the fishing industry a particularly urgent task. From the 1890s onward, Japan's military expansion had two important spin-off effects for pelagic fisheries. First, war stimulated government support for the private shipping and shipbuilding sectors, which benefited the fishing industry. Second, acquisition of overseas territories expanded the scope of Japan's fishing rights, making it possible for the Japanese fleet to exploit a larger pool of resources.[43] As Richard White has identified cattle as the fuel for expansion in North America, fish fueled Japanese imperial expansion in East Asia.[44]

With the outbreak of the First World War in 1914, Japan declared war on Germany and occupied its leasehold in Qingdao. Japan's fishing fleet arrived in the wake of the military, coming to Qingdao to supply fish to Japanese troops and expatriates. Responding to a boom in fishing activities, in 1916 the Japanese colonial administration put regulations in place that required all fishing enterprises to obtain official approval and register with Qingdao's military command. The Japanese also made all fishermen join a cooperative association that would work to "reform and develop the fishing industry, protect the reproduction of fish species, correct the harmful trade practices of cooperative members, and promote their mutual benefits."[45]

Japanese vessels came to Shandong each spring for fishing season and entrusted their boats and gear to Qingdao's fishing cooperative when they returned to Japan in the fall. The cooperative worked in conjunction with a central marketing facility that extended credit to Japanese fishing enterprises and monopolized the sale of all fish landed in the port.[46] Although supply fluctuated on a seasonal basis, mechanized refrigeration facilities enabled the market to store fish and sell it at periods of peak demand. This system safeguarded credit, expanded sales channels, and facilitated financial transactions between producers and merchants.[47]

By the 1920s, these measures had made Qingdao the center for Japanese fishing activities off the northern coast of China in the Bohai and Yellow Seas. The Qingdao-based Japanese fleet sold much of the fish it caught in these waters in north China.[48] Wang Wentai claimed that Japanese had stifled China's fishing industry by driving down prices and forcing out domestic producers, while competition from Japanese trawlers in the Yellow Sea reduced the catches of Chinese boats. Initially, as Wang stated, "Because their ambition was to control the seas in perpetuity, they enact protections for the reproduction and spawning of lower-level fish stocks, and the gear they used did not impede reproduction." However, overfishing with "severe" fishing gear still had the potential to "decrease or extinguish" production.

When talk of handing Qingdao over to China grew more frequent in the early 1920s and the Japanese expected to lose the fishing center, Japan allegedly sent large numbers of mechanized trawlers to fish rapaciously in the Yellow Sea. Japan and the nations of Europe and North America strictly prohibited these vessels in their coastal waters because they "overfish and impede spawning," but the Japanese actively encouraged them to fish off the coast of Qingdao.[49] Trawlers damaged the spawning of bottom-dwelling species, so restrictions on this technology had to be put in place. "In the future, regardless of whether or not that nation's fishing trawlers come to our seas to wreak havoc, precautions should be taken and prohibitions placed on steam trawlers to prevent overfishing."[50] Wang called for restrictions like ones Japan used to limit trawling activities off its coast, thereby protecting small-scale domestic producers and shifting the burden of modern technologies to more distant waters.

Given the conflation of maritime space and sea power, Japanese incursions on fishing grounds off the coast of China appeared to violate China's national sovereignty. As Wang Wentai put it, "Fisheries build up the nation's sea power (*liguo haiquan*). No nations in the world today permit fishers from other nations to carry out trade in their territorial waters. Qingdao must be entirely handed over to our nation on the basis of this principle."[51] To counter the threat, Wang called for China to reclaim Japanese fishing organizations in Qingdao and consolidate the nation's fishing rights in the Yellow Sea.[52] This move to assert Chinese control over the sea's resources had a global inspiration. "In all nations of the world today, the sale of fish is carried out via fish markets. Although their structure and regulations are different, their character is to regulate prices, expand markets, and benefit the hygiene of citizens. For this reason, fish markets are well developed in all the nations in Europe, America, and Japan, while those run by the Japanese in Dalian and Lushun have also met with excellent results." After China reclaimed Qingdao, it would keep the infrastructure that the Japanese had used to make its fishing industry successful. As Wang concluded, "The original spirit of this market should not be suddenly changed."[53] After Japan ceded Qingdao to China in 1922, Chinese merchants organized a market of their own, but it soon went out of business and Japanese enterprises retained dominance in Shandong's fishing industry.[54]

Nevertheless, Japan still acted as the inspiration for Chinese fisheries reforms throughout the 1920s and 1930s. Following the blueprint presented by Japan's possessions in Qingdao, in 1921 China's Ministry of Agriculture and Commerce announced an agenda for the revitalization of the country's fishing industry. The Chinese government planned to set up state-run marketing facilities and collect fees to fund education and relief for the fishing population. Same-trade associations would be promoted to further fishermen's mutual interests.[55]

Japan's reorganization of Qingdao's fisheries acted as an "outside stimulus" for China's move to develop its fishing industry. Additional impetus came from Japanese-trained experts such as Wang Wentai, who pressed to implement their fisheries-development proposals.[56] With this encouragement, China's Ministry of Agriculture and Commerce ordered surveys of coastal areas in 1924 to find ports suitable for modern fishing harbors equipped with marketing facilities, transport, and refrigeration equipment like those found in Japan.[57] Fisheries development also appeared in Sun Yat-sen's *Industrial Plan* (*Shiye jihua*), which called for construction of modern fishing harbors along China's coast to open up the nation's marine resources and expand its fishing territories.[58]

The goal of remaking China's fishing industry in the image of Japan's took on greater urgency in the 1920s and 1930s due to incursions by Japan's fishing fleet. After discovering abundant bream fishing grounds outside of Jiaozhou Bay in 1917, Japanese vessels converged on them, assisted by subsidies from Qingdao's military command. Fishing season lasted from May to October of each year, when "mountains of bream piled up in the market."[59] It took less than a decade for bream stocks to decline due to overfishing by mechanized Japanese vessels.[60] After Japan's fleet exhausted bream stocks, it moved to yellow croaker fishing grounds off China's southeast coast. Japan's trawlers sold most of their fish in Shanghai, where the unequal treaties signed in the nineteenth century allowed Japanese to land and market their catch without impediment. Chinese fishing enterprises urged their government to keep technologically superior Japanese vessels out of China's coastal waters. But Japan's ability to support its fishing industry with diplomatic pressure and the threat of military force prevented China from limiting Japanese access to these fishing grounds.[61]

Even as Japanese vessels placed greater pressures on fish populations, China struggled to counter foreign competition and control fishing territories by expanding domestic production and marketing. The same drive to fortify national wealth and power by controlling marine resource space that motivated imperial Japan's move into China's coastal fishing grounds motivated Chinese efforts to resist these incursions.

Beginning in the mid-1930s, China's Nationalist government prepared to open a central fish market in Shanghai. China's Ministry of Industry sent a team of fisheries experts led by Hou Chaohai, who had trained in Japan, on a fact-finding mission to Japan in 1933 to gather information on how the Japanese government regulated the marketing of fish.[62] The Shanghai Fish Market opened for business in June 1936, and the Nationalist government took control of fish sales in China's largest consumption center.[63] But any assertion of Chinese control did not last for long, since the Japanese military occupied Shanghai in 1938 following the outbreak of war with China.

Persistence of Japanese Influence in China's Fisheries after 1949

Since the beginning of the twentieth century, Japanese-trained Chinese fisheries experts advocated modern science and technical expertise to achieve more rational and efficient exploitation of the marine environment. Prior to 1949, fisheries experts fell short of implementing plans to remake relationships between society and nature. Nevertheless, their developmental vision exerted a direct influence over fisheries policies carried out under the People's Republic of China (PRC). In the 1950s, the PRC realized Republican-period plans when they set up state-run marketing facilities to control the pricing and distribution of fish, along with cooperatives that provisioned gear and supplies to fishing boats. These development measures extended from the effort to rationalize exploitation of the marine environment according to high modernist models from Japan.[64]

It is not at all difficult to explain these continuities. Japan-trained experts who staffed fisheries offices under the Chinese Nationalist regime held leadership positions in the PRC's education and research institutes well into the 1950s.[65] The difference before and after 1949 was that the PRC, unlike its Nationalist counterpart, actually had the capacity to carry out these plans. Yet the PRC could not eliminate international pressures from the rebuilt and expanded postwar Japanese fleet, which returned to waters off the coast of China in the 1950s.[66] By the 1970s, China and Japan overexploited fish populations in the Yellow Sea and East China Sea. Once-abundant bream and yellow croaker stocks, as well as other commercially important species, soon reached the brink of collapse.[67] The average trophic levels of catches from the two seas decreased (a phenomenon called "fishing down the food web") as demersal fish such as yellow croaker declined and small pelagic species increased. The annual catch per unit effort (CPUE) in the Yellow Sea fell from 3.46 tons per unit horsepower (thp) in 1962 to 0.03 thp in 2001, and annual CPUE in the East China Sea declined from 1.89 thp in 1961 to 0.01 thp in 2001.[68] Modern fisheries management had proven disappointing at best.

Conclusion

In Japan and China, strengthening the nation by efficiently developing natural resources through technology and science was central to the modern project.

During the Meiji period, Japanese reformers adopted Western models of fisheries management, and during the early 1900s these discourses traveled from Japan to China. Fisheries experts in Japan and China endeavored to rationalize exploitation of the environment through centralized, scientific management, thereby augmenting the nation's geopolitical power. Japanese and Chinese approaches to fisheries management closely resembled those prevalent in nineteenth-century Europe and the United States, which expressed a strong developmental bias and held that scientific and technological interventions could eliminate waste, achieve efficient utilization, and make nature endlessly productive.[69]

The discipline of fisheries management acquired particular significance upon its reception under distinctive circumstances prevailing in Japan and China.[70] Developing the ocean's wealth through application of modern technology and scientific expertise fortified the power of the nation-state. In this formulation, the marine environment was imagined as a site of geopolitical competition for resources. This spatial order rendered legible only components of the ocean relevant for spurring economic growth, exploiting resources, and maintaining military defense.

The disciple of fisheries management posited the marine environment as "dominated space" that the state and its expert advisors controlled and transformed with modern technologies. The ocean as an "appropriated space" that served the needs of fishing communities was not part of this spatial construction.[71] People who fished appeared only at the margins of writings by fisheries experts. The only role for these benighted social groups was as beneficiaries of enlightenment and progress promised by state-run fishing associations. Marginalization and control went hand in hand with the construction of maritime space.

Finally, by constructing the sea as a space of geopolitical struggle, scientific discourses of fisheries management fueled the transformation of the marine ecosystem. In a power-centered international system, national strength required developing marine resources and making exploitation as efficient as possible. Any nation that squandered nature's wealth risked forfeiting it to outsiders who could utilize resources more efficiently. Careless use of the natural environment was anathema only because it would hinder the interests of the nation in the prevailing world order.

Notes

1. Marcia Yonemoto, "Maps and Metaphors of the 'Small Eastern Sea' in Tokugawa Japan (1603–1868)," *Geographical Review* 89:2 (1999): 170–171.

2. Julia Adeney Thomas, *Reconfiguring Modernity: Concepts of Nature in Japanese Political Ideology* (Berkeley: University of California Press, 2001).

3. Akira Iriye, *China and Japan in the Global Setting* (Cambridge, MA: Harvard University Press, 1992), 8.

4. Ibid., 37.

5. Ibid., 15.

6. Philip E. Steinberg, *The Social Construction of the Ocean* (Cambridge: Cambridge University Press, 2001).

7. James C. Scott, *Seeing Like a State: How Certain Schemes to Improve the Human Condition Have Failed* (New Haven, CT: Yale University Press, 1998).

8. Angus Lockyer, "Japan at the Exhibition, 1867–1970." Doctoral diss., Department of History, Stanford University, 2000.

9. Tessa Morris-Suzuki, *The Technological Transformation of Japan: From the Seventeenth to the Twenty-first Century* (New York: Cambridge University Press), 82.

10. Kokuritsu kyōiku kenkyūjo, ed., *Nihon kindai kyōiku hyaku nen shi*, vol. 9: *Suisan kyōiku 1* (One-hundred-year history of education in modern Japan, vol. 9: Fisheries education) (Tokyo: Kyōiku kenkyū shinkōkai, 1973), 784.

11. Ibid., 785.

12. John L. Kask, *Fisheries Education and Research in Japan* (Tokyo: General Headquarters, Supreme Commander for the Allied Powers, Natural Resources Section, 1946), 12.

13. Brett L. Walker, "Meiji Modernization, Scientific Agriculture, and the Destruction of Japan's Hokkaido Wolf," *Environmental History* 9:2 (2004).

14. Kokuritsu kyōiku kenkyūjo, *Nihon kindai kyōiku*, 805.

15. Ibid., 795.

16. Ibid., 797.

17. Ibid., 798.

18. Ibid., 818.

19. See Richard J. Samuels, *"Rich Nation, Strong Army": National Security and the Technological Transformation of Japan* (Ithaca, NY: Cornell University Press, 1994).

20. *Shanghai yuye zhi* (Shanghai fisheries gazetteer) (Shanghai: Shanghai shehui kexue yanjiuyuan, 1998), 545.

21. Li Shihao and Qu Ruoqian, *Zhongguo yuye shi* (A history of China's fisheries) (Shanghai: Shangwu yinshuguan, 1937), 42, 154–156.

22. *Dongfang zazhi* (Eastern miscellany) (hereafter DFZZ), September 1904, 112.

23. DFZZ, March 1906, 27–28.

24. Ibid., 26–27.

25. *Shanghai yuye zhi*, 546–547.

26. Wang Tang, "Duiyu zhengdun Zhongguo yuye zhi guanjian" (Ideas on the reform of China's fisheries), in *Shenbao* (Shanghai daily) (hereafter SB), June 22, 1924 (supplement): 2.

27. "Zhongguo shuichan xuehui huiyuan lu" (China Fisheries Studies Association membership record), in *Zhonghua minguo shuichan xuehui huibao* (Bulletin of the Republic of China Fisheries Studies Association) (1934): 101–112. Shanghai Municipal Archives: Y4-1-225.

28. Gu Mingsheng, trans. *Shuichanxue xinbian* (Fisheries studies: New edition) (Shanghai: Shanghai kexue shuju, 1911), 1–2.

29. Ibid., 128.

30. Ibid., 21.

31. Ibid., 22.

32. Ninohei Tokuo, *Nihon gyogyō kindai shi* (History of modern Japan's fisheries, Tokyo: Heibonsha, 1999), 105–111.

33. "Zhongguo shuichan xuehui huiyuan lu," 112.

34. "Wang Wentai chen song Haizhou yuye jihuashu cheng gao" (Report from Wang Wentai on draft plan for Haizhou's fisheries), February 20, 1920, in *Zhonghua minguo shi dang'an ziliao huibian* (Collection of archival materials on the history of the Republic of China) (hereafter ZMDZH) (Nanjing: Jiangsu guji chubanshe, 1991), vol. 1, 3, 682–683.

35. Ibid., 785.

36. Takahashi Yoshitaka, "19 seiki matsu Nihon ni okeru suisan seikaku no tokuchō to dōjidai shiteki ichi" (The special characteristics of fisheries policy in late nineteenth-century Japan and their world-historical meaning) *Nihon shi kenkyū* (Researches in Japanese history) 533 (2007): 23–46.

37. Paul R. Josephson, *Resources under Regimes: Technology, Environment, and the State* (Cambridge, MA: Harvard University Press, 2004), 48.

38. Ninohei Tokuo, 58, 60–61, 93–97, 102; Okamoto Nobuo, *Kindai gyogyō hattatsu-shi* (History of modern fisheries development) (Tokyo: Suisansha, 1965), 257; Nihon kyōiku kenkyujo, *Nihon kindai kyōiku*, 808–809.

39. Okamoto, *Kindai gyogyō hattatsushi*, 111–112.

40. Nihon kyōiku kenkyūjo, *Nihon kindai kyōiku*, 797, 814.

41. Li and Qu, *Zhongguo yuye shi*, 19.

42. "Wang Wentai chen song Haizhou yuye jihuashu cheng gao," 683.

43. Nihon kyōiku kenkyūjo, *Nihon kindai kyōiku*, 815; Yamamura Kozo, "Success Ill-gotten? The Role of Meiji Militarism in Japan's Technological Progress," *Journal of Economic History* 37:1 (1977).

44. Richard White, "Animals and Enterprise," in *The Oxford History of the American West*, ed. Clyde A. Milner II, Carol A. O'Connor, and Martha A. Sandweiss (New York: Oxford University Press, 1994), 237–274.

45. "Haizhou yuye jishu chuanxisuo wei baosong Qingdao yuye diaocha baogao shu cheng gao" (Draft of investigation report on Qingdao's fisheries from the Haizhou Fisheries School), April 7, 1922, ZMDZH, 705.

46. Ibid., 695, 701–707.

47. "Wang Wentai mibao Ri ren jingying Qingdao yuye you ai woguo haiquan yuli ji jieshou shi sheshi jielüe gao" (Abridged draft of secret report from Wang Wentai on the impediments to our country's sea power and fishing rights from Japanese fishing enterprise in Qingdao and measures for retrocession), ZMDZH, 716–717.

48. "Haizhou yuye jishu," 704–706. See also Li and Qu, *Zhongguo yuye shi*, 199–200.

49. "Wang Wentai mibao Ri ren jingying Qingdao yuye you ai woguo haiquan yuli ji jieshou shi sheshi jielüe gao," 716.

50. Ibid., 721.

51. Ibid., 719.

52. Ibid., 720–725.

53. Ibid., 722.

54. Chintao suisan kumiai, *Chintao suisan no gaikyō* (The condition of Qingdao's fisheries) (Qingdao: Chintao suisan kumiai, 1936), 4, 7.

55. SB, July 14, 1921, 11.

56. Ibid.

57. SB, March 3, 1924, 15.

58. Sun Yat-sen, *The International Development of China* (Taibei: China Cultural Service, 1953), 155–159.

59. Chintao suisan kumiai, *Chintao suisan no gaikyō,* 4.

60. Ibid., 111, 125.

61. Micah S. Muscolino, "The Yellow Croaker War: Fisheries Disputes between China and Japan, 1925–1935," *Environmental History* 13:2 (2008).

62. Shanghai yuye zhi bianzuan weiyuanhui, *Shanghai yuye zhi,* 549.

63. *Shanghai shi nianjian* (Shanghai municipal yearbook) (Shanghai: Shanghai shi tongzhiguan, 1937), Q 71.

64. Micah S. Muscolino, *Fishing Wars and Environmental Change in Late Imperial and Modern China* (Cambridge, MA: Harvard University Asia Center, 2009), chapter 7.

65. *Shanghai yuye zhi,* 547–549; *Zhejiang sheng shuichanzhi* (Zhejiang Province fisheries gazetteer) (Beijing: Zhonghua shuju, 1999), 1008–1009, 1015–1016.

66. Henry N. Scheiber, *Inter-Allied Conflicts and Ocean Law, 1945–1953: The Occupation Command's Revival of Japanese Whaling and Marine Fisheries* (Taipei: Institute of European and American Studies, Academia Sinica, 2001).

67. Terazaki Makoto, "Recent Large-scale Changes in the Biomass of the Kuroshio Current Ecosystem," in *Biomass Yields and Geography of Large Marine Ecosystems,* AAAS Selected Symposium 111, ed. K. Sherman and L. M. Alexander (Boulder: Westview Press), 37–65.

68. *PICES Special Publication: Marine Ecosystems of the North Pacific* (Sidney, Canada: North Pacific Marine Science Organization, 2004), 70–71.

69. Arthur McEvoy, *The Fisherman's Problem: Ecology and Law in the California Fisheries, 1850–1980* (Cambridge: Cambridge University Press, 1986), 108; Josephson, *Resources under Regimes,* 5–6, 197–198.

70. David N. Livingstone, *Putting Science in Its Place: Geographies of Scientific Knowledge* (Chicago: University of Chicago Press, 2003).

71. Henri Lefebvre, *The Production of Space,* trans. Donald Nicholson-Smith (Oxford: Blackwell, 1991), 164–167.

CHANGING LANDSCAPES | II

4

Talking Sulfur Dioxide

Air Pollution and the Politics of
Science in Late Meiji Japan

TAKEHIRO WATANABE

"Is it not the case, gentlemen, that the copper poisoning crisis . . . was caused by scientific progress deviating from the principles of civilization?" alleged parliamentarian Mutō Kinkichi during a 1909 Diet session on an air pollution case in eastern Ehime Prefecture, on the Japanese island of Shikoku.[1] The legislator had just returned from a tour of the agricultural area devastated by sulfur dioxide emissions from the Shisakajima Refinery, which stood in the middle of the Inland Sea on four uninhabited islands and was operated, along with the nearby Besshi Mine, by the Sumitomo industrial conglomerate. In speaking of "the withering of crops, grass, and trees" and "cattle and horses unable to produce offspring,"[2] he was following the oratory style of a former Diet member, Tanaka Shōzō, Japan's early antipollution leader and the inspiration for Mutō's career-defining campaign against this toxin. The lawmaker argued that it was "a problem for politicians to decide based on the advice of scientists," and a turn to ethics would steer science back to serving society.[3]

This chapter explores the politics of scientific knowledge during two related Meiji-period air pollution cases in Ehime Prefecture: the Niihama Refinery Pollution Incident, which began in 1893, and the Shisakajima Refinery Pollution Incident, which began in 1905. In these cases, the copper refineries released sulfur dioxide into the atmosphere, which oxidized into sulfuric acid, damaged crops, and harmed the local economy. After farmers staged violent protests and village leaders invited government experts to conduct investigations, a series of negotiations with the company and state officials resulted in Japan's first government-monitored air pollution policy, which included a compensation program for the affected region, a planned series of meetings that spanned four decades, and a production schedule synchronized with the agricultural cycle.[4] What made this intervention possible was a historical confluence of the protest traditions of the local peasantry, the recruiting of experts by village officials to conduct investigations, and the state's attention to the epistemological difficulties in using scientific data.

The outcome was extraordinary at a time when the natural environment was being sacrificed for industrial expansion. In the "sociotechnical imaginary"[5] of Meiji Japan, copper production was central to its modernization effort not only because it was the key material used in the conduction of electricity, but also because it financed industrialization projects, brought in technological knowledge, and fueled the building of a modern infrastructure. Pollution, therefore, was seen as an unfortunate but necessary sacrifice for nation building. Many other antipollution movements—most significantly the long, bitter campaign led by Tanaka against the Ashio Mine—failed to win concessions for the victims or stop environmental degradation. The outcome was telling of the priorities of the nation-state: as the land became barren and the erosion gave way to devastating floods, entire farming communities vanished or were forcibly relocated, while copper production continued. Like the Furukawa conglomerate, Ashio's operator, Sumitomo Zaibatsu, had deep government connections: the head of the merchant clan, Sumitomo Tomoito, was a brother of Saionji Kinmochi, Japan's prime minister during the Shisakajima case.

Yet, the local communities in Ehime successfully pushed the state and the company to cut emissions and make reparations. After a trouble-ridden offshore relocation of the offending refinery, the antipollution leaders persuaded the national government to mediate between the farmers and the company in the Air Pollution Compensation Talks (Engai Baishō Kyōgikai), the first one of which occurred in 1909, and they were held every two to three years until the last meeting in 1939. In these talks, the company agreed to a production schedule that matched the agricultural calendar, launched a reforestation program, and developed a technology to remove the toxin from the emissions. The company also compensated victims and later gave donations for, among other things, "edifying ideology [shisō], improving public good for society, and preserving scenic beauty."[6]

Historians have written about these Besshi cases as a triumph of local communities against the state-industry alliance—a social historical narrative about the awakening of a grassroots political consciousness that challenged modern capitalism and the Meiji regime.[7] My retelling of this story focuses on science's role in the political construction of sulfur dioxide, the chemical compound that the negotiating parties identified as the primary cause of damage to plant and animal life. Before the advent of modern chemistry, the pollutant was referred to as smoke (kemuri) or "ore poison" (kōdoku). But when it became apparent that science could deliver proof of the toxin's existence, a struggle ensued over the legal status of the evidence derived from observations and experiments. Modern science was fast becoming a secular religion, its myths and rituals praising society's growing capacity to understand nature and harness its powers, but large-scale environmental disasters, especially those generated by the industrial application of science, often prompted society to question this new expertise.[8] In the Besshi cases, however, power maneuvered truth through negotiations, trials, and investigations amid armed protests in a game that was rigged so that science would always emerge victorious.

By the late Meiji period, science supplied the discursive currency for the negotiations between the farming communities, the company, and state actors. The state technocracy, driven by the urgency to modernize, was expanding as rapidly as the cadre of scientists and engineers hired by the nation's industrialists. Government agronomic programs introduced modern uses of pest control, fertilizer, and seed varieties, thus building local capacity to conduct surveys and execute action plans—methods later used by the village officials to document sulfuric acid deposition—as well as plugging local leaders into a national network of government experts.[9] But while the village elites recognized the value of scientific investigation, the tenant farmers, who knew about the local mining pollution from the past two centuries, saw science as offering ineffective and confusing solutions to what was at the core a political problem. When the company stonewalled the talks by insisting on further investigations, the farmers grew impatient and resorted to armed collective action in the style of peasant uprisings (*ikki*), which had gained popularity during the Freedom and Popular Rights Movement of the 1880s.[10] These protests dovetailed later on in eastern Ehime with the tenancy disputes of the 1920s and 1930s.[11]

The antipollution leaders therefore had to answer the doubts of unconvinced farmers and the skepticism aired by the mining conglomerate. Science enabled investigators to identify sulfuric acid, but it could not grant the chemical legal objectivity without the help of the state.[12] To overcome this impasse, the Ministry of Agriculture and Commerce became engaged in the task of building a consensus by recognizing the constructed and limited nature of technoscientific knowledge, drawing a sharp boundary between science and politics, and establishing procedural regularity for investigations and negotiations.[13] The state underwrote science's authority by distancing the talks from the scenes of social unrest and shielding the data from political and economic interests.

These talks centered on sulfur dioxide, which emerged not only as a noxious compound but also as an ideological abstraction and a target of regulation. Already in the Tokugawa period, the polluting agent was engaged in "the mixing of natural and social worlds,"[14] as it helped shape not only the region's ecosystem and geology but also landownership patterns, labor-management relations, and even shogunal tax policy. But it truly emerged as a "quasi-object" during these pollution cases, inspiring hired scientists to detect its existence and capitalize on its chemical potentials.[15] The discovery of its usefulness in the industrial production of synthetic nitrates—a chemical of world-historical importance because it made possible the mass production of artificial fertilizer and explosives[16]—triggered shifts in the social meaning of sulfur dioxide from being an obstacle hindering Japan's development to a solution for "the problem" of tenant unionization, as well as a substance indispensible to the nation's military ambitions. Finally, the burden of measuring the amount of toxin and their effect on the livelihood of the farmers proved to be too great, as calculated compensations, based on elaborate formulas, were replaced by lump-sum donations. When science identified sulfur dioxide, however, it ceased to be only a political construct and emerged as a powerful historical agent, shaping society's relationship to the environment.

Scientific Skepticism

Since 1690, when the Sumitomo merchant family began mining at Besshi, quarrying, smelting, and logging operations had contaminated rivers, denuded forests, and caused landslides, often with disastrous consequences. In late Meiji, technological modernization widened Besshi's environmental footprint and exacerbated the already tense relationship between the industrial giant and local agricultural communities. Smelters had always released sulfur dioxide, which upon contact with air or water oxidizes into sulfuric acid. But the introduction of the reverberatory furnace technology, which required the use of coal, increased production and toxic output. High concentration of sulfuric acid is known to damage plants, desiccating leaves and stunting growth: in the two modern-day cases at Besshi, it was reported that "reddish streams" of smoke were visible to the naked eye,[17] had a "strong, acerbic scent,"[18] and burned off the buds during the crop's budding season. The relocation of refineries also intensified the damage, as the smelters in the mountains were moved down to the foothills because the pollution-induced deforestation and landslides made operations untenable. This operational overhaul paralleled the effort to follow the vein downward, which was shaped like a curtain cutting vertically into the crust: as the vast network of mineshafts, which began from twelve hundred meters above sea level, inched closer to sea level, it was more efficient to have mine openings, and hence the refineries, near the port. By 1893, when the pollution began to noticeably damage crops, the company had just completed a comprehensive modernization project that included the consolidation of the once-scattered refineries to the new Sōbiraki plant, a network of modern tunnels and mountain railroads, a hydroelectric dam, and the rationalization of labor management by eradicating a legacy system of subcontractor middlemen.[19]

Local villagers immediately blamed Sumitomo, but because they could not get the prefecture to publicly recognize the pollution, they petitioned the company, and later the national government, to conduct investigations of the contaminated land. Meanwhile, the villagers staged demonstrations that at times turned violent. The frustration felt by the local community stemmed from its experience with two centuries of pollution: even before the construction of the Sōbiraki Refinery, the villagers in 1884 filed a grievance accusing Sumitomo of never paying compensation for the polluted water and noting concern that "this project will also release smoke or contaminated water that will seep into the earth and cause immeasurable damage."[20] In September 1893, when the pollution was already doing damage, representatives from Niihama village visited Sumitomo's local office and demanded that they conduct a survey to determine the cause of the crop failure. But the company denied any wrongdoing and instead named pest infestation as the cause.[21] A few hundred farmers, upon learning of this denial, surrounded the office, only to be quelled by police intervention. The following year saw more crop injury, and in July farmers from Kaneko village met at a local shrine and marched to the office with bamboo spears and flags. When the police arrived, a scuffle ensued and twenty-three were arrested—of whom twelve were charged for gathering with intent to cause civil unrest—a few years before the protesters of the Ashio pollution case were detained based on the same law.

Shortly after, the local landlords visited the company in Osaka. Sumitomo, by promising to investigate and report the findings to the Ministry of Agriculture and Commerce, maintained scientific skepticism. This position stalled their effort, as the company refused to admit guilt and insisted on further investigation because the crop failure could have had any number of causes, such as disease, pest infestation, and the weather.[22] This was also the same year that Sumitomo began to acquire agricultural land in the Niihama region. Separately, plans were under way for the central government to conduct a nationwide survey of copper mining pollution cases, prompted by the troubles at Ashio. After an investigative team, as part of this survey, visited Niihama, the Osaka Office of Mines in 1898 issued a directive that ordered the company to relocate the refinery and "stop the use of the current ore refinery method."[23] An internal government report, which may have been used as a basis for this directive, stated that "the decline in agricultural output within the affected areas is directly caused by smoke pollution" and that fumes from the refinery "contained . . . , without doubt, sulfuric acid gas and particles of copper sulfides," which "directly cause the stems and leaves of agricultural products to rot."[24]

Sumitomo, however, was silent about the causal link between pollution and crop damage when it relocated the copper refinery to Shisakajima, a cluster of four islands in the Inland Sea chosen because the site was believed to be distant enough from land for the pollutants to not affect agriculture. The company also prevented unrest by becoming the largest landowner in the region;[25] by 1902, Sumitomo owned 12.7 percent of agricultural land in the areas surrounding the plant.[26] Later, when fumes from Shisakajima caused crop damage, Niihama farmers "had to accept the pollution and swallow their tears in secret," because "Sumitomo owns many plots in this area."[27]

Science as Political Capital

The offshore relocation of the refinery, which was part of Sumitomo's continuing effort to modernize their operation, doubled copper output within a decade: in 1905, 3,902 tons of refined copper were produced; by 1915, the figure increased to 7,889 tons.[28] But the basin-like topography of the Inland Sea area offered favorable conditions for the chemical's wide distribution, as the fumes slid across the sea unimpeded, curling up in concentrated amounts against the mountain ranges of Shikoku and Honshu, where they caused damage to farmland in the counties of Ochi and Shūsō in eastern Ehime, as well as to areas near Hiroshima on the opposite coast.

Unlike in the earlier Niihama case, the company had less influence in the affected counties. The tactic of buying up polluted land was later proposed by Ōura Kanetake, at the time the minister of agriculture and commerce,[29] but what made this option a nonchoice was the dominance of the local landlord class. During the Tokugawa period, these landowning families flourished as the local suppliers of goods for the mining industry, benefiting from the acquisition of landholdings contaminated by the pollution, as well as the shogunal tax reductions from 1702 to 1870 that were implemented because of pollution-related reduction in agricultural output.[30] In the Meiji period, these landlords maintained political power as village officials; by the late Meiji, national tax, agronomic, and public health initiatives strengthened the capacity of local governments to carry out countywide investigations. When the 1873 Land Tax Reform took effect, Ehime Prefecture ordered villages to conduct their own investigation to measure land, land use, and the amount of harvest and then compared their findings across villages to sort out discrepancies.[31] Agronomic programs, such as the promotion of new plant strains and pest control,[32] had also put into use networks of data collection offices and trained villagers in the logistics of scientific investigations.

So when faced with the possibility of crop failure, the town mayors and village heads in Shūsō and Ochi counties organized investigation teams to conduct surveys and map the damage. The Pollution Investigation Association of Shūsō County, for example, consisted of the heads of two towns and twelve villages who were responsible for completing, on a daily basis, forms for recording smoke density and crop damage.[33] In July 1906, upon separate requests from the mayor of

Nyūgawachō in Shūsō and the mayor of Tomitamura in Ochi, investigators from the prefecture and the county collected specimens of injured crops, which they sent for testing.[34] By August, Ochi County leaders had organized several "smoke-poison" investigations and sent samples to labs run by the Ministry of Agriculture and Commerce in Nishigahara, Tokyo, which concluded that the spots on the leaves of the rice plant were caused by the fumes. On September 1, village heads in Shūsō met in Nyūgawachō and decided to send a petition to the Osaka Office of Mines demanding an end to the air pollution. Similar petitions were sent to the prefecture and Sumitomo.[35]

An important initiative of the villagers was to invite a high-ranking ally to collect data. In 1906, the Agricultural Union of Ochi commissioned Okada Yutaka, who was then a technician for the prefectural agricultural association, to conduct an investigation. In a report compiled later that year, he unequivocally concluded that "the direct cause of the crop damage that suddenly appeared this year in Ochi and Shūsō counties is the smoke from Shisakajima" and that "the fumes from the Shisakajima Refinery contain large amounts of sulfuric acid gas" which is "injurious to crops."[36] The report was the first step in the creation of sulfur dioxide as a legally actionable object. Likening the damage to the injury to plants near volcanoes, the report established the observable effect of sulfuric fumes on vegetation, such as the browning of the leaves due to their "desiccation at the cellular level."[37] In one section, the report linked the emissions to the refinery process by explaining that six to twelve parts of sulfur were released for every part of refined ore and determining that the local topography and weather patterns were the main factors in the geographical variations of the damage.[38] The report also dismissed alternative explanations such as disease, pests, soil degradation, excessive rain, and drought. To discredit disease, for example, it cited six pieces of counterevidence, including the lack of microscopic spots (which are signs of infection), the sprouting of new leaves (which does not occur with an infection), and the fact that while bacteria affects different plants differently, the damage in Ochi was uniform across species. Strong wind, another claimed possibility, was disproved by tracking the daily changes in wind—direction, strength, and temperature—over a span of two months in Ochi, as well as in Matsuyama for comparison.

When this report became available, the governor of Ehime Prefecture submitted a request, jointly with a Sumitomo representative, for the government to conduct an investigation. In 1908, the Ministry of Agriculture and Commerce sent a team of investigators—a livestock specialist from Tokyo University, an engineer from the ministry's Office of Forestry, an engineer from the Kyoto School of Silk Industry, and two agricultural specialists from Nishigahara—for a six-month investigation.[39] During August of the same year, Nakata Kinkichi, the general manager of Sumitomo's Osaka office, visited Ochi. Upon Kinkichi's arrival on August 25, over five thousand farmers gathered in Ochi, while in Shūsō twenty-five hundred farmers gathered the following day to hear an update on the negotiation. The farmers, concerned about Sumitomo's inaction, marched four thousand strong to the company office in Niihama, despite injunctions from the police.[40] That same year, the director of the Bureau of Mining in Osaka visited with a team of scientists, as did the governor of Ehime Prefecture, several Diet members, and Minister Ōura.

Amid this tense atmosphere, the village leadership sent two petitions to the government, signed respectively by 760 farmers from Ochi and 780 from Shūsō. The letters accomplished, for the first time, the task of entering a substantial set of evidence into the public record.[41] The petitions—which Mutō and fellow Seiyūkai Party member Natsui Tamoshirō, a representative from Ehime, submitted to the Diet—asked for a revision of the mining laws that would set up a legal mechanism for pollution victims to receive compensation from offending companies. Attached as an appendix was a twenty-six-page summary of the Okada report outlining the history of the pollution at Besshi, the sulfur content of the Besshi ore, and the extent of the damage.

Of particular importance were sections that sought to prove the effect of pollution over time by experimentation and documentation. In one section, figures on airborne sulfuric acid over a twenty-six-day period were supplemented with the results of a controlled experiment. The first data set recorded the volume and weight of sulfuric acid found in one hundred cubic centimeters of air: during the fifteen days during which fumes were visible, the meter responded six times. Based on another experiment in which dry farm and rice paddies at different stages of the crop cycle were exposed to three different levels of smoke density, the report concluded that exposure during the crop's budding and pollination periods, compared with other phases of development, resulted in the greatest harvest loss. Rice paddies exposed uninterrupted to air that contained 40,725 grams of sulfur per 10 million grams of air would result, according to these findings, in a 42.6 percent harvest loss.[42] The appendix also cited daily records of the smoke in Sakurai village, Ochi County, from March 15 to October 15, which documented visual density, wind direction, and the weather. Organic specimens, such as rice and cedar bark, were taken from twenty locations, including both affected and unaffected areas, in order to measure sulfuric acid exposure. Other sections had charts displaying the amount of crop loss in terms of weight, size of damaged area, crop type, and market price across forty-two villages and over time, from 1905 to 1908.

The appendix also alluded to the pollution's role in discrediting science for tenant farmers. In a section titled "Blocking the Spread of Science," the report called attention to how local villagers were no longer "lending their ears" to "the technicians and other advisors from the prefecture and county levels" who administered the state's agronomic programs. Farmers were first convinced that the high level of harvest—"the best in the prefecture for years 1902 and 1903"—was due to the introduction of different seeds and fertilizer, but as the yields dropped due to the pollution, they had lost their "enthusiasm for scientific application."[43] This widespread mistrust of agronomy was reported as part of a growing suspicion toward science (gakuri): villagers "lost faith" in technicians who wrongly identified the cause of crop failure and in local leaders whose campaign to document the pollution had at that point made no headway in curbing pollution.[44]

The letter prompted the first negotiations between the company, the pollution victims, and government officials, which took place from April 20 to May 1, 1909, dubbed "the Onomichi Talks" after the city in Hiroshima Prefecture in which these discussions were held. The company, however, refused to pay compensation (baishō) and instead suggested an agricultural and forestry subsidy (nōringyō shōreikin). Isshiki Kōhei, the antipollution movement's most visible leader, condemned the company's proposal by arguing that "donating subsidies is to disguise the compensation sum that they are obligated to pay."[45] The negotiations ended without any resolution, but the demand for compensation set the stage for science's central role in future talks.

Unsettled by this setback, the farmers had begun to publicly vent their frustration with the local leadership in oratory meetings—by that time an established way of expressing political dissent. On May 26, 1909, an event became so unruly that movement leaders complained to the police for not doing enough to put an end to the protest. When the orator accused the governor of Ehime of receiving bribes from Sumitomo and distributing the money to local village heads, "the listening audience erupted, screaming praises and clapping their hands in approval," but the local "police did not make any arrests," even when, at a later point, the speaker "stood behind [Isshiki] with an upside-down empty beer bottle in his hands, gesturing to hit him."[46]

It was in this tense atmosphere that the village leaders set out for Tokyo for the negotiations. The prefecture and the Ministry of Agriculture and Commerce, upon receiving yet another letter from the village leaders, worked to bring Sumitomo back to the negotiating table.[47] Minister Ōura, after a trip to Ehime, invited the village leaders and Sumitomo representatives to the minister's mansion for the first Air Pollution Compensation Talks.

Science's Possibilities and Limits

The 1910 inaugural session began by arriving at a consensus on the rules of negotiation. These procedural guidelines created a space that allowed for a plurality of perspectives and a method for dealing with discrepancies between the figures presented by the company, the state officials, and the village leaders. The fact that the meetings were held in Tokyo was crucial to their success because of their distance from the site of the pollution and the local response. In this first round of talks, the parties came to an agreement on the compensation sum and the terms for reducing ore production, in addition to meta-level issues such as the duration of the contracts and how to arrive at figures used in calculating the compensation sum. The state guaranteed a space of discursive freedom by allowing each group the opportunity to present the results of their investigation and mutually check their respective research methods. The minister of agriculture and commerce, during a pretalk dinner, announced the goal: "In this negotiation, the ministry hopes that the resulting agreement will emerge out of a fruitful debate in which the participants, based on their own free will [*jiyū ishi*], will make their assertions known."[48] Later, Sumitomo also acknowledged the state's authority by saying that "we will enter negotiations by following the principle of free will as explained by the minister" and called for "a discussion in which both sides can maintain their viewpoint" (*Shisakajima engai baishō*, 5).

The villagers, however, expressed doubt about such promises. To get the company to admit fault, Isshiki asked if the corporation was willing "to accept or not accept the results of the [ministry's] report," despite the company's push for its own data (*Shisakajima engai baishō*, 20–21). The representatives, who attributed the failure of the earlier Onomichi talks to "the relative lack of survey information," expected a better outcome because "these negotiations will be held with fairness and frankness and based on the survey results of the Ministry of Agriculture and Commerce" (5). But when Sumitomo rejected the ministry's data, the village leaders accused the corporation of denying the objectivity of the data gathered by "precise investigation and orderly method, which scientifically and procedurally is of high quality and should be trusted" (51).

At each turn, Sumitomo representatives and village leaders demanded explanation of each other's research method. The forestry section chief, in response to queries by the village leaders, described the difference between the "mildly damaged" and "heavily damaged" areas as based on the number of flowers on twenty-year-old trees and comparing those figures against trees in areas with no discernible pollution damage (*Shisakajima engai baishō*, 31). Sumitomo and the ministry's agriculture section also described their procedures for quantifying crop damage, such as setting up a testing site and extrapolating from the results (28). These methodological inquiries allowed for data comparison and helped in determining an agreed figure. For example, the ministry and Sumitomo had reported different numbers for the amount of harvest loss per year, but the final figure ended up between the two, favoring the ministry's results. A similar technique was used to come to an agreement on production caps and the number of days the refinery was to be closed.

The first meeting ended with a consensus on many issues, including a compensation program and an emissions reduction. During the subsequent three decades of the talks, however, two key developments changed the way the pollution was imagined: philanthropic aid and desulfurization technology. Acceptance of corporate philanthropy signaled the recognition of the logistical limits of scientific investigation to document all of the effects of sulfur dioxide. While many village leaders at first resisted the idea of receiving philanthropy rather than compensation from the company, they soon came to realize that the negotiators could not settle on a precise indemnity sum for damages that defied precise, quantitative measurement, such as long-term psychological and social problems caused by the pollution. In the first round of talks, the representatives asserted that the reparation sum should be greater than the market value of crops destroyed by the pollution because it must also account for effects such as discouragement among farmers, conflicts and ill-will between tenants and landlords, drop in the market price of tenancy rights, the undermining of local government initiatives due to reduced tax revenues, and the decrease in lumber output due to forest damage. The village heads were disappointed, however, as the company refused to have these issues reflected in the compensation sum (*Shisakajima engai baishō*, 29). Another problem with compensation was that it required the burdensome and expensive task of recording the pollution and calculating the cost of damage—a point often raised by both sides. So in the later sessions, the victims pushed for adding philanthropic donations to the compensation sum.

By the third round of talks in 1916, the villagers began to openly demand donations to address the issue of unquantifiable costs. Because the company explicitly presented these sums as donations rather than compensation, this agreement gave the farmers a way to ask for reparations for items that fell outside the strict definition of "pollution damage." Ishihara Minotarō, a village representative who called for an increase in subsidies, explained that "compensation makes up for the loss [caused by pollution damage], but it does not contribute to the development of agriculture" (*Shisakajima engai baishō*, 252). During the 1919 talks, a village leader stated that "during the period without compensation payment, the farmers were in a self-destructive state" and that "the sulfuric acid would strike just when the farmers had invested all their financial assets and knowledge in their work. . . . Thus they lose all hope in the mutual development of agriculture and mining" (*Shisakajima engai baishō*, 191). In the same session, Katō Tetsutarō, another local leader, gave a speech that was the closest expression of a conservation ethic from the villagers. His message appealed to a rhetoric that linked nature worship to State Shinto:

As for the damage to the impressive sacred trees on shrine grounds, the spiritual condition of the farmers is to be noted. When grammar school children visit these shrines and temples to pray, the damage affects their minds and it disturbs us to think that this image scars the minds of children. . . . The minister of the interior called for spiritual cultivation and nurturing of healthy citizens, for the purpose of strengthening and preserving the national polity [*kokutai*]. The air pollution, which interfered with the economic activity of the farmers in eastern Ehime, also ravaged shrines and temples, thus destroying the basis for defending the national polity. (*Shisakajima engai baishō*, 368–369)

The political aestheticization of nature was rare among the villagers, compared to the elaborate glorification of the Besshi mountain by the corporation. Yet in this argument, the village headman separated the scientifically measurable from the ideological to stress the ideological damage caused by the pollution.

If the adoption of philanthropy marked science's limit, desulfurization technology pointed to its unlimited potential. Sulfuric dioxide, as part of the nitrogen fixation procedure, promised to solve local, national, and international problems. The company mentioned their research on this process as early as the first session, when it pleaded for a reduction of the compensation amount to defray the cost of procuring and developing this technology (*Shisakajima engai baishō*, 21, 183, 435). At the time, the corporation reported that they planned to acquire the Haber-Bosch process, an industrial chemistry technology that, if reengineered, promised to remove the sulfur dioxide from the emissions by combining it with ammonium to manufacture ammonium sulfate. The technology was essential for modern warfare, since the process allowed for the industrial production of explosives without relying on saltpeter, a limited natural resource. Thus the company touted its significance for the nation, both militarily and agriculturally. Later, Sumitomo succeeded in importing the process by enlisting the help of the government and other *zaibatsu* (family-controlled commercial combines).

The manufacturing of ammonium sulfate was also viewed as a solution to the threat of class conflict that had dominated the political imaginary of interwar Japan. When Sumitomo, during the 1919 talks, suggested that the desulfurization technology would lead to "the defeat of the class supporting democracy [*minponshugi*] and the improvement of the gap between the rich and the poor" (*Shisakajima engai baishō*, 326), the reference was to two class-based antagonisms: the labor and tenant unionization movements. The corporation therefore purported that desulfurization, which would curb emissions so that ore production could continue and benefit farmers with synthetic fertilizer, was a magic bullet that promised social equity and cooperation between agriculture and industry. Implied also was that this chemical process would pacify the tenant farmers seeking to overthrow their landlords—an appeal, most likely, to their negotiation counterparts. The possibilities of this technology also bolstered the corporation's position that it must continue to produce copper so that it could "compete with foreign capitalists on the world stage" and engage "in activities that are of benefit to society [shakai kōeki]" (Shisakajima engai baishō, 327).

Conclusion

In late Meiji Japan, technoscientific knowledge expanded the power to extract value from the natural environment—its air, rocks, soil, and living organisms (including human bodies). These Besshi pollution cases, when viewed in the context of the increasing demand for raw materials across industries, appear as conflicts over natural resources rather than occasioning the birth of a grassroots green movement. The antipollution activists in Besshi rarely called for the preservation of nature as an index of progress, as was the case, for example, in air-pollution cases in New York during the same time period.[49] Nor was the focus on public health—the issue in many of the postwar pollution cases in Japan[50]—even though, for example, a village near the Niihama Refinery reported in 1901 that "in recent years there have been increasing cases of respiratory illnesses."[51] Rather, the dispute was over damage to private property, caused by the reliance on the atmosphere as a commons—the mining industry freely dumping their waste into it and the agricultural industry using it freely to grow foodstuff.

The village elites and the mining company shared a similar class position in their respective industries, and both were instrumental in adopting technoscience to increase production capacity. In both the metal and the agricultural industries, the same expansionary logic of capitalism regulated the bodies of the workers in the mines, the factories, and the rice paddies. Perhaps because of these affinities, they also subscribed to the idea that science can offer a solution to social problems. During the same period as the pollution cases, the company confronted the radicalization of mine and factory workers: in 1907, mine workers staged a violent revolt against a new management system that gave the corporation direct control over the workers; in the 1920s, the company set up schools for their workers to combat labor radicalism.[52] Landowners, too, had to deal with tenancy disputes that broke out in Nii, Uma, and Shūsō counties—areas closest to Besshi and most affected by industrial pollution. In fact, the first tenant organization in Ehime was founded in Nyūgawa, which was also the center of antipollution activism.[53] Sumitomo later launched a pro-company farmers union, which was ironic, given that the industrial pollution may have been the initial inspiration for the unionization of tenants.

In the negotiations, the village elites suggested that the unrest among their tenants stemmed from the pollution, which undermined their position of authority and instilled doubt about modern science. But when the leaders denounced the use of bamboo spears in favor of words and numbers, they signaled that rules and procedures were important and that they accepted science as the language of negotiation. By silencing their own tenants, they were expressing their commitment to the protection of a lawful space of discourse in which participants can speak without physical threats. It is, however, important to remember that the commitment was not to the science of pure research but of the expert witness. Bruno Latour describes experts as a walking contradiction because they are scientists who "occupy the throne of supreme court judge, cloaking their testimony in the incontrovertible authority of the facts as judged."[54] In modern environmental disasters, experts who speak on behalf of the state and the industry testify in the court of public opinion. In these Besshi cases, the village officials defended science's judiciary power by isolating the experts and the exchange of expertise from the vigorous and, at times, arms-bearing judgment of the tenant farmers. By doing so, they also effectively separated the talks from the judgment of nature, the verdict for which the region, as well as the nation, is to this day answering.

Notes

1. Yonemaru Chūtarō, *Shisakajima seirenjo engai mondai no katei to engaichi ni shosuru nōkō ni tsuite* (Ehime-ken Tōyo Ichishi Shigun Shisakajima Engai Jogai Kisei Dōmeikai, 1930), 134.

2. Ibid., 136.

3. Ibid., 140.

4. Kenneth E. Wilkening, *Acid Rain Science and Politics in Japan: A History of Knowledge and Action toward Sustainability* (Cambridge, MA: MIT Press, 2004). See also Jun Ui, *Industrial Pollution in Japan* (Tokyo: United Nations University Press, 1992).

5. Sheila Jasanoff and Sang-Hyun Kim, "Containing the Atom: Sociotechnical Imaginaries and Nuclear Power in the United States and South Korea," *Minerva* 47 (2009): 119–146.

6. Isshiki Kōhei, ed., *Ehime ken Tōyo engai shi* (Nyūgawachō: Shūsō Gun Engai Chōsakai, 1926), 8.

7. Sugai Masurō, "Nihon shihonshugi no kōgai mondai: Yon dai dōzan kōdoku engai jiken," part 1, *Shakai kagaku kenkyū*, 30 (4): 94–162 and part 2, *Shakai kagaku kenkyū*, 30 (6): 75–150. A similar focus appears in human rights handbooks for local children, such as *Hokoreru furusato: Ittemiyō jinken mappu* (Tōyo: Tōyoshi Jinken Keihatsu Sentā, 2003).

8. Gregory Clancey, *Earthquake Nation: The Cultural Politics of Japanese Seismicity, 1868–1930* (Berkeley: University of California Press, 2006).

9. Penelope Francks, *Technology and Agricultural Development in Pre-War Japan* (New Haven, CT: Yale University Press, 1984), 144–176.

10. Irokawa Daikichi, *Meiji no bunka* (Tokyo: Iwanami Shoten, 1970).

11. Shimazu Toyoyuki, ed., *Ehime-ken no hyakunen* (Tokyo: Yamakawa Shuppansha, 1988).

12. Bruno Latour, "Scientific Objects and Legal Objectivity," trans. Alain Pottage, in *Law, Anthropology and the Constitution of the Social: Making Persons and Things*, ed. Alain Pottage and Martha Mundy (Cambridge: Cambridge University Press, 2004), 73–113.

13. Sheila Jasanoff, *The Fifth Branch: Science Advisers as Policymakers* (Cambridge, MA: Harvard University Press, 1998). See Thomas Gieryn, "Boundary-Work and the Demarcation of Science from Non-Science: Strains and Interests in Professional Ideologies of Scientists," *American Sociological Review* 48 (1983): 781–795.

14. Timothy Mitchell, *Rule of Experts: Egypt, Techno-Politics, Modernity* (Berkeley: University of California Press, 2002), 27.

15. Bruno Latour, *We Have Never Been Modern* (Cambridge, MA: Harvard University Press, 1993), 55.

16. Vaclav Smil, *Enriching the Earth: Fritz Haber, Carl Bosch, and the Transformation of World Food Production* (Cambridge, MA: MIT Press, 2001).

17. "Besshi Dozan engai torishirabesho," 6, File #2A-038-07-Ashi00034100–001, filed in Meiji 38, in the National Archives of Japan, Tokyo.

18. Okada Yutaka, "Engai chōsa sho," 26. A photocopy of the document, dated 1907, is archived at Tōyo Kyōdokan, Saijō.

19. In 1893, the amount of freighted ore was 48,183 tons (12,848,905 *kan*). The amount almost doubled in 1894 (83,803 tons, or 22,347,585 *kan*) and again in 1897 (165,382 tons or 44,101,899 *kan*). Sumitomo Kinzoku Kōzan Kabushiki Kaisha Sumitomo Besshi Kōzan Shi Henshū Iinkai, ed., *Sumitomo Besshi Kōzan shi*, vol. 3 (Tokyo: Sumitomo Kinzoku Kōzan Kabushiki Kaisha, 1991), 430–432.

20. Sugai Masurō, "Besshi Dōzan engai jiken," *Shakai kagaku kenkyū* 29:3 (1977): 166.

21. Kabushiki Kaisha Sumitomo Honsha, *Besshi kaikō nihyakugojūnen shiwa* (Osaka: Kabushiki Kaisha Sumitomo Honsha, 1941), 396.

22. Sugai, "Besshi Dōzan engai jiken," 168.

23. Ehimeken Keizaibu Nōmuka, "Ehimeken Tōyo chihō in okeru Besshi Dōzan engai mondai no katei" (1940), 6.

24. "Besshi Dōzan engai torishirabesho," File #2A-038-07-Ashi00034100–001, filed in "Meiji 38," in the National Archives of Japan, Tokyo.

25. Niihama-shi, ed., *Niihama sangyō keizai shi* (Niihama: Niihama-shi, 1973), 103–105, 114–116. See also Niihama Shi Shi Henshū Iinkai, ed., *Niihama shi shi* (Niihama: Niihama shi, 1962), 597.

26. This figure is a total from four villages: Niihama, Kaneko, Takatsu, and Shingō. Sugai, "Besshi Dōzan engai jiken," 171.

27. Niihama-shi, *Niihama sangyō shi*, 187.

28. Sumitomo Kinzoku Kōzan Kabushiki Kaisha Sumitomo Besshi Kōzan Shi Henshū Iinkai, *Sumitomo Besshi Kōzan shi*, vol. 3 (Tokyo: Sumitomo Kinzoku Kōzan Kabushiki Kaisha, 1991), 221.

29. A transcript of the 25th Diet session (1909) in Yonemaru, *Shisakajima seirenjo*, 141.

30. Iwahashi Masaru, ed., *Tōyo shakai to Sumitomo: Sono shiteki tokushitsu to kyōseiteki kankei* (Matsuyama: Matsuyama Daigaku Sōgōkenkyūjo, 2002), 42.

31. Tōyo Shi Shi Hensan Iinkai, ed., *Tōyo shi shi* (Tōyo: Tōyo shi, 1987), 555–568.

32. For example, the archival records of Tōyo Kyōdokan, Saijō, show that among the

sixty-one prefectural and county directives that reached Yoshii village in 1899, four are related to forestry, two to pest and agricultural disease, and two to husbandry.

33. These associations also documented the price of seeds, real estate, fertilizer, and labor, and the amount of local land owned by Sumitomo. The 1908 bylaws of these associations also noted the importance of keeping records of their expenses. In the archives of Tōyo Kyōdokan, Saijō.

34. Sugai, "Besshi Dōzan engai jiken," 181.

35. Isshiki, *Ehime ken Tōyo engai shi*, 15–16.

36. Okada, "Engai chōsa sho," 66–67.

37. Ibid., 6.

38. Ibid., 9–10.

39. Yonemaru, *Shisakajima seirenjo*, 5–6.

40. Isshiki, *Ehime ken Tōyo engai shi*, 27.

41. There was, however, a confidential documentation by the government from the first Mining Pollution Investigation, which included reports on the Niihama case. These reports are in the National Archives of Japan, Tokyo.

42. The numbers are from a chart in Yonemaru, *Shisakajima seirenjo*, 108, reproduced below:

	Cylindrical container that reproduces the condition of a *dry farmland*		
	Large amount	Medium amount	Small amount
Germination phase	4.2	3.2	1.0
Vegetative (growth) phase	8.4	6.3	2.2
Flowering phase	11.5	6.3	4.3
Ripening phase	4.2	3.3	0.0
All phases	17.7	11.5	8.4

	A wooden box that reproduces the condition of a *wet paddy*		
	Large amount	Medium amount	Small amount
Germination phase	12.6	9.4	8.8
Vegetative (growth) phase	16.1	14.0	8.8
Flowering phase	19.5	11.0	9.6
Ripening phase	1.8	1.7	0.6
All phases	42.6	25.7	23.1

43. Yonemaru, *Shisakajima seirenjo*, 126.

44. Ibid., 127.

45. Ibid., 43.

46. Isshiki, *Ehime ken Tōyo engai shi*, 44–45.

47. Sugai, "Nihon shihonshugi no kōgai mondai: Yon dai dōzan kōdoku engai jiken," part 1, 97.

48. *Shisakajima engai baishō kyōgi kai kaigi roku,* vol.1-2, 2. In the archives of Tōyo Kyōdokan, Saijō. Further citations of this work are given in the text as (*Shisakajima engai baishō*).

49. David Stradling, *Smokestacks and Progressives: Environmentalists, Engineers, and Air Quality in America, 1881–1951* (Baltimore: Johns Hopkins University Press, 1999).

50. For example, the Minamata mercury poisoning case and Yokkaichi air pollution case.

51. Niihama-shi, *Niihama sangyō keizai shi,* 122.

52. Ibid., 182–184, 275–286.

53. Ehime Ken Nōchi Bu, ed., *Ehime ken nōchi kaikaku gaiyō* (Matsuyama: Ehime Ken Nōchi Bu Nōchi Ka, 1952), 46–47.

54. Latour, "Scientific Objects and Legal Objectivity," 109.

5

Constructing Nature

PHILIP C. BROWN

The history of the Echigo Plain encapsulates the particularly intense dialog between Japanese society and natural erosional processes, a negotiation that continues today. Its story reminds us that natural processes radically transformed Japan's geography even during historical times. The forces underlying these changes continue to challenge human efforts to live off the land despite improvements in materials, machinery, and funding for large-scale, environment-transforming projects. Its history also exemplifies some of the striking, unanticipated conundrums created by human alteration of the natural environment in order to make it more amenable to human use, problems with which Japan continues to wrestle.[1]

The discussion that follows contradicts some common understandings that often characterize views of Asian and Japanese societies' relationship to the natural environment. First, they question the orientalist idealization of man's relationship with nature that presumes a more harmonious and less intrusive Asian cultural orientation toward the natural environment, at least before capitalism and economic modernization. One common Japanese version of this loss of innocence focuses on postwar growth of the so-called constructionist state that radically reengineered Japan's coasts, rivers, and mountains.[2] Such approaches minimize or ignore the kinds of activities examined here—activities demonstrating that Japan's "controlling urge" has a history that extends well before nineteenth-century industrialization. Early objectives concentrated on improvement of agricultural outcomes, not undergirding a modern industrial economy. Nonetheless, people eagerly acted upon their urge to control nature whenever they could marshal the resources. Viewed in a somewhat different light, if one presumes that large-scale efforts to manipulate the natural environment mark "the modern," then Japan, along with many parts of Asia, was "modern" long before Commodore Perry's arrival.

Modern economic development supplied new resources for civil engineering projects both directly and indirectly. Funds from Japan's imperial expansion exemplify the latter. From this perspective, the history of the Echigo Plain lies within the mainstream of Japanese history and its march to the beat of imperialism. It also fits the framework of modern riparian engineering elsewhere.[3]

Two Construction Methods

Recent human activity has extensively transformed the environment, yet such activities are arguably dwarfed throughout history—and even today—by climatic, tectonic, erosional, and similar natural forces. Natural forces are as much major actors in environmental histories as humans. They may lack will and intent, but their effects and the stimuli they provide to human action are undeniable. Skeptics need only look at the recent Tohoku earthquake and tsunami. We begin our discussion with an examination of natural forces that shaped the Echigo Plain— what I refer to here as "natural construction"—and then turn to some of the ways in which human society has sought to alter the plain to make it safer for human habitation. Here I focus on one of the natural forces seen as subject to direct human engineering (as opposed to prayer and supplication): efforts to ameliorate flooding.

NATURAL CONSTRUCTION

The Echigo Plain's story begins in prehistoric times, when erosion of uplands and soil deposition created the plain. Geologically speaking, the plain is a very recent creation, a product of highland water and wind erosion and the consequent soil deposition. Its rivers altered course substantially even within recent historical times. These processes transformed regional topography as dramatically as explosive volcanoes and shattering earthquakes.

Less than seven thousand years ago, today's Niigata City area was heavily populated by fish, whales, and crustaceans; its chief crops were multiple varieties of seaweed. It was underwater. Figure 5.1 depicts the ancient coastline over a modern relief map, its black line creating a horseshoe-shaped opening toward the map's top. The area within the horseshoe, between the short stream to the Sea of Japan and the longer stream that branches off to the right, constitutes much of Niigata City's center. The precursors of the Shinano and Agano rivers, the major waterways flowing through Niigata today, were broader and followed different courses seven millennia ago than they do today. (On the map, modern river courses are light gray and those of seven thousand years ago are dark gray.)

Jumping ahead, about a thousand years ago (fig. 5.2), sedimentation from rivers and wind action had created immense coastal sand dunes and produced a coastline similar to its modern counterpart. Nonetheless, rivers flowed in channels much broader than at present even when they followed a near-modern course.

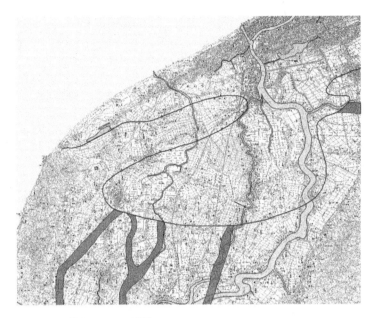

FIGURE 5.1 Niigata area 6,800 years ago. (MAP BY PHILIP BROWN)

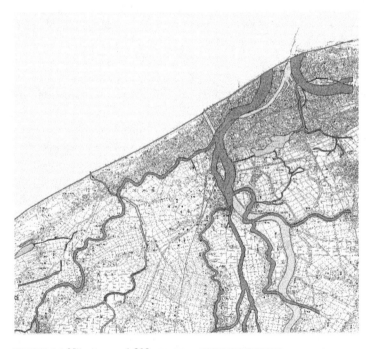

FIGURE 5.2 Niigata area 1,000 years ago. (MAP BY PHILIP BROWN)

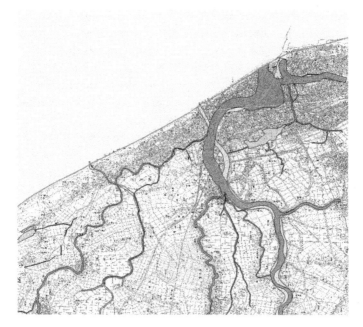

FIGURE 5.3 Early Edo era Niigata. (MAP BY PHILIP BROWN)

FIGURE 5.4 Meiji lakes and swamps, Niigata. (MAP BY PHILIP BROWN)

Erosion and deposition processes continued over the next half millennium to create the topography depicted in figure 5.3, the lower Shinano during the early Edo period. While sedimentation pushed rivers into courses close to their twenty-first-century form, a notable exception can be seen in the Niigata City area. The Agano River no longer flowed directly into the Sea of Japan (contrast figs. 5.2 and 5.3) but joined the Shinano to create a pool that flooded land that is the heart of the modern city.

These maps convey the rapidity of change in the Echigo Plain; nonetheless, they understate the degree to which the area was simultaneously at the mercy of water and dependent upon it. Even the presence of modern lakes and swampy areas on the preceding maps does not tell the whole story. Figure 5.4, depicting Meiji-era Niigata, provides some hint of how extensive these lakes and swamps had been, but even this map reflects earlier conscious and successful efforts to drain waterlogged terrain.

Additional evidence demonstrates that the people of the lower Shinano lived lives delicately balanced between the benefits and hazards of water. Modern travelers see orderly rice paddies, but such vistas do not reflect even recent historical experience. Into the mid-twentieth century, rice cultivation in much of the lower Shinano flood plain depended heavily on boats to haul seedlings for transplant through the "fields" as well as to move the harvest in the fall (figs. 5.5–5.7). Farmers waded hip-deep in muck to cultivate their crop.

FIGURE 5.5 Transplanting rice seedlings by boat. Iokawa Kiyoshi et al., Shinanogawa Okōtsu Shiryōkan *Okōtsu bunsuji monogatari: Shinanogawa Okōtsu Shiryōkan gaidobukku,* Nagaoka: Kokudo Kōtsūsho Shinanogawa Kasen Jimusho, 2006, 9.

FIGURE 5.6 Farming by boat. *Shashinshū Mizu to tsuchi to nōmin, Kameda kyōdo tochi kairyōku* 51.

FIGURE 5.7 Lowland harvesting, Kameda district, Niigata. *Shashinshū Mizu to tsuchi to nōmin, Kameda kyōdo tochi kairyōku* 16.

FIGURE 5.8 Niigata canals. Iokawa et al., Shinanogawa Okōtsu Shiryōkan, 7.

Niigata City's nickname, "The City of Rivers," suggests its sodden condition. Historically, it had such an abundance of streams that it bore a considerable resemblance to Venice. In 1878, British traveler Isabella Bird wrote, "It is correctly laid out in square divisions, formed by five streets over a mile long, crossed by very numerous short ones, and is intersected by *canals, which are its real roadways. . . . [E]verything comes in by boat,* and there are few houses in the city which cannot have their goods delivered by canal very near to their doors" (emphasis added; see fig. 5.8).[4]

Another Western traveler to Niigata, Richard Henry Brunton (1841–1901), brought an engineer's perspective: "The Shinano's discharge, gauged by me while there, was 1,500,000 cubic feet per minute, its summer flow being calculated as 700,000 cubic feet per minute, and its flood discharge 14,000,000 cubic feet per minute. . . . As the Thames discharged 400,000 cubic feet per minute and the Shannon in Ireland, the largest river in the British Isles, only 5,000,000 cubic feet per minute in flood, some idea may be obtained as to the relative size of this Japanese stream."[5] A large volume of water flowed between its banks, but the Shinano was a shallow river. Brunton noted that upstream, the riverbed was as much as three miles wide but only three feet deep.

Even into the 1960s, major sections of the Nuttari district of the city looked more like Venice than today. Peddlers brought goods to households by boat. Water taxis ferried folk from one place to another.

HUMAN CONSTRUCTION: AN OVERVIEW

Since its first agricultural settlements, Japanese have had a complicated relationship with their natural environment—one simultaneously appreciative of the bounty it provides and aware of its potential to destroy human settlements. But as in many other parts of the world, Japan has a long history of efforts to dominate and transform nature, too. This is especially true in the realm of agricultural water supply.

From the time of Japan's late sixteenth-century pacification under Toyotomi Hideyoshi and Tokugawa Ieyasu, we see increasingly successful efforts to dominate, subdue, and control natural forces quite aggressively. More efficient revenue assessment and collection by daimyos (barons) and broader effective regional political control improved rulers' ability to undertake more and larger public works projects than previously, even when the technologies echoed those long employed on the continent by China's imperial regimes. Such projects boosted agricultural output, which the overlords taxed.[6]

An enduring peace produced a double dividend. On the one hand, it eliminated military campaigns and conscription of labor, which impeded villagers' efforts to improve and maintain water control and distribution facilities. On the other hand, it freed up funds from military expenditures that could now be turned to investments in expanded revenue-enhancing activities such as land reclamation and improved irrigation. Further, relieved of incessant demands of widespread, constant civil war of the late fifteenth and sixteenth centuries, domain administrators had time to contemplate such investments. Indeed, deprived of the opportunity to expand their revenues by conquest, they had little choice but to exploit their domain resources fully if they hoped to bolster revenues.

Daimyo investments began a long-term process whereby human forces reconstructed the Echigo Plain. Whether financed locally or by the domains, the number of projects accelerated, particularly from the eighteenth century. Figure 5.4, by implication, shows the extent of these human manipulations: creating it called for the cartographer to depict on a twenty-first-century base map the small lakes and swamplands present in the mid-nineteenth century. Two hundred years earlier, these inland water bodies were even bigger and more numerous.

Figure 5.9 provides a striking example of the outcome of human activities, depicting how different modern Niigata City is compared to the city Bird and Brunton witnessed. The thick gray lines represent the broader Meiji River channel, while the light-gray stream and shorelines within it mark the narrower modern channel. Clearly, residents subdued, domesticated, and trained much of the old floodplain to support extensive urban construction.

In general, societies have two options in dealing with natural hazard risks. The first is to avoid dangerous locations; the second is to use technology to protect

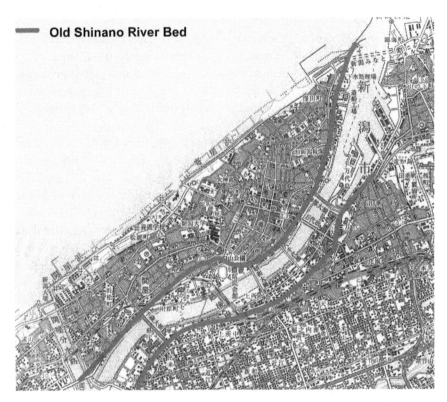

FIGURE 5.9 Modern and Meiji (thick gray lines) Shinano riverbanks.

human populations from the hazard or to limit its impact. An example of the first is zoning: creating flood hazard zones to keep people from conducting significant activities in high-risk areas and identifying zones of lesser risk in which people may live and work while bearing a degree of risk, such as paying higher insurance premiums. Engineering earthquake-resistant buildings represents a well-known example of the second approach.

Historically, Japan has relied heavily on the construction of riparian facilities to address flood hazard risks as well as to provide water for irrigation and urban populations. The tendency is understandable: the Japanese are literally squeezed between high, steep places onto narrow valleys and coastal plains that channel runoff to the seas. High population density in limited lowland areas compounds the challenge, so Japanese have long pushed the limits of usable land to raise crops.

Three civil engineering projects—two Tokugawa examples and one that transcends the early modern and modern eras—illustrate Japan's controlling urge.

The Matsugasaki project redirected the Agano River away from the Shinano River to enter the Sea of Japan directly. The Nishi and Shin river project created a river where none had existed before. The Okotsu diversion channel provided a relief valve for floodwaters on the lower Echigo Plain.

Rebuilding Nature

Tokugawa-era villagers demonstrated considerable creativity in addressing hazardous conditions that threatened their farms and homes, a creativity that draws admiration even today.[7] On the "soft," nonengineering side, they created place names that reflected the risk presented by particular locations. Naming a town Oshimizu (literally "pushy water," modern Ishikawa Prefecture) clearly served notice of flood risks even if not accompanied by zoning prohibitions. In areas prone to landslides, hamlet names such as Oshidashi (literally "pushed out") and Ochida (literally "fallen fields") can be found.[8] In other instances, villagers exercised joint ownership of arable land (*warichi*) to assure that residents shared all the different natural risks present in the village, creating a risk-diversified portfolio of cultivation rights for each shareholder.[9] No family could accumulate rights to only the best land. These communities also reallocated access to lands in the village, typically by lottery, after significant changes in arable land area from reclamation, landslides, or flooding.

TOKUGAWA RIPARIAN PROJECTS

Overwhelmingly, however, villagers and their governors resorted to "hard" approaches, and over time they developed a broad array of ingenious mechanisms to increase irrigation, improve river navigability, and reduce flood damage. Many irrigation projects, while intended primarily to bolster agricultural productivity, also helped to limit flooding by storing water for later release or transport elsewhere. Japanese villagers and their samurai overlords not only built irrigation channels, they developed aqueducts, mastered the principles of siphons to move water uphill, and in other ways advanced water control technology that conditioned the planning of many modern efforts.[10]

While some crops could be cultivated in swampy areas, greater productivity was typically possible when surplus water could be drained. The Three Lagoons (Sangata) district just south of Niigata presented one such case. Building drainage channels in such districts meant exercising ingenuity as well as initiative and organizational ability.

Several projects illustrate premodern (especially pre-Meiji) efforts to reshape nature. They provide some sense of the variety of approaches people took. While the following examples represent the high-cost end of the civil engineering spectrum, readers should bear in mind that myriad small-scale efforts transformed early modern landscapes.

By the early nineteenth century, people in the lower Shinano planned their own channel to facilitate drainage south of Niigata, our first example. Geography created a critical problem: the need for a drainage channel to cross a river rather than to drain water into it. The existing river, the Nishi, was itself subject to frequent flooding, and thus it was inappropriate as the outlet for additional water. Engineers solved this problem by creating Japan's first riparian underpass. Construction of the new channel, not surprisingly called the "New River" (Shinkawa), was begun in 1818. Creating a tunnel under the Nishikawa at the village of Uchino, water was drawn directly to the Sea of Japan at Ikarashi. Completed in 1820, it continues to function today with modern modifications.

Other instances show attempts to reshape rivers. At the beginning of the Tokugawa era, only two rivers on the Echigo Plain, the Shinano and the Arakawa, emptied into the Sea of Japan. All other rivers on the plain were tributary to these two. Up to the early eighteenth century, even the large Agano River joined the Shinano. From the early eighteenth century, several new channels were excavated to drain waters directly into the Sea of Japan. The Ochibori River was completed in 1721. It helped to drain the Shiunji Lagoon as part of a program of land reclamation.[11] The larger Matsugasaki Diversion Channel was completed in 1730 as a means of directing the Agano's overflow into the Sea of Japan, but its dike collapsed and the channel was reconstructed to make it a permanent extension of the Agano, transporting water directly to the sea.

Finally, although not constructed until the twentieth century, the present Okōtsu Diversion Channel is a direct descendent of Tokugawa efforts to reengineer nature. Had it been funded, this channel would have been the fourth major Edo-era project on the Echigo Plain. Its ultimate construction finally took place two centuries after its initial proposal.

In the early eighteenth century, a provincial merchant, Honmaya Kazuemon, first proposed construction of the diversionary channel as a way to reduce local flood hazard and improve agricultural output. Honmaya's repeated entreaties to the Bakufu got nowhere. His namesake son joined his father's efforts, continuing them long after Kazueimon senior's death. While few details are known about either man, their idea exerted a powerful attraction for local residents long after their deaths.[12]

Like the Matsugasaki project, Honmaya conceived of a barrier on the west bank high enough to keep the Shinano's water level at its normal, nonflood depth so that the stream could still be used for transportation. At the planned overflow point on the river, the east bank would have a dike that was higher than the west bank. This configuration allowed high water to flow over the top of the lower dike and into a newly constructed diversion channel. This design released water from the Shinano only when the river reached flood stage. This overflow barrier, called an *araizeki*, was widely used throughout Japan. It required no complex mechanism to regulate the river's water level. The flood control mechanism was automatic.

But the Okōtsu Channel faced unique, formidable challenges. Unlike the Matsugasaki, Shinkawa, and Ochibori projects, where sandy alluvial deposits were easily dug out and transported, the Okōtsu project had to go through much more challenging, hard Tertiary rock formations. In addition, the channel was longer than the other three projects—about ten kilometers. When shogunal officials prepared estimates of costs for the channel in 1842, they rejected the idea as too expensive. One estimate calculated that the project would require the labor of 8 million people![13]

Further, planners faced the considerable challenge of constructing a west-bank barrier strong enough to withstand floodwaters of the river, which carried more water than any other in Japan. Recall that the Matsugasaki project on the Agano had failed shortly after its completion. Its barrier was composed largely of rock, and Honmaya's plan likely employed a similar design (no drawings or details of the structure they planned remain). Could a dike of sufficient strength be constructed? That question became a central theme in public discussions of the Okōtsu project's merits.

Just as with major civil engineering projects today, the Tokugawa Okōtsu proposals engendered considerable opposition from powerful quarters of society.[14] As with the Matsugasaki, Shinkawa/Nishikawa, and other projects that might affect the flow of water into its harbor, Niigata merchants and officials saw the proposals as a threat to their businesses and revenue bases.[15] They feared that diverting water from the Shinano would increase sedimentation and reduce the harbor depth. The proposed use of an overflow design did not assuage the opposition. Opponents argued that at some point the dike would fail, just as it had at Matsugasaki. They and the Tokugawa officials reviewing the proposal had evidence of problems other than Matsugasaki, e.g., failure of similar projects on the Kiso River.[16]

A second related concern arose with Commodore Perry's arrival in the nineteenth century. Niigata was designated the second international treaty port, and from the 1860s existing concerns about harbor depth were exacerbated by the deeper draft of Western ships. Opponents worried that the Okōtsu project would reduce stream flow and increase soil deposition, making the harbor much too shallow for international shipping. Such concerns focused squarely on the effects of the processes of erosion and soil deposition that initially built the lower Echigo Plain. Bird pointedly observed,

In the freshets, which occur to a greater or less extent every year, enormous volumes of water pour over these [riverbed] wastes, carrying sand and detritus down to the mouths [of streams], which are all obstructed by bars. Of these rivers the Shinano . . . is the most refractory, and . . . at its entrance . . . there is only a passage seven feet deep, which is perpetually shallowing. The minds of engineers are much exercised upon the Shinano, and the Government is most anxious to deepen the channel and give Western Japan what it has not—a harbour.[17]

The preceding sampling of civil engineering projects demonstrates the important role played by the controlling urge even in premodern times. Furthermore, these projects built a record that generated a degree of confidence in large-scale civil engineering projects, confidence that they could be created, not fail repeatedly, and arguably improve the lot of Echigo Plain populations. Tokugawa thinkers developed plans for projects that would shape mid-nineteenth- and early twentieth-century projects, the primary example of which is the Okōtsu Diversion Channel, a project ultimately brought to completion in the twentieth century after one false start.

THE FIRST OKŌTSU CONSTRUCTION, 1870–1875

Advocates for the Okōtsu project were persistent. Finally, in 1870 (Meiji 3), the new Meiji leadership started construction of the channel.[18] That year, the Shinano River Diversion Channel Office (Shinano Bunsui Yakusho) was established with a budget of 1 million *ryō*: 400,000 *ryō* from the Imperial Court, 150,000 *ryō* from the central government, and 450,000 *ryō* from local sources.[19]

Even as construction began, the debate over the project continued. Niigata City residents still feared that the diversion channel would reduce scouring of the riverbed and increase sedimentation. In addition, downstream farm communities worried about floods and potential loss of irrigation water should the weir ever collapse.[20] Protests against the project erupted. Major landslides occurred during excavation of the channel, and opponents saw in them further evidence of the project's impracticality.[21]

Continued dissent and concern about project viability led Minister of the Interior Okubo Toshimichi to send two European engineers to evaluate. One, Englishman Richard Henry Brunton, primarily employed to develop lighthouses, conducted the first measurements of stream flow volume in Japan. The other, Dutchman Isaac A. Lindo (1847–1941), worked on water control projects, notably on the Tone River.

Brunton visited Niigata in June 1871 and March 1872, in part at the instigation of Sir Harry Parks at the British legation. His overall evaluation of the diversion plan was as sharp as it was terse: "This scheme . . . is an extraordinary instance of perverted intelligence [and] would have the undoubted effect of still further silting up the mouth of the channel at Niigata." Brunton's (and the British) interest lay in opening the harbor to international trade, and his most specific recommendations focused on ways to channel flood-stage waters to scour and deepen the harbor.[22]

Lindo made an extended visit in October of the following year (Meiji 6, 1873). His judgment was more tempered. He concluded that the channel construction, while possible, had significant problems beyond those Brunton identified. He was concerned particularly about possible landslides.[23]

In the end, both men concurred with the Niigata opposition: the project imperiled the harbor's ability to dock deep-draft vessels. They also raised questions about its impact on other parts of the river. They even questioned the efficacy of a diversion channel as a flood control mechanism, and their statements played an important role in publicly justifying a change in government support for the project.

Okubo ordered a halt to construction in 1875 (Meiji 8). By this time, the channel had largely been dug. The *araizeki* alone remained to be completed.[24] Disregarding the significant investments to date, further construction was canceled.

Despite the reliance on the Brunton/Lindo evaluations, a core reason for canceling the project was surely financial. By 1875, Okubo and other leaders had become fully aware of the enormity of the financial burdens that the Meiji government had undertaken—paying the costs of domain debt, declassing the samurai, and building a modern army and navy. In this context, cutting funding for projects like the Okōtsu project was a part of broader efforts to get a firm handle on expenditures; it constituted an admission that even though meritorious, such projects had to take a back seat to other more pressing issues facing the new government.

Setbacks notwithstanding, local leaders such as Tazawa Yoichirō (1823–1883) and his son, Miiri (1852–1928), felt a continued need for increased protection from flooding of the Shinano. In Meiji 14 (1881), diversion channel backers—large and small local landowners, small businessmen, and the like—formed the Shinanogawa Chisui Kaisha to raise funding to restart the Okōtsu project.[25] They also advocated for and ultimately won approval of new dikes along particularly vulnerable stretches of the lower Shinano drainage basin.[26] In addition to promoting the business interests of the Chisui Kaisha backers, the stability of agriculture, and the amelioration of floods and their consequent destruction of property, both kinds of projects benefited local small farmers by providing paid work as construction labor. Even for dikes the process of obtaining funding was contentious, given the limited revenues available. Although officials conducted investigations in response to the pleas of the Chisui Kaisha and others, no major construction was undertaken. Small projects advanced slowly, based entirely on local funding.[27] Construction of stronger dikes with national and prefectural assistance began in 1886 and continued into the 1890s.[28] Yet such efforts did not sate local demand for a much larger effort, an effort that continued to draw opposition from shippers and merchants in Niigata port and downstream farmers and boatmen concerned about possible harbor and river shallowing on the one hand and destruction of fields and irrigation systems on the other, should there be an incident similar to the Matsugasaki collapse.

THE SECOND OKŌTSU CONSTRUCTION, 1909–1931

All of the projects undertaken in the wake of Okubo's decision to cancel the nearly completed diversion channel were small scale. Broader plans could be implemented only if there were an increased sense of urgency or an increased supply of available funding. Late nineteenth-century events fulfilled both requirements and enabled successful construction of the Okōtsu project.

As is frequently the case, nature itself prompted a renewed, urgent sense of the need for flood control. Along with much of the country, the lower Shinano River basin suffered massive inundations from the heavy, continuous rains of the summer of 1896 (Meiji 29). Dikes in Yokota village (modern Tsubame City) gave way, and the swollen Shinano pushed onto the plain. Photographs taken three weeks after this Yokota Break show villages and fields still swamped. Record-setting in scale, the Yokota Break was the first of repeated, significant floods over the next several years, all reminders of the pressing need to do more to protect fields and villages (fig. 5.10).[29]

FIGURE 5.10 Yokota area three weeks after the levee break.

These floods demonstrated the limitations of existing dike construction along the lower Shinano and its tributaries. Dike construction was the path urged by Brunton and, indirectly, by Lindo. Local communities and the prefecture had pursued this course of action; nonetheless, floods continued to take lives and destroy property.

Availability of funding was also critical, and in this regard Japan's early imperial successes provided funds. Money for the project was not simply redirected from other budget lines or new tax levies; finance resulted directly from Japan's victory in the Sino-Japanese War. Coincident with the floods Japan suffered, negotiations for the final settlement of the Sino-Japanese War gave Japan large reparations. In due course, the Meiji government diverted a 100-million-yen share of reparations to construction of flood control projects, ultimately financing Okōtsu and other projects throughout Japan.

Finally, with full central government support, construction of the redesigned Okōtsu Diversion Channel began in 1909. It employed modern construction materials, not just wood and stone as in the past. The new design incorporated modern mechanical water gates similar to those used in the Panama Canal, on which one of the project designers, Aoyama Akira, had worked. Modern explosives and power equipment, not traditional hand tools, blasted, excavated, and transported rock and soil.

The new technologies controlled some construction risks and increased chances of success. Cement and new metal products could create stronger structures than ever before. Their worth had been demonstrated in recent decades in projects that improved the viability of Niigata Harbor and elsewhere nationwide.[30]

When completed, the Okōtsu Diversion Channel was the largest civil engineering project in East Asia.[31] Basic statistical information conveys its scale. The channel was ten kilometers long and lined with dikes. In the shallower sections, excavation extended 2 to 2.5 meters deep, and in the hills it was 6 to 18 meters deep. Some 29,218,869 cubic meters of soil and rock were removed and used to fill lowland reclamation areas and the Enjōji wetlands. Over the life of the project an estimated 1 million people labored on it. The original budget for the project was 23.5 million yen, but significant cost overruns, especially from three large landslides, added over 10 million yen.

This listing of expenditures suggests one additional attraction of the diversion project for adherents and planners: it produced fill to turn swampy areas into productive agricultural land. The filling of Enjōjigata was but one episode in a series of projects that removed from the face of maps almost all the wetlands visible in figure 5.4. Okōtsu-related reclamation projects provided economic benefits beyond flood relief, increasing agriculturally productive lands and tax revenues at all levels of administration.

The use of expensive modern construction techniques notwithstanding, the Okōtsu project confronted major challenges. Landslides that occurred during the construction provided one of the first indications of the risks borne when seeking to alter nature. One might attribute landslides during the first construction to inadequate, old-fashioned Edo period materials and methods; however, the twentieth-century construction commenced when the materials and methods employed demonstrated Japan's recent technological modernization. Nonetheless, construction began prior to the general use of soil boring samples; estimates of excavation site wall stability were largely seat-of-the-pants.[32] While deaths did not result, major landslides slowed the project, generated cost overruns, and inflicted collateral damage on areas not directly associated with the project. South of the channel's mouth on the Sea of Japan, Teradomari Harbor suffered from major mudflows, and once the debris was removed a jetty was added to the project to prevent channel sediment from silting up the harbor.[33]

Landslides and mudflows hinted at the larger disaster to come. As evident even in the aftermath of the recent Tohoku earthquake and tsunami, choices in construction design and materials have consequences that cannot always be predicted, and in the case of the Okotsu Diversion Channel that limitation was manifest in the dam that controlled the flow of surplus water from the Shinano into the runoff channel. The dam allowed a downstream flow that proved too much for the structure.[34] On June 24, 1927, a movable portion of the dam collapsed, its foundation undermined by hydraulic action of the channel stream in the five years since water first flowed through it. The weir's collapse completely blocked the flow of water to the lower Shinano. The entire contents of the river then flowed directly down the diversion channel into the Sea of Japan.

The worst fears of the project's opponents had been realized. Villagers who had predicted that inevitably there would be a disastrous collapse of the weir now had proof: the paddies in fifty-one villages totaling 27,300 hectares were starved of irrigation water and completely lost to cultivation.[35] Those who feared the diversion channel would interfere with water transport downstream and in Niigata Harbor could point to the fact that the disaster literally grounded all water transport between Niigata and Nagaoka. Unanticipated problems arose: Niigata City and eight towns lost their water supply. With no water flowing through the lower river, seawater and raw sewage backed upstream. Emergency measures provided some relief, but it took considerable time to restore the full flow.[36]

Despite complaints and reinvigorated calls to ditch the entire project, plans quickly developed to repair the dam and restore the main channel. Rebuilding took another four years, at a cost of nearly 4.5 million yen. Chief engineer Aoyama Akira and his lieutenant, Miyamoto Takenosuke, replaced the failed gate with a new one placed upstream of the old dam. They took steps to harden the river floor and strengthen the foundation of the new dam.[37] The new structure reduced the flow of water downstream, ameliorating the hydraulic forces in play at the dam site. This formula worked.

Happily Ever After?

Since the 1920s, there has been no further disaster, and with several later renovations the Okōtsu channel has continued to function smoothly. Its success encouraged construction of a number of other projects that run the gamut from modernizing dikes and levees to new diversion channels and drainage facilities. As Okōtsu's history suggests, early modern engineering of nature set a pattern for modern Japan, and at the end of the Tokugawa era there were only four streams on the Echigo Plain that emptied directly into the Sea of Japan; today there are twenty.

From the perspective of local residents, civic leaders, and businessmen, the positive effects of riparian construction are considerable. There is now more effective and complete drainage of the lower Shinano. Farmers no longer navigate their fields in boats. Irrigation supply has improved. Agricultural productivity has increased, and today Niigata is very well known for the high quality of its rice and sake. In Niigata City, urban development occurred where no one dared to build before. In the smaller towns, now suburbanized, new modern houses sprout where rice once grew.

Yet all is not bright. Technological controls on natural processes, even if successful at one level, often generate new problems.[38] Disastrous flooding continues in the Echigo Plain. For example, in July of 2004, slow rains stalled over Niigata. The Shinano did not flood, but the Ikarashi, Kariyata, and Nakanokuchi rivers in the suburban districts south of Niigata City did—with a vengeance. Modern dikes were undermined in scenarios reminiscent of the collapse of the weir at Okōtsu.[39] The results of civil engineering on the Echigo Plain and nationally are not black and white. On the positive side of civil engineering accomplishments, major flooding takes fewer lives now, and the total area affected by flood disasters has declined. While civil engineering has contributed to these developments, lower loss of life in particular is largely the result of better meteorological understanding and improved warning systems. From the Meiji era, meteorological and hydrological data has been gathered and studied, and lessons have been learned. In combination with better understanding of weather patterns, telegraph, telephone, and wireless communication have increasingly permitted rapid dissemination of reliable flood warnings.

One additional trend suggests that when engineering brought clear successes, societal reaction negated their impact. While areas damaged and lives lost from floods have declined, the value of property lost has increased substantially. This is a broad national trend in postwar Japan.[40] Why? Because people have a pervasive, implicit sense that modern technology will protect them, and that confidence leads to individual decisions that place people and their property at greater risk than they realize.[41] Consequently, the increased sense of safety attendant on the construction of modern riparian works has encouraged people to claim for human use lands previously considered subject to high flood risk and therefore unusable.[42] People vote confidence in modern riparian works with their pocketbooks. In downtown Niigata, much of the area close to the Shinano has been built up, becoming expensive urban landscape (see fig. 5.9). New levees along the Nakanokuchi and other streams have encouraged building of houses where long-time residents, made aware of flood risk by stories of their elders, would never have built. In all these cases, "hard" solutions succeeded in some sense but induced behaviors that counteracted their beneficial impacts. When floods occur now, the economic loss is greater than in similar past events.

Overconfidence in modern technologies is abetted by another problem: lack of public access to data on hazard risk and public policy based on it. Heavy investment in land long made owners wary of any effort to define high-risk areas and to implement zoning restrictions that could limit flood damage—they fear a decline in property values. The Kobe earthquake led to widespread production of urban hazard maps; nonetheless, the first efforts at systematic crafting of risk-related zoning regulations for Niigata and other areas have only just begun.[43] Meanwhile, absent risk data, suburban immigrants buy homes, blithely unaware they are located in traditionally flood-prone areas and confident of the protection offered by modern dikes.

"Hard" solutions—all the new dikes, dams, and diversionary channels—further contribute to a new problem far more pervasive than building in risky areas: the rapid pace at which the lower Shinano River basin is sinking. The Echigo Plain is one of Japan's worst subsidence areas. Rates vary by place and year but are as high as five centimeters a year and as much as eight centimeters over five years.[44] With growing confidence in the efficacy of civil engineering, the population increased, and with it so did industrial and personal consumption of groundwater. Further, engineering reduced the deposition that had filled in the sea to create Niigata. Both developments increased subsidence to such a degree that much of Niigata City now lies below sea level (fig. 5.11). Such circumstances present challenges from tsunami as well as flooding. The Niigata earthquake of 1964 caused major direct damage, but like its recent Tohoku counterpart, major seismic waves also swamped the city. Water pooled and did not drain for weeks. Continued subsidence expanded the acreage subject to tsunami damage and has created new pockets where water will stand after any future flooding.[45] In sum, if the first plotlines

FIGURE 5.11 Sections of Niigata City below sea level. Darkest areas are those of greatest subsidence and represent greatest depths below sea level (more than 1 meter; max. more than 2.5 meters); midtone areas represent elevations between 0 and –1 meters; the most lightly shaded areas are above sea level. White sections are outside the survey area.
SOURCE: NIIGATA-KEN KENMIN SEIKATSU KANKYŌBU.

of human interaction with erosional forces were those of plucky resilience in the face of natural hardships and the rise of technological triumphalism, the more recent story line might be hubris humbled.

Reflections

Beyond the economic and geological impacts of the Okōtsu Diversion Channel and similar projects, riparian construction produced environmental changes. Rivers are ecological systems themselves, nested in still larger systems. Altering river flows dramatically restricted rivers and flood plains and rendered some sections of channels uninhabitable by once-prosperous species of fish, including salmon. Small lakes and swamplands that dotted the mid-nineteenth-century map have largely been drained, reducing the feeding and breeding grounds of swans and other waterfowl that once populated the entire Echigo Plain. The presence of rivers in ordinary peoples' lives has changed; rivers are more psychologically distant. Children can no longer go down to the rivers and streams and play as they did before the Niigata earthquake. Rivers have become more dangerous in one sense: many are now little more than cement tubes that make it more difficult for children to extricate themselves should they fall into a stream.

Ecological, psychological, and economic costs evoke the dilemmas in Edward Tenner's thoughtful ruminations on "why things bite back."[46] Technological solutions engender new, unanticipated problems. The Okōtsu project suggests the veracity of that perception, but it also indicates that people often seek a solution to an immediate problem with limited perception of what the proposed solution's broader impact might be. The most recent evidence and economic concerns dominate decision making. Based on the preceding material and research still in progress, I think it is fair to conclude that into the first postwar decades, concern to limit flood damage locally, combined with concerns to increase agricultural output, constituted the motive forces behind projects such as those discussed above. This generalization holds even for opponents of a project. For example, in the case of the Okōtsu Diversion Channel, opponents' concerns focused on damage to downstream navigation and the serviceability of Niigata as an international port based on some of the negative outcomes of the Matsugasaki project.

Orientalist portrayals of the high value that Japanese and Asian culture generally places on nature notwithstanding, Japan's efforts to transform nature clearly have an extended history, as did similar projects in ancient Chinese and South Asian Harappan civilizations. Japan has taken the same direction as have many other societies over the past several centuries, especially densely populated places such as China and South Asia.[47] In the process, Japanese have shown incredible initiative and creativity in designing "hard" solutions. Early projects like the first Okōtsu Diversion Channel were sometimes very large scale and were funded out of traditional agricultural revenue bases, not those of a modern, industrialized economy.

The adoption of modern carbon-powered technologies certainly extended the range and scale of possible projects, but the basic thrust of efforts to enhance safety, agriculture, and transportation were firmly established much earlier. Again, the completed Okōtsu Diversion Channel is illustrative. When opened in 1922, it represented the fulfillment of an eighteenth-century dream, enabled by reparations from the Sino-Japanese War.

These trajectories elide the commonly presumed divide between premodern and modern societal attitudes toward nature. The ability of industrialized, heavily capitalized societies to act on their urge to control natural forces, to develop new materials, and to harness new forms of energy certainly permitted larger-scale efforts than in the past, and planning has extended to grander projects. Travelers in Japan's scenic mountains pass hillside after hillside blanketed in cement structures installed in an effort to reduce the incidence of landslides. Parallel vistas greet those cruising seaside routes: shores are often lined with cement tetrahedrons placed to reduce shoreline erosion. Examination of successive maps of Tokyo Bay reveal the degree to which it, too, has been filled (e.g., Haneda Airport) and reshaped by landfill (*umetate*), programs that present subsidence problems similar to those of the lower Echigo Plain.[48] Seawalls in areas such as Japan's Tohoku region have been erected to protect against tsunami. Nonetheless, the Japanese, like a number of premodern Asian societies, harbored grand dreams of transforming their environment—dreams on which they acted.

The use of hard solutions in the Echigo Plain—such as landslide reduction, tsunami amelioration, and landfill—presented new problems even as they had identifiable successes. The Matsugasaki and Okōtsu collapses, especially the latter, suggest that while big efforts can constrain ordinary flood threats, when the facility fails the human costs are larger than otherwise would be the case. In the recent Tohoku tsunami, even where seawalls did not collapse, river diking channeled floodwaters, directing their flow, increasing their velocity, and shaping the resulting damage. Drainage of low-lying areas, now often dependent on electric pumps, was slowed by the loss of power, limiting relief and prolonging the disaster. These and similar lessons have been hard for contemporary planners (as well as their historical counterparts) to encompass. Today, in response to the Tohoku tsunami, we now have a plan for a higher, more extended seawall, rather than attempts to address problems via "soft" solutions such as zoning.[49]

Thus, in many important ways, the history the Echigo Plain encapsulates both the dilemmas Japanese face today in dealing with flood hazards (including tsunami) and the mixed outcomes of efforts to ameliorate risk. It reflects the broad Japanese struggle to improve upon their natural environment to support economic development and increase safety. In the Echigo Plain's history, we witness the degree to which natural forces remain constantly present actors, today as well as in the past. To understand the evolution of the Echigo Plain and much of the rest of Japan, it is useful to begin with a recognition that both natural and human forces work interactively to reshape the land.

Notes

1. Linda Nash, "The Agency of Nature or the Nature of Agency?" *Environmental History* 10:1 (January 2005): 67–69.

2. Alex Kerr, *Dogs and Demons: Tales from the Dark Side of Japan* (New York: Hill and Wang, 2001); Brian Woodall, *Japan under Construction: Corruption, Politics and Public Works* (Berkeley: University of California Press, 1994); Tessa Morris-Suzuki, *Re-Inventing Japan: Time, Space, Nation* (Armonk, NY: M. E. Sharpe, 1998); Julia Adeney Thomas, *Reconfiguring Modernity: Concepts of Nature in Japanese Political Ideology* (Berkeley: University of California Press, 2001).

3. Skim, for example, dam histories such as Nicholas J. A. Schnitter, *A History of Dams: The Useful Pyramids* (Rotterdam: A. A. Balkema, 1994).

4. Isabella L. Bird, *Unbeaten Tracks in Japan* (San Francisco: Travelers' Tales, 2000), 128.

5. Richard Henry Brunton, *Building Japan, 1868–1876* (Sandgate, UK: Japan Library Ltd., 1991), 41–42.

6. William Cronon, "A Place for Stories: Nature, History, and Narrative," *Journal of American History* (March 1992): 1347–1376. On daimyo control, see Philip C. Brown, *Central Authority and Local Autonomy in the Formation of Early Modern Japan: The Case of Kaga Domain* (Stanford, CA: Stanford University Press, 1993).

7. Both the Shinkawa and Okōtsu projects are major tourist attractions in Niigata, just to name two examples directly related to this essay.

8. Nakamura Keizaburō, *Yamakuzure* (Tokyo: Iwanami Shoten, 1934), 128–135.

9. Philip C. Brown, *Cultivating Commons: Joint Ownership of Arable Land in Early Modern Japan* (Honolulu: University of Hawai'i Press, 2011).

10. See, for example, Kensetsu Daijin Kanbō Gijutsu Chōsa Shitsu, *Furusato doboku shi* (A history of rural civil engineering, Tokyo: Keizai Chōsa Kai, 1990), 152–160.

11. Okuma Takashi, "Echigo heiya no kaihatsu to jisui no rekishi: Bunsui no tame no zeki suimon gijutsu wo chūshin to shite," in Iokawa Kiyoshi, ed., *Okōtsu bunsui sōsho Shiryō hen 5: Dai ichiji kōji, Shinanogawa chikutei kōji, dai niji kōji* (Niigata: Hokuriku Kensetsu Kōzaikai, 2005), 8.

12. "Honmaya Kazuemon," in Iokawa Kiyoshi, ed., *Okōtsu bunsui sōsho shiryō hen 2: Mizu no shisō* (Niigata: Hokuriku Kensetsu Kōzaikai, 2003), 4–5.

13. Chino Yasuaki, "Chisui ni okeru kinsei seki gijutsu no hensen ni kansuru kenkyū," PhD diss., Niigata University, 1994, 255–258.

14. Bunsui Chōshi Hensan Iinkai, ed., *Bunsui chōshi, shiryō hen 2* (Niigata-ken: Bunsui Machi, 2005), 368–412. Koizumi Sōken's mid-nineteenth century "Echigo kuni Shinanogawa setsu Okōtsu horiwari soneki," *Okōtsu bunsui sōsho shiryō hen 2: Mizu no shisō*, 14, defends the project from its downstream critics.

15. Charles David Sheldon, *The Rise of the Merchant Class in Tokugawa Japan, 1600–1868* (London: J. J. Augustin, 1958); Kigoshi Ryūzō, *Zeniya Gohei* (Kanazawa: Hokkoku Shuppansha, 2001); and Wakabayashi Kisaburō, *Zeniya Gohei: Bakamatsu hansei kaikaku to umi no gōshō* (Kanazawa: Hokkoku Shuppansha, 1982).

16. Kiso San Kawa—Sono Ryūiki to Kasen Gijutsu Henshū Iinkai, ed., *Kiso san kawa: Sono ryūiki to kasen gijutsu* (Nagoya: Kensetsushō Chūbu Chihō Kensetsukyoku, 1988), 850.

17. Bird, *Unbeaten Tracks in Japan*, 126.

18. The shogun showed a more positive attitude in 1867, just before its demise. Niigata Kenshi Hensan Iinkai, ed., *Niigata Kenshi: Kenshi shiryō 12* (Niigata: Niigata Prefecture), 618.

19. Okuma, "Echigo heiya no kaihatsu," 13.

20. Iokawa Kiyoshi, ed. *Okōtsu Bunsui sōsho shiryō hen 3: Shinanogawa chisui nikki shō, Shinano kikō* (Niigata: Hokuriku Kensetsu Kōzaikai, 2004), 5.

21. *Okōtsu Bunsui sōsho shiryō hen 3*: "Shinanogawa chisui nikki shō," 27.

22. Brunton, *Building Japan*, 42. Chapter 7, "Taming the Rivers." Note that a "levees only" policy failed to protect lower Mississippi through the early twentieth century where levees also failed to effectively scour the river channel. O'Neill, *Rivers by Design*, 132 and 143.

23. See *Niigata Kenshi: Kenshi shiryō* 14, 195 for Lindo's report in Japanese. For other perspectives, see Niigata Kaikō Hyakunen Shi Iin, ed. *Niigata kaikō hyakunen* (Niigata: Niigata, 1969), 173–174.

24. Takahashi Kenzō, "Shinanogawa chisui nikki shō," 35.

25. Kensetusho Hokuriku Chihō Kensetsukyoku Nakaoka Kōji Jimusho, *Shinanogawa Okōtsu bunsui shi* 1 (Nagaoka: Kensetusho Hokuriku Chihō Kensetsukyoku Nakaoka Kōji Jimusho, 1968), 100.

26. The first session of the Niigata Prefecture Parliament created an overall plan in Meiji 12 (1879) but had no funds. Some projects were undertaken later based on subprefectural funding. Shirone Shi Shi Hensan Iinkai, *Shirone shi shi Tsūshi-hen* (Niigata: Shirone, 1985), 649–651; Takahashi's diaries note similar projects without details. *Sosho Shiryō* hen 3, 62, 65 (note), and 63 respectively. For one listing of local expenditures on dikes, see *Shinanogawa Okōtsu bunsui shi* 1, 135–136.

27. *Shinanogawa Okōtsu Bunsui shi* 1, 99.

28. *Shirone shi shi Tsūshi*, 651.

29. Niigata Ken Shi Kenkyū Kai, ed., *Niigata ken hyakunen* 1 (Niigata: Niigata-shi, 1968), 616.

30. *Niigata kaikō hyakunen shi*, chapters 2 and 3.

31. *Bunsui chōshi Tsūshi*, 501.

32. Test borings were conducted only at the site of the main weir. See *Bunsui shi dai 2 shū*, 154–157.

33. *Shinanogawa Okōtsu bunsui shi* 2, 132–135.

34. *Bunsui chōshi Tsūshi*, 501.

35. Ibid., 509.

36. Ibid., 510.

37. See *Bunsui chōshi Tsūshi* 511 for a summary. See also *Shinanogawa Okōtsu Bunsui shi* 2, 219–235, for details.

38. Edward Tenner, *Why Things Bite Back: Technology and the Revenge of Unintended Consequences* (New York: Vintage Books, 1996), 347; Charles Perrow, *Normal Accidents: Living with High-Risk Technologies* (Princeton, NJ: Princeton University Press, 1999).

39. Okuma Takashi, "2004.7.13 Niigata suigai no tokuchō kara kongo no chisui no arikata wo kangaeru," in Takahama Nobuyuki et al., *Heisei 16 nen 7 gatsu Niigata/ Fukushima, Fukui gōu saigai ni kansuru chōsa kenkyū* (Niigata: Niigata Daigaku Sekisetu Chiiki Saigai Kenkyū Sentaa, 2005), 1–9, especially 4–5.

40. Kokudō Kōtsushō Hokuriku Chihō Seibi Kyoku, Kanazawa Kasen Kokudō Jimusho, "Kasen gyōsei no genjō to kadai" (Kanazawa, 2007).

41. For example, Tenner, *Why Things Bite Back,* 94–95.

42. This paradox, parallel to that James Scott explored in *Seeing like a State: How Certain Schemes to Improve the Human Condition Have Failed* (New Haven, CT: Yale University Press, 1999), focuses on individuals rather than states.

43. Discussions at Niigata-ken Nadare Jisuberi Kenkyū Sentaa, Myōkō-shi, January 28, 2008.

44. Yamagishi Tsuneo, "Niigata Heiya kaigan no dosa shūshi no ichi rei," *Niigata Oyō chishitsu kenkyū kaishi* (Niigata Journal of Applied Soil Geology) 50, n.d., 24; Niigata-ken, Kenmin Seikatsu Kankyōbu, "Niigata Heiya no jiban chinka," March 2007 (n.p.).

45. Takahama Nobuyuki and Urabe Atsushi, "Echigo Heiya no '0-m[eetoru] chitai'

to shinsui higai yosoku," *Niigata daigaku saigai kenkyū nenpō* 27 (2005): 11–18; Yamagishi, "Niigata Heiya kaigan," 22, 23.

46. Tenner, *Why Things Bite Back*. For literature on hazard and risk, see Susan L. Cutter, *Living with Risk* (New York: Edward Arnold, 1993).

47. These areas and South Korea comprise the top six nations building large dams. World Commission on Dams, *Dams and Development: A New Framework for Decision-Making* (London: Earthscan Publications Ltd., 2000).

48. Kansai Airport in Osaka Bay may be the most well-known reclamation project based on landfill, a project famous for its anticipation of subsidence and provision for jacking up the facility to compensate. Landfill-based reclamation has a long history in Japan, as does the controversy surrounding it. For critical perspectives, see, for example, Nihon Kagakusha Kaigi Setonai Iinkai, *Umetate jigoku no setonai engan: Kaihatsu no shōrai wa kore de yoi ka,* Shohan, ed. (Kyoto: Hōritsu Bunkasha, 1985). Kaoru Yamamoto, *Umi wa minna no mono: Yokourawan umetate o meguru jūmin undō no kiroku* (Wakayama-ken Nishimuro-gun Shirahama-chō: Yamamoto Kaoru, 1989).

49. The proposal for one such plan, noting pre-tsunami and planned post-tsunami seawall size in Tanohata village, Iwate Prefecture, is posted at www.reconstruction.go.jp/topics/田野畑村セット.pdf, viewed December 31, 2011.

6

Toroku

Mountain Dreams, Chemical Nightmares

TIMOTHY S. GEORGE

When Americans imagine harm caused by environmental pollution, they may think of spotted owls or melting glaciers. The images that come to mind for Japanese are likely to be the ravaged bodies of human beings, particularly the victims of congenital mercury poisoning in Minamata.[1] Poisons human beings release into the environment have also returned to destroy human bodies in many other places in Japan, including Toroku, a tiny mountain hamlet. For eight years after the Toroku arsenic mine opened in 1920, Tsuruno Masaichi and his wife, Kumi, processed the ore, crawling into a crude kiln to scrape out the white arsenic trioxide powder. In 1921, their first child was stillborn.

Dreams and Border Crossings

J. R. McNeill writes that "some of the most dramatic and revealing work in environmental history to date concerns frontier transformations, where one system of human ecology replaces another."[2] Donald Worster suggests that environmental history must be approached on the three levels of nature, technology, and ideology and emphasizes changing "modes of production," his term for relationships between human society and the environment.[3] Toroku's environmental history illustrates the results of such frontier transformations and changing modes of production powerfully. The tiny hamlet of thirty-three households—there once were over fifty—is strung along a narrow, steep, remote river valley in the mountains of northern Miyazaki Prefecture on the island of Kyushu.[4] It is six kilometers upriver from Ama no Iwato Shrine in Takachiho, the spot where the sun goddess Amaterasu hid in a cave and was enticed out to return light to the world. A villager described the most important event in Toroku's history—the discovery and opening of the mine, probably in the late sixteenth century—as follows:

The Toroku mine . . . developed rapidly after the Bungo merchant Morita San'ya opened it as a silver mine at the start of the Edo period.

> "Who first dug the Toroku mine?
> San'ya of Funai, *yō*, he first dug it
> *Tokotōtō, tokotōtō*
> A thousand blacksmiths' furnaces roar
> The birds that dance in the sky, *yō*, they all fall down
> *Tokotōtō, tokotōtō.*"

That's the Toroku furnace song. . . . It was apparently bustling with hundreds of miners. . . . There's a legend . . . called "Dream-Buying San'ya". . . . :

One day, as San'ya was crossing the mountains from Bungo to peddle his goods in Hyūga, he met up with a man. . . . While the two of them were sitting down talking, the man fell asleep, and when he woke up he said: "I had a strange dream. . . . Bees were digging in the earth, and they came out with gold dust in their mouths." San'ya . . . said, "You have to sell me that dream!" He handed the man some coins, found the place the man had seen in the dream, and dug his pickaxe into the ground. That's how he opened the Toroku silver mine.

San'ya, whose silver mine made him a millionaire overnight, was resented by the lord of Funai, Hineno Yoshiaki. They say that he and all his family were killed.[5]

Movements of people, things, technologies, and even dreams across borders, in and out of this frontier area, mark turning points in Toroku's history. Many involved dreams of wealth, and some turned into nightmares. In the Edo period (1600–1868), San'ya's silver mine caused the deaths of birds and then of San'ya himself. In the twentieth century, the mine produced arsenic and brought devastation and death to the environment and people, and Toroku's arsenic poisoning became the fourth officially designated pollution disease in postwar Japan.

The best known of the first three officially recognized pollution diseases was organic mercury poisoning, which occurred in two places: in Minamata, where a factory dumped mercury into the sea, and along the Agano River in Niigata. In Toyama Prefecture, cadmium mine waste caused victims' bones to become painfully brittle in what was known as Itai-Itai ("ouch-ouch") disease. In Yokkaichi, air pollution from a petrochemical complex caused severe respiratory diseases. Patients in these cases filed lawsuits between 1967 and 1969 and won between 1971 and 1973.

For a time in the 1970s and occasionally thereafter until 1990, Toroku's arsenic poisoning joined these other pollution diseases on front pages. Today, however, few Japanese recognize the name "Toroku," though they know the other officially recognized pollution diseases.[6] Still, Toroku is not insignificant. The costs of modern industrial development are often painfully visible in bodies and lives of people who live and work close to sources of pollution. Richard White's study of Island County, Washington, shows how the environmental history of one small place can have a broader meaning.[7]

Toroku's environmental history, and much of environmental history in general, involves repeated crossings of the indistinct borders between humans and "nature," center and periphery, local and national, and domestic and foreign. Toroku has been repeatedly linked by its underground resources to the nation and world, and each such link has changed it. This illustrates the fact that in environmental history there is no such thing as a story about just one small place, and that environmental history is an integral part of Japanese history. Toroku's key historical moments remind us that definitions of "remote" and "peripheral" are fluid, that events on the national stage had local repercussions quite early, that Japan's contact with the Western world in the sixteenth and seventeenth centuries helped transform its environment, that rice growing was not in fact at the center of agriculture virtually everywhere in Japan until recently, and that globalization and its environmental effects reached far into the mountains of Japan early in the twentieth century.

Early Human History in Toroku

Toroku's history is both a human story and the result of its particular physical environment. There was a latent agency in its mountainscape. In the Jōmon (late Neolithic) period, it was likely not a peripheral or frontier region, and human beings were already beginning to transform its ecology. The megafauna were extinct by about 13,000 BP, so Jōmon hunters depended on the smaller game that remained up to contemporary times in the Sobosan mountain range (including Sobosan itself, 1,756 meters high and one of Japan's "hundred famous mountains").[8] One of the many ways that "Toroku" was written in the past was 猪鹿, a compound combining the characters for wild boar and deer, and Neolithic tools have been found in Toroku.[9] Many Jōmon settlements and hunting and trading routes were in the mountains rather than the lowlands where river crossings were difficult, so Toroku was literally not far off the beaten path.[10]

However, the agricultural revolution that began in the Yayoi period, in the first millennium BCE, turned Toroku into a backwater as rice paddies slowly spread through lowland areas. Slash-and-burn (swidden) agriculture continued to be practiced in remote mountain areas into the 1950s.[11] It was called *yabosaku* in the region around Toroku, where an old villager explained the process:

You cut down a thicket of bamboo and trees, and after three or four months, when it's dry, you set fire to it.

Then when you sow seeds, the ashes serve as fertilizer, and millet, soy beans, and azuki beans grow well. . . .

Where the slope is steep or the ground is rocky, the soil washes away and in five or six years the field goes back to being barren. Then you cut down a different thicket and start over again there. It's easy to do, so in Toroku until after the war, millet *yabo*, buckwheat *yabo*, and daikon *yabo* were common.[12]

A 1609 land register shows Toroku in transition from slash-and-burn to dry fields; there were no wet rice paddies. This change happened as regional and central authorities exerted more control over remote areas. The new overlords encouraged farming, as production from permanent fields is not only greater than from hunting, gathering, and slash-and-burn agriculture, but also easier to measure and tax. Paddies were first listed for Toroku in a 1732 register but did not cover a substantial area until irrigation systems were built in the mid-nineteenth century.[13]

Toroku as Remote Refuge:
Satō Dōgen

Humans were present in Toroku in Jōmon times, but there is no hard evidence enabling us to date the first permanent settlement. There is only a legend. The story of Satō Dōgen is the first of many events, dreams, or border crossings that transformed Toroku and linked it to national events while simultaneously marking it as peripheral, remote, and overlooked.

Part of the story is well known through literature and drama, including the epic *Heike monogatari* and one of the most popular Kabuki plays, *Yoshitsune senbonzakura*. Satō Tadanobu (1161–1186) was a general and retainer to Minamoto Yoshitsune, half brother of Minamoto Yoritomo, the first shogun. After Yoshitsune helped Yoritomo defeat the Heike clan, Yoritomo turned on him and ordered his arrest. The fugitives escaped into the mountains of Yoshino, where Satō Tadanobu urged Yoshitsune to flee while he impersonated Yoshitsune to draw off the pursuers. Both Tadanobu and Yoshitsune, at least in some versions of the story, were eventually caught and committed suicide.

According to legend, Satō Tadanobu's son Tadaharu was sent to safety in a temple in distant Kyushu, taking the Buddhist name Dōgen. In search of a peaceful, remote location, he settled in the Sobosan mountains. A pass entering Toroku on the west is named after him. A shrine in Toroku is dedicated to Hachiman, god of war and of the Minamoto family, and near it is the supposed site of Dōgen's villa (Dōgen yashiki ato).[14]

FIGURE 6.1 Hachiman Shrine. © TIMOTHY S. GEORGE.

The people of Toroku consider Dōgen the founder of their hamlet. When commoners took family names in the nineteenth century, nearly all families in Toroku chose Satō. Family names are therefore rarely used in Toroku. *Yagō*, or "house names," are used instead. A man might therefore be described as "Hinokuchi no Tsuyoshi-san," or "Tsuyoshi of the Hinokuchi house," where "Hinokuchi" is the *yagō*. The *yagō* may also be a place name, since the most important house in an area often takes its place name as its *yagō*. The *yagō* remains even if one family moves out and another moves in.

Toxic Wealth: Morita San'ya

Literature and legend surround the founding of Toroku's mine, as they do the founding of the settlement itself. Ihara Saikaku apparently modeled the protagonist of his story "From Kyoto's Streams to Bungo's Baths" on Morita San'ya.[15] Yorozuya San'ya of Funai in Bungo Province (now Oita City, Oita Prefecture) becomes "the leading millionaire of Kyushu" but dissipates his fortune on his mansion, on concubines brought from Kyoto, and on shipping water from Otowa Falls in Kyoto for his bath.[16] After the death of his senior clerk, who had worked to protect his master's wealth, San'ya's "misfortunes accumulated, until his own life became forfeit, and all that had yet remained to him was confiscated by others."[17]

There are several versions of the legend of "Dream-Buying San'ya" related by the Toroku villager at the beginning of this chapter.[18] San'ya actually lived from 1584 to 1647. The site of his mansion is indicated by a historical marker in Oita. He is supposed to have decorated the mansion with imported treasures, including some from Europe. Above a ceiling of glass, there were colorful swimming goldfish. When the daimyo visited, San'ya laid on his back and pointed out the ceiling with his foot, and this disrespect was the pretext for which he and his family were put to death.[19]

As the birds falling from the sky in the Toroku furnace song suggest, the mine harmed its immediate environment as well as its owner in the Edo period. Another verse in the song includes these lines: "In the garden of San'ya of the Toroku silver mine / Even though it's summer, yō, frost falls."[20] The white powder that settled on Toroku was arsenic trioxide (As_2O_3) in the smoke from the furnaces processing silver ore, which also included arsenic. At high temperatures, it sublimes (changes from a solid to a gas). When it cools, the gas becomes a solid again. The same powder settled on land, water, plants, animals, and people around other mines, including Japan's largest silver mine at Iwami and the copper mine at Ashio. It was sold in the Edo period as "Iwami Silver Mine Rat Poison."[21]

The increased production, wealth, and poison produced by mines in the Sengoku period (the period of civil war that preceded Japan's 1600 unification) and early Edo period resulted from a mining boom enabled in part by technological advances.[22] The daimyos, in search of wealth and of iron for weapons, put mines under their direct control. Previously, many mines had been discovered and even operated by *yamabushi* mountain priests, known for esoteric understanding of nature and for magical abilities. They were also known for their fighting abilities, and some served as military advisors to the daimyos, who vied for power up to the late sixteenth century. The daimyos also incorporated foreign technology and techniques into their fighting forces and at the same time imported foreign mining technology and even mining specialists. After domestic warfare ended in 1600, the Tokugawa shogunate took control of major mines and focused on increasing production, particularly of copper, silver, and gold needed for coins and domestic and foreign trade. Thanks to these efforts and new domestic and foreign technologies, including horizontal shafts and better ventilation and pumping systems, Japan may have been the world's largest producer of silver in the seventeenth century.[23]

Morita San'ya may have used foreign technology and knowledge to extract wealth from Toroku. A resident related a story about the origins of the name of the hamlet:

> At the start of the Edo period, when Morita San'ya of Bungo developed the silver mine, it seems that a Portuguese mining engineer was invited, and

taught new technologies such as western furnaces. That foreigner's name was Yosefu Torofu, and to commemorate Torofu the place was given the name Toroku.

There probably isn't any basis for this theory. In the reports from Hideyoshi's land survey, which took place earlier, is the line:

1. amount 14 *koku, 7 to, 9 gō*   Toroku

So the place name Toroku existed earlier, and maybe after the Portuguese engineer came to Toroku, he took the name Torofu. "Toroku" seems to mean a remote place. Deeper into the mountains than this, there are no human settlements.[24]

Another version of the story has the Portuguese taking the Japanese name Toroku Yotarō, giving the name Toroku to the hamlet.[25] The villager is probably right, however, that Toroku did not take its name from a Portuguese mining engineer, but such a person may have been there and come to be known as Toroku or Torofu. Bungo, Morita San'ya's base, was involved in trade with Europeans, and Morita could well have brought in a Portuguese mining expert.

Toroku was therefore first linked to the world beyond Japan in the sixteenth or seventeenth century. Its mountains and their mines—both called *yama*—were removed from the world of magic and priests and transformed by global flows of trade and technology. Toroku produced more wealth as a result. But as in the twentieth century, when extraction of its mineral wealth again brought new ties between Toroku and the world, that wealth went elsewhere, while Toroku suffered its poisonous effects.

Meiji Transformations: Ditches, Paddies, and Community Governance

One of Toroku's late nineteenth-century transformations was shared with the rest of Japan: the modernizing authorities of the Meiji period (1868–1912) extended tentacles of direct central government control into the hamlet for the first time. Another transformation had been experienced by most of Japan earlier: wet rice paddies became Toroku's dominant form of agriculture. A third change was the closing of the mine. The fourth was a response to the others: an organization was formed to help withstand the economic and social stresses of the new age and soon took over most functions of hamlet government.

Toroku's environment and human relationships to it were dramatically transformed by two major irrigation ditches in the 1850s and 1860s. For one, a tunneling specialist named Kumagorō worked for a year to dig a 130-meter tunnel through mountain rock.[26] These ditches made possible the construction of rice

FIGURE 6.2 Rice fields in Toroku. © TIMOTHY S. GEORGE.

paddies. Back-breaking work was required to build terraces in this steep terrain. Impressive work was done by a woman named Moka-san. By the time she died in 1912 at the age of 81, she and her husband had transformed mountain slopes into thirteen paddy fields totaling 0.25 hectares (0.6 acres) and sixteen dry fields totaling 1.1 hectares (2.75 acres). Moka-san did not live to see what the reopening of the mine to produce arsenic did to her fields. Arsenic poisoned the land and people, forcing some to give up farming and work in the mines. The mine owners were able to buy nearby farmland cheaply. Moka-san's fields were bought and used as a dumping ground for slag from the furnaces that produced arsenic trioxide, and for many years they were barren. After Toroku's poisoning became a national issue in the 1970s, visitors were shown "Moka-san's stone walls," one section of which is eight meters high and thirty meters long.[27] Today Moka-san's fields are covered by new forest, but pieces of partially burned arsenic ore are still visible. Moka-san embodies Toroku's shared historical memories of struggles against nature, and the fate of her fields symbolizes the destruction in the twentieth century of Toroku's livelihood, lifestyles, and environment by arsenic.

During the Tokugawa period, the mine came under the control of the daimyo of Takanabe in Hyūga (now Miyazaki Prefecture). In the 1850s it was taken over by the daimyo of Higo (now Kumamoto Prefecture). In the Meiji period, under several private owners, it produced decreasing amounts of silver, copper, and lead, and it was closed in 1900. Toroku's residents returned to depending almost exclusively on agriculture.[28]

Because of the land reforms, circumstances for farmers in Meiji Japan were very different from those of the Tokugawa period. They could legally own their fields, and they were required to pay land taxes in cash to the government rather than in kind to the daimyo. Tenancy increased as farmers were forced in bad years to sell land in order to pay taxes.

In 1890, a remarkable new organization was created in Toroku in order to keep the community together and avoid having to sell land to outsiders. The Wagōkai was started by Satō Zen'en, a Buddhist priest of the True Pure Land Sect (Jōdo Shinshū), modeled on organizations he had seen in his travels and based on Buddhist principles. Zen'en had left Toroku at the age of fourteen to study in Hikone in Ōmi (now Shiga Prefecture). He returned to serve in Senpukuji, the nearest temple to Toroku, several kilometers downstream in the village of Iwato, to which the hamlet of Toroku was appended. The Wagōkai was originally designed to be a kō—a mutual savings and assistance association. Most kō were centered on a temple or shrine, and all of Toroku's families were affiliated with Jōdo Shinshū, so it was natural for Zen'en to chair the association. A resident recalled Zen'en's founding of the organization:

> He gave up [his position at the temple] and came back to Toroku . . . about 1889. He lived by himself in an outbuilding at "Nageshi" [the yagō for his family's home], and since he didn't have any fields, he raised silkworms and opened a private school where young people of the hamlet came to learn to read and write.
>
> 1890 was a year of panic. Some people had to sell their land to pay back their loans. If Toroku's fields were handed over to people from other hamlets, negotiations over water rights and planting would be difficult. The harmony of the hamlet would be destroyed. . . . Zen'en . . . came up with the idea of creating a financial organization to save the poor people.[29]

Zen'en drew up a twenty-one-article charter. Interest on loans from the organization would be 1 sen per month, property would not be sold to people from other hamlets, and the purpose of the organization was to help those in need. Those who broke the rules would lose their rights as members of the community. With the approval of the mayor of Iwato, the Wagōkai was established in September 1890. Meetings were held in May and November, and members were fined for absence or tardiness. They discussed not only loans and their repayments "but even issues like the raising of cattle and horses, education for the children, improvement of roads and bridges, punishment of thieves, and whether couples who had eloped should be made to apologize. So it was the highest decision-making organization in the hamlet."[30]

Although Toroku was administratively part of Iwato, the Wagōkai made it largely independent. The Wagōkai enabled virtually all families to pay their taxes without selling land to outsiders or taking out high-interest loans, and it even served as an agricultural cooperative that bought and sold supplies and products. Toroku received government awards for the quality of the horses, cows, and honey it produced. The Wagōkai continued to exist into the 1960s, when it was replaced by a branch of Nōkyō, the Central Union of Agricultural Cooperatives.[31] In the late Meiji period, thanks to the Wagōkai, Toroku must have come closer than most hamlets to being the sort of independent, harmonious, successful farming settlement envisioned by Tanaka Shōzō, the village headman, Diet member, and activist who fought for the victims of pollution from the Ashio copper mine in the late nineteenth and early twentieth centuries. But that changed when Toroku's boundaries were again crossed by outside forces and the mine reopened to produce arsenic. These forces and the poison from beneath the earth brought new threats that the Wagōkai discussed as early as 1923 but proved unable to manage.[32]

Chemicals, Global and Local

The first half of the twentieth century was an age of chemicals: gasoline, pharmaceuticals, fertilizers, pesticides, plastics, and chemical weapons. The intrusion of this new age into Toroku linked this small hamlet and the poison it produced to global wars, the global economy, and the global environment. A resident recalled the discussion at a Wagōkai meeting in 1923:

> The topic was the arsenic trioxide poisoning. Someone said: "This spring, my *shiitake* plants didn't produce any mushrooms." . . . Voices were heard from around the floor saying "My *shiitake* plot was the same," and "Same here." *Shiitake* are one of Toroku's important products. Money from their sale was used to pay taxes and provide funds that farm families needed. . . .
>
> Soybeans, which are used to make miso, soy sauce, and *yuba* [dried bean curd, or "tofu skin"] were the main source of protein. . . . Throughout Toroku the soybean plants had withered. Setsuzō-san of Kōji, across the river from the mine, said: "Last fall, my *kabosu* [a citrus fruit] never ripened"; someone from Sōmi *kumi* said: "The leaves on my bamboo turned red"; and someone from Minami *kumi* said: "My plum trees lost their leaves twice last year." The talk was all about strange occurrences like these.
>
> When the persimmon leaves appear, the honeybees start making hives. So it was about time for hive-making, but . . . that year for some reason the honeybees were slow getting going. Honeybees are also one of Toroku's important products. . . . The money from them would buy a year's supply of

iriko [dried sardines], *katsuobushi* [dried bonito flakes], sugar, and oil. There were some beekeeping families with over a hundred boxes of them. So for bees to be affected was really serious. And . . . someone from near the mine said: "My cows are losing weight and won't eat their fodder." . . . When even cows and horses were being harmed, you couldn't make a living anymore. If this were ignored it would be really serious.

All of the changes happened after the burning of arsenic began at the mine. Considering the fact that they gradually spread from the area around the mine to places farther away, anyone could clearly see that the cause was the mine. The meeting passed a unanimous resolution:

"All members unanimously request that the manager responsible, in order to prevent poisoning, not carry out any further operations without equipment that is fully effective."[33]

Toroku was being poisoned because of the expanding global market for arsenic, particularly arsenic trioxide, which was used in pigments, medicines, and insecticides. Germany was the major producer before World War I, and in the war it used poison gas made from arsenic trioxide. Japan's chemical industry took off after the war, and Japan became a major producer of arsenic trioxide and products made from it.[34]

Pesticides containing arsenic had been used since the nineteenth century to combat grape blight in Bordeaux, gypsy moths in Massachusetts, and Colorado beetles infesting potato crops in North America and Europe. Lime arsenite, also called calcium arsenate, was used against the boll weevils that infested all of the cotton-growing regions in the United States by the 1920s. Huge amounts of this white powder were sprayed from the air on cotton fields until it began to be replaced in the 1940s by DDT. A report from 1938 lists the United States as the largest foreign destination of Toroku's arsenic trioxide.[35]

These global changes made it profitable to reopen the Toroku mine in 1920 for its arsenopyrite, an ore containing arsenic that had previously been discarded. But first a process for producing arsenic trioxide from the arsenopyrite had to be developed. Two years earlier, the Ashio mine had begun extracting arsenic trioxide from the smokestacks of its copper smelters. Ashio used new technology—electrostatic precipitators recently developed by Frederick Cottrell at the University of California—which reduced pollution, increased profits, and made Ashio Japan's largest producer of arsenic trioxide.

Toroku's method of arsenopyrite processing, however, was the lowest cost and least technologically advanced imaginable. Satō Kiemon inherited the mine and the surrounding land and hoped that reopening it would bring him a profit. A husband and wife known as kiln- or furnace-making specialists were invited to

Toroku, and with the help of a hamlet stonemason named Takaichi they built a kiln and succeeded in producing arsenic trioxide in 1920. Their process, called in Toroku *ahiyaki*, or "arsenic-burning," was increased in scale but fundamentally unchanged throughout the entire period of production, until the mine was finally closed in 1962. In 1920, the reopening of the mine was welcomed by residents of Toroku:

> Some sort of completely white powder was taken out of the kiln. . . . The news spread through the hamlet immediately. "The mine is starting up again!" The whole hamlet got excited. No one was worried. Those times were different from today; it was a time when there weren't many ways to make money. If the mine opened up, you could sell firewood. You could sell timbers. If you went down in the mine, you could get paid wages. People who owned land at the mine site could get rent.[36]

Arsenopyrite was dug from under Toroku with picks and shovels and carried out of the mine shafts in *karui* (straw backpacks). Later it was hauled out in mine carts, with networks of cables strung across the valleys to deliver the ore to furnaces. The ore was broken up, mixed with mud, and shaped into softball-sized balls. The entire processing operation was initially carried out by three people.[37] The ore was broken up by a hammer-wielding character called by the locals "the old drifter," supposedly a veteran of the 1869 battle at Hakodate in Hokkaido that was the Tokugawa shogunate's last stand against the Meiji revolutionaries. The crumbled ore was then formed into balls called *dango* (dumplings) by Tsuruno Kumi, a young woman who along with her husband, Masaichi, had been persuaded by Satō Kiemon to work for the mine. The pay was low, but the work appealed to Kumi and especially to Masaichi, who needed to pay off family debts that had forced him to be an indentured servant (*hōkō*) and then a *nago* to the "Hinokuchi" house. (A *nago* was a landless peasant who was virtually a serf, though by the twentieth century the term might well have meant simply a dependent menial worker.)

Kumi's *dango* were burned in the kilns to produce arsenic trioxide. The kilns, made of stone and clay, used technology that had been available for several centuries. A series of box-shaped chambers was built on a slope. In the lowest chamber, Masaichi built a fire with wood and charcoal, inserted the balls of ore, and sealed the door. The ore burned for a week to ten days (during which time Masaichi got little sleep), and the smoke and gas passed through exhaust holes at the top rear of each chamber into the next. Beyond the combustion chamber were three collecting chambers. Beyond the last of these, an exhaust pipe connected to a short smokestack. As the arsenic trioxide cooled, it turned from a gas into a white

FIGURE 6.3 Mine employees, 1924; Kumi in second row holding baby, Seiichi in back row, far right. PHOTO COURTESY OF KAWAHARA KAZUYUKI.

powder that collected on the floors and sides of the collecting chambers. A tenth or more of the arsenic trioxide, however, remained in gaseous form and flowed out of the smokestack, which was covered with a crude filter of straw, and then precipitated on the surrounding mountains, fields, and homes as "arsenic frost."

When the fires were out, Kumi and Masaichi, only their eyes visible beneath protective layers of clothing, entered the collecting chambers to scrape out the white arsenic trioxide powder, which was boxed and transported down the narrow mountain road. The ashes and slag, which still contained arsenic, were dumped nearby, often into the Toroku River, and later on in Moka-san's fields. Satō Tsuru, born in 1940, recalls playing in the piles of ashes as a child. Her family moved farther from the mine to try to escape its effects, but she was the only one of twelve children to survive.[38] As Linda Nash has shown for California, human industry in Toroku polluted the environment, and human bodies, as part of that environment, were polluted, damaged, and destroyed as well.[39]

A villager described the horrific effects on Tsuruno Kumi and Masaichi:

Kumi-san, who worked the crumbled ore with her bare feet and shaped it with her hands, had black spots covering her hands and feet. If the arsenic trioxide powder got on their bodies, they'd jump into the bath right away.

obvious to Tsuruno Kumi and Tsuruno Masaichi by 1921, to the Wagōkai and the entire hamlet by 1923, and to local government authorities by 1925. Despite repeated petitions by the Wagōkai and requests by the mayor of Iwato that the prefecture investigate, the pollution continued unchecked and the problem was never reported beyond the local newspapers. Not until 1971, when pollution problems had become a national issue, did Toroku's situation become widely known. In 1973 the Environment Agency recognized Toroku arsenic poisoning as a pollution disease. Victims sued Sumitomo Metal Mining in 1975 and won in 1984, and after appeals to higher courts the Supreme Court imposed a *wakai* (perhaps best described as a court-imposed out-of-court settlement) in 1990. Over 170 people have been certified as victims and over 70 others deemed eligible for assistance.[48] The main support group for the Toroku victims, the Toroku Matsuo Tō Kōdoku no Higaisha o Mamoru Kai, evolved into the Asia Arsenic Network, a globally active nongovernmental organization working on behalf of arsenic victims outside of Japan, particularly in Bangladesh. The bare hillsides of Toroku were covered with forests again by the time of the 1990 settlement.

   Toroku is part of a story that includes more than Japan's remarkable, rapid turnaround from wanton pollution to strict controls. Toroku's population is aging and shrinking. The surrounding mountains are now dotted with brown trees suffering from acid rain, as the winds much of the year come via Beijing, Seoul,

FIGURE 6.6 Empty, crumbling old houses and new graves are common sights in Toroku today.
© TIMOTHY S. GEORGE.

Shanghai, and the industrial sites of northern Kyushu. Our transformations of the environment have put us far beyond the point, as Bill McKibben noted two decades ago, of being able to restore "nature" or let it restore itself.[49] But how all of these things happened and what border crossings were involved are further chapters in the environmental history of the hamlet of Toroku.

Notes

This chapter is part of a larger project on the environmental history of Toroku supported by grants from the Northeast Asia Council of the Association for Asian Studies, the University of Rhode Island Center for the Humanities, the University of Rhode Island Council for Research, the University of Rhode Island Foundation, and the J. William Fulbright Foreign Scholarship Board. For assistance, advice, information, and hospitality, I thank Satō Mariko, Satō Shin'ichi, Satō Tsuru, Akutagawa Jin, Kawahara Kazuyuki, Ueno Noboru, Shimotsu Yoshihiro, the members and staff of the Asia Arsenic Network and the Toroku Matsuo Tō Kōdoku no Higaisha o Mamoru Kai, Norimatsu Kazue, Norimatsu Setsuo, Okamoto Kōichi, and Horikawa Saburō.

1. See W. Eugene Smith and Aileen Mioko Smith, *Minamata* (New York: Holt, Rinehart and Winston, 1975); and Timothy S. George, *Minamata: Pollution and the Struggle for Democracy in Postwar Japan* (Cambridge, MA: Harvard University Asia Center, 2001). On pollution and human bodies in Japan, see Brett L. Walker, *Toxic Archipelago: A History of Industrial Disease in Japan* (Seattle: University of Washington Press, 2010).

2. J. R. McNeill, "China's Environmental History in World Perspective," in *Sediments of Time: Environment and Society in Chinese History,* ed. Mark Elvin and Liu Ts'ui-jung (New York: Cambridge Universtiy Press, 1998), 45. Brett L. Walker pioneered the study of frontiers and borderlands in Japan's environmental history in *The Conquest of Ainu Lands: Ecology and Culture in Japanese Expansion, 1590–1800* (Berkeley: University of California Press, 2001).

3. Donald Worster, "Transformations of the Earth: Toward an Agroecological Perspective in History," *Journal of American History* 76:1 (March 1990): 1087–1106.

4. Satō Shin'ichi provided the information on the number of households in Toroku in a personal interview on May 18, 2008, and is the best source of information on Toroku's people, animals, geography, society, farming, and history.

5. A resident of Toroku, in Kawahara Kazuyuki, *Kuden ahiyakidani* (Arsenic-burning valley: An oral history, Tokyo: Iwanami, 1980), 2–3. This oral history collection, hereafter abbreviated KAYD, does not give speakers' names. Funai in Bungo Province is now Oita City in Oita Prefecture. Hyūga Province is now Miyazaki Prefecture.

6. Japan's best-known arsenic poisoning case is not Toroku but the 1955 contamination of Morinaga Milk's "MF" brand baby formula, which poisoned thousands and killed hundreds. Shōji Kichirō and Sugai Masurō, "The Arsenic Milk Poisoning Incident," in *Industrial Pollution in Japan,* ed. Ui Jun (Tokyo: United Nations University Press, 1992), 77–102.

7. Richard White, *Land Use, Environment, and Social Change: The Shaping of Island County, Washington* (Seattle: University of Washington Press, 1980).

8. Conrad Totman, *Pre-industrial Korea and Japan in Environmental Perspective* (Leiden: Brill, 2004), 25.

9. Kawahara Kazuyuki, *Jōdo mura Toroku: bunmei to inochi no shiki* (Toroku, village of the Pure Land: A chronicle of civilization and life, Tokyo: Chikuma Shobō, 1988), 102, 104, 109–110.

10. Gina L. Barnes, *The Rise of Civilization in East Asia: The Archaeology of China, Korea, and Japan* (London: Thames and Hudson, 1993), 89.

11. Robert Hall and Toshio Noh, "Yakihata, Burned-field Agriculture in Japan, with its Special Characteristics in Shikoku," *Papers, Michigan Academy of Science, Arts, and Letters* 38 (1953): 315–322. Yukawa Yōji, *Yama no minzokushi* (Records of mountain folk customs, Tokyo: Yoshikawa Kōbunkan, 1997), 90–105, describes Itsuki, another Kyushu mountain village with both a mine and slash-and-burn agriculture.

12. "A villager over sixty," in Kawahara, *Jōdo mura Toroku*, 109.

13. Kawahara, *Jōdo mura Toroku*, 110, 113, 116.

14. On Satō Dōgen, see Kawahara, *Jōdo mura Toroku*, 18–24.

15. Ihara Saikaku, "From Kyoto's Streams to Bungo's Baths," book 3, story 2 in *The Japanese Family Storehouse, or The Millionaires Gospel Modernised,* trans. G. W. Sargent (Cambridge: Cambridge University Press, 1959), 63–66. Sargent believes Yorozuya [Morita] San'yasuke of Funai was the model for the character Yorozuya San'ya; see note 6, 184–187.

16. Ihara Saikaku, 64.

17. Ibid., 66.

18. One example is Takachiho Kyōiku Iinkai, "Yume kai San'ya" (San'ya the dream-buyer), www.komisen.net/minwa.htm. Kawahara discusses San'ya in *Jōdo mura Toroku*, 55–63.

19. Watanabe Katsumi,"Shinsetsu, San'ya Chōja: Saikaku sakuhin no haikei o genchi ni motomete" (San'ya the millionaire, the true story: Seeking the background to Saikaku's story on location), *Kyūshūjin* (People of Kyushu), September 1980, 24–43.

20. Sung by Satō Yoshio of Toroku, quoted in Kawahara, *Jōdo mura Toroku*, 72–73.

21. On "arsenic frost" and Iwami Silver Mine Rat Poison, see "Genroku nenkan ni mo endoku: Toroku chiku" (Smoke pollution in the Genroku period too: The Toroku District), *Miyazaki nichinichi shinbun*, January 21, 1972, and Kawahara, *Jōdo mura Toroku*, 72–74, 76–84.

22. Totman, *Pre-industrial Korea*, 130.

23. William Wayne Farris, *Japan's Medieval Population: Famine, Fertility, and Warfare in a Transformative Age* (Honolulu: University of Hawai'i Press, 2006), 243–244.

24. KAYD, 9.

25. Kawahara, *Jōdo mura Toroku*, 63.

26. Ibid., 116–117.

27. Kawahara, *Jōdo mura Toroku*, 117–118, 179.

28. On ownership of the mine from founding to closing, see Nakazawa Takao, "Gyōsei igaku o utsu" (Attacking bureaucratic medical science), in Toroku Matsuo Tō Kōdoku no Higaisha o Mamoru Kai, *Onmin no fukken,* 154–156.

29. KAYD, 36–37.

30. Ibid., 37.

31. On the early years of the Wagōkai, see also Tanaka Tetsuya, *Kōgai: Toroku jiken* (Industrial pollution: The Toroku incident, Tokyo: Sanseidō, 1981), 90–91, and Kawahara, *Jōdo mura Toroku*, 118–123.

32. For Wagōkai meeting minutes and mine-related petitions, see Toroku Matsuo Tō Kōdoku no Higaisha o Mamoru Kai, *Onmin no fukken*, 46–53.

33. KAYD, 32–34.

34. On the early years of the chemical company Nihon Chisso Hiryō (which caused Minamata disease), see Barbara Molony, *Technology and Investment: The Prewar Japanese Chemical Industry* (Cambridge, MA: Harvard University Council on East Asian Studies, 1990).

35. Report submitted to Miyazaki-ken Sangyō buchō (Director of the Miyazaki Prefecture Department of Industry) by Iwato Kōzan (Iwato Mine), July 15, 1938, in the document collection assembled by Kawahara Kazuyuki and housed in the Nonohanakan in Takanabe-shi, Miyazaki-ken. On insecticides containing arsenic, see Edmund Russell, *War and Nature: Fighting Humans and Insects with Chemicals from World War I to Silent Spring* (Cambridge: Cambridge University Press, 2001), 6, 111.

36. KAYD, 6.

37. See the description by a villager in KAYD, 15–18.

38. Satō Tsuru, personal interview, Toroku, May 17, 2008.

39. Linda Nash, *Inescapable Ecologies: A History of Environment, Disease, and Knowledge* (Berkeley: University of California Press, 2006).

40. KAYD, 18.

41. Hotta Nobuyuki, ed., *Mansei hiso chūdoku kenkyū: shōkōgaku teki apurōchi* (Chronic arsenic poisoning: Symptomatological studies, Kumamoto-ken, Kumamoto-shi: Sakuragaoka Byōin, 2008), collects studies on arsenic poisoning in Toroku and elsewhere.

42. Hotta Nobuyuki et al., "Toroku kōdokubyō (mansei ahi chūdokushō) no rinshōteki kenkyū" (Clinical studies of Toroku Mine disease [Chronic arsenic poisoning]), in Hotta, *Mansei hiso chūdoku kenkyū*, 19.

43. Tanaka, *Kōgai: Toroku jiken*, 84–87.

44. Toroku Matsuo Tō Kōdoku no Higaisha o Mamoru Kai, *Onmin no fukken*, 61.

45. On use of Toroku's arsenic trioxide in poison gas, see the series "Doku gasu no shima" (Poison Gas Island) by Kawahara Kazuyuki, particularly "Genryō seisan de mo tsume ato" (Production of raw ingredients also left scars), *Asahi shinbun*, September 15, 1995, 17. For an interview with a worker in the poison gas plant on Okunoshima, see Haruko Taya Cook and Theodore F. Cook, *Japan at War: An Oral History* (New York: New Press, 1992), 199–202.

46. On wartime environmental history, including other examples of reduced environmental damage during wartime, see William M. Tsutsui, "Landscapes in the Dark Valley: Toward an Environmental History of Wartime Japan," *Environmental History* 8:2 (April 2003): 294–311.

47. Saitō Masatake, "Toroku kōdoku jiken kokuhatsu to watashi (sono 2)" (My role in indicting [those responsible for] the Toroku Mine pollution, part 2) *Kōdoku* (Mine Pollution) 7 (May 1975): 13.

48. For a timeline of events in Toroku from 1920 to 1992, see Toroku o Kiroku Suru Kai, ed., *Kiroku: Toroku* (Toroku: A documentary record) (Miyazaki-ken, Higashimorokata-gun, Takaoka-chō: Honda Kikaku, 1993), 598–608.

49. Bill McKibben, *The End of Nature* (New York: Random House, 1989).

BETWEEN BODIES | III

7

Fecal Matters

Prolegomenon to a History of Shit in Japan

DAVID L. HOWELL

Poop is yucky. As a rule, yuckiness is socially constructed, but poop is different. Our dislike of the stuff is hardwired into us. Neuroscientists confirmed this in an experiment designed to locate regions of the brain involved in "the response to disgusting stimuli presented in the olfactory modality."[1] Poop's yuckiness is an insistent plea for us to stay away; it protects us from the critters that live in it and could cause illness or even death if ingested. Yuckiness is good, at least with regard to poop. At the same time, poop is more than just yucky; it's necessary, too, and not just in the usual sense of giving form to food the body cannot or will not digest. Babies are born with sterile guts. They must acquire intestinal microflora for their immune systems to develop properly. They pick up these vital bacteria from Mommy's feces on the journey through the birth canal or, barring that, from unwittingly helpful caregivers and well-wishers in the maternity ward.[2]

Poop's yuckiness presents a challenge to the aspiring historian of shit. In Tokugawa and Meiji Japan, people readily acknowledged the essential yuckiness of poop, but they also looked beyond it and indeed embraced shit as an object of utility. In the pages that follow, I will discuss a number of possible topics for a comprehensive history of shit in Japan. In every case, my emphasis will be on shit as something useful—a source of benefit for the individual and the nation. I will, moreover, meditate briefly on notions of the nature of excrement—the shittiness of shit—particularly from an agronomic perspective. Yet, at the end of the day, despite the rich variety of angles from which to look at it, it's still shit we're talking about—yucky poop, disgusting as ever in the olfactory modality.

The Shittiness of Shit

In his discussion of night soil (and fertilizer more generally), Miyazaki Yasu-sada, the author of the agricultural manual *Nōgyō zensho* (The agricultural compendium), first published in 1697, cites what he calls an old proverb.[3] Looking at the characters alone, the reader will want to read the proverb as "*Jōnōfu wa kuso o oshimu koto, kogane o oshimu ga gotoshi*"—something like, "The superior farmer values shit as he values gold." Actually, however, Yasusada glosses the character 糞—normally read *kuso* or *fun*, "shit"—as *koe*, "fertilizer." He does this, in fact, throughout his entire discussion of fertilizer.[4] Now, the usual character for *koe* is 肥, the *hi* of *hiryō* 肥料, "fertilizer," and *himan* 肥満, "obesity." Yasusada uses this character as well, but he uses it to describe the beneficial results of the application of fertilizer. This suggests a slippage in meaning—"shit" 糞 is not waste but rather anything that nourishes and enriches the land and makes it literally "fat," *koechi* 肥地, be it excrement, compost, green fertilizer, or the mud of streambeds.[5]

Yasusada divides fertilizers into various categories depending on their source and use, but he eventually settles on a broad differentiation between "miscellaneous shit" (*zōgoe* 雑糞) and "superior shit" (*jōgoe* 上糞); in both cases, I'm using "shit" in his capacious sense. Night soil is "superior shit," along with things such as oil cake (the dregs of cottonseed and sesame seed that have been pressed for oil), dried sardines, and the remains of whale meat and bones boiled and pressed.[6] He makes no mention of night soil per se as a commodity, though the other items in the "superior shit" category were commercial fertilizers. In any case, he is certainly cognizant of agriculture as a commercial enterprise. He cautions against using "superior shit" on crops that won't return a high price or in fields without the labor to make the most of its potent power. Don't invest more in fertilizer, in other words, than the crop is worth.[7]

I should like to stress that even useful shit is still yucky; but its utility trumps its yuckiness. Hiraga Gennai made this point in his 1776 treatise, "On Farting" ("Hōhiron"). Here I quote William Sibley's elegant translation:

> All things that lie between heaven and earth array themselves naturally into categories of high and low, lofty and base. Among them, surely the lowest of the low, the basest of the base, are urine and excrement. In China they have various pejorative figures of speech in which things are compared to "ordure," "coprolith," etc., while in Japan we simply say of things we don't care for that they're "like shit." Yet this loathsome filth, we should not forget, is turned into fertilizer and thereby nourishes the millions.[8]

Gennai's essay on farting was intended to amuse his readers. Conversely, a lecturer named Furuichi Matsuo, speaking in 1915, was not joking when he said, "As you all know, excrement is bad smelling, foul looking, dirty stuff. Yet, for we farmers, it's deeply important—treasure, really." In fact, Furuichi continued, it's not proper to think of excrement as dirty, for shit is nothing less than rice transmuted:

"If rice is important, so too is shit (*kuso*)." Unfortunately, some people just don't get it—especially folks in Tokyo, who call farmers "poop handlers" (*kuso nigiri*) and "turd tinkers" (*kuso ijiri*). He concluded ominously that such people might change their tune and stop looking down on farmers if they stopped collecting their night soil—in ten days Tokyo would be inundated in a sea of shit and piss.[9]

Without being quite so angry or aggressive, other writers made the same association between rice and shit as Furuichi did. The author of a short essay entitled "Which Is More Precious, Shit or Rice?" reads much into the characters used to write "shit," 糞 and 屎 (either can be read *kuso*).[10] The first combines the characters for "rice" 米 and "different" 異, the second "rice" and "corpse" 尸. In either case, he argues—invoking an appealing but incorrect folk etymology—that the characters demonstrate that shit is the transmutation of rice.[11] Hence, "rice and shit are of the same essence but manifest themselves in somewhat different forms. Man depends on rice to live; shit depends on man to be formed; and rice depends on shit to grow. Rice becomes shit and shit becomes rice in an endless cycle of birth and rebirth." Indeed, it's only because rice goes in the mouth and shit comes out the anus that we think of the one as pure and the other as filthy. After all, when we eat rice, it's like we are indirectly eating shit. We're getting into pretty disgusting territory here, and by the point the author declares, "In this world, nothing is as important as shit," one senses that he is not being entirely serious. Nevertheless, the basic circle-of-life storyline is one repeated frequently in Japanese discourses on shit.

Shit as a Natural Resource

Another late seventeenth-century farm manual, *Hyakushō denki* (The farmer's memoir), devotes one of the work's fifteen fascicles to a discourse on *fujō*, "the unclean."[12] Although the anonymous author explicitly defines *fujō* as "excrement and urine" (*daishōben*), much of the fascicle is given over to a general discussion of fertilizer in its myriad forms, including varieties of green fertilizer from land and sea and animal products ranging from horse manure, bird droppings, and dried sardines to dried turtle meat, bivalves, and gastropods. Whatever the source—animal, vegetable, or human—because fertilizer requires careful curing and preparation before use, the author devotes much of his account to detailed instructions on the alchemy required to transform raw shit into useful fertilizer. For night soil, the basic task of curing meant leaving excrement in a closed container for about a year to kill harmful bacteria and parasites; only then could yucky poop realize its destiny as an object of utility.

Despite the author's ecumenical view of shit, he lavishes the most detail on human excrement and urine, with detailed tips on best practices for their collection and use. "Waste not a single drop of shit," he exhorts the reader, for "shit nourishes the land" and ensures the cultivator his livelihood and prosperity. In elite households, he tells us, *setchin* is the word for a toilet in the northern part of the house. If it's in the western section it is a *saijō*, and in the east, it is a *tōen*. But surely the most elegant place to do one's business is in the southern part of the house, in the "fragrant-fragrant" *kōkō*.[13] Ordinary folk without the wherewithal to indulge in fancy toilet construction should place their privies where the excreta will be protected from rain, which disrupts the curing process. Chamber pots should be placed discreetly around the dwelling for the convenience of women and children who, out of incontinence or fear of the dark, may not be able to make it to the toilet; besides, it's inconvenient and a waste of time to go all the way to the toilet to fulfill one's needs. Indeed, "waste not, want not" is the author's constant theme—don't waste time, don't waste shit, don't even waste dishwater, for it too is a useful form of "shit."

Not all shit is created equal. For one thing, different crops require different types of fertilizer. For example, seaweed harvested in the sixth and seventh months is excellent for barley and potatoes, provided the earth is not inordinately wet. The meat of fish, turtles, and shellfish can be extremely efficacious in fertilizing rice paddies, but they must be prepared and used with great care, for they are so potent that rice plants will easily overdose. Indeed, when using any type of oily fertilizer on rice, it's best to inquire of experienced local farmers what works best.[14] Even as a by-product of human digestion, not all shit is created equal. "The shit of people whose diets are rich in flavorful foods, with lots of fish, is particularly potent, while that of those who eat simply does not nourish crops well. Therefore, villages that gather shit from prosperous areas (*hanjō no chi*: i.e., urban areas) and use it to fertilize their paddies and fields enjoy bountiful harvests of grain and vegetables."[15]

The idea that some people's feces are particularly potent was widely accepted in Japan. Night soil collectors in Edo routinely paid a premium to empty the privies of the well-born and well-fed residents of daimyo mansions and high-end Yoshiwara brothels. In modern times, night soil from military barracks was considered to be the best because soldiers ate a lot of meat. Excreta from the pleasure quarters was generally highly regarded as well, though connoisseurs engaged in contentious debates over questions like the relative quality of different red-light districts and whether cheap brothels, with their legions of young customers, might not be better sources of robust poop than fancy joints.[16] Farmers in the eastern outskirts of modern Tokyo claimed to be able to discern a household's economic status with a glance at its shit: the poop of the rich was greasy and plump, whereas the turds of the poor simply bobbed forlornly in the slurry.[17]

Quality in, quality out: the logic is unimpeachable, and poop scientists in the early twentieth century endorsed this commonsensical view with studies that demonstrated that diets rich in protein rendered poop high in nitrogen.[18] Still, surely the tea farmers of Uji in the 1830s needn't have insisted on using night soil from only two streets in the tony Kamigyō district of Kyoto to fertilize their oldest and best tea plants.[19]

The noted agronomist Satō Nobuhiro lists thirty-six different types fertilizer—animal, vegetable, and mineral—in his comprehensive treatise on crop fertilization, *Baiyō hiroku* (Secrets of fertility), but reserves pride of place for human excrement. Its oiliness warms and nourishes, and its volatility ensures that essential salts are quickly infused into the plant; crops treated with night soil grow strong and true.[20] In another work, *Jūjigō funbairei* (Annotated guide to manuring), Nobuhiro presents a series of sometimes rather elaborate fertilizer recipes, cooked up to suit diverse crops, climates, and soil conditions; despite the variety, the great majority feature night soil as a principal ingredient.[21]

Nobuhiro's contemporary, Ōkura Nagatsune, the "technologist" celebrated by Thomas C. Smith, starts his discussion of night soil with the comment that excrement is so well known among farmers as an efficacious fertilizer that there is no need for a detailed discussion. True to his word, he does little more than caution his readers against applying insufficiently cured, lumpy night soil to plant roots for fear of causing the plant and its neighbors to die of a nutrient overdose.[22]

Rather than preach to the choir on the virtues of shit, Nagatsune dwells on urine, which is much appreciated as a fertilizer in the Kansai region but disdained by peasants in the environs of Edo, who think it poorly suited to the local soil. Nagatsune concedes that raw urine can kill plants but insists that, with proper curing, it works extremely quickly and effectively, particularly on stems and leaves, making it ideal for leafy vegetables, eggplant, green onion, and watermelon (just the sort of crops, in fact, that truck gardeners in the outskirts of Edo produced). The urine of people who engage in hard physical labor is concentrated and particularly potent, so—in contrast to excrement—the poor are a better source of pee than the rich.[23]

If Tokugawa agronomists were connoisseurs, ever ready to debate the goût de terroir of regional shits, their counterparts writing during the golden age of stercorary science in Japan—roughly the 1890s through the 1910s—were simple utilitarians who pooh-poohed the notion that differences in fecal quality were significant enough for the average farmer to worry about.[24] Their concern instead was that farmers were not sufficiently aware of the value of night soil or that even if they were, their methods of processing the stuff did not maximize the potential return on Japan's GNP—Gross National Poop—a figure estimated in 1914 to be something like 106 million *koku*, or a bit more than 5 billion gallons of raw shit, assuming an average annual output of about 2 *koku* (95 gallons) for each of Japan's 53 million men, women, and children.[25]

Koshikawa Zenshichi, writing in 1901, runs his readers through a series of quick calculations of the value of their own output of poop. A rural household of five produces about 10 *koku* of excrement per year, to which is added 3 *koku* of water to make 13 *koku* (618 gallons) of fertilizer base. This is equivalent to 43.3 loads (*ni*) of night soil, worth 3.90 yen at 0.09 yen per load retail. In addition, let us assume that each household member produces around 1 *shō* 1 *gō* (just over half a gallon) of urine each day, or about 4 *koku* per year. The 20 *koku* (950 gallons) of urine produced by the entire household is worth 3.333 yen, assuming a retail price of 0.05 yen per load. Hence, one household produces about 7.233 yen worth of excrement and urine per annum. Since it would cost 25.037 yen to buy the chemical nutrients found in the family excreta, the household actually saves 17.844 yen per year—a significant sum in 1901—by using its own night soil. But wait, there's more! If that same family employed Koshikawa's new and improved system for curing night soil, they could extract even greater value—33.097 yen worth of nutrients—from their 7.233 yen of poop. That's an annual savings of 25.864 yen![26] And, of course, the more you poop, the more you save.

If Koshikawa had been writing during the Tokugawa period, he might have been satisfied to begin and end his sales pitch with an appeal to the individual profit-maximizing instincts of Japan's many rational peasants. But since he was writing in the Meiji era, it figures that his story is ultimately a national one: the nation as a whole actually produces enough shit to nourish its agricultural lands, but waste and inefficiency lead to the loss of two-thirds of the nitrogen and other nutrients housed in that shit. Instead of self-sufficiency, the nation has to expend valuable resources on chemical and other commercial fertilizers. Other writers confirmed Koshikawa's basic point: in 1913, night soil accounted for only 22 percent of the fertilizer market by value, but the figure is low only because night soil was so cheap. Replacing the nutrients with other sources would cost the nation dearly.[27]

Koshikawa wasn't the only one thinking about the possibilities of shit. "The progress of culture [is] a question of sewage," wrote the German chemist Justus von Liebig in the mid-nineteenth century, expressing a sentiment that his colleagues in Meiji Japan would have found eminently sensible. Liebig was concerned that the land would be irredeemably depleted unless nutrients were returned to it in the form of human and animal excreta. Indeed, he attributed "the singular continuity of Chinese culture across millennia" to the "exemplary perfection" of the Chinese in recycling their excreta.[28] Other Western observers, including James Madison, concurred.[29] By the end of the century, Liebig's ideas had inspired others to extol the fertilizing properties of poop. In 1896, a group of German technocrats published a massive study titled "The Use of Urban Waste Material," and planners in Berlin and a number of cities in the western United States implemented ambitious if ultimately short-lived schemes to commodify shit, projects that foundered once flush toilets and chemical fertilizers became widely available.[30]

Shit as a Commodity

By the latter part of the Tokugawa period, urban centers such as Edo and Osaka were major sources of night soil for peasants in the surrounding countryside. The night soil trade is the one aspect of the history of shit in early modern Japan that has been covered reasonably extensively. Scholars have focused particularly on the implications of night soil use for urban hygiene and on the complexities of the market for night soil in the countryside. Among those writing in English, Louis Perez examines the night soil trade panoramically, with a focus on the eighteenth century.[31] Susan B. Hanley, who is concerned with the quality of life in early modern Japan, argues that the commodification of shit helped make Edo, Osaka, and other Japanese cities far more sanitary and livable than large urban centers in Western Europe.[32] In the hinterland of Edo, the development of the agricultural economy in the eighteenth century fostered the development of a lively market for night soil and with it the emergence of a complex array of overlapping and sometimes conflicting rights. Anne Walthall, looking at the poop wars from the countryside, has examined the strains on regional solidarity among villages.[33]

Aratake Ken'ichirō describes how the night soil trade worked in one village near Osaka around the beginning of the nineteenth century. Well-to-do residents of Hashiramoto, a community on the western bank of the Yodo River, contracted with forty-five landlords in three urban wards to pay 25 *monme* in silver annually for rights to the contents of the landlords' latrines. Twice a month, three groups of four villagers each went into the city the collect the merchandise. Aratake speculates that rather than do the dirty work themselves, the villagers likely hired proxies from the ranks of their less fortunate neighbors. In any case, the work was so onerous that the teams invariably spent at least one night—and sometimes as many as three—in Osaka each time they went on their poop-scooping rounds. After the raw night soil was delivered to the village by boat, the contracting villagers took what they needed themselves and sold the leftovers to their neighbors.[34] Iwabuchi Reiji describes a similar arrangement in Edo on the eve of the Restoration. About half the residents of Tokumaru village participated in a night soil syndicate, in which they exchanged cash, eggplants, fresh and dried daikon radishes, and pickles for the excrement of 146 households in three Edo neighborhoods.[35]

Tokumaru was in the western suburbs of Edo, where the lack of convenient water transportation routes retarded the development of a large-scale retail market for poop. East of Edo, however, night soil was a big business, and it remained so until the early decades of the twentieth century. The ready availability of night soil for fertilizer encouraged the development of truck gardening, with the result that the eastern suburbs supplied most of the city's fresh vegetables, fruit, and flowers until industrialization and urban sprawl swept over the area in the period after World War I.

Although many villages east of Edo contracted directly with urban landlords for the contents of their toilets, a lot of night soil was moved by brokers who hired workers to empty privies and carry the contents to wharves on the rivers in the east of Edo, where it was loaded onto boats and carried upstream as far as forty kilometers from the city. Brokers sometimes owned their own night soil boats, but often they simply hired boats worked by owner-operators who lived aboard their vessels with their families. The night soil boats and their operators were famous for their gaudy appearance and for the pride they took in running boats clean enough to haul vegetables back to the city after they had been emptied of their yucky cargoes upstream. They were also occasionally accused of dirty tricks like adding river water—and toilet paper—to the night-soil buckets as they went upstream, proffering increasingly watery shit to beleaguered farmers in the capital's exurbs. Although all sorts of cargo moved in and out of Edo/Tokyo on the intricate network of rivers and canals that once characterized the city, night soil was surely the most voluminous of all: according to figures compiled by the government of Tokyo in 1872, almost a quarter (1,564 of 6,545) of the vessels in the prefecture were night soil boats.[36]

Competition for night soil led to all sorts of conflict. Landlords might sell their tenants' shit to individual peasants, villages, or night soil brokers; in some cases, the income from the toilets might exceed the rent collected on a tenement's apartments. As demand for night soil grew in the late eighteenth century, consumers eager to get their hands on raw shit participated in bidding wars that drove up the price of night soil significantly. Peasants priced out of the poop market occasionally banded together in an effort to persuade the shogunal authorities to intervene and either force down the price of night soil by fiat or drive brokers—whom peasants blamed for ratcheting up prices—out of the market altogether. Major conflicts occurred at least four times between 1789 and 1867; the first instance embroiled more than a thousand villages in Musashi and Shimōsa provinces.[37]

Urine was another matter altogether. Farmers in the hinterland of Edo had little interest in using urine as a fertilizer, notwithstanding the efforts of Ōkura Nagatsune and other boosters to persuade them otherwise. A few enterprising entrepreneurs did set out urinals in the city, but almost all of early modern Edo's pee ended up at the site of relief, be it the side of the road or the side of a building. In western Japan, however, urine was highly valued as a fertilizer. In urban tenements, residents ceded rights to their feces to the landlord or building manager, but their urine was theirs to sell to the highest bidder. In Osaka that was likely to be a urine jobber (*shōben nakagainin*) or a member of the urine guild (*shō-ben nakama*), a group that claimed members in around four hundred villages by the time of the Meiji Restoration. (Incidentally, some villages in the hinterland of Osaka bought night soil but not urine, others urine but not night soil, and still others bought excreta of all sorts.)[38]

Passersby in Osaka could empty their bladders at one of the many public urinals (*tago*) placed around the city. The men and women who found relief there (women stood to pee everywhere except in polite Edo society, we're told) probably did so without much regard for the conflicts over rights to the contents of public urinals that raged almost incessantly in the city from the early eighteenth century until shortly after the Meiji Restoration.[39]

The problems started in 1740, when the city authorities gave the elders of Watanabe village, the most important outcaste community in western Japan, the right to set out public urinals. The gesture was a mark of gratitude to the outcastes for their efforts in fighting a major fire; moreover, the income stream from the urinals would help compensate the Watanabe village elders for ensuring that their community fulfilled its particular feudal duties. Unfortunately, in the zero-sum world of Osaka urine, the granting of rights to the outcastes meant that townsmen who had apparently previously enjoyed rights to manage public urinals were hurt. The aggrieved commoners tried everything to break the outcastes' monopoly: they put out their own illegal urinals; they damaged and destroyed the outcastes' pissoirs; they even sabotaged the basins' precious cargo by pouring sand into the containers. If such problems were not enough, the outcaste urinal managers had to deal with incidents like the case of Chūbei, a peasant caught pilfering pee from an outcaste-owned urinal in 1743. The authorities invariably supported the outcastes when disputes came to court, yet they seemed unable to put a decisive end to the conflict.[40]

As Kobayashi Shigeru argues, it was only because urine was such a valuable commodity that people cared enough to sabotage urinals or steal pee outright. And indeed it was valuable: as early as 1776, the outcastes estimated their urinal income to be enough to buy three hundred *koku* of rice—roughly enough to feed three hundred people for a year. In the decades that followed, the demand for urine increased, and so did complaints about unscrupulous dealers who adulterated the urine they sold and householders who turned their noses up at the daikon radishes they had once happily received in exchange for their pee and instead demanded cotton yarn, high-grade rice, and other luxuries.[41]

In all the tussles over night soil and urine, the winner was the guy who got his hands on the excreta. Although "purity" and "pollution" are key words in discussions of traditional Japanese culture, they don't come up in the writings of those who pondered poop as a resource or commodity. Sure, people saw excrement as yucky and disgusting, but collecting, transporting, and handling the stuff was not defiling. Nor did working in the poop industry jeopardize one's standing as a commoner. Unlike the carcasses of livestock—whose handlers were inevitably marked as outcastes—night soil was dirty but not polluting. Shit isn't blood.

The institutions governing urban shit began slowly to change after the Meiji Restoration of 1868. In 1874, the Osaka prefectural government disbanded the night soil league (*shimogoe kumiai*) that had represented 309 local villages and regulated the collection of night soil directly, instituting a series of anal rules concerning the storage and transport of raw shit: keep it covered, don't leave it out on the streets when collecting, move it only at night, don't move it at all when there's a lot of traffic on the roads and rivers, and so on.[42]

Aratake notes that throughout the regulations, there is a consistent and wholly novel concern with smell: poop has always been stinky, but its stinkiness was the object of official concern only in the 1870s. He argues that this was probably due to the fear of cholera, which reached Japan in 1858 and whose spread was linked by officials and the public to malodorous smells. A major cholera epidemic in 1877 upset the balance between the production of night soil in the city and its consumption in the countryside. During times of anxiety about cholera, peasants refused to come into the city to empty privies.[43]

The real turning point in the history of shit came after World War I. As Tokyo grew and its populace simply produced far more shit than the local agricultural economy could absorb, a teeming latrine became a liability, and urbanites were forced to pay others to relieve them of their shit. In Hongō ward in the eastern section of Tokyo, the tipping point came in 1918, when in response to residents' complaints of a "deluge of excrement," the authorities were finally forced to hire night soil men to haul away excess shit in some neighborhoods; emboldened carriers reneged on their contracts and refused to empty toilets until they received a fee. The toilets emptied for a fee still provided night soil to local farmers: in 1935, the ward supplied over 61,000 loads of night soil to agricultural associations in Chiba, Saitama, and Tokyo prefectures.[44] In Yokohama the crisis occurred a bit later, in 1921, but the storyline is very similar: peasants, realizing that the supply of shit in the booming metropolis far outpaced demand, abruptly stopped paying for night soil and demanded a fee instead. The city, faced with the problem of disposing of 5,150 loads of night soil every day, had no choice but to capitulate to the farmers' demands.[45]

Shinoda Kōzō, in his nostalgic look back at Meiji Tokyo, contrasts his childhood memories of the family poop man, an uncultured but kind-hearted rustic from a village near the Tama River, with the privy cleaners of the present day—that is, the early 1930s—men who just don't give a shit: it's all waste to them, so they're surly, they don't mind spilling, and if anyone complains they'll carry the grudge (with stinky consequences, no doubt). Back in the day, when a farmer would come with his oxcart to receive oh so gratefully the precious contents of the loo, you could "shit to your heart's content (*kuso shihōdai*)," but now. . . .[46]

Coda: Who Gives a Crap about the Environment?

Poop is yucky, especially when it's underfoot or in the water supply. Yuckiness abounded in the cities of early modern Europe; in Japanese cities, not so much. Much credit goes to the night soil man for making a city like Edo a relatively healthful place to live, but as Susan Hanley notes, good water helped as well. Abundant rain and freshets of melted mountain snow flushed pollutants from the rivers that supplied the city with its water; cleverly designed aqueducts helped keep the clean river water clean for many of the city's residents.[47]

Edo was a green city; London was brown. Wonderful—but were the city fathers thinking green when they laid out Edo's infrastructure? Reading Ishikawa Eisuke's bizarrely chauvinistic celebrations of premodern Japan, one would think so: indeed, in his presentation, the French might have avoided the Black Death and their revolution had they only thought to value shit as the Japanese did.[48] Less ostentatiously celebratory is Itō Yoshiichi, who has detailed Edo's surprisingly sophisticated system for disposing of the garbage produced by prosperous commoners: contractors hauled it away for use in landfill or occasionally to sell to rural farmers for use as yet another form of organic fertilizer. (Commoners in poor neighborhoods and samurai in general had to deal with their own garbage, which they did, often in unsanitary ways.)[49]

Iwabuchi Reiji sounds a note of caution.[50] Cities like Edo may have been relatively sanitary, but one shouldn't equate green results with green intentions. And in any case, clean compared to eighteenth-century London isn't necessarily very clean at all. The Japanese recycled garbage and marketed shit not because they wanted to preserve the environment per se, but because it made practical sense to do so. When given the opportunity to be bad custodians of their surroundings, they often took it.[51]

An incident from 1784 illustrates this point. Villagers from the hinterland of Edo, apparently heeding Ōkura Nagatsune's advice to embrace the fertilizing powers of urine, petitioned to place urinals in the streets of Edo. Commoner officials, pondering the question at the behest of the city magistrates, opposed the scheme. They complained that urine buckets in narrow city streets would hinder commerce and obstruct traffic during the day and pose the risk of injury to passersby stumbling across them at night. They fretted over the possibility of insulting the sensibilities of the city's most exalted residents—it would hardly to do for the shogun to glimpse a pissoir while passing through the commoner wards on procession (*onari*), and since many shops in the city were official provisioners to daimyo mansions, stinky pee smells mustn't mar their wares. Hiding urinals in back alleys was hardly better: alleys were even narrower than main streets, and the people back there already had toilets in their tenements. And in any case, what's the big deal about peeing into drainage ditches or directly onto the ground?

In a conciliatory gesture, however, the officials said that they wouldn't mind if the urinals were set out in poorer neighborhoods—Fukagawa and Honjo might be good choices—so long as the petitioners avoided areas where there already were more than 160 public urinals put out by enterprising night soil men. Incidentally, 160 public urinals may sound like a lot—or not: Edo had more than a million people, after all—but even with all those urinals around, more than half of Edo's urban wards (*chō*) remained without public facilities until the end of the Tokugawa period, despite a series of petitions similar to the one in 1784.[52]

As Nesaki Mitsuo argues, the episode strikes the modern reader as odd. Potties are a convenience, yet the officials seem to have considered them a nuisance best relegated to marginal districts: Edoites could drain their bladders at home, use an acquaintance's facilities, or take a leak into a ditch in an emergency. To be sure, they had some sense that urine would make good fertilizer, but it does not seem to have occurred to them that the urinals would contribute to making Edo a cleaner, more livable city—notwithstanding that all parties openly acknowledged the foul smell of urine and all excreta.[53]

All this talk about the environmental consequences of people's toilet habits would surely have mystified people in early modern Japan. They didn't share our concept of or concern with the environment, so it figures that they didn't care whether their shit was green or brown so long as it remained an object of utility: stinky and yucky but useful all the same. That, much more than conservation or sanitation, is the story of shit in Japan.

Notes

1. Maike Heining, Andrew W. Young, Glavkos Ioannou, Chris M. Andrew, Michael J. Brammer, Jeffrey A. Gray, and Mary L. Phillips, "Disgusting Smells Activate Human Anterior Insula and Ventral Striatum," *Annals of the New York Academy of Sciences* 1000 (2003): 380–384.

2. Lars Å. Hanson, Marina Korotkova, Samuel Lundin, Liljana Håversen, Sven-Arne Silfverdal, Inger Mattsby-Baltzer, Birgitta Strandvik, Esbjörn Telemo, "The Transfer of Immunity from Mother to Child," *Annals of the New York Academy of Sciences* 987 (2003): 199–206.

3. Miyazaki Yasusada, *Nōgyō zensho* (1697) (*Nihon nōsho zenshū*, vols. 12–13), ed. and annot. Yamada Tatsuo et al. (Tokyo: Nōsangyoson Bunka Kyōkai, 1978), vol. 12, 101.

4. Ibid., 91–105; the section on fertilizer is simply entitled "*Koe.*"

5. Ibid., 93.

6. Ibid., 98.

7. Ibid., 101–102.

8. Fūrai Sanjin [Hiraga Gennai], "Hōhiron" (On farting), trans. William Sibley, in *Readings in Tokugawa Thought* (Chicago: University of Chicago Center for East Asian Studies, 1993), 149–156.

9. Furuichi Matsuo, "Jinpunnyō no hanashi," in *Guntai nōji kōenshū*, 2 vols. (Tokyo: DaiNihon Nōkai, 1915), vol. 2, 244, 245, 246.

10. "Kuso to kome to wa izure ga tōtoki ka," *Nihon nōgyō zasshi* (1909), reprinted in Tsubame Sakuta, *Shimogoe* (Tokyo: Yūrindō, 1914), 191–199.

11. See the etymological discussion in Morohashi Tetsuji, ed., *Dai Kan-Wa jiten,* 13 vols. (Tokyo: Taishūkan Shoten, 1955–1960), s.v. 糞,屎.

12. Anon., *Hyakushō denki,* 2 vols., ed. and annot. Furushima Toshio (Tokyo: Iwanami Shoten, 1977), vol. 1, 156–185. The text was produced in Tōtomi or Mikawa (modern-day Aichi Prefecture), most likely around 1681 to 1683. See Fukaya Katsumi, "Kinseiteki hyakushō jinkaku: *Hyakushō denki* ni arawareta," *Waseda daigaku daigakuin bungaku kenkyūka kiyō* 26 (1980): 157–166.

13. *Hyakushō denki,* vol. 1. 157–158.

14. Ibid., 170–171.

15. Ibid., 168.

16. Anne Walthall, "Village Networks: *Sōdai* and the Sale of Edo Nightsoil," *Monumenta Nipponica* 43:3 (autumn: 1988): 295; Hori Mitsuhiro, "Tōkyō kinkō nōson ni okeru shimogoe riyō no shosō," in *Nihon minzoku fiirudo kara no shōsha,* ed. Inokuchi Shōji (Tokyo: Yūzankaku, 1993), 120.

17. Hori, "Tōkyō kinkō nōson," 119.

18. Koshikawa Zenshichi, *Shinshiki jinpunnyō toriatsukai benpō: Ichimei nōji kairyō daigen* (Tokyo: Yūrindō, 1901), 50–55. Koshikawa cautions, however, that in addition to diet, many other factors affect the quality of a person's excrement, particularly age and general health. Tsubame, *Shimogoe,* 25, notes that although the feces of people with high-protein diets is indeed rich in nitrogen, people with low-protein diets produce feces with other types of nutrients.

19. Ōkura Nagatsune, *Nōka hibairon* (1830s), 25–137 in *Nihon nōsho zenshū,* vol. 69, *Gakusha no nōsho 1,* ed. Tokunaga Mitsutoshi (Tokyo: Nōsangyoson Bunka Kyōkai, 1996), 50–51.

20. Satō Nobuhiro, *Baiyō hiroku* (1840), 153–391 in Tokunaga, *Nihon nōsho zenshū,* vol. 69, 241–242.

21. Satō Gen'an and Satō Nobuhiro, *Jūjigō funbairei,* ed. Oda Kanshi (n.p.: Oda Kanshi, 1872). Gen'an was Nobuhiro's great-grandfather. In his agronomic works, Nobuhiro always presented himself as merely passing down the techniques and knowledge of his ancestor. See Morita Hideki, "Edo no shinyō sehi jijō," *Toshi to haikibutsu* 36:2 (2006): 51–54.

22. Ōkura, *Nōka hibairon,* 49–51. See Thomas C. Smith, "Ōkura Nagatsune and the Technologists" (1970), reprinted in Smith's *Native Sources of Japanese Industrialization, 1750–1920* (Berkeley: University of California Press, 1988), 173–198.

23. Ōkura, *Nōka hibairon,* 37–39.

24. Hara Hiroshi, *Hiryōhen* (Tokyo: Hakubunkan, 1892), 71.

25. Tsubame, *Shimogoe,* 24. The population figure excludes Korea.

26. Koshikawa, *Shinshiki jinpunnyō toriatsukai benpō,* 36–39.

27. Ibid., 36–38. See Tsubame, *Shimogoe,* 6, for the value of night soil as a percentage of the entire fertilizer market; Furuichi, "Jinpunnyō no hanashi," 245, for a lamentation of the high cost of replacing night soil's nutrients with chemicals from other sources.

28. Joachim Radkau, *Nature and Power: A Global History of the Environment,* trans. Thomas Dunlap (Washington, DC: German Historical Institute; New York: Cambridge University Press, 2008), 12–13.

29. Steven Stoll, *Larding the Lean Earth* (New York: Hill and Wang, 2002), 39.

30. Radkau, *Nature and Power,* 145, 208.

31. Louis G. Perez, *Daily Life in Early Modern Japan* (Westport, CT: Greenwood Press, 2002), 217–226.

32. Susan B. Hanley, "Urban Sanitation in Preindustrial Japan," *Journal of Interdisciplinary History* 18:1 (summer 1987): 1–26.

33. Walthall, "Village Networks," 293–302.

34. Aratake Ken'ichirō, "Kinsei kōki ni okeru shimogoe no ryūtsū to kakaku keisei," *Ronshū kinsei* 24 (2002): 1–21, especially 3–8.

35. Iwabuchi Reiji, "Kinsei toshi no toire to shinyō mondai no genkai," *Rekishi to chiri* 484 (December 1995): 52–53.

36. Ibid., 53–55. On the night soil boats and their operators' tricks, see Hori, "Tōkyō kinkō nōson," 118, 120. On the night soil wharves in Edo, see Iwabuchi Reiji, "Edo no shimogoe no kashi ni tsuite," *Chihōshi kenkyū* 262 (August 1996): 4–9.

37. Walthall, "Village Networks," discusses the 1789 protest in detail. On conflicts in the nineteenth century, see Kobayashi Shinado, "Kinsei kōki Edo shūhen chiiki ni okeru shimogoe ryūtsū no hen'yō: Tenpō, Kōka-ki no shimosōjidai hikisage negai to gijō o chūshin ni," *Senshū shigaku* 38 (2005): 42–105, and Kobayashi Shinado, "Keiōki no shimogoe nesagerei to shimogoe ryūtsū," *Senshū shigaku* 43 (2007): 125–152.

38. On the distribution of rights to urine, see Iwabuchi, "Kinsei toshi no toire," 50. On the urine guild in Osaka, see Kobayashi Shigeru, *Nihon shinyō mondai genryūkō* (Tokyo: Akashi Shoten, 1988), 68–69.

39. On women routinely standing to urinate, see Iwabuchi, "Kinsei toshi no toire," 50, and "Shōbenkō," *Kokkei shinbun,* no. 159, reprinted in Tsubame, *Shimogoe,* 204–206.

40. Kobayashi, *Nihon shinyō mondai genryūkō,* 70–73. Hanley, "Urban Sanitation in Preindustrial Japan," 10, briefly discusses disputes over Osaka urinals.

41. Kobayashi, *Nihon shinyō mondai genryūkō,* 73–78.

42. Aratake Ken'ichirō, "Meiji zenki Ōsaka ni okeru shinyō mondai," *Ōsaka Shiritsu Kōbunshokan kenkyū kiyō* 15 (2003): 3–19. See also Yoshimura Tomohiro, "Toshi buraku ni okeru shinyō shori mondai no tenkai: Shiiki hennyūki no Ōsaka Minami-ku Nishihama-chō no gutaizō," *Sekai jinken mondai* 6 (2001): 157–173. Similar rules were instituted in Tokyo in 1872: Nesaki Mitsuo, "Edo no shimogoe ryūtsū to shinyōkan," *Ningen kankyō ronshū* 9:1 (2008): 19.

43. Aratake, "Meiji zenki Ōsaka."

44. Hongō Kuyakusho, ed., *Hongō ku shi* (Tokyo: Hongō Kuyakusho, 1937), 899–901. Many thanks to Jordan Sand for guiding me to this source.

45. Kira Yoshie, "Shinyō shori o meguru toshi to nōson: 1921-nen no Yokohama shigaichi to kinkō chiiki," in *Yokohama kinkō no kindaishi: Tachibana-gun ni miru toshika, kōgyōka,* ed. Yokohama Kindaishi Kenkyūkai (Yokohama: Yokohama Kaikō Shiryōkan, 2002), 103–132.

46. Shinoda Kōzō, *Meiji hyakuwa,* 2 vols. (Tokyo: Iwanami Shoten, 1996), 163–166.

47. Susan B. Hanley, *Everyday Things in Premodern Japan: The Hidden Legacy of Material Culture* (Berkeley: University of California Press, 1997), 111.

48. Ishikawa Eisuke, *Ōedo risaikuru jijō* (Tokyo: Kōdansha, 1997), 158.

49. Itō Yoshiichi, *Edo no yumenoshima* (Tokyo: Yoshikawa Kōbunkan, 1982).

50. See Iwabuchi Reiji, "Edo no gomi shori saikō: 'Risaikuru toshi,' 'seiketsu toshi' zō o koete," *Kokuritsu Rekishi Minzoku Hakubutsukan kenkyū kiyō* 118 (February 2004): 301–336. Iwabuchi Reiji, "Kinsei no toshi mondai," *Rekishi to chiri* 560 (December 2002): 1–16, deals mostly with garbage disposal in the service of the same argument.

51. With regard to garbage, Japan was not so different from the West in the age before mass production. Susan Strasser, *Waste and Want: A Social History of Trash* (New York: Henry Holt & Co., 2000).

52. Nesaki, "Edo no shimogoe ryūtsū to shinyōkan," 16–19; Iwabuchi, "Kinsei toshi no toire," 50–51.

53. Nesaki, "Edo no shimogoe ryūtsū to shinyōkan," 19.

8

Weathering Fuji
Marriage, Meteorology, and the Meiji Bodyscape

ANDREW BERNSTEIN

My body may not be a rugged man's,
but my striving spirit
is second to none.

—NONAKA CHIYOKO (1871–1923)[1]

A half shell split from the world,
I wonder, after a hundred years,
will someone pick me up?

—NONAKA ITARU (1867–1955)[2]

Exploring the Bodyscape

On the first of October in the twenty-eighth year of the Meiji emperor's reign
(1895), Nonaka Itaru began recording meteorological phenomena on Mount Fuji's
summit with the ambitious goal of taking measurements every two hours, day and
night, for an entire year. In an age when the Japanese press eagerly celebrated tales
of scientific discovery in dangerous, exotic places,[3] Itaru's project offered something unique: a bracingly raw view of the most familiar of mountains. Fuji, after
all, was anything but distant. Easily seen from the streets of the capital and climbed
each summer by thousands, it was a national icon. Yet no one had ever endured
the long, harsh winter of Japan's highest summit. Beginning in early autumn, heavy
snows covered any trace of human presence on the upper reaches of the volcano
and effectively transformed this well-trafficked peak into a terra incognita.[4] Itaru's
scientific exploit made headlines precisely because it occurred within a terrain

located not in a far-off land but at Japan's geographical and cultural heart, offering Japanese the distinct pleasure of regarding the old anew.[5]

When Itaru's wife Chiyoko decided to join her husband without his knowledge and against her in-laws' wishes, an already remarkable story became a family drama. Entrusting her baby daughter to her parents, Chiyoko made the trek up Fuji, arriving on the summit twelve days into her husband's grueling routine. Itaru ordered her back down the mountain, according to Chiyoko's serialized diary ("Fuyō nikki"), but she stood her ground, determined to serve both husband and nation with her "useless" woman's body.[6] In the end, living in a tiny stone shelter on a bitterly cold mountaintop with thin air, inadequate supplies, and little to no exercise severely weakened *both* of their bodies. Thus their published accounts focus as much on coping with physical suffering as on producing meteorological data.

Enduring and recording their suffering was integral, not merely incidental, to their advancement of science in two ways. First, vividly relating their sacrifices increased the value and circulation of their hard-won findings. After all, why undergo extraordinary hardships unless the goals were extraordinarily worthwhile? Comparable to the austerities of religious ascetics, the Nonakas' hardships constituted an acceptable price to pay in search of a higher truth, one made all the higher, in their own and others' accounts, by those very hardships. Second, in an age when high-altitude medicine—along with high-altitude meteorology—was in its infancy, recording varieties of bodily distress amounted to the revelation of scientific truth in its own right. By chronicling not just the weather but also the conditions and manifestations of their suffering, they contributed data to those seeking to understand and ultimately minimize the impact of high-altitude living on human bodies.

Making sense of the Nonakas' multidimensional experience as both observers and victims of Fuji's weather, as well as promoters and objects of their story in the Japanese media, entails exploring a bodyscape particular to Fuji yet incorporated into the far more extensive bodyscape of Meiji Japan. By "bodyscape" I mean an assemblage of human and nonhuman bodies—constituted both physically and discursively—that is coherent yet always changing. Writers working in various genres often use "landscape" in a way that acknowledges the complex traffic between bodies and their surroundings, but no matter how broadly and dynamically construed, the word retains a linguistic bias toward the total and solid in contrast to the varied and fluid. Freed of this semantic burden, "bodyscape" declares unequivocally that the perceived whole is a function of its parts: bodies that grow and decay, encompass and divide, cooperate and clash.

Integral to the bodyscape of the Nonakas' story were, most obviously, the bodies of Chiyoko and Itaru. But so were those of many other actors, ranging from humble porters to the Meiji emperor. Moreover, if we use the word "body" to indicate a discrete, physical entity that can just as well be inorganic as organic—the sun as "celestial body," for example—then Fuji can be considered a historical agent with a (sometimes violent) body of its own. In fact, from ancient times to today, Fuji worshippers have referred to the volcano as a *goshintai*, literally "god body," and the lava caves at its base as *tainai*, or "wombs." As we will see, the Nonakas, too, personified Fuji—in a paradoxically "dehumanizing" manner—as they struggled to transform the wintry summit into an object of scientific investigation.

By comprehending Fuji as a fellow body in the bodyscape, I aim to bridge the gap that too often separates histories of the body from those of the environment, a gap indicative of a deeper and widely accepted conceptual dichotomy separating humans from nonhumans, biological and otherwise. In *Inescapable Ecologies*, a study of the changing relations between environment and disease in California's Central Valley, author Linda Nash challenges this "modern dichotomy that separates human beings from the rest of nature" by attending carefully to the human body as an element *of*, not merely set amid and against, the environment.[7] Whereas environmental historians have "typically reinforced the modern dichotomy by placing humans and their creations on one side and everything else—nonhuman nature—on the other," Nash approaches her subject in such a way that "the boundary between the human and the nonhuman world, the actors and their objects, becomes much more fuzzy and the distinction much more tenuous."[8] Likewise, my choice to join body and landscape in the unified field of the bodyscape calls attention to the often-overlooked physical and discursive processes through which humans and the environment mutually construct (and destroy) each other.[9]

To fully appreciate these processes as they played out in the story of Chiyoko, Itaru, and Fuji requires situating them in the nationalized bodyscape of Meiji Japan—and there, the human body that mattered most was the Meiji emperor's. This is not because individual Japanese necessarily valued his life over their own (though, tragically, it appears some did) and not because the emperor was especially adept at initiating change (far more change was made *through* than *by* him), but because, starting from his ascension to the throne in 1868, the mere fact of his body determined time itself. Until the emperor's death in 1912, his subjects accepted as perfectly natural that they should count the passing years in reference to his reign (just as westerners presumed that time should be indexed to the birth of Christ). Whether in speech or in writing and no matter what the subject, to state the year meant to invoke the emperor. As a result, the word "Meiji" appears again and again in the writings of the Nonakas and their contemporaries. When compounded across time and space, these shared habits of notation were like water carving a canyon. By sheer repetition in the most diverse circumstances, the practice of defining time in terms of the sovereign's reign made the Meiji emperor an especially potent and pervasive body of authority, even if the emperor rarely exercised this authority on his own initiative.

Like many other Japanese, the Nonakas chose to nourish the body of imperial authority in ways more self-conscious than the mundane recording of time. A dramatic case in point appears in Chiyoko's "Fuyō nikki," which states that she and Itaru, despite suffering from altitude sickness and bitter cold—analogous to a "short sword plunging in and out"[10]—decided to honor the emperor's birthday by crawling out their observatory window (the door was frozen shut) and prostrating themselves in the ice and snow in the direction of the imperial palace in Tokyo.[11]

The Nonakas' act of submission did not simply reflect the emperor's authority, and Chiyoko and Itaru were not mere conduits[12] for the imperial cult. After all, imperial power was not a Platonic form waiting to be realized in this and other instances of devotion. Rather, it was *generated* by such instances, each one unique in obvious or not-so-obvious ways. Maybe the Nonakas' singular performance was concocted after the fact to enhance their image. Yet given their circumstances, one can imagine why Chiyoko and Itaru would actually have gone through with it. For exerting their bodies to participate in an observance shared by millions would have confirmed, if only for a short while, that they were not the sum of their suffering. It would have allowed them to engage a wider world of meanings that their pain had been "unmaking" over the prior weeks.[13]

It is also important to acknowledge that Chiyoko and Itaru chose to winter on Fuji not because they were inherently slavish but precisely because they were so strong willed. In important respects, they were downright rebellious. Itaru defied his father's wishes by quitting medical school at the age of twenty-two to enter the nascent field of high-altitude meteorology. Chiyoko not only disobeyed her in-laws and deceived her husband by climbing Fuji on her own but also (as we will see) butted heads with Itaru's mentor at the Central Meteorological Station (Chūō Kishōdai) in Tokyo. By willfully mediating different bodies of authority, not just serving them, the Nonakas helped to shape the Meiji bodyscape even as they negotiated it.

Nature, Nation, and the Middle Stratum

No trace of rebellion appears in the group portrait of Fuji, Itaru, and Chiyoko published in the January 5, 1896, issue of *Taiyō*, a general interest magazine aimed at highly educated readers (fig. 8.1). Here the Nonakas dominate Fuji in conventional respectability and individual glory, befitting their social status as former samurai members of Japan's elite. The family lineages of Chiyoko and Itaru—who were cousins as well as spouses—had served the Maeda lords in Kyushu for generations, and Itaru's father Katsuyoshi worked as a judge in Tokyo.[14] Many of *Taiyō*'s readers were of samurai origin as well, but like the metropolitan Nonakas they increasingly prided themselves on composing a hardworking, *future*-oriented

FIGURE 8.1 Fuji and the Nonakas. *Taiyō* 1:2 (January 1896), front matter.

"middle stratum" (*chūtō*) of Japanese just as eager to "distinguish themselves from the aristocratic ideals of hereditary privilege and inherited wealth" as from "the unenlightened life of an archaic past."[15]

Although Chiyoko and Itaru engaged in the most modern of ventures, the positioning of their circular portraits over Fuji repeats a pattern that had persisted for centuries. The image in figure 8.2, painted by Kano Motonobu in the 1500s, is a famous example of the many Fuji mandalas ("sacred maps") produced in Japan from the sixteenth century on.[16] To the mountain's left is the moon and to its right the sun, the former embodying yin/female energy and the latter yang/male energy. The Nonaka portraits obviously echo these celestial counterparts, with Chiyoko occupying the yin/female position of the moon and Itaru the yang/male position of the sun.[17]

The evocation of yin-yang iconography links the pursuit of the sacred to the practice of science. At the same time, it establishes an implicit yet dramatic contrast between the *naturalized* Fuji of the Nonakas and the *institutionalized* Fuji of shrines and pilgrims. The mandala showcases the built environment of the lower slopes, and a string of pilgrims continues the human presence up to the stylized,

FIGURE 8.2 *Fuji Mandala Zu,* by Kano Motonobu. OWNED BY FUJISAN HONGŪ SENGEN TAISHA.

Buddha-inhabited peak.[18] It is a bodyscape composed not of "natural" features but "power" features—human and divine—articulated through the institutions clustered at Fuji's base. The *Taiyō* Fuji is a different mountain altogether. Devoid of human structures, it provides no clue that pilgrims had long taken advantage of facilities clustered into "stations" (*gōme*) along the climbing routes and on the summit.

The *Taiyō* image banishes humans from the mountain proper, but it presents a countryside shaped by them. In fact, a hut occupies the composition's lower right-hand corner. Remarkable about this building, compared to the impressive ritual structures shown in the Fuji mandala, is just how *un*remarkable it is. It anchors the corner of a landscape that clearly produces tea, a crop particular to southwestern Japan, but due to its generically rustic appearance it signifies the Japanese countryside more generally. In sum, while the mandala proclaims Fuji to be a place structured by local institutions with site-specific rituals, the magazine depicts Fuji as a wonder of nature looming above an agricultural landscape, implicitly making it the property of *all* Japanese, whether they were located in the volcano's vicinity or not.

Portraying Fuji in this manner was, to a large degree, nothing new. Tokugawa-period artists (most famously Hokusai and Hiroshige) had already popularized images of Fuji as a naturalized mountain integrated into scenes of everyday life. But the *Taiyō* composition was different not only in its allusion to—and thus its tacit contrast with—depictions of Fuji as mandala, but also because it furthered a growing trend in the 1890s to regard Fuji as a natural symbol of the modern nation. Fuji assumes a place of honor, for example, in Shiga Shigetaka's bestselling paean to the Japanese landscape, *Nihon fūkeiron,* published just a year before the Nonakas' expedition. Shiga extols Fuji not because it is unique in its own right but because it is a splendid example of the volcanic activity that makes the landscape of Japan superior to that of other nations (one of which, China, was at war with Japan when *Nihon fūkeiron* was published).[19] By presenting Fuji as a volcano par excellence in a nationalized volcanic landscape, Shiga presses it into service for a larger ideological project that Kären Wigen aptly terms "geographical enlightenment"[20]—a project integral to a still broader "discovery of landscape" that Karatani Kōjin demonstrates to have occurred in/through various fields of cultural production in 1890s Japan. This discovery was characterized by a "relentless defamiliarization of the familiar" that "does not describe landscape but always creates it," bringing "into existence landscapes which, although they had always been there, had never been seen."[21] By establishing a dramatic contrast between the urbane Nonakas and the rustic countryside, *Taiyō*'s group portrait implied not only that Fuji belonged to all Japanese but that an enlightened elite would reveal to the nation a Fuji that had never been seen.

Bodily Enlightenment

Itaru and Chiyoko explored Fuji-as-nature through the practice of meteorology, which had evolved since the late eighteenth century (first in Europe and increasingly elsewhere) from an amateur endeavor into a systematic science, and as a result "the meaning of locality changed from its status as an exclusive end of investigation to a specimen in a larger entity, a point on the grid."[22] By the time modern meteorology took hold in Japan, it had developed standard techniques—such as the creation of weather charts and maps—for comparing local phenomena on a grid that was national and increasingly global in scope. Japan's government consolidated the application of these techniques in the Central Meteorological Station, established in Tokyo in 1875 under the auspices of the Home Ministry and linked to a network of local observatories by telegraph in the 1880s, making the practice of meteorology an instrumental part of the Meiji regime's growing technocracy.[23]

Unlike the laboratory-based sciences, meteorology was a body of knowledge and practice that continued to be produced largely "*inside* its own subject matter."[24] It thus shared with other field sciences a lack of control far greater and a boundary between subject and object far more permeable than that experienced in the confines of the lab. As Gregory Clancey shows in his history of Japanese seismology, any discipline constructed outdoors is particularly vulnerable to unexpected shocks delivered by the nonhuman world.[25] It is also susceptible to *human* forces on the loose, complicating the formation of a tidy body all its own. In fact, alpine meteorology's unconfined nature made it attractive to Itaru and unexpectedly accessible to Chiyoko in ways that a bureaucratized lab science never could.[26]

After all, Itaru primarily saw himself not as a data-collecting drone (though his work required machinelike discipline) but as a gentleman-adventurer. By leaving the security of medical school in 1889 to study high-altitude meteorology, he sought to join the company of intrepid elites forging into uncharted regions around the world. Central Meteorological Station technocrat Wada Yūji did provide Itaru with the necessary instruments and training for his mission—and pressured Itaru's father to release funds originally set aside for medical studies—but only *after* he had been approached by Itaru, who came to him in 1894 with his dream of spending the winter on Fuji's peak.[27] In other words, Itaru did not come to Fuji through meteorology but to meteorology through Fuji. His plan was clearly conceived as part of a mainly Western (if increasingly global) mountaineering tradition and its cult of heroic masculinity.[28]

Through his physical encounters with Fuji, Itaru demonstrated heroic masculinity while enacting, in the most immediate of ways, the middle-stratum colonization of the volcano celebrated in *Taiyō*.[29] To prepare for his mission, he made two exploratory climbs on January 2 and February 14, 1895.[30] Significantly, they started in Gotenba—not Ōmiya, Yoshida, Subashiri, or Suyama, where the centuries-old routes up Fuji originated—the reason being that Gotenba was easily accessed by train from Tokyo.[31] Itaru's accounts of both ascents begin by noting the times of his departure from Tokyo and his arrival in Gotenba, thus locating his climbs within the methodical framework of railroad timetables. The modern division of time, along with a topographical map, accompanied Itaru up the mountain, making him akin to Western travelers in pre-Restoration Japan who "had the white man's confidence that their chronometric system was nearly universal in the world outside this eccentric island," as Masao Miyoshi puts it.[32] Tellingly, Itaru chose not to apply the metric scale to gauge the progress of his ascents but instead used the well-established convention of referring to Fuji's stations. This enabled him to colonize the traditional system for signifying elevations on Fuji by indexing it to Anders Celsius' universalizing centigrade scale.

Upon his arrival at each station, Itaru used a watch and thermometer to record the time and temperature, creating a quantified world in which his body not only *moved* but also *felt*. Here is his description of the third station on his February climb:

> I arrived at the third station at 8:55 a.m., and when I looked back, it appeared that rain was trailing from a band of clouds in the direction of the Tarōbō [an inn located on Fuji's lower slopes]. Gusts of wind from the summit drove fine particles of snow down the snowpack from the station above, making it seem just as if it were really snowing. Not only was it difficult to breathe, it was impossible to look forward, and I wondered if the snowy wind hitting my face would pierce right through me. Here the temperature was 1.7 degrees [centigrade].[33]

Itaru provides no cultural markers to orient the reader in this passage. Gone are the summertime slopes of Fuji, dotted with shelters and the climbers who used them. In their place, we encounter a bodily experience available to anyone in the right meteorological conditions, bracketed by clockwork on one end and the centigrade scale on the other. That is, instead of describing a familiar pilgrimage site—one defined at Fuji, as at other sacred mountains, by local institutions and practices and circulated for generations through travelogues, guidebooks, and word of mouth—Itaru's text links the most immediate and intimate of physical sensations to the most abstract and universal of measurements, advancing an extensive—and highly *intensive*—project of bodily enlightenment through the practices of meteorological science.

As the decision to refer to stations rather than meters demonstrates, Itaru did not discard older forms of knowledge so much as encompass them. Mainly through his friendship with Satō Yōheiji, owner of the Tarōbō inn, he successfully positioned himself as a mediator between local and cosmopolitan knowledge. In addition to providing emotional and material support, Satō shared his considerable experience with all things Fuji, including quickly changing weather patterns, the construction of stone shelters, and the use of snowshoes. Itaru's writings convey gratitude and respect toward Satō and his family, but they also make clear that only an educated and motivated gentleman such as himself could put local expertise to scientific work. Reading his account of the February climb, for instance, we learn that Itaru wore the snowshoes recommended to him by Satō from the third station to the seventh. To continue up Fuji, however, he found it necessary to replace the time-honored contraptions used by local hunters with nail-studded shoes of his own making, a physical exchange of the old for the new that supposedly allowed him to go higher up the volcano in winter than anyone had ever managed.[34] The lesson: local knowledge can take you only so far.

Misbehaving Bodies

Itaru's project took a dramatic turn when Chiyoko chose to join her husband on Fuji's summit, thereby transforming an incipient tale of "heroic masculinity" into one of "heroic domesticity." Despite vigorous opposition from her mother-in-law (and aunt) Tomiko, who relied on Chiyoko to breastfeed Itaru's two-year-old sister Kotoko, Chiyoko left for Gotenba in early August 1895 with her own two-year-old child Sonoko in tow.[35] Chiyoko spent the next few weeks at Satō's home coordinating the purchase and transport of supplies for the observatory and living quarters (primitive wooden structures connected by a passageway and covered with stones) under construction on the peak. Ignorant of his wife's ultimate goal, Itaru stayed on the summit to oversee the building effort—plagued by foul weather, altitude sickness, and a work stoppage instigated by laborers seeking higher pay—while Chiyoko surreptitiously stockpiled provisions for *two* people instead of one.[36]

After the facility was completed at the end of August, Itaru descended to Gotenba for several days before heading back up Fuji. With an alarm clock at his side, he planned to record the summit's temperature, air pressure, wind speed, and humidity every two hours, day and night, from October first to the beginning of summer—in effect, transforming his body into a highly disciplined, machinelike extension of the weather instruments provided by Wada. Chiyoko explains in her diary that she worried Itaru could not possibly keep up such a demanding regime on his own, adding, "Even with my useless body, I thought I should accompany him so I could at least prepare his meals."[37] So once Itaru returned to the summit, she did not go back to Tokyo as everyone had expected but took Sonoko to her home village in Kyushu and left her in the care of her parents. Disregarding Itaru's parents' appeals to return to Tokyo, she eventually made it to Itaru's observatory on October 12.[38]

Chiyoko disobeyed her in-laws and deceived her husband by climbing Fuji, but *Taiyō* transformed the headstrong rebel into a conventional helpmate. Situating Chiyoko in the yin position of the moon—a heavenly body that produces no light of its own but shines only because it reflects the light of the sun[39]—put Chiyoko in her place, literally and figuratively, as a woman. Although Chiyoko's portrait was the same size as Itaru's, the apparent symmetry was ultimately a picture of inequality. And yet the yang-privileging deployment of yin-yang logic, or "encompassed asymmetry,"[40] to use Angela Zito's words, presumes that yin and yang are poles on a continuum of change, not opposites in a hard-and-fast dichotomy. The principle of polar reciprocity allows (even requires) *all* humans to take up positions of yin and yang—that is, positions of submission and agency—in different circumstances to achieve different ends.[41] Thus a mother in relation to her son frequently occupies a yang position even if, in a generic sense, women are categorized as yin. Although her options are usually more limited than a man's, a woman operating through this polar logic can choose to occupy yin and yang positions either to enforce the status quo or to destabilize it by pitting one body of authority against another.

This complex dynamic is readily apparent in "Fuyō nikki." Take the poem that appears at the beginning of this chapter, in which Chiyoko laments her "useless" female body only to reveal that it houses a powerful spirit:

> My body may not be a rugged man's,
> but my striving spirit
> is second to none.[42]

Here it seems Chiyoko considered her yang spirit the equal of any man's—even the superior, as it had to contend with the added burden of inhabiting a woman's yin body.[43] Chiyoko's ability to turn her yin status into a yang advantage is also on display in the audacious letter she wrote to Itaru's mentor, Wada Yūji, just before her climb up Fuji. It justifies her decision to join her husband by invoking the authority of the Nonaka lineage, virtuously announcing, "To protect one's household (*ie*) is the way of a woman (*onna no michi*)."[44] Toward the end of her letter, Chiyoko also informs Wada that she is sending the membership fee to join the all-male Meteorological Association (Kishō Gakkai) in the hope that a woman might be admitted.[45]

Once on the peak with Itaru—who tried unsuccessfully to send her back down the mountain—Chiyoko took charge of domestic chores in challenging circumstances.[46] By the end of October the observatory was encased in so much ice and snow that when, on October 28, two members of Gunji Shigetada's expedition to the Kuril Islands (see note 3) paid the couple a surprise visit, they had to enter the snowbound shelter rear-end first through a small window.[47] The thin air, poor hygiene, inadequate nutrition, lack of exercise, and perilously low temperatures (any liquid not within a foot of the stove immediately froze) took a terrible toll on Chiyoko and Itaru. As Chiyoko put it, "Working in a dark cave like small bugs and lacking adequate food, our bodies and minds grew feeble."[48] Both suffered severe headaches, loss of appetite, and edema; and by early December, Itaru—feverish and hardly able to move—was in especially bad shape.[49]

Because Chiyoko was better off than Itaru, it fell to her to take over the task of recording weather data, as the *Yomiuri shinbun* matter-of-factly reported.[50] This story was borne out decades later in interviews conducted by Nitta Jirō, meteorologist-turned-author, who published a historical novel about the Nonakas' experience (told mainly from Chiyoko's imagined standpoint) in 1975. The Japanese government opened a permanent, all-season observatory on Fuji's summit in 1932, and Nitta worked there three to four times a year from its opening until 1937. He met Itaru personally, and when writing his book years later, he conducted interviews with the Nonakas' eldest son and other people who knew them well. Based on this oral history, it is hard to doubt that Chiyoko did indeed take over the meteorological work in December. In fact, according to Nitta, Chiyoko began calibrating instruments and taking readings as early as October.[51]

The Nonakas' own accounts finesse this sensitive subject. Both merely note that the meteorological work continued uninterrupted during Itaru's decline.[52] Yet their vivid descriptions of Itaru's condition imply that he could not have adhered to the grueling schedule of around-the-clock readings. Also, Itaru's words indicate that he regarded his wife more as teammate than helpmate. A telling example is his description of the edema that afflicted Chiyoko. Using terminology usually associated with the battlefield, he wrote, "This illness was the root cause of my comrade's defeat (*mikata haiboku*)."[53] Apparently Itaru viewed his wife as a fellow soldier in a war against a common foe. In fact, the memoirs of both Nonakas make clear that bodily suffering, combined with a determination to endure their battle with the elements, was an inescapably shared experience that diminished, if not entirely eliminated, gender distinctions.

Depicting their hardship through the language of war not only turned spouses into comrades but also anthropomorphized Fuji into a paradoxically *de*human-ized enemy. In describing his "comrade's defeat," Itaru likened the summit's low air pressure to a "military tactic" (*sakusen keikaku*) employed by a sinister, calculating foe.[54] This merciless Fuji was unlike the temperamental yet ultimately beneficent and approachable deity worshipped by the shrines at its base and the pilgrims who wound their way up its slopes each summer. While the volcano's eruptions, rockslides, and hard-to-predict weather had inspired fear for ages, that fear had been akin to what one might feel toward an occasionally angry parent, not a devious, cold-hearted enemy.[55]

By the time another intrepid pair (two local men delivering greetings from family and friends) visited the couple on December 12, Itaru and Chiyoko looked so wretched they broke into tears at the sight of them. Itaru stoically urged the visitors not to reveal their plight to those down the mountain.[56] Yet upon returning to Gotenba, the men leaked the bad news, and a rescue effort quickly ensued. Acting on orders from the minister of education, Wada led a team of local men to retrieve the Nonakas, but when he and the other rescuers reached the observatory (on December 22), Chiyoko and Itaru refused to budge.[57] Despite the fact that "Mr. Nonaka was so pale and emaciated he did not even appear to be of this world," he told Wada he preferred death to cutting his mission short, reported the *Yomiuri shinbun*.[58] In response, Wada bluntly asserted his authority, telling Itaru he acted on direct orders from the Ministry of Education. Itaru acquiesced—though according to Chiyoko, only *after* extracting a promise from Wada to "build a large imperial observatory [on Fuji] in the future."[59]

Even after her husband had agreed to submit, sickly but defiant Chiyoko argued that she wanted to continue the project alongside her husband even if both of them froze to death.[60] Whereas Wada put Itaru in his place as an instrument of the state, he put Chiyoko in her place as a woman, angrily yelling, "How can a woman be so unreasonable?!"[61] He then chastised her for not considering the condition of her husband, leveling the charge that she was "disloyal and unfilial." "Unexpectedly moved to tears," according to her memoir, Chiyoko stopped resisting.[62]

Thus began the last phase of a rescue mission that was, at the same time, Wada's way of putting an end to an experiment that had spun dangerously out of control. His team wrapped the Nonakas' ailing bodies in thick blankets, put them on porters' backs, and transported them down the perilous slopes. When they finally arrived at Satō's home on the evening of December 23, the weary party encountered a throng of family, friends, journalists, and curiosity seekers eager to greet the newly famous couple and their rescuers.[63] Later that evening, Tokyo University pathologist Miura Moriharu raced to Gotenba to give the couple a thorough medical exam.[64] Thus no sooner had Wada employed his bureaucratic power to end the Nonakas' act of exploit science than the government's medical establishment asserted its own authority by examining their bodies.

The Nonakas proved to be willing patients—one, for the sake of their immediate health, and two, to transform bodily failure into potentially useful data for the field of high-altitude medicine, an area of scientific inquiry closely intertwined with high-altitude meteorology. In fact, in his report to the Meteorological

Association (published in the association's journal), Itaru offered up the results of Miura's examination in full, down to such details as the quantity and quality of his urine.[65] Unable to subject Fuji's body to the universalizing measurements of meteorology for an entire winter, Itaru underscored the scientific value of subjecting his own body to the universalizing measurements of the medical establishment. While the first half of his report details the observatory's construction, the value of Fuji as a site for meteorological study, and the performance (and failure) of weather instruments, the second half conveys the lessons learned not as a detached observer but as a biophysical being fighting to survive the very object of his study. Itaru's ultimate aim was to promote future research, so after cataloguing numerous mistakes concerning nutrition, hygiene, heating, and so on, the report suggests remedies ranging from the provision of lemon water to building a corridor for regular exercise. Simple measures such as these would ensure the success of future research on Fuji, states the report, an optimistic outlook reinforced by the observation that "even the weak body of a woman can handle it."[66]

Bodies in Print

Twelve days after the rescue, *Taiyō* published its composite portrait of Chiyoko, Itaru, and Fuji—as well as an account written by Wada.[67] The press had been reporting the Nonakas' story every step of the way, but Wada was the first of the dramatis personae to publish a firsthand recollection. His piece starts by explaining Itaru's decision to enter the field of alpine meteorology and the development of his relationship with Wada. It then makes the case for taking wintertime weather readings on Fuji's summit, describes Itaru's facility, and discusses ways to improve living conditions in the future. Only at the very end, seemingly as an afterthought, does the technocrat make the briefest mention of Chiyoko, noting that she was a virtuous woman for "standing at her husband's side."[68]

Just two days after Wada's article appeared, the newspaper *Hōchi shinbun* began publishing Chiyoko's version of events. While Wada's account is matter-of-fact and scientific in tone, the serialized "Fuyō nikki" is rich in metaphors, emotions, and classical allusions. Chiyoko may have been excluded from the narrowly determined public sphere of science, but by situating herself in a literary tradition shaped to a great degree by female writers—exemplified famously by Murasaki Shikibu, author of *The Tale of Genji*—she could project her viewpoint into the more broadly defined public sphere of the printed word.[69]

Chiyoko's account constituted yet another challenge to Wada. "Fuyō nikki" broadcasts her bold letter to him; implies, if never declares, that she engaged in scientific work without official training or approval; and puts Wada on the spot by trumpeting his promise to Itaru to build an observatory on Fuji's peak. Viewed as a whole, moreover, "Fuyō nikki" portrays Itaru as a gutsy yet cultured gentleman ultimately superior to the technocratic Wada. No mention of Wada's tutelage appears in Chiyoko's account. Rather than portray Wada as the "yang" brains directing Itaru's "yin" brawn, she immediately puts the spotlight on her husband's aesthetic aptitude, writing that he found solace in composing poetry. To emphasize Itaru's unself-conscious love of poetry—the mark of a *true* gentleman—she claims he spontaneously jotted down poems in moments of overpowering emotion.[70]

Several of Itaru's poems compiled in "Fuyō nikki" express heroic determination, but others, like the one that appears at the beginning of this chapter, reveal despondency and self-doubt:

> A half shell split from the world,
> I wonder, after a hundred years,
> will someone pick me up?[71]

Here we meet Itaru the misfit, unappreciated in his time and wondering if his work will be recognized. Yet viewed in the larger context of "Fuyō nikki," it serves not to diminish its author but to enhance him. Just as Chiyoko's spirit seems all the stronger for having to contend with a "useless" woman's body, so Itaru's machine-like discipline becomes all the more admirable when the reader realizes Itaru is not, after all, a bloodless automaton, but a human being wrestling with doubts and fears. Several of Chiyoko's poems express insecurity as well, showing that it was not only physical suffering and the determination to endure it that united the Nonakas but also the ability to communicate emotional responses amid this suffering through the discipline of poetry.

Chiyoko's celebration of poetry in such daunting circumstances inspired Ochiai Naobumi, an accomplished poet and "national literature" (*kokubungaku*) activist who founded the publishing house Meiji Shoin with the goal of introducing classic works of Japanese literature to the public.[72] Drawing mainly on "Fuyō nikki" but including excerpts from Itaru's publications, he published a book-length account of the Nonakas' experience in the fall of 1896 called *Takane no yuki* (Snows of the lofty peak).[73] The Nonakas' story was an ideal choice for Ochiai, who used it to promote interest in Japanese literature while providing his nascent publishing house with a book that would sell. After all, Chiyoko and Itaru were celebrities, their tale having been featured not only in the press but also on the stage.[74]

One only has to look at the photographs of Chiyoko and Itaru on display in Ochiai's book (fig. 8.3) to perceive a clear difference between *Takane no yuki*'s portrayal of the Nonakas and *Taiyō*'s. In the book, as in the magazine, symmetry is established—not only through the shape and size of the portraits but also through their juxtaposition with an idealized etching of the observatory, drawn

FIGURE 8.3 The Nonakas and the Fuji Observatory. *Takane no yuki,* front matter.

as if composed of perfectly equal halves. Yet unlike the portraits in *Taiyō*, spaced literally a mountain apart, these nearly abut one another. Another obvious difference: the book's photographs show Chiyoko and Itaru not in the formal attire of Japan's middle stratum but in the exotic, fur-sporting outfits worn on Fuji. Moreover, the contrast between Chiyoko's constrained hairdo in *Taiyō* and her deliberately unkempt hair in *Takane no yuki* is stark. The former announces conventional respectability, the latter bold adventure. In short, while gender distinctions certainly appear in the *Takane no yuki* photographs, their symmetry signals a measure of equality absent in the yin-yang *Taiyō* composition.

This makes sense in light of Ochiai's mission to encourage Japanese, male *and* female, to study national literature and contribute to it.[75] Although Ochiai's book does convey the raw suffering that united Chiyoko and Itaru, it focuses far more on the bond they developed through writing poetry.[76] By the same token, it gives the overall impression that nature is less a brutal force to be measured and resisted than it is a wondrous source of poetic inspiration. After all, while Itaru may have colonized Fuji with a thoroughly modern mode of understanding the physical world, and while he may have repeatedly portrayed his hardship as a "battle" against the elements, when it came time to express his sense of alienation from the human world, he chose to identify with a decidedly nonhuman product of nature: a half shell.

Since the publication of Ochiai's book, the Nonakas' tale has occasionally been retrieved from the sands of time and re-presented to the world. Itaru did it himself in 1901 by publishing *Fuji annai*, which comprises not only a guidebook to climbing Fuji (in summer) but also his previously published articles.[77] Moreover, he continued to campaign for the establishment of a permanent weather station on Fuji, and in 1912 he built a new storehouse on the summit toward that end.[78] "Fuyō nikki" was Chiyoko's only foray into print,[79] but she, too, remained active in the effort to build a new weather station.

After Chiyoko died of influenza in 1923, Itaru never spoke again of spending another winter on Fuji.[80] Yet he did support others who hoped to follow in his footsteps; and in August 1932, when a government-funded observatory finally began year-round operations on the summit, he climbed the mountain with his youngest daughter (the Nonakas had five more children after Sonoko) to inspect the new facility.[81] While showing her the site where he and her mother had performed their celebrated act of exploit science decades earlier, Itaru apparently found the peg Chiyoko had used to hang her fur coat. According to Nitta Jirō, he made sure to carry it back down the mountain.[82]

The Nonakas' story never stopped circulating among those, like Nitta, who worked as meteorologists on Fuji. But it was largely forgotten by the public until 1948, when Hashimoto Eikichi, relying on *Takane no yuki*, published *Fuji sanchō*, a novelistic version of the Nonakas' tale clearly meant to inspire a defeated people by celebrating a Japanese man and woman who had endured the unendurable.[83] Nitta thought Hashimoto failed to give Chiyoko due credit, however, so he published his Chiyoko-centered *Fuyō no hito* nearly three decades later.[84] The Nonakas then fell back into obscurity until 2006, when Heibonsha republished "Fuyō nikki" and *Fuji annai* in a single volume. Their story was timely once again, now because of publicity surrounding the closure of the Fuji observatory in 2004.[85]

Here I present yet another incarnation of Chiyoko and Itaru's story, one that embraces *both* the physical and narrative bodies that composed it. For stories do not speak for themselves, and although conceptual bodies take on lives, they are never lives of their own. *People* tell stories; *people* make concepts. And when they create and employ distinctions between nature and culture, yin and yang, local knowledge and scientific truth, they rarely do so for theory's sake but rather to achieve concrete ends within a given (though always changing) bodyscape. In fact, it is the *tacit* employment of conceptual divisions—by different people for very different purposes—that invests them with power, ingraining them so deeply that to many they appear constitutional rather than provisional. And since humans are storytelling animals who make sense of a particular bodyscape in order to survive (and hopefully to thrive) in it, they enact these divisions through their physical bodies as well as their discursive ones—producing inconsistent and even contradictory results. After all, one can paint Itaru and Chiyoko as middle-stratum emissaries of nationalism and science who appropriated local knowledge for cosmopolitan ends, articulated a dehumanized Fuji stripped of traditional associations, and helped forge modern links between the weather as experienced and the weather as measured. But it is also fair to view them as social misfits and rebels who used their bodies to challenge middle-stratum conventions and deployed their poetic training to enter intellectually and emotionally satisfying dialogues with both nature and tradition. By gathering these different "Chiyokos" and "Itarus" into one text, by treating them as living, suffering, *and* narrating bodies, I have aimed to explore the tensions and collaborations between men and women, mountains and humans, nature and tradition, science and poetry, and privilege and rebellion that shaped not only the Meiji bodyscape but also, by extension, our own.

Notes

1. "*Tatoe mi wa masura onoko ni arazu tomo, tsukusu kokoro wa otoraji mono o.*"
Nonaka Chiyoko, "Fuyō nikki," orig. pub. in *Hōchi shinbun*, January 7 to February 1, 1896 (in seventeen installments); reprinted in *Fuji annai, Fuyō nikki*, ed. Ōmori Hisao (Tokyo: Heibonsha, 2006), 204.

2. *"Yo ni awanu katagai naredo momo to se no, nochi ni wa hirou hito mo arinamu."* Ibid., 202.

3. Take, for example, Fukushima Yasumasa's solo trek on horseback across Siberia in 1892 and Gunji Shigetada's expeditions to the Kuril Islands in 1893 and 1894. Nihon Kagaku Shi Gakkai, ed., *Nihon kagakujitsu shi taikei*, vol. 11 (Tokyo: Dai'ichi Hōki, 1968), 95–100.

4. The "blankness" of Fuji in winter made it akin to the polar regions, where explorers "literalized the colonial fantasy of a tabula rasa where people, history, and culture vanish," allowing for "a new kind of imperial theatre with all its colonial and scientific trappings." Lisa Bloom, *Gender on Ice* (Minneapolis: University of Minnesota Press, 1993), 2–3.

5. Modern instruments and methods had already been used to register meteorological phenomena on Fuji's summit, but not during the winter. Shizaki Daisaku, *Fujisan sokkōjo monogatari* (Tokyo: Seizandō, 2002), 2–7; and Arakawa Hidetoshi, *Nihon kishōgaku shi* (Tokyo: Kawade Shobō, 1941), 8–9.

6. Nonaka Chiyoko, "Fuyō nikki," 180, 195. "Fuyō nikki" appeared serially in the *Hōchi shinbun* between January 7 and February 1, 1896.

7. Linda Nash, *Inescapable Ecologies: A History of Environment, Disease, and Knowledge* (Berkeley: University of California Press, 2006), 8.

8. Ibid.

9. My approach also accords with "actor-network-theory" (ANT) as articulated by Bruno Latour in *Reassembling the Social: An Introduction to Actor-Network-Theory* (New York: Oxford University Press, 2005). ANT practitioners seek to trace, step-by-step, the complex connections formed between human and nonhuman actors (or "actants"); and in order to describe the complexity of "actor-networks" as fully as possible, they refrain from segregating their actors into the rigid compartments of the "social" and the "natural." The term "bodyscape" is akin to Latour's "collective," a concept used by Latour "to designate the project of assembling new entities"—human and not—that the more limited terms "society" and "nature" fail to accommodate.

10. Nonaka Itaru, "Kanchū taigaku ki," in *Fuji annai, Fuyō nikki*, 99.

11. Nonaka Chiyoko, "Fuyō nikki," in *Fuji annai, Fuyō nikki*, 199–200.

12. Or "intermediaries," to use Bruno Latour's terminology in *Reassembling the Social*, 37–42.

13. Elaine Scarry, in *The Body in Pain: The Making and Unmaking of the World* (New York: Oxford University Press, 1985), analyzes the dynamics and ethical implications of this "unmaking," a process that derives from the fundamental "unsharability" of pain and its concomitant "resistance to language." As Scarry puts it, "Physical pain does not simply resist language but actively destroys it, bringing about an immediate reversion to a state anterior to language, to the sounds and cries a human being makes before language is learned" (4).

14. Ochiai Naobumi, *Takane no yuki* (Tokyo: Meiji Shoin, 1896), 2–10.

15. Mark Jones, "Children as Treasures: Childhood and the Middle Class in Early Twentieth Century Japan," PhD diss., Columbia University, 2001, 10.

16. This mandala depicts a pilgrimage route up Fuji that starts at Suruga Bay, proceeds through Sengen shrine and the Murayama *shugendō* complex, and ends at the summit, where the Buddhas Yakushi, Amida, and Dainichi are seated.

17. The moon and sun appear to the left and right of the mountain in virtually all Fuji mandalas.

18. See note 16.

19. Shiga Shigetaka, *Nihon fūkeiron,* orig. pub. 1894 (Tokyo: Iwanami Shoten, 1995), 94–97.

20. This enlightenment was accomplished in the "homeland" (*naichi*) through the invention of the "Japanese Alps," a geographical construct that "threw the Shinano highlands into sharp relief for the Japanese public for the first time" and set the stage for "writing new emotional scripts for the responses that landscape might provoke." Kären Wigen, "Discovering the Japanese Alps: Meiji Mountaineering and the Quest for Geographical Enlightenment," *Journal of Japanese Studies* 31:1 (winter 2005): 2, 6.

21. Karatani Kōjin, *Origins of Modern Japanese Literature* (Durham, NC: Duke University Press, 1993), 29.

22. Vladimir Jankovic, *Reading the Skies: A Cultural History of English Weather, 1650–1820* (University of Chicago Press, 2001), 11.

23. The Tokyo-based system of collecting and interpreting weather data was mostly based on methods worked out in the United States by the Smithsonian Institute, which had, during the mid-nineteenth century, set up a far-reaching network of volunteers and professionals to process numerous observations into coherent sets of data. Arakawa, *Nihon kishōgaku shi,* 62. See also James Rodger Fleming, *Meteorology in America, 1800–1870* (Johns Hopkins University Press, 1990).

24. Vladimir Jankovic, *Reading the Skies,* 3.

25. Gregory Clancey, *Earthquake Nation: The Cultural Politics of Japanese Seismicity, 1868–1930* (Berkeley: University of California Press, 2006).

26. Significantly, the first character in the neologism devised in the Meiji period for "science," the *ka* in 科学 *kagaku,* connotes an official department within a bureaucracy.

27. Nonaka Itaru, "Fuji sanchō kishō kansokujo setsuritsu no tenmatsu," in *Fuji annai, Fuyō nikki,* 58.

28. Peter Bayers, *Imperial Ascent: Mountaineering, Masculinity, and Empire* (Boulder, CO: University of Colorado Press, 2003), 2. The importance of keeping high-altitude meteorology from being the "sole province of Europeans and Americans" was central to Itaru's unsuccessful appeal to well-off Japanese to help defray the costs of his mission, which he promoted "for the sake of the nation" as well as the advancement of science. Nonaka Itaru, "Fuji sanchō kishō kansokujo setsuritsu no tenmatsu," in *Fuji annai, Fuyō nikki,* 61–62.

29. I use the term "colonization" in this context not to diminish the word's power in its geopolitical sense but to acknowledge that similar mechanisms of appropriation and domination were at work in the internal colonization of the Japanese homeland by Meiji elites.

30. Nonaka Itaru, "Dai ikkai tōki tozan ki" and "Dai ni kai tōki tozan ki," in *Fuji annai, Fuyō nikki,* 65–86.

31. The Gotenba trail opened in 1883. Nonaka Itaru, *Fuji annai,* in *Fuji annai, Fuyō nikki,* 25.

32. Masao Miyoshi, *As We Saw Them: The First Japanese Embassy to the United States* (New York: Kodansha International, 1994), 111.

33. Nonaka Itaru, "Dai ni kai tōki tozan ki," 79.

34. Ibid., 74, 80–81.

35. Nonaka Chiyoko, "Fuyō nikki," 181. Tomiko was unable to produce enough milk to satisfy her daughter, so Chiyoko had been making up the difference.

36. Nonaka Itaru, "Kengamine kansokujo no keiei" and "Kanchū taigaku ki," in *Fuji annai, Fuyō nikki,* 88–97.

37. Nonaka Chiyoko, "Fuyō nikki," 180–181.

38. Chiyoko was accompanied by the Satōs' son Gorō, the boss of a station shelter named Jūsaburō, and Itaru's younger brother Kiyoshi, who had decided to lend his support. Nonaka Chiyoko, "Fuyō nikki," 194–195.

39. Feminist Hiratsuka Raichō made this same point in her 1911 manifesto, "Restoring Women's Talents," which asserts, "In the beginning, woman was the sun and a true being. Now woman is the moon. She lives through others and shines through the light of others. Her countenance is pale, like a patient." Translation from David Lu, *Japan: A Documentary History*, vol. 2 (Armonk, NY: M. E. Sharpe, 1997), 398.

40. Angela Zito, *Of Body and Brush: Grand Sacrifice as Text/Performance in Eighteenth-Century China* (Chicago: University of Chicago Press, 1997), 145.

41. "Something can be yin only in relation to something that is yang—and everything in the cosmos is thought to be so positioned, including people in the Five Bonds. The father whose sons obey him do so because he has given them the example of his own filial obedience. They are yin to him as he is yin to his own father. (The filial food chain tops out with Heaven)." Zito, *Of Body and Brush*, 212.

42. Nonaka Chiyoko, "Fuyō nikki," 204. See note 1 for the Japanese.

43. In this respect, Chiyoko behaved much like Matsuo Taseko, the peasant poet who "deliberately remade herself into a political figure" amid the turmoil leading to the Meiji Restoration. In her biography of this determined woman, Walthall shares several of Taseko's poems concerning her "weak" woman's body. These lamentations did not stop Taseko from intervening in an explicitly male realm. In fact, she highlighted her physical weakness as a way to emphasize her inner strength, just as Chiyoko did. Anne Walthall, *The Weak Body of a Useless Woman: Matsuo Taseko and the Meiji Restoration* (Chicago: University of Chicago Press, 1998), 7.

44. Nonaka Chiyoko, "Fuyō nikki," 193.

45. Ibid.

46. Itaru's memoir emphasizes that his wife's presence turned out to be a blessing. With Chiyoko melting ice into drinking water, tidying the shelter, mending clothes, and rousing him every two hours during the day (he kept himself awake at night), he could turn his full attention to the work at hand. Nonaka Itaru, "Kanchū taigaku ki," 99.

47. Nonaka Chiyoko, "Fuyō nikki," 196.

48. Ibid., 205.

49. Ibid., 198, 201, 205–209; Nonaka Itaru, "Kanchū taigaku ki," 99–105; and "Kanchū hachi jū ni nichi kan no kansoku ki," in *Fuji annai, Fuyō nikki*, 137–140.

50. "Nonaka Itaru-shi, fusai gesan no moyō," *Yomiuri shinbun*, December 26, 1895, 5.

51. Nitta Jirō, *Fuyō no hito* (Tokyo: Bungei Shunjū, 1975), 143–148.

52. Nonaka Itaru, "Kanchū taigaku ki," 104; and Nonaka Chiyoko, "Fuyō nikki," 214.

53. Nonaka Itaru, "Kanchū taigaku ki," 102.

54. Ibid.

55. Renowned ascetic Kakugyō (1541?–1646) referred to the Fuji deity as the "original mother and father" (*moto no chichihaha*), as did Jikigyō Miroku (1671–1733), the successor to Kakugyō's teachings who starved himself to death on Fuji's upper slopes. Significantly, several caves at the foot of the volcano were (and still are) referred to as "wombs" (*tainai*). For more on Kakugyō and Jikigyō, see Royall Tyler, "The Tokugawa Peace and Popular Religion: Suzuki Shōsan, Kakugyō Tōbutsu, and Jikigyō Miroku," in *Confucianism and Tokugawa Culture*, ed. Peter Nosco (Princeton, NJ: Princeton University Press, 1984), 92–119.

56. Nonaka Itaru, "Kanchū taigaku ki," 104–05; and Nonaka Chiyoko, "Fuyō nikki," 209–212.

57. Nonaka Chiyoko, "Fuyō nikki," 216; Nonaka Itaru, "Kanchū taigaku ki," 105; and "Nonaka Itaru-shi," 5.

58. "Nonaka Itaru-shi," 5.

59. Nonaka Chiyoko, "Fuyō nikki," 218.

60. "Nonaka Itaru-shi," 5.

61. Nonaka Chiyoko, "Fuyō nikki," 219.

62. Ibid. According to the *Yomiuri shinbun*, Wada pointedly asked Chiyoko, "Are you callously willing to kill your husband?" "Nonaka Itaru-shi," 5.

63. Nonaka Chiyoko, "Fuyō nikki," 220–223; Nonaka Itaru, "Kanchū taigaku ki," 106–108; and "Nonaka Itaru-shi," 5.

64. Nonaka Chiyoko, "Fuyō nikki," 223.

65. Nonaka Itaru, "Kanchū hachi jū ni nichi kan no kansoku ki," 141–143.

66. Ibid., 140.

67. Wada Yūji, "Nonaka Itaru-shi no Fujisan kansokujo," *Taiyō* 1:2 (January 1896): 195–200.

68. Ibid., 200.

69. In the 1890s, a truly nationalized (and anthologized) canon of Japanese literature took shape; and since much of it consisted of women's writing, especially that of the Heian period (794–1185), there was a receptive audience for a product like Chiyoko's, which told her story through culturally familiar and critically validated norms. For more on the process of literary canonization in Japan, see Haruo Shirane and Tomi Suzuki, eds., *Inventing the Classics: Modernity, National Identity, and Japanese Literature* (Stanford, CA: Stanford University Press, 2000).

70. Nonaka Chiyoko, "Fuyō nikki," 178.

71. See note 2 for the Japanese.

72. Yamamoto Sansei, ed., *Ochiai Naobumi shū, Sasaki Nobutsuna shū*, vol. 3 of *Gendai tanka zenshū* (Tokyo: Kaizōsha, 1930), 185.

73. Ochiai Naobumi, *Takane no Yuki* (Tokyo: Meiji Shoin, 1896).

74. Unfortunately, there seems to be no record of the play's content. It was performed at Tokyo's Ichimuraza in February 1896. Ōmori, *Fuji annai, Fuyō nikki*, 253.

75. In addition to canonizing works by female authors, Ochiai also founded a women's literature society (*joshibun no kai*) in 1892; and in the following year, he began leading a *tanka*-writing group in his home, "Senkōsha," which consisted of women as well as men. Yamamoto, *Ochiai Naobumi shū, Sasaki Nobutsuna shū*, 182–184.

76. Notably, however, the book has a brief forward by Wada that honors Itaru for "sacrificing his body for the sake of learning and the nation" but makes no mention whatsoever of his wife. Ochiai, *Takane no Fuji*, 1.

77. *Fuji annai* is republished in its entirety in *Fuji annai, Fuyō nikki*.

78. Wada had faded from the picture. During the Russo-Japanese War (1905–1906) he established observatories in Korea and Manchuria and remained on the continent when the war was over. Shizaki, *Fujisan sokkōjo monogatari*, 16; Arakawa, *Nihon kishōgaku shi*, 114.

79. It was consolidated and republished in *Shōkokumin* 11:14 (July 1899).

80. Shizaki, *Fujisan sokkōjo monogatari*, 17.

81. Nitta, *Fuyō no hito*, 239.

82. Ibid.

83. Hashimoto Eikichi, *Fuji sanchō* (Tokyo: Kamakura Bunko, 1948). The book was made into a movie (also released in 1948).

84. Nitta, *Fuyō no hito*.

85. Most of the data it had been collecting could be gleaned by satellites instead.

9

Animal Histories
Stranger in a Tokyo Canal

CHRISTINE L. MARRAN

On August 7, 2002, a bearded seal (*Erignathus barbatus/Agohige azarashi*) was spotted in the Tama River, far beyond its usual Arctic Ocean habitat. Over the course of a few days, onlookers grew into the hundreds. Newspaper reporters and television crews flooded the area to document not just the seal but the astounding human interest in the slippery stranger. One television crewmember commented that the seal was treated as a kind of messiah: "People would follow it along and scream whenever it raised its head above the surface. Everybody was walking along slowly, watching its every move. It was like some mass exodus. There must have been over 200 reporters from TV, radio and print media. God, they even had the company helicopters tracking the seal."[1] In calling this mass interest in the seal an "exodus," the crewmember infers that the creature was akin to a religious prophet leading Tokyo dwellers to a promised land. Spectators followed like true believers as Tama swam from the Tama River (Tamagawa) to Yokohoma's Tsurumi River (Tsurumigawa), presumably by returning to the bay and then entering the new river, then to the Katabira River (Katabiragawa) that flows through Yokohoma, the Ōoka River (Ōokagawa), then the Naka River (Nakagawa), and from there to the Ara River (Arakawa).[2] The arctic seal that deftly navigated his way through the complex engineered water systems of the global commercial hubs of Tokyo and Yokohama for nearly two years was christened "Tamachan."

The frenzy to spot the seal certainly illustrates a contemporary habit of the urban human to turn animals into spectacle. John Berger's point that animals have receded from our everyday lives only to return in commodity form rang true in the various cakes, towels, and other objects created in Tamachan's likeness. Yet, the joy expressed every time the seal bobbed his wet head above the surface of the water implied a reluctance to reduce animal to mere spectacle and a fervent desire to make this animal the messenger and promise that Berger referred to as a precapitalist urge—a time when animals were "subjected *and* worshipped, bred *and* sacrificed."[3] Tamachan came from over the horizon, a survivor under incredible odds, like a long-lost friend from an idealized natural past, an imagined wild world in which living can be more authentic.

The appearance of an arctic seal in Tokyo Bay, utterly beyond its normal habitat, invites reflection on how it managed to swim such a distance in the first place. For animals, the impetus to migrate or move can be a genetic or active adaptation to changes in the environment. The movement from a birth habitat to another location is called "biological dispersal" and varies for each organism. There are differing motivations, ranges, and mechanisms for dispersal, but all animals (and plants) move or are moved in some way. In this sense, human and nonhuman animals are similarly mobile creatures. Humans move or emigrate in active adaptation for better economic or educational opportunities. They get displaced from their original home because of war, famine, or natural disaster and actively adapt to a new environment. These dispersals of human populations have led to the formation of multigenerational diasporic communities that influence urban design and the political concerns of a place.

Biological dispersal of nonhuman animals takes place either as a matter of seasonal change or under particular constraints that may be unnatural, such as habitat fragmentation caused by human land use. Human technologies can also increase dispersal of some organisms. Mosquitoes can increase their range by riding ships into new habitats. Polar bears may move beyond their usual geographic range because of human-induced changes to their environment, such as the melting of the Arctic ice cap, rather than a self-directed choice to propagate across a wider terrain. Bearded seals, of which Tamachan was one, are migrating animals that move with the advance and retreat of the Arctic ice. This brings the seals farther south as the ice grows in the winter months and farther north when the ice retreats in warmer months. Bearded seal pups have been spotted as far south as Hokkaido, though no adults had ever been seen that far south. A different bearded seal was spotted out of its normal migration range in 2005, but the discovery of its dead body a year later in August 2006 shows that the dispersal caused mortal stress to the seal. This makes Tamachan's appearance and relatively long survival in the Tokyo area a substantial anomaly.

With its unusual appearance in Tokyo's urban rivers, the arctic seal was quickly cast as a figurative symbol for how radically humans have become distant from the natural world. For many spectators who stared out into the dismal suburban landscape of cemented riverbanks and opaque green water, the seal was a reminder of a distant past—a symbiotic ruralscape of humans in nature that has since succumbed to urban development and manufactured landscapes. An electric bulletin board created by the Keihin Rivers Bureau (with jurisdiction over Tokyo and Yokohama rivers) for the thousands of stories, photos, pictures, and poems that flooded the government agency had the following post:

> During the summer of Tamachan, I followed television and newspapers and studied the relationship between humans and animals and the problem of protecting plants and animals. One night, the family's radishes went missing. Deer had eaten them, so my mother-in-law stretched out a net, hung a clapper, and planned to borrow the big dog next door [to keep the deer away]. It made me indignant at the Japan that exterminates deer who lay waste to farm fields, and felt that my own home standing before my very eyes should not exist.[4]

The writer laments that her own home has caused the displacement of deer who, like badgers, raccoons, possums, and other animals of the urban environment are exiled from their normative habitat. Their experience of exile is hardly analogous to Tamachan's. Displaced suburban wildlife is not embraced as messenger and promise that rescues the willing from the revulsion of urban human life and exults those who recognize animals' vulnerability. Rather, they are treated as vermin, while Tamachan is treated, as his name suggests, as a rare gem (*tama*) of a nostalgic past and symbol for an ecological future.

The endowment of Tamachan with subjecthood, with a name, and with a photographic face gave him more resonance as a conduit onto which to project dreams of abandoning this polluted world in favor of something else. That Tama is from a distant place hardly familiar to most humans makes his appearance all the more gratifying. The complexity of seal life is mostly ignored in favor of affirming the seal as savior who brings the human back into proximity with nature. That Tama appeared alone, a young male seal in foreign waters, likely made his status as ecological messiah all the greater. Tama was credited for curing illness and for awakening environmental consciousness.[5] Elderly woman Kobayashi Hiroko, a recluse (*hikikomori*) who had not ventured outside in recent years, expressed her gratitude to Tamachan, who coaxed her out of her home and "reminded her to treat nature well, enjoy living, and be grateful for being alive." Tamachan has been credited with healing others suffering from a condition that is increasingly considered a social problem in Japan and other forms of depression by unwittingly coaxing them out of their rooms. As Nishiwaki Matsuko put it on the memory gallery board, "All of Japan was surprised, laughed and then was *cured* (*iyasareta*)."

One of the popular discussions around Tamachan involved global warming and pollution. One person suggested that "The issue of the environment has started to attract more attention. Some people say Tamachan has taught them there is a danger: they recognize the seal came because of climate change."[6] Others, such as the Pana Wave religious group, believed Tama's appearance proved what they had known all along: the earth is being poisoned by human-created electromagnetic waves, and this environmental problem has led Tamachan away from his natural environment. For Pana Wave, Tama was both a messianic figure and a sign of the apocalypse. One American environmentalist group with no interest in religious affiliation with Pana Wave cooperated with them to try to capture the seal because it worried, along with a number of secular Japanese scientists, that Tamachan risked death if he continued to be isolated from his fellow seals in the dirty rivers of Tokyo.[7] Some, suspicious of the group, claimed that Pana Wave had created a pool in which to keep Tamachan as a celebrated mascot to proselytize their message.[8] An article as recent as 2008 claimed that the Katabira River "where Tamachan had swum" was gradually ridding itself of the multicolored dyes that had polluted it, and that *ayu* fish populations were returning to normal. This reference to the seal nearly half a decade after his disappearance suggests the haunting presence of the seal as messenger of ecological wisdom.[9]

As the various reactions to the arctic seal's appearance in Tokyo suggest, when knowledge about animals is minimal, "the images and values created for these [animals] have very little to do with the animal themselves as they are virtually unknown like a legendary or fictional animal from outer space."[10] This was particularly the case in the commotion caused over the awarding of a residency card (*jūminhyō*) to Tama by the city of Yokohoma, which raised serious discussions about citizenship within Japan, not to mention the question of Japanese sovereignty in East Asia. Both the issue of rights for foreigners in Japan and the question of sovereignty of the disputed Liancourt Rocks (known as Dokdo by the Koreans and Takeshima by the Japanese) came to the fore in foreigners' demand for scrutiny of long-standing laws for Koreans and Chinese living in Japan for generations.

Capitalizing on Tamachan's popularity, the city of Yokohama officially registered Tama as "Nishi Tamao" after he had appeared in various Kanagawa rivers. After February 7, 2003, when the Nishi ward office of Yokohama city government announced its intent to issue a certificate of residence to the seal, there was public outcry from a number of foreigners' groups.[11] Dave Gutteridge of the foreign rights campaign group "The Community" argued, "There are many second and third generation Chinese and Koreans who cannot get a residence permit. Also, there are many tax-paying foreign residents who cannot get a *jūminhyō*, and thus have no say in the government they pay tax to. . . . I think the city government were [sic] acting lightheartedly, but were unable to connect the issues (of residency for a seal and no residency for the foreign community)."[12] Edward Crandall wrote for the Japanese-language *Saga shinbun* (Saga newspaper), "It would be better if Japan should become a country where foreign-born residents' human rights are respected and afforded at least the same privileges as seals."[13] His group took up the issue at the end of February by dressing up as seals and submitting a formal request for the same rights as Tamachan to the Yokohama Nishi Ward Office on February 24, 2003. One member said it was one of the most successful awareness-raising campaigns he has been involved in because the group received enough media attention to elicit a formal response from the Nishi Ward bureaucrat Kimizuka Michinosuke, who stated that Tama received only a "Special Residency Certificate" (Tokubetsu Jūminhyō), not one based on the "Basic Residency Records Law" (Jūmin Kihon Daichō Hō). Takano Fumio, member of an advocacy group for foreigner rights in Japan, suggested that Korean and Chinese communities, which have a long history in Japan, were particularly upset by the designation.[14] As he put it, the problem is that most Japanese don't worry too much about residency or what it means to not have it and therefore think "giving a seal a *jūminhyō* is happy news." This "feel good" act of bringing Tama into the human social and political system shone a bright light on the intolerability of inclusiveness for some humans in Japan. While the effort to make Tama a citizen was a strategy to teach ecological practice through commodifying the animal, it threw the seal out with the seawater, so to speak, by ignoring human rights as well as the environmental conditions that made this ecological perversion of an arctic seal's appearance in the Tama River possible in the first place by offering a false sense of *inclusiveness* for the animal. As one protestor suggested, perhaps only half sarcastically, equity should be extended not only to all humans but all animals, not just this charismatic individual.

The other discussion that involved the Japanese government and the seal was a far less public one. Environmental studies scholar Kumi Kato argued that the announcement by the Korean Ministry of Environment in 2002 to create a national park on and around the Dokdo and Ulleung islands, combined with the Japanese Ministry of Environment's nearly simultaneous decision to amend the Wildlife Protection Act to include three sea-grass mammals—dugongs, bearded seals, and hair seals—is sure to make any remaining seals on these islands hostages of international dispute.[15] However, for now there is no particular species on which the government can hang its hopes for making claims to the island. The last sighting of a seal was approximately three decades ago. If seals are sighted, the governments are ready to manipulate the doe-eyed creatures in asserting sovereignty over the islands.

Daydreams and Nightmares

Years after the first gawkers stood on the banks of the Tama River, stragglers continued to travel to the watery mecca for a glimpse of Tamachan. Others daydreamed nostalgically about the vanished creature. The occasional blogger remarks at calling out to the river, "Tamachan, are you there?" A year or more after Tama's final disappearance in 2004, writer Miyazaki Shinpei visited the banks where Tama had appeared and asked local residents to speak about their experience of the years that Tama had been there. Commenting on his interview of a resident at Tsurumigawa who knew that the river was too dirty to support wildlife but hoped and imagined that one day it would be possible, Miyazaki wrote this thoughtful passage:

> Looking at it from others' perspective, it may seem that the kind of [vibrant] river with a seal and other creatures that this woman hopes for is perhaps hard to realize (*jitsugen no muzukashii*) and hers is just a way of dealing with it through simple imagination (*tan-naru sōzō*). But I want to support this imagination. The ability to imagine takes us one step closer to the possibility of realizing [a healthy river]. So I decided to emulate this lady and dream of such a river.[16]

John Berger has written in his essay about looking at animals that "the image of a wild animal becomes the starting point of a daydream: a point from which the day-dreamer departs with his back turned."[17] Berger's claim is that the wild animal, the state or plight of the wild animal, is eventually ignored for a more pleasant daydream. The daydreamers dream of a world in which animals and humans coexist and the rivers shine like clear blue jewels. Miyazaki Hayao's two-dimensional animated worlds in which pollution can be pulled out from the guts of a living river in one stroke and trees can newly erupt from the soil in green profusion in a matter of minutes illustrate that daydream.

But these daydreams camouflage nightmares. The daydream of Pana Wave was that Tamachan could save the world, but what were the more serious circumstances of the global pollution that led to Tamachan's appearance in the river in the first place? And what of other animals made media spectacle? What dreams and nightmares do their lives reveal? How have celebrated zoo giraffes been taken from their central and south African habitats? How are dolphins captured in annual dolphin slaughters off the coast of Taiji "saved" for transport to global sea worlds that only sometimes bother to masquerade as education centers? These histories of particular traveling animals get mostly ignored in commodity culture. One reporter said that the media frenzy over Tamachan revealed "more about social and environmental problems here than the natural history of the animal itself."[18] This is true in the sense that it reveals the ease with which a particular animal's history will be erased for a daydream. The bestowing of citizenship or a name upon one animal gives the illusion of sympathy for the rest. Nowhere is this clearer than in the journey of the sea park dolphin. When a sea zoo representative acquires a dolphin in Taiji, a number of mammals are set aside to become named individuals. Others are merely nameless entities in pods to be culled and slaughtered for dog food. While Japan is not the only country to capture and sell dolphins to sea zoos, since the release of the award-winning film *The Cove*, Taiji has become the best-known place for international trafficking of dolphins. It is likely not an exaggeration to say that Taiji's dolphin hunts and captures are still taking place because the trade of live dolphins is so lucrative. The fishermen increase their rate of sale twenty- to sixtyfold when they sell captive dolphins to the entertainment industry. Some in Taiji, recognizing the lucrative profits from dolphin sales for zoos and aquariums, now train dolphins before selling them. Those dolphins not chosen for training during the annual culls are taken to nearby processing factories where their meat is packaged. The World Association of Zoos and Aquariums that purports to teach "conservation and education" in zoos implicitly condones this practice by allowing global exploitative entertainment programs to acquire dolphins from the hunts. In these acquisitions, individual animal histories are both erased and created. The acquisition of two dolphins from the Japanese Enoshima Aquarium by the Vancouver Aquarium began with an anthropomorphizing media release. The *Vancouver Sun* reported on October 17, 2005, "Dolphin duo arrives in Vancouver: A pair of rehabilitated Japanese dolphins checked into their new home at the Vancouver Aquarium Sunday, and will provide much-needed company for current residents." Upon their celebrated arrival at the sea parks, the dolphins are named. Contests are held, dolphins are christened. Visitors to the park are taught to identify them individually by their fins. These survivors are treated like hotel guests. While the Vancouver Aquarium did not buy wild-caught dolphins, many irresponsible entertainment programs in the world do not have such strictures. New acquisitions are given a new history, while anonymous others are unceremoniously processed for food. So Tokyo spectators at the riverbanks worry whether Tamachan has made it "home" or is dead, while his pinniped harp seal cousins most certainly are dead but completely absented from our vision and imagination. The daydream of the single animal that is imagined as similar to us, with humanlike agency, must supplant the nightmare of the powerless and nameless many (human and animal, foreign and domestic), or it is unbearable.

The Vanishing Elephant

This discussion of a seal that disappeared as suddenly as he appeared concludes with a story of another disappearing animal, but one in literature. I turn to this story partly because literature can help move us beyond usual structures of knowledge that guide our thinking and can limit our perspective on animals and environment, and because this story in particular addresses the ways in which animals can disappear as easily as they become spectacle. This story describes how a man's quiet attention to an animal's everyday life changes his perspective on the world. "The Elephant Vanishes" is a fairly melancholic work of literature by Murakami Haruki that describes the way a man is moved toward a different way of being in the world through watching an elephant. The anonymous narrator begins his story by describing an anonymous elephant that has been chained in a small yard with a small shed for years by a town that received the elephant after the land on which the elephant's former zoo had stood was bought by developers. The town acquired the land, donated by developers, for the elephant's new abode with the agreement that it would be used for development only after the elephant's death. Just as with Tamachan, the city celebrated the elephant's arrival to the town with fanfare. Schoolchildren wrote essays for the elephant with titles like "Please live a long and healthy life, Mr. Elephant." Art classes visited the elephant to draw it.

The elephant had grown to be a feature of the town, and when he went missing, everyone in town searched high and low for him, but to no avail. It didn't take long for the elephant to be mostly forgotten. The town went back to business as usual. As the protagonist put it,

> The disappearance of one old elephant and one old elephant keeper would have no impact on the course of society. The earth would continue its monotonous rotations, politicians would continue issuing unreliable proclamations, people would continue yawning on their way to the office, children would continue studying for their college-entrance exams. Amid the endless surge and ebb of everyday life, interest in a missing elephant could not last forever.[19]

The narrator obliquely critiques the way in which animals vanish in modernity in the absence of media that turns them into spectacle.

Toward the end of the story, the narrator reveals to a virtual stranger how the elephant escaped. He claims to have seen the size of the elephant and the keeper change, so that both became the same size. The narrator can't decide whether the elephant had gotten smaller or the keeper had gotten bigger or both simultaneously, but he simply knew that "to some extent the difference between them had shrunk."[20] The balance between them had changed. He makes the discovery through peeping—surreptitiously watching the keeper and the elephant from a hillside as he often did in the evening: "It was a mysterious sight. Looking through the vent, I had the feeling that a different, chilling kind of time was flowing through the elephant house—but nowhere else. And it seemed to me, too, that the elephant and the keeper were gladly giving themselves over to this new order that was trying to envelop them—or that had already partially succeeded in enveloping them."²¹ For the elephant to be free from its confinement as zoo dweller and object of spectacle on a tiny speck of land tied to a short chain, he and his owner had to become equivalent in size. The usual scale of things had to change.

And it had—not just for the elephant and keeper, but for the narrator as well. The nameless protagonist of "The Elephant Vanishes" is unable to go on with life as usual. Something has shifted within him: "I would begin to think I wanted to do something, but then I would become incapable of distinguishing between the probable results of doing it and of not doing it. I often get the feeling that things around me have lost their proper balance. . . . Some kind of balance inside me has broken down since the elephant affair, and maybe that causes external phenomena to strike my eye in a strange way."²² Not only was the protagonist unable to carry on with the mundane tasks of everyday life, the elephant's disappearance meant the land would be available for development, but the desolate space of withered grass remained empty. The ghostly blank of land that was neither wild nor developed was like the river where Tamachan swam—neither clean nor uninhabitable; a green canal haunted by a ghostly presence.

In this sense, the forgotten elephant appears to be similar to the "spectral" animal of modernity as described by scholar Akira Mizuta Lippit. The spectral animal, considered generally, disappears into the shadows of human language, immortalized as *the* animal. But particular animals become the object of metamorphosis for the human. The elephant's keeper had a "dark, ruddy look, small eyes" and "perfectly circular ears [that] stuck out on either side with disturbing prominence." The human and elephant become a reflection of one another and when they do, they disappear. The Tamachan event reveals the desire to make particular animals figure differently than others.

One can talk about the spectrality of the animal, the numbing of the animal in the human world, the relegation of it to the category of the "undead," but not without considering the problem of the human imagination. As philosopher Jacques Derrida has shown, humans seem to suffer an incapacity for keeping animals alive in any recuperative sense. Animals become apparitions in mournful daydreams because they haunt memories absent of the passion of the present that philosopher Derrida describes in looking at his cat as he stood naked before it wondering, for the first time, how it looks at him:

> And in these moments of nakedness, under the gaze of the animal, everything can happen to me, I am like a child ready for the apocalypse. *I am (following) the apocalypse itself,* that is to say, the ultimate and first event of the end, the unveiling and the verdict. I am (following) it, the apocalypse, I identify with it by running behind it, after it, after its whole zoo-logy. When

the instant of extreme passion passes, and I find peace again, then I can speak calmly of the beasts of the Apocalypse, visit them in the museum, see them in a painting . . . ; I can visit them at the zoo, read about them in the Bible, or speak about them as in a book.[23]

Derrida here speaks to a fleeting moment of excitement when the world looks as though it can be written anew and less anthropocentric ways of thinking about animals will emerge. But that excitement soon passes, and animal bodies are relegated to symbol and taxonomy. That initial jubilance diminishes and is replaced by a usual quotidian gaze upon the animal through common institutions of viewing and commodification. The "beast" has been moved from one epistemological category to another—from the messianic to the agnostic, from creature of the rich wild to dweller of a conservationist reserve. Most people who once combed the river horizon for a sighting of Tamachan have all but forgotten the seal. Only a few followers, his parishioners, still linger at the banks of the river waiting for the stranger to reappear.

Notes

1. This refers to the English-language site for the *Mainichi Daily News*, "Slick Seal Slips Past Stumbling Local Media," September 4, 2002, http://mdn.mainichi-msn.co.jp/waiwai/archive/news, accessed June 18, 2007.

2. Wikipedia provides a chart of some of the dates and locations of Tamachan: August 7, 2002, to August 17, 2002, Tamagawa; August 25, 2002, to August 30, 2002, Tsurumigawa; September 12, 2002, to September 13, 2002, Katabiragawa; September 15, 2002, to September 24, 2002, Ootsunagawa; September 29, 2002, to March 14, 2003, Katabiragawa; April 20, 2003, to April 23, 2003, Nakagawa; April 30, 2003, Arakawa.

3. John Berger, *About Looking* (New York: Vintage, 1992), 4.

4. Kawakami Etsuko, Keihin Kasen Jimusho, "Tamachan Memori- Gyarari-," http://www.ktr.mlit.go.jp/keihin/whole/tamachan_memory/gallery/no03.htm#contents, accessed July 24, 2008.

5. A new research group was started in 2005 at the University of Tokyo called "Hopology" to address a perceived widespread problem of "hopelessness" in Japan, especially among youth. Some participants are Komorida Akio, director of the Institute of Social Science, University of Tokyo; Genda Yuji, Nakamura Naofumi, Sato Kaoru, and Nagai Akiko, all associate professors of the Institute of Social Science, University of Tokyo; and Masahiro Yamada, professor of Tokyo Gakugei University.

6. Francoise Kadri, "Tama-chan Tells Serious Story about Japan's Woes," *Viet Nam News*, February 8, 2003.

7. BBC News, "Japan Seal Slips Through Net," March 11, 2003, http://news.bbc.co.uk/2/hi/asia-pacific/2840083.stm, accessed 18 June 2007; Howard French, "Japanese Cult Vows to Save a Seal and the World," *New York Times*, May 14, 2003; Benjamin Dorman, *Religion in the News* 6:2 (summer 2003), http://www.trincoll.edu/depts/csrpl/RINVol6No2/Latest%20Japanese%20Cult%20Panic.htm, accessed 18 June 2007.

8. Jonathan Watts, "A Nation's Fate is Sealed," the *Guardian*, May 12, 2003, http://www.guardian.co.uk/world/2003/may/09/japan.worlddispatch, accessed June 18, 2007.

9. On August 24, 2008, the *Mainichi* reported that the *ayu* fish populations for the Katabiragawa, "where Tamachan had been spotted in 2002," would move back to normal levels in 2009 with the inclusion of new fish ladders and cleaning of industrial waste, including dyes that had been dumped in such large amounts that the river would change color. See "Katabiragawa: Ayu sojō e gyodō rakusa-bu ga samatage, Asahi-ku no san-ka sho secchi kentō," *Mainichi shinbun*, http://mainichi.jp/area/kanagawa/news/20080824 ddlk14040137000c.html, accessed July 24, 2008.

10. Kumi Kato, "Love You to Death: Tale of Two Japanese Seals," the *Environmentalist* 24 (2004): 150.

11. Barry Brophy, "Kawaii Sea Lion Back in Spotlight," *Japan Times*, February 11, 2003, http://search.japantimes.co.jp/print/fl20030211zg.html, accessed June 18, 2007.

12. Ibid.

13. Edward Crandall, "Residency Certificates and Foreigners," *Saga shinbun*, February 12, 2003 (trans. Crandall), http://www.debito.org/TheCommunity/tamachanmoreinfo.html, accessed June 18, 2007.

14. Brophy, "Kawaii Sea Lion Back in Spotlight."

15. Kato, 149.

16. Miyazaki Shinpei, "Tamachan no ita machi," *Daily Portal*, November 12, 2004, http://portal.nifty.com/koneta04/11/05/02/, accessed August 14, 2008.

17. Berger, *About Looking*, 17.

18. Kadri, "Tamachan Tells Serious Story."

19. Murakami Haruki, *The Elephant Vanishes*, trans. Alfred Birnbaum and Jay Rubin (New York: Vintage International), 318.

20. Ibid., 325.

21. Ibid., 325–327.

22. Ibid., 327.

23. Jacques Derrida, *The Animal That Therefore I Am*, ed. Louise-Marie Mallet, trans. David Wills (New York: Fordham University Press, 2008), 12 (emphasis is author's).

VISTAS AND VANTAGE POINTS | IV

10

Inventorying Nature

Tokugawa Yoshimune and the Sponsorship of Honzōgaku in Eighteenth-Century Japan

FEDERICO MARCON

Our friend Robinson Crusoe learns this by experience, and having saved a watch, a ledger, ink and pen from the shipwreck, he soon begins, like a good Englishman, to keep a set of books. His stock-book contains a catalogue of the useful objects he possesses, of the various operations necessary for their production, and finally of the labour-time that specific quantities of these products have on average cost him.

—KARL MARX, CAPITAL

Channeling Luck, Controlling Resources

Ihara Saikaku (1642–1693), chronicler of merchant life in early modern Japan, seemed to share his contemporaries' belief that chance was the most important source of business prosperity: "Fortune be to merchants, luck in buying and happiness in selling!" he recited at the beginning of his *Seken munezan'yō* (Worldly mental calculations, 1692).[1] On the other hand, Saikaku's urban heroes nicely fit John Stuart Mill's definition of *homo economicus* when they act in his merchant tales as "a being who desires to possess wealth, and who is capable of judging the comparative efficacy of means for obtaining that end."[2] His shopkeepers, artisans, and wholesale traders are well aware that if chance is a fundamental component of success, there are also means at the disposal of ingenious and industrious businessmen to catalyze luck: "Getting rich," Saikaku explained, "is a matter of luck, we say; but this is simply an expression. In point of fact, a man builds his fortune and brings prosperity to his family by means of his own wit and ingenuity."[3]

The preoccupations of Saikaku's townsmen with financial prosperity—what renders Saikaku's stories so familiar to us—reveal the degree of how, already by the end of the seventeenth century (just less than a century after the founding of the Tokugawa regime), the lives of Japanese of all social classes had increasingly adjusted to the logic of the market and of profit. The monetization of trade that had begun in the fifteenth century encompassed now almost all economic activities. With the establishment of the Dōjima Rice Exchange (Dōjima Kome Ichiba) in 1697, the logic of the market came to exercise a strong influence over political affairs simply by controlling the exchange rate of rice, the *formal* unit of measurement of wealth and power among the samurai political elites, for money, the *actual* measurement of wealth in the larger field of economic transactions. In other words, the incremental separation of the political and the economic spheres—a structural creation of the compound regime of the Tokugawa that Yoshimune's reforms accelerated—created a situation in which the wealth of the ruling elites was increasingly at the mercy of the ups and downs of the market.

Channeling luck into more profit and managing misfortunes with back-up plans were certainly central concerns for wealthy peasants, artisans, and merchants, as Saikaku's lively stories show. As the growing volume of trade in international and, especially, domestic markets required the ruling samurai elites to exercise an active role in the economic life of the various domains, the necessity of "managing" luck became a matter that called for political attention.

This chapter reconstructs the organizational effort of a massive survey campaign of all vegetal and animal species living and growing in Japan, carried on under shogunal oversight between 1734 and 1736 and resulting in a load of statistical data unprecedented in world history for quantitative and qualitative magnitude.[4] The pharmacologist Niwa Shōhaku, the mind behind the formidable organization of the resource inventory, acted under the aegis of Tokugawa Yoshimune to mobilize retainers of all domains to carry on the survey locally at the smallest village level. Like one of Saikaku's shopkeepers, Shōhaku knew that to channel luck and secure profit one had to take control over one's labor and resources. The first days of the New Year, Saikaku instructed, are "the time for merchants to bind their ledgers, take inventory, and open the vaults to inspect their silver." What Shōhaku achieved was the creation of "national ledgers" where an inventory of the natural riches of the state could be recorded in an orderly fashion.

The organization of the surveys under Yoshimune brought fundamental changes to the study of nature in early modern Japan. Under his rule, the bakufu sponsored scholars such as Abe Shōō, Norō Genjō, Uemura Saheiji, Aoki Kon'yō, Niwa Shōhaku, and Tamura Ransui as collaborators and executors of a massive reform project aimed at restructuring shogunal control over the land and coping with financial and agricultural difficulties that arose after the economic bubble of the preceding Genroku period (1688–1704). Yoshimune's plan involved these scholars in three main projects: to produce a complete survey of all species of plants and animals that could be found in Japan, to implement agricultural technology in the cultivation of alternative pest-resistant crops and vegetables sustainable in times of famine, and to establish a state-sponsored medicinal garden to supply internal demand for pharmacological substances and enable Japan to end its reliance on Chinese and Korean imports.

State sponsorship of specialized scholars affected in particular the structure and stakes of the field of *honzōgaku*. Usually translated as "pharmacology" or "materia medica," the term *honzōgaku* designated a field of learning devoted principally to the study, interpretation, and translation of Chinese encyclopedias of material medica that by the first half of the eighteenth century had developed into an eclectic discipline of nature study consonant with what was known in early modern Europe as "natural history." Shogunal patronage of these scholars and their involvement in various agricultural reform projects influenced the ways they studied, understood, manipulated, and explained nature to produce sophisticated descriptions of the morphological, organographical, physiological, and anatomical aspects of plants and animals. In the long run, the unforeseen consequences of this transformation would entail a radical change of the Japanese conception of "nature" and natural "species" and a complete reclassification of human and natural space.

The Classification of All Things

Shobutsu ruisan, left unfinished by the death of its author Inō Jakusui in 1715, was a first attempt to give a comprehensive classification of all existing species of plants and animals. It was a very erudite enterprise of monumental proportions, attempting to give an ultimate systematization to information about plants and animals contained in the most authoritative encyclopedias of natural knowledge produced in China.

It was never published, and after Jakusui's death none of his students continued his work. In 1719 Maeda Tsunanori donated the original manuscript to the shogunal library. At the turn of the nineteenth century, Chief Librarian Kondō Morishige recorded in his memoirs that on the "11th day of the 9th month of 1719 Matsudaira Kaga-no-kami [Maeda Tsunanori] offered a copy of *Shobutsu ruisan* as a result of a direct request from the shogun to Lord Kaga-no-kami the 29th day of the 7th month of the same year."[5] The intermediary agent of the transaction was Hayashi Hōkō, at the time the head of the Shōheikō, a shogunal academy of neo-Confucian studies. According to Ueno Masuzō, Yoshimune appreciated the importance of Jakusui's work and regretted that Tsunanori did not charge anybody with the task of completing his encyclopedia.[6] It was only in 1734 that Niwa Shōhaku, a former student of Jakusui and official physician of the shogunate for twelve years, began the compilation of the remaining 638 volumes of Jakusui's original plan. He named, described, and classified a total of 3,590 species of plants and animals and specimens of various kinds of metals, earths, stones, and jewels.

To bring the project to completion, shogunal authorities issued a permit allowing Shōhaku to move freely through the country. He was to have free access to all territories and was entitled to receive assistance from local authorities whenever needed. Shohaku's mission was preceded by an ordinance dispatched by the senior councilor Matsudaira Norisato to all domainal lords, temples, and regional magistrates:

> In the case that the physician Niwa Shōhaku, in charge of the revision and expansion of *Shobutsu ruisan,* would need it, it is requested that all deputy magistrates (*daikan*) of shogunal territories (*tenryō*), all Lords (*ryōshu*) and estate managers (*jitō*) of private domains (*shiryō*), and all administrative officials of territories controlled by temples and shrines (*jisharyō*), comply to any form of request regarding names, forms, typology of natural products (*sanbutsu*) in all provinces of the realm that the aforementioned Shōhaku may have.[7]

Niwa Shōhaku was born in Matsusaka in 1691 in Ise Province, at that time a part of the domain controlled by the Kii Tokugawa family of Yoshimune. His father was a physician of samurai origins. Shōhaku was destined to follow in his father's professional footsteps and did so for several years, until he decided to enter Inō Jakusui's school to study *honzōgaku.* He distinguished himself among Jakusui's students for his interest in fieldwork and herb collecting, activities that differentiated him also from his master's strictly lexicographical interests.[8] It is known that he practiced as a town physician (*machi isha*) in Edo between 1720 and 1721, and it was in that year that the shogunate first contacted him to conduct herbal expeditions in the Nikkō and Hakone mountainous regions. His enlistment as official physician of the shogunate followed in 1722, and Ueno has argued that the expeditions were probably an examination to judge his actual abilities in the field.[9]

Shōhaku is today mostly famous for bringing *Shobutsu ruisan* to completion and for organizing the first official survey of Japanese natural resources on a national scale. It is, however, worth mentioning that his first activity as shogunal physician was to establish the Office for Japanese Pharmacology (Wayaku Aratame Kaisho) that would later become part of the shogunal Institute of Medicine (Igakukan), which was responsible for the importation, cultivation, distribution, and instruction regarding pharmacological herbs. Shōhaku's task was to facilitate an agreement among the major pharmaceutical dealers (*yaku don'ya*) to organize an oligopolistic cartel under the control of the Office for Japanese Pharmacology.

In 1729, the office sponsored the publication of a manual coauthored by Shōhaku that was designed to provide an introductory education for the general population on the utilization of 155 herbs in the preparation of fundamental drugs, primarily general analgesics and antipyretics.

In 1734, Yoshimune officially commanded Shōhaku to finish *Shobutsu rui-san*, along with a national census of vegetable and animal life in Japan. These surveys were conducted on a regional level in the form of *sanbutsuchō*, or "product reports" that every domain was required to complete and dispatch back to Edo. Of the original official letters that Shōhaku sent in 1735 to the Edo residences of domainal lords requesting the compilation of a *sanbutsuchō* of their realm, many are lost, but we may have a glimpse of their contents from a surviving one sent to chief-retainer Hanabusa Iemon of the Fukuoka domain. The letter reproduced Shōhaku's instructions on how to compile a *sanbutsuchō*:

Produce Report of the _____ Province, _____ Domain
Compiled by _____

— Grains:
Early rice (*wase* わせ), specify quantity and region of production
Second rice (*nakate* なかて), "
Late rice (*okute* おくて), "
Mochiine (糯稲), "
Foxtail millet (*awa* 粟), "
Barnyardgrass (*hie* 稗), "
Sugarcane (*kibi* 黍), "
Wheat (*komugi* 小麦), "
Barley (*ōmugi* 大麦), "
Buckwheat (*soba* 蕎麦), "
Soybeans (*daizu* 大豆), "
. . .

All kinds of crops must be written in this order: additional species should be added at the end in the same fashion.

— Vegetables:
Leafed vegetable (*sai* 菜), "
Japanese radish (*daikon* 大根), "
Etc. etc., "

As can be seen from the examples above, the list should include name, form, quantity, and region of production not only of herbs and trees, but all edible vegetables. The same should be done for the following:

— mushrooms
— watermelons
— fruits
— trees
— herbs
— bamboo

The lists should be as exhaustive as possible and should follow the order of *Shobutsu ruisan:*
— fish:
loach (*dojō* 泥鰌)[10]
etc.
etc.
— shellfish
— birds:
crake (*kuina* くいな)
etc.
— beasts:
Japanese serow (*kamoshishi* かもしし)
etc.
— insects:
snails (*maimaitsuburi* まいまいつぶり)
etc.
— snakes:
adder (*mamushi* まむし)
etc.

Of all previous categories, all species living in the region must be included, without considerations for their edibility.[11]

The letter continued with a request to local authorities to investigate among the peasant population all possible usages of "all products generating from the earth."[12] In another passage, Shōhaku reported that he was authorized to inquire about "all species [growing and living] in that region without exception."[13] Local authorities were not to impose geographic limitations on their surveys and were requested to distribute copies of *sanbutsuchō* forms in every village of the domain to be compiled and collected. In addition to the distribution of survey models to all domains, in 1735 Shōhaku requested a meeting with the managers (*rusui*) of the Edo mansions belonging to the various domainal lords to provide further instructions and clarification on the practical execution of the surveys. Yasuda Ken, the professor of agronomy who first discovered and studied the *sanbutsuchō,* reported that the diaries of one such caretaker had been found. Ōkubo Okaemon, an Edo *rusui*, recorded in his diary his meeting with Niwa Shōhaku in the fourth month of 1735.[14] At a certain point in the meeting, Ōkubo asked Shōhaku: "Since plants and animals of the Okayama domain are more or less similar to those of the surrounding countryside of Edo, I was wondering whether we should report only the strangest and rarest of the plants and animals of the Okayama region." At this, Shōhaku replied, "As you rightfully observed, the majority of the species of plants and animals of the different provinces of the realm are the same. Nevertheless, I beg you to ensure that all mineral, vegetable, and animal produce of your region is carefully recorded without exception."[15]

Beginning in the fourth or fifth month of 1735, almost every village in Japan received a copy of the survey.[16] As recorded at the end of these surveys, those who actually conducted the censuses were members of the peasant class: *shōya* (village headmen) or members of the *hyakushō sōdai* (village councils). These men were charged with the task of returning them within a few months time (two or three months was the average) to a specially established office of the domainal administration, the Sanbutsu Goyōdokoro. This office had the duty of assembling the compiled surveys, copying them into a single booklet, and resolving statistical errors when data were missing or recorded in a confusing manner. The data from the various villages were assembled differently in each domain. Some put them in order of distance from the main castle town of the domain. Others followed the administrative divisions of the province. All surveys had to be dispatched back to Edo by the twelfth month of 1735.[17]

Unfortunately, many of these regional surveys have been lost, either partially or completely. It is known that they were each labeled "Produce Report of _____ Domain of _____ Province." All entries were sequenced in the order provided by Shōhaku—similar to the order in which entries were arranged in *Shobutsu ruisan*. All names had to follow the standard provided by Shōhaku himself. This meant that every regional Sanbutsu Goyōdokoro had to address inconsistencies and indicate the standard name of a species for those that had been recorded in local forms with the names in dialect.[18] We know, for example, that the produce report of the Kaga domain recorded 386 species of trees, 210 species of herbs, 223 species of birds, and 200 species of fish.[19] These statistics also distinguished regional variations of certain species and noted the distribution of different species by region. For example, the produce report of the Morioka domain, in the northern part of Honshu, distinguished 13 species of Scolopacidae and 24 species of Anatidae, while Okayama distinguished 20 different species of crabs, 12 species of bees, 9 species of dragonflies, and 8 species of flies.[20]

These surveys were conducted on a massive scale, and it is easy to see why hundreds of new species were added to those previously described in Chinese encyclopedias. The thoroughness of the national survey was, for Shōhaku, more important than the rapidity of their execution, as we gather from a number of letters he wrote granting extensions of deadlines. Delays, imprecision, and negligence were surely only a few of the difficulties that a project of this scale must have suffered. Niwa Shōhaku, once having received a complete report from a domain, checked it for any mistaken, contradictory, or incomprehensible data. He then sent the reports back to the various domains for additional information. He marked with a circle any species he wanted to be illustrated and with a triangle any entry for which he needed more thorough information. Entries marked with the triangle usually required additional specifications added in the margins. All species marked with the circle required as precise and detailed a drawing as possible.[21]

The realization of accurate drawings of plants or animals was probably a demanding task for local authorities. The species for which Shōhaku requested an illustration were often rare, difficult to find, or in case of animals, hard to capture. Each domain had to hire a skilled painter to portray the requested plant or animal. It was not rare, Yasuda explained, for Shōhaku to request illustrations for one hundred or even two hundred species. Of plants or trees, in particular, Shōhaku required the artists to reproduce them in the various phases of their growth or their changes in accordance with seasons. The images were then bound together and entitled "Illustrated Albums of Produce of the _____ Domain in the _____ Province." Nothing is known of the authors of the illustrations.

Today, these surveys are useful sources of information regarding species now extinct in Japan such as the *kawauso*, a Japanese subspecies of the Eurasian river otter, the *toki*, a species of crested ibis, and the Japanese wolf, *ōkami* (fig. 10.1).[22]

These surveys provide important historical documentation of vegetal and animal species, but they still await full study. They are presently regarded as the largest and most comprehensive surveys of natural resources to have ever been attempted in East Asia—and probably in the world. Surprisingly, however, when Niwa Shōhaku presented the 638 volumes that completed Inō Jakusui's *Shobutsu ruisan*, no trace of the immense quantity of data obtained from the regional *sanbutsuchō* was included, other than a list of regional and dialect names for various species. The encyclopedia was quickly catalogued in the shogunal library, and Shōhaku was promoted to a higher position in the Institute of Medicine.

A further supplement of fifty-four volumes was added to the encyclopedia in 1745, but the data collected ten years before was still not mentioned. Why did the shogunate devote such a large quantity of resources to complete this inventory, explicitly designed to support Shōhaku's revision and enlargement of Inō Jakusui's encyclopedia, if Shōhaku did not use all the information collected? Jakusui's project was structurally and intentionally lexicographical, aimed at developing an

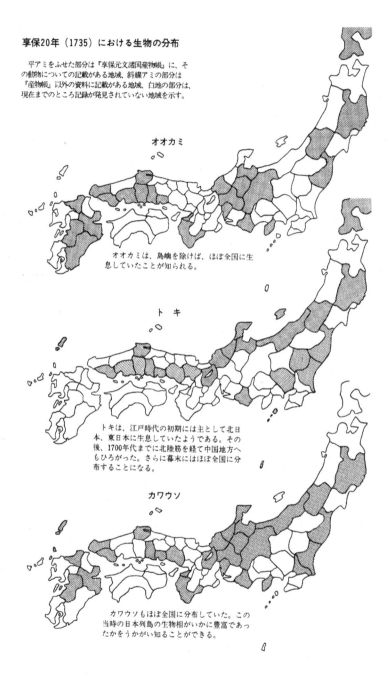

享保20年（1735）における生物の分布

平アミをふせた部分は『享保元文諸国産物帳』に、その動物についての記載がある地域、斜線アミの部分は『産物帳』以外の資料に記載がある地域、白地の部分は、現在までのところ記録が発見されていない地域を示す。

オオカミ

オオカミは、島嶼を除けば、ほぼ全国に生息していたことが知られる。

ト　キ

トキは、江戸時代の初期には主として北日本、東日本に生息していたようである。その後、1700年代までに北陸筋を経て中国地方へもひろがった。さらに幕末にはほぼ全国に分布することになる。

カワウソ

カワウソもほぼ全国に分布していた。この当時の日本列島の生物相がいかに豊富であったかをうかがい知ることができる。

FIGURE 10.1 The distribution of the Japanese wolf, the Japanese crested ibis, and the Japanese river otter (in order) throughout the Japanese main islands as indicated in the 1735 surveys. SOURCE: SHIMONAKA, *SAISHIKI EDO HAKUBUTSUGAKU SHŪSEI*, 69.

all-inclusive and rational arrangement of all *honzōgaku* sources and a definitive classificatory system. Stylistically and substantially, Shōhaku faithfully followed Jakusui's model. Since that was the case, what was then the purpose of the surveys? If Shōhaku aimed only to order once and for all the regional and dialect variations of the names of plants and animals, why bother to request so many illustrations? Why not utilize or insert those images in his *Shobutsu ruisan*?

These questions still await an answer. Yasuda's view is that Shōhaku exploited shogunal resources and authority to satisfy his own scientific curiosity.[23] Indeed the mystery remains, particularly because there is speculation over the legal status of the surveys, and mere curiosity does not seem a satisfactory hypothesis.[24] Aside from the official 1734 letter assigning Shōhaku the task of organizing the general census of natural resources and the final report summarizing the collected data, there is no trace of the original surveys among the official documents in the shogunal archives.[25] *Shobutsu ruisan* itself, once stored in the shogunal library, was never printed or published, and access to it was limited to those who could obtain authorization from the assembly of senior councilors.

The secrecy surrounding the encyclopedia, the "disappearance" of some the surveys, and the great power and authority at Shōhaku's disposal—unprecedented for a physician—all suggest a much greater interest in the project on the part of the government and, in particular, of Yoshimune. Surveys may be interpreted as one of the strategies Yoshimune adopted to achieve his objective to control the realm, which might provide an explanation for the secrecy surrounding them. Indeed, together with the massive production of maps by the shogunate throughout the early modern period, this inventorying endeavor suggests a conscious plan of the Tokugawa to extend the reach of their hegemonic control over the islands.[26]

Another motivation for the organization of national surveys of natural resources was the rural crisis of 1729–1735, also known as "the Kyōhō famine." A general worsening of agricultural output reached its apex in 1732, when bad weather during the winter and spring and a locust infestation in summer produced a widespread famine responsible for the death of more than one hundred thousand persons in western Japan. From a fiscal standpoint, this famine resulted in a cut of tax income for the shogunate and the domains. Yoshimune responded to the famine by ordering a shipment of rice from the eastern reserves, but that measure was not sufficient to contain the effects of malnutrition. Throughout the fall of 1732 and the spring of 1733, incidents and local revolts convinced Yoshimune to increase the amount of rice distributed to the area.

The crisis of 1732–1733 induced Yoshimune to adopt an agricultural policy aimed at encouraging the research and production of alternative and pest-resistant crops. The surveys of 1734–1735, I believe, were a major component of his program of agricultural reform. The famine was a likely motivating force for the expansion of Jakusui's research, as it would be hard to otherwise explain why Yoshimune did not order the enlargement and revision of *Shobutsu ruisan* after he acquired it in 1719 or after he hired Shōhaku in 1722 and did so only after the Kyōhō crisis of the 1730s.

Surveying and Surveillance

Survey campaigns were a common phenomenon in emerging states of the early modern period. In Europe, the young Carl Linnaeus (1707–1778) traveled to Lapland with a grant from the Royal Swedish Society of Science to complete a survey of its botanical resources, which he later published in 1737 under the title *Flora Lapponica*. This journey, besides having scientific purposes, was motivated by the economic interests of the Swedish government in the area.[27] The value of Linnaeus' classificatory system was exponentially increased by virtue of his students, who became known as "Linnaeus' apostles," who were sent around the world with the task of recording, describing, and classifying as many new species as possible.[28] Linnaeus' system of classification was simple and malleable enough to be accommodated to new species of plants. Linnaeus' "apostle" Pehr Kalm (1716–1779) traveled in North America between 1749 and 1751 with a grant from the Royal Swedish Society of Science. Daniel Solander (1733–1782) embarked on James Cook's HMS *Endeavour* to gather botanical specimens for the English Royal Society. Fredric Hasselquist (1722–1752) gathered specimens in Palestine, while Carl Peter Thunberg (1743–1828) traveled in South and East Asia with the Dutch East India Company. It is impossible to separate these scientific enterprises from the economic and political interests of the emerging European colonial empires or to separate "pure" scientific curiosity from interested commitment. As Peter Raby has argued regarding the African expeditions of Joseph Banks (1743–1820), "The 'pure' impulse to add to European knowledge went hand in hand . . . with the utilitarian: the word commerce was not mentioned, but perhaps did not need to be."[29] Scientific knowledge and imperial possession of the most remote parts of the world were two sides of the same coin.

Similarly, Yoshimune's national inventory of all species of plants and animals can be interpreted as an enterprise to acquire precise data on land productivity and exploitable resources. This is evident from Yoshimune's patronage of *honzōgaku* experts whom he dispatched on herbal tours in the provinces for the establishment of medicinal and botanical gardens under the direct control of the shogunate or of domainal authorities. Niwa Shōhaku is remembered as having acquired the highest official title among them, but other scholars enjoyed the fruits of Yoshimune's patronage as well. Of these it is worth remembering Norō Genjō and Uemura Saheiji, who, like Niwa Shōhaku, both came from Ise Province.

Material Nature, Abstract Nature

The survey campaigns organized by Yoshimune's administration—along with other similar projects that soon followed at the local, domainal level—had several dramatic consequences for the field of nature studies. Through the financial and political support of the shogunate, the discipline of *honzōgaku* acquired enough institutional authority and financial prosperity to sustain a larger community of specialists. Governmental patronage recruited *honzōgaku* specialists as shogunal officials, employees of the Institute of Medicine, or the Office for Japanese Pharmacology. *Honzōgaku* practitioners and the study of plants and animals both acquired cultural value due to natural history's connection to matters of economic livelihood and national prosperity.

Bakufu- and domain-sponsored herborizing expeditions in "deep valleys and steep mountains" had the unforeseen result of secularizing and opening up a space that had been traditionally described and quarantined as "sacred space," the abode of deities and demons, and turning it into reservoirs of natural resources (*sanbutsu*). In Kaibara Ekiken's words, "I climbed tall mountains. I penetrated into deep valleys. I followed steep paths and walked through dangerous grounds. I have been drenched by rains and lost my way in fog. I endured the coldest winds and the hottest sun. But I was able to observe the natural environment of more than eight hundred villages."[30]

A mass of local myths and legends—codified and categorized during the Middle Ages into folk stories, Buddhist moral tales (*setsuwa*), oral performances, and so on—narrated stories of vicious goblins and demons, *tengu* and *kappa*, tricking humans who dared to enter a deep forest or who lost their way in a solitary mountain path.[31] Both Shintō rituals and Buddhist practices regarded the realm of *yama* and *mori*—literally "mountains" and "forests," but often used as synonyms for such otherworldly wilderness—as a realm thoroughly separated from "human space," marked by visual landmarks such as small Shintō portals (*torii*) or little rock statues of Jizō.[32] Mountains and forests were the domain of shamans and ascetics—a three-dimensional material mandala where the initiates performed ascetic pilgrimages as spiritual exercises.[33]

Naturalists involved in herborizing expeditions invaded a world traditionally separated from human space and opened it up to exploration and exploitation.[34] As Inō Jakusui wrote in *Saiyaku dokudan* (Handbook of herbology), "Whenever I have spare time from my work on the Classics, I like to investigate the nature of birds, beasts, herbs, and trees, why they fly or lurk in the ground, how they move or grow. To that purpose, I climb steep mountains and enter deep valleys and wild fields. I gather [specimens] in woods and valleys and observe them in their minutest detail."[35]

The routinization of such expeditions and, most importantly, the reclassification of *yama* and *mori* into a space available to economic production and resource exploitation contributed to secularize "woods" and "mountains." As a result, the commodification of their resources transformed that space into an abstract and quantifiable realm whose objects could be inventoried, counted, measured, relocated, transformed, and consumed.[36]

The vanishing of the invisible texture of metaphysical relations that held together sacred and human spaces was the effect of a long, unplanned, and contingent series of intellectual, economic, political, and cultural processes of which Yoshimune's surveys stand as a symbolic watershed, deeply affecting both scholarly and economic practices. On a cognitive level, a variety of disciplines of nature studies more or less directly associated with *honzōgaku* knitted together these processes. The ensuing secularization of nature sprang from a parceling of nature in a myriad of discrete objects to be described, analyzed, consumed, or accumulated in the form of standardized and quantifiable units as products, natural species, or collectibles.[37] *Honzōgaku* scholars and amateurs tended to examine plants and animals as intellectual commodities in isolation from their ecosystems, to be catalogued as concrete samples of abstract species in encyclopedias, albums, monographs, and collections. This tendency derived in part from the adherence of early *honzōgaku* scholars to the explanatory style of canonical texts such as *Honzō kōmoku*, which tended to treat mineral, vegetal, and animal species as *meibutsu*, or "names," in the form of discrete encyclopedic entries revealing their pharmacological properties. The treatment and manipulation of individual species disconnected from their ecosystem developed in concomitance with the recruitment of naturalists in state-funded missions to inventory plants and animals as *sanbutsu*—"products" or "resources"—and to experiment with medicinal herbs (*yakuhin*) and pest-resistant crops in botanical gardens. A burgeoning popular interest in plants and animals contributed to their transformation into objects of curiosity (*suki*) to be collected, admired, exchanged, and exhibited as spectacles (*misemono*).

On a socioeconomic level, the increasing commercialization of agricultural production—which included the farming of rice and other grains as well as protoindustrial activities like fishery, textiles, sake brewing, dyeing, and so on—led to the commodification of plants and animals and their transformation in resources to inventory and accumulate for the needs of agricultural growth and the demands of the expanding market of medicinal substances.

At once material and intellectual commodities, plants and animals constituted, as *specimens*, the myriads of things that populated the world (*banbutsu*). But as *species* to be studied, produced, or traded, plants and animals became concrete bearers of abstract characteristics. Through their collecting, observing, and representing, *honzōgaku* scholars reduced nature to a collection of material objects that were manipulated to manifest increasingly abstract qualities. These species-essential morphological properties were abstracted from the variety of individual specimens to fit them into different classificatory standards, depending on whether they were encyclopedia entries, agricultural products, medicinal substances, or merely curiosities. These social practices—intellectual, artistic, political, economic, but more often a mixture of them all—secularized nature by transforming what was once the enchanted realm of unfathomable divine forces and metaphysical principles into a multiplicity of "objects" that could be grasped and manipulated through protocols of descriptive, observational, and reproductive techniques.

By the second half of the eighteenth century, accurate pictures of plants and animals constituted the focal point of natural historical atlases and monographs, a process undoubtedly put into motion by the important role that Shōhaku attributed to them in editing the surveys in *sanbutsuchō*. "True-to-nature" illustrations—or *shashin*, as they came to be known—had a double function. On the one hand, they distilled the results of shared protocols of observation to pictorially represent species-specific morphological characteristics of each species. On the other, as epistemic paradigms they trained the naturalist's eye to recognize species in nature by distinguishing morphological and quantitative features of plants and animals. The practical function of *shashin* illustrations was to help scholars to precisely identify a species of plant or animal without reference to the lexicographical authority of canonical sources. As such, they had the same impact as Linnaeus' *systema naturae* in teaching naturalists to "see systematically," as Michel Foucault put it, by molding the expert's observing gaze to the necessities of the system.[38]

The assumption behind *shashin* illustrations was that the bodies of plants and animals revealed their membership in a precise species. Hence, their accurate pictorial description in atlases and manuals and their preservation through increasingly refined drying and embalming techniques became standardized instruments to represent species. This accompanied and in certain instances replaced the traditional lexicographical approach of early *honzōgaku* scholars. As I have argued, Shōhaku himself requested accurate illustrations to accompany regional catalogues of species precisely to avoid confusion in identifying species due to local names, synonyms, and homonyms.

The transformation of individual, concrete specimens into material bearers of a set of universal, species-specific abstract features reified epistemological norms. The assiduous labor of *honzōgaku* scholars and their collaborators involved inventorying, collecting, growing, breeding, exchanging, drying, storing, cataloguing, painting, and describing. Specimens-as-species representatives embodied intellectual and material practices contrived to convert particular examples into universal exemplars, which as "social hieroglyphics" concealed social labor.[39]

Specimens-as-species representatives, therefore, were "sensuous things which [were] at the same time suprasensible or social."[40] Their homology with commodities is particularly revealing. Like commodities, species (*shu*) were a product of human labor, an abstraction performed through an array of intellectual and manual practices. Natural species—unless perhaps considered from their cladogenetic history—are by no means natural kinds but social constructs.[41] In that sense, the operations performed by *honzōgaku* scholars were not qualitatively different from those of contemporary Linnaean naturalists.[42] Furthermore, the search for accurate, "true-to-nature" pictorial representations of plants and animals, in Europe as well as in Japan, concealed in the lifelike appearance of specimens-as-species representatives in atlas illustrations the fact that those representations were the result of human labor performed under historically determined social conditions.

Yoshimune's surveys initiated a process of parceling nature into myriads of objects to be inventoried, accumulated, and consumed as material and intellectual commodities. A century later, the thinker Satō Nobuhiro would bring this process to completion by conceptualizing and putting into practice a system of human dominion over nature—mediated by a reorganization of labor, a transformation of the role and scopes of knowledge, and the development of new useful instruments and technologies—which rested on the belief that the natural environment was a potentially inexhaustible reservoir of resources to be exploited for human need.[43] The discipline of *honzōgaku* legitimated this process by giving it doctrinal and institutional authority. As a result of this transformation, *honzōgaku* facilitated the adoption of Western science before and after the Meiji Restoration of 1868. Most importantly, the utilitarian inclination that characterized it since the 1736 surveys helped the Meiji government to mobilize natural knowledge to stimulate industrialization, with all the benefits and costs for the human and natural worlds that characterize the modern world.

Notes

1. Ihara Saikaku, *Seken munezan'yō,* in Taniwaki Masachika, Jinbō Kazuya, Teruoka Yasutaka, eds., *Ihara Saikaku shū,* vol. 3 (Tokyo: Shōgakukan, 1996), 337. I follow the English translation of Ben Befu in *Worldly Mental Calculation: An Annotated Translation of Seken munezan'yō* (Berkeley: University of California Press, 1976), 31.

2. John Stuart Mill, "On the Definition of Political Economy, and on the Method of Investigation Proper to It," originally published in October 1836 in the *London and Westminster Review,* reprinted in *Essays on Some Unsettled Questions of Political Economy,* 2nd ed. (London: Longmans, Green, Reader & Dyer, 1874), essay 5, paragraphs 38 and 48.

3. Ihara Saikaku, *Seken munezan'yō,* 369. English translation in Befu, *Worldy Mental Calculation,* 52.

4. A xerographic reproduction of the survey papers can be found in Morinaga

Toshitarō, Yasuda Ken, eds., *Kyōhō—Genbun shokoku sanbutsuchō shūsei*, 21 vols. (Tokyo: Kagaku Shoin, 1985).

5. Kondō Morishige (Seisai), *Kondō Seisai zenshū* (Tokyo: Kokusho Kankōkai, 1905–1906), vol. 12, 293.

6. Ueno Masuzō, *Hakubutsugakusha retsuden* (Tokyo: Yasaka Shobō, 1991), 11.

7. Quoted in Yasuda Ken, *Edo shokoku sanbutsuchō: Niwa Shōhaku no hito to shigoto* (Tokyo: Shōbunsha, 1987), 25.

8. Ueno, *Hakubutsugakusha retsuden*, 19.

9. Ueno, *Hakubutsugakusha retsuden*, 20. There are no historical sources revealing whether there was any contact between Yoshimune and Shōhaku before 1722, but it is reasonable to believe that Yoshimune may have at least indirectly heard about the young and talented physician-*honzōgakusha* practicing in one of the most vibrant castle towns of his domain, Matsusaka.

10. *Misgurnus anguillicaudatus.*

11. Quoted in Yasuda, *Edo shokoku sanbutsuchō*, 27–29.

12. Yasuda, *Edo shokoku sanbutsuchō*, 29. In Japan before the nineteenth century there was no single term like the English word "nature" that united the entirety of natural phenomena as well as the laws that regulated their existence. Instead, *honzōgaku* scholars conceived of their research on plants and animals in terms of the social function of their intellectual and practical labor. In other words, the names and uses of rocks, plants, and animals depended on their instrumental value for society and the economy. For example, plants and animals for physicians, apothecaries, and orthodox *honzōgaku* scholars were called *honzō* or *yakubutsu*, "medicinal herbs or substances," whereas for encyclopedists and lexicographers they had been *meibutsu*, "names of things." For agronomists and naturalists engaged in survey projects, they were "products," or *sanbutsu*. *Honzōgaku* scholars frequently used the clumsy serial term *sōmokukinjūchūgyokingyokudoseki*, translated as "herbs-trees-birds-beasts-insects-fish-metals-jewels-grounds-stones." And when plants and animals became the focus of popular entertainment, they might be referred to as *misemono*, things for exhibitions and spectacle, or *sukimono*, "curiosities."

13. Ibid.

14. Ibid.

15. Ibid.

16. Ibid.

17. Instructions on how to record various crops were very detailed. For example, in many domains the production of food crops like rice followed different rhythms. Rice was usually recorded under three different rubrics—*wase, nakate,* and *okute*—that is, the first, second, and third harvest of the year, which had to be precisely dated. The problem was that different villages in the same domain might have followed different harvesting calendars or had different numbers of yields. In that case, the Sanbutsu Goyōdokoro collected the data in *wase, nakate,* and *okute,* specifying, however, in explicatory notes the crop yield in villages that did not follow the average harvesting calendar. Yasuda, *Edo shokoku sanbutsuchō*, 31.

18. In case the name did not appear in Shōhaku's guidelines, they followed Ekiken's nomenclature in *Yamato honzō*.

19. Morinaga and Yasuda, *Kyōhō—Genbun shokoku sanbutsuchō shūsei*, vol. 1.

20. Yasuda, *Edo shokoku sanbutsuchō*, 32.

21. Ibid.

22. In order, *Lutra lutra whiteleyi, Nipponia nippon,* and *Canis lupus hodophilax.*

23. Yasuda Ken, "Niwa Shōhaku," in Shimonaka Hiroshi, ed., *Saishiki Edo hakubutsugaku shūsei* (Tokyo: Heibonsha, 1994), 64.

24. That a minor member of the shogunate such as a physician of the Igakukan contacted directly local authorities through their Edo estates managers (*rusui*) was unprecedented. Yasuda, "Niwa Shōhaku," 64.

25. Now in the National Archives of Japan, Kokuritsu Komonjōkan.

26. Mary Elizabeth Berry, *Japan in Print: Information and Nation in the Early Modern Period* (Berkeley: University of California Press, 2006), 54–103.

27. See Wilfrid Blunt, *Linnaeus: The Compleat Naturalist* (Princeton, NJ: Princeton University Press, 2001), 38–70; and Lisbet Koerner, *Linnaeus: Nature and Nation* (Cambridge, MA: Harvard University Press, 1999).

28. See Blunt, *Linnaeus*, 185–197; Patricia Fara, *Sex, Botany, and Empire: The Story of Carl Linnaeus and Joseph Banks* (New York: Columbia University Press, 2003); and Nishimura Saburō, *Rinne to sono shitotachi* (Tokyo: Asahi Sensho, 1997).

29. Peter Raby, *Bright Paradise: Victorian Scientific Travellers* (Princeton, NJ: Princeton University Press, 1997), 45.

30. Quoted in Ueno, *Nihon hakubutsugaku shi*, 66.

31. A repertoire that would be later appropriated by nativist thinkers such as Ueda Akinari (1734–1809) and Hirata Atsutane (1776–1843) and that would contribute to construct the archaic memory of the Japanese "nation" in the works of Yanagita Kunio (1875–1962) and Orikuchi Shinobu (1887–1953). On medieval folktales, see Komine Kazuaki, *Setsuwa no mori* (Tokyo: Taishūkan Shoten, 1991). See also Komatsu Kazuhiko, *Kamikakushi: Ikai kara no izanai* (Tokyo: Kōbundō, 1991); and Kaneda Hisaaki, *Mori no kamigami to minzoku* (Tokyo: Hakusuisha, 1998).

32. See Massimo Raveri, *Itinerari nel sacro: L'esperienza religiosa giapponese* (Venice, Italy: Cafoscarina, 1984).

33. See Massimo Raveri, *Il corpo e il paradiso: Esperienze ascetiche in Asia Orientale* (Venice, Italy: Marsilio, 1992); and Barbara Ambros, *Embracing Pilgrimage: The Ōyama Cult and Regional Religion in Early Modern Japan* (Cambridge, MA: Harvard University Press, 2008). See also Henri Lefebvre, *The Production of Space* (Malden, MA, and Oxford: Blackwell Publishing, 2005).

34. Incidentally, *honzōgaku* scholars became increasingly disinterested in the complex neo-Confucian cosmological apparatus that used to frame earlier encyclopedias of materia medica. While neo-Confucian notions like *tenchi* ("heaven and earth") continued to be utilized by naturalists, by the eighteenth century they were emptied of their metaphysical implications.

35. Quoted in Ueno, *Hakubutsugakusha retsuden*, 9–10.

36. It is for precisely this reason that forestry could develop into a full-scale national industry in the Tokugawa period, as Conrad Totman has demonstrated. See Totman, *The Green Archipelago: Forestry in Preindustrial Japan* (Berkeley: University of California Press, 1989).

37. This description echoes Max Weber's notion of Entzauberung, or "disenchantment," which he adopted from Friedrich Schiller to describe the decline of the network of magical and symbolic correspondences characteristic of the premodern conceptions of the world as a result of the instrumental rationalization and bureaucratization of modern capitalist society. See Max Weber, "Science as a Vocation," in *The Vocation Lectures: "Science as a Vocation," "Politics as a Vocation,"* D. S. Owen and T. B. Strong, eds. (Indianapolis: Hackett,

2004), 1–32. Here I use "disenchantment" in a looser sense—much closer to the one that Theodor W. Adorno developed in *Negative Dialectics* (New York: Continuum, 1973)—mainly to emphasize how various forms of intellectual and manual practices focused on discrete natural objects such as minerals, plants, and animals—analyzed, represented, and manipulated in isolation from their ecosystem. As a result, notions of an integrated, organic, autopoietic cosmos simply ceased to be central in the discourses of Tokugawa intellectuals: totalizing metaphysical constructions simply disappeared from the majority of scholarly texts of the period to leave space for more instrumentally oriented approaches.

38. Michel Foucault, *The Order of Things: An Archaeology of the Human Sciences* (New York: Vintage Books, 1994), 134.

39. The expression comes from Karl Marx, *Capital: A Critique of Political Economy*, vol. 1, trans. Ben Fowkes (London: Penguin Classics, 1990), 167.

40. Modified from Marx, *Capital*, 165.

41. See the two excellent essays, Alexander Bird and Emma Tobin, "Natural Kind," in *Stanford Encyclopedia of Philosophy* (2008) at http://plato.stanford.edu/entries/natural-kinds/ (accessed October 14, 2010), and Marc Ereshefsky, "Species," in *Stanford Encyclopedia of Philosophy* (2010) at http://plato.stanford.edu/entries/species/ (accessed October 14, 2010). See also John Dupré's two articles, "Natural Kinds and Biological Taxa," *Philosophical Review* 90:1 (1981): 66–90, and "In Defense of Classification," *Studies in History and Philosophy of Biological and Biomedical Sciences* 32:2 (2001): 203–219; and John Wilkins, *Species: The History of the Idea* (Berkeley: University of California Press, 2009).

42. See John Dupré, *The Disorder of Things: Metaphysical Foundations of the Disunity of Science* (Cambridge, MA: Harvard University Press, 1993), and John Wilkins, *Species*. See also Nishimura Saburō, *Rinne to sono shitotachi* (Tokyo: Asahi Sensho, 1997).

43. See chapter 14 of my forthcoming *The Name of Nature: Intellectual Networks and Natural History in Early Modern Japan*. See also Ine Yūji, *Satō Nobuhiro no kyozō to jitsuzō* (Tokyo: Iwata Shoin, 2001).

11

Japanese Literature and Environmental Crises

KAREN THORNBER

Ecosystems are always in motion. Some of their changes result directly from human actions and some occur independent of people, while the majority result from a more nebulous combination of human behaviors and nonhuman dynamics. For many millennia, anthropogenic transformations of environments were relatively separate local phenomena, but in the last several centuries these changes have expanded to become subnational, national, regional, and ultimately global events. The greater the anthropogenic modifications of an ecosystem, the more likely this environment is regarded as damaged or in crisis. Since the 1970s, many have argued that the planet itself is in crisis, in large part as a result of human behaviors.

Limiting further degradation and remediating damaged ecosystems require significant cultural change, including "new learning, a changed ethos, and vigorous action."[1] Essential to these endeavors is developing deeper, more nuanced understandings of the fluid relationships among people and ecosystems in specific places and moments, as well as over time and across spaces. Writing, reading, and analyzing literature, in the sense of openly imaginative writings with clear aesthetic ambitions, can perform important roles in this undertaking. As Lawrence Buell has argued, "For technological breakthroughs, legislative reforms, and paper covenants about environmental welfare to take effect, or even to be generated in the first place, requires a climate of transformed environmental values, perception, and will. To that end, the power of story, image, and artistic performance and the resources of aesthetics, ethics, and cultural theory are crucial."[2] Literature's regular and often blatant defiance of logic, precision, and unity enables it to grapple more insistently and penetratingly than most scientific discourse and conventional environmental rhetoric with the contradictory interactions among people and ecosystems. More specifically, literature's intrinsic multivalence allows it to highlight and negotiate—reveal, (re)interpret, and shape—the ambiguity that has long suffused interactions between people and environments, especially those interactions that involve human damage to ecosystems.[3] Ambiguity here emerges not primarily as an ethical or aesthetic value but as a symptom of epistemological uncertainty that is parsed both sympathetically and exactingly as a deficit of consciousness and/or implicit confession of the impotence of writers and literary characters.

This is particularly true of Japanese literature, where the nonhuman plays a central, often dominant role.[4] The attention Japanese literature has devoted to nature since the *Kojiki* (Record of ancient matters, 712 CE), Japan's oldest extant text, and the *Man'yōshū* (Collection of ten thousand leaves, eighth century), the earliest surviving collection of Japanese poetry, is often cited as confirmation of Japanese "love of nature." So consistently have Japanese literature and other art forms discussed, celebrated, and demonstrated sensitivity toward the nonhuman that this "love of nature" has been said to have "uniquely distinguished Japan since before the advent of agriculture."[5] Japanese literature, like Japanese culture, has conventionally been associated with celebrations of "nature" and with touching portraits of relatively harmonious human integration with the nonhuman, nature serving as a refuge from society for dreamers, travelers, and recluses. But in fact, when Japanese literature is read from an ecocritical perspective concerned with the larger environmental implications of human/nonhuman interactions, numerous texts reveal much more complex dynamics among people and their environments than the ecophilia that has generally been assumed.[6] This is not surprising considering the extent of the anthropogenic changes to the archipelago's ecosystems across the millennia.

To be sure, as Edwin Cranston has asserted, "the feeling for the divinity and beauty of the land is one of the most attractive aspects of Man'yō poetry."[7] But some verses in this collection that praise Japan's wondrous terrain also appear to be celebrating people's notable reshaping of it. These include the anthology's second poem: "There are crowds of mountains in Yamato, and among these is Heavenly Mount Kagu. When I [Emperor Jomei, 593–641 CE] climb Mount Kagu, and look out over the land, above the plains the smoke rises and rises (*kunihara wa keburi tachitatsu*); above the seas, the gulls rise and rise (*unahara wa kamame tachitatsu*). A beautiful land, Dragonfly Island, land of Yamato."[8] This verse describes a "land-looking" (*kunimi*) ritual, whereby a ruler would climb a mountain and look out over the land to affirm his power and the prosperity of his terrain.[9] The poem celebrates Emperor Jomei's authority over both parts of his realm; his power is such that he can see water not actually visible from the diminutive Mount Kagu.[10] To be sure, the smoke in this poem often is interpreted as manifesting the spirit of the land and the gulls as manifesting the spirit of the sea. But what are the implications of smoke, presumably from human activity, embodying the spirit of the land? Emperor Jomei's reign (629–641 CE) coincides with the early decades of Japan's "ancient predation" (600–850 CE), an era of construction and logging on a scale never before seen in that country. Its rulers, inspired by the introduction of large-scale architecture from the Asian continent, "dotted the Kinai basin with a plethora of great monasteries, shrines, palaces, and mansions" and eventually felled all the old-growth stands in the region.[11] Read ecocritically and taking into consideration historical circumstances, the poem leaves open the possibility that although gulls and presumably other animals continue to flourish at sea, people have completely overtaken the land. Moreover, the emperor seems not the least disturbed by these changes; in fact, he applauds them. The smoky land not only is declared "beautiful" but also is referred to as "Dragonfly Island" (Akizushima), a common appellation for Japan. Flying animals give the land its name, but the fact that they no longer are mentioned as flying above the land is taken as a sign of progress.

Like most literatures, Japanese literature over the centuries has explored a broad range of human interactions with environments. Although never absent from the corpus of Japanese literature, explicit concern with environmental degradation is most common in twentieth-century creative works. During the Meiji period, Japan's rapid industrialization began damaging landscapes more widely, seriously, and quickly than ever before. Miyazawa Kenji's (1896–1933) moving portraits of diverse ecologies and Shiga Naoya's (1883–1971) descriptions of the Ashio Copper Mine incident (1880s) are among the most frequently cited examples of early twentieth-century environmentally conscious Japanese literature.[12] But they are not anomalous. Although focusing largely on human tragedy, early poetry and prose on the atomic bombings of Hiroshima and Nagasaki often also address devastation of the nonhuman. After the mid-1950s, Japanese literature began to play a more dynamic role in exposing and protesting against the destruction of the nonhuman. Most notable have been creative works that grapple with environmental pollution.

The remainder of this chapter analyzes two of these texts: Ishimure Michiko's (1927–) novel *Kugai jōdo: Waga Minamatabyō* (Sea of suffering and the Pure Land: Our Minamata disease, 1969) and the anthology *Genbakushi 181 ninshū, 1945–2007 nen* (Atomic bomb poetry: Collection of 181 people, 1945–2007, 2007), edited by Nagatsu Kōzaburō, Suzuki Hisao, and Yamamoto Toshio.[13] As their titles suggest, these creative works deal with two of modern Japan's greatest and most persistent human tragedies: the Minamata disease and the atomic bombings of Hiroshima and Nagasaki. *Sea of Suffering* and *Atomic Bomb Poetry* consist for the most part of personal accounts of these disasters, including emotional discussions of the physical and psychological wounds from which many people died and with which even greater numbers continue to live. But these texts also incorporate documentary sources, interweaving government reports as well as journalistic, scientific, and medical articles/accounts, some of which rely heavily on statistics. Ishimure's and Nagatsu's texts validate these more objective sources even as they undermine them, revealing their limits—particularly their inability to convey human and nonhuman suffering.

Significantly, the great anguish about which *Sea of Suffering* and *Atomic Bomb Poetry* speak is not just that of the Japanese people. Not only do both texts, and *Atomic Bomb Poetry* in particular, go out of their way to depict humans around the world as suffering from the effects of nuclear proliferation and industrial pollution. Their many references to global human and nonhuman affliction also advocate what Ursula Heise has identified as eco-cosmopolitanism, or "environmental world citizenship."[14] On the other hand, while advocating eco-cosmopolitan consciousness, *Sea of Suffering* and *Atomic Bomb Poetry* reveal relationships between people and their environments as characterized by substantial ambiguity. These contradictions in human/nonhuman interactions clarify the need for but also in many ways impede the attainment of truly eco-cosmopolitan attitudes, not to mention behaviors. Most simply, Ishimure's and Nagatsu's texts depict people as both determined polluters and haplessly polluted, harmed, and even killed by damaged environments. Notably, under these conditions people continue and in fact often escalate behaviors detrimental to their own vitality and that of other parts of their ecosystems. Ishimure's and Nagatsu's texts examine motivations and means: What drives people to destroy themselves and their surroundings? What allows them to continue doing so even when the consequences of their behaviors become undeniable, if not deadly? When both people and nature are imperiled, to what extent should concern for human health/suffering overshadow concern for the nonhuman? Even more significant, at least as far as interactions among people and the nonhuman are involved, how much environmental suffering can be tolerated? What human displacement of the nonhuman is just, what is unjust, how and by whom is justice determined, and how and by whom should injustice be addressed? Conversely, what are the attitudes of human beings toward nonhuman (re)generation amid continued human suffering, and how are these attitudes modulated? *Sea of Suffering* and *Atomic Bomb Poetry* in general do not ask, much less answer, these questions explicitly. Instead, as is true of many creative works, these diverse texts script environmental-ethical concern, in the words of Lawrence Buell, "not as if it could be translated readily into the terms of prevailing ethical or political programs but as a thought experiment: i.e., in exploratory, often tentative ways complicated by multiple agendas and refusal to take fixed positions."[15]

Contours of Suffering: *Sea of Suffering* and Minamata Disease

The symptoms of Minamata disease, which affected well over three thousand people in and around Minamata (a village on the Shiranui Sea in western Kyushu), are well known even outside Japan, thanks in part to W. Eugene Smith and Aileen M. Smith's powerful photographic volume *Minamata:* severe brain damage, neurological degeneration, physical deformities, numbness, slurred and involuntary speech, involuntary movements, unconsciousness, and death.[16] To this day, Minamata patients, their families, and activists continue to struggle for recognition and compensation.

A creative writer, activist, and native of Minamata, Ishimure has been "by far the most important person in the movement on behalf of Minamata disease patients."[17] The first part of her trilogy on Minamata, *Sea of Suffering* is a patchwork of the narrator's own experiences, moving stories of Minamata sufferers told from multiple points of view, poetry, documents including medical, scientific, and journalistic reports, accounts of the region's rich cultural history, and lyrical depictions of its nonhuman landscapes. The novel both openly defies narrow definitions of genre and, more important, underlines the interdependence of scientific, social scientific, and humanistic interpretations of the experienced world. Chronologically, it loops backward and forward in time, denying suffering a beginning and an end. Demonstrating an eco-cosmopolitan consciousness, it additionally denies suffering any clear spatial borders. Not only does the narrator speak repeatedly of the Ashio Copper Mine incident and of Niigata Minamata disease, the latter of which she describes as creating a vision of a "deep, chasm-like passage that with a cracking sound ran the length of the Japanese archipelago."[18] *Sea of Suffering* also moves outside Japan, exposing the Chisso Corporation's controversial history in colonial Korea, including its damming of the Yalu River between China and Korea and the plight of Koreans under Japanese control more generally, including Korean deaths in the atomic bombings of Hiroshima and Nagasaki.

Sea of Suffering most obviously condemns how readily human life has been sacrificed in the quest for economic prosperity. But Ishimure's text also raises important questions concerning human/nonhuman relationships. The narrator portrays people in the Minamata area as having enjoyed years of harmonious interactions with the natural environment; the novel's opening passage depicts ecosystems before the arrival of the Chisso Corporation as "healthy," as places where people, their cultural artifacts, and the nonhuman flourished and boundaries among the three regularly blurred.[19] Ishimure's next pages depict these allegedly peaceful days as long gone: people have polluted the water with lethal chemicals that have worked their way up the food chain: "Organic mercury never attacked from the front. It lurked densely in the mullets, the clear sea octopuses, and the nocticulae that were such an important part of people's daily lives. It infiltrated deep into the human body together with people's food, their sacred fish."[20] The very animals that sustained people, the very animals on whom the fishers depended for livelihood and life, for physical and spiritual fulfillment, now hasten their deaths, economic and corporeal.

But there is more to the story. Although depicting both people and animals as suffering greatly, *Sea of Suffering* exposes the ready privileging of human anguish. The novel portrays the nonhuman as being discussed and examined—by government and corporate officials, scientists, journalists, teachers, activists, and fishers alike—primarily in relation to its service to the human, whether as a vital source of physical and spiritual nourishment or as a convenient space for depositing waste. People are depicted as alarmed by the mercury levels in fish primarily because they depend on the fish for nourishment. Likewise, people become concerned when confronted with cats with visible symptoms of Minamata disease primarily because they think the fate of the cats might soon be their own; for their part, scientists study cats because they believe the suffering of these animals will provide insights into human distress.

This all is to be expected considering the severity of human suffering caused directly by fish and prefigured by cats. Likewise, human-on-human violence is a central part of the Minamata story and one that, as the hybrid and whirling narrative structure of *Sea of Suffering* suggests, needs to be continually repeated in words, lest it be repeated even more vigorously in actions. But the privileging of human suffering does have ambiguous implications for understanding relationships among people and the nonhuman. How severely must environments harm people before people are motivated to remediate environments? Is preventing or repairing devastation of the nonhuman important only when the health of people is clearly at stake?

Sea of Suffering also posits troubling congruencies between certain aspects of local people's behaviors and attitudes toward nature and the behaviors and attitudes of the Japanese government and the Chisso Corporation. The narrator describes the people of Minamata as long having used the waters around their town as a source of nourishment. To be sure, the narrator remarks concerning one Minamata couple, "They never took more fish than they needed; they spent their days fishing in moderation."[21] This is true even for the fishers who believe the sea their own. One local resident asserts, "I've neither rice paddies nor fields to leave my family. Just the sea, which I think of as my own sea."[22] Yet there is no indication that he has taken more from the sea than he needs. Without question, corporate pollution usually involves disruption and destruction of the nonhuman on a much larger scale than do fishing, hunting, and farming by local peoples. But how fundamentally different is a corporation's using a body of water as its dumping ground from a town's using the same nonhuman body as its source of nourishment? As monographs such as Jared Diamond's *Collapse* have revealed, there is little to prevent seemingly sustainable use from eventually bringing about massive devastation of the nonhuman.[23] Where, then, should/can/must lines be drawn? *Sea of Suffering* gives few answers. In fact, the narrator establishes a sharp dichotomy between the villagers' (directly) killing animals for survival (killing based on need) and Chisso's (indirectly) killing animals for profit (killing based on greed); the former is depicted as preserving human bodies, the latter as destroying both human and nonhuman bodies. But a persistent question remains: What will happen when nonhuman reproduction no longer keeps pace with human reproduction?[24]

Exposés of conflicting attitudes toward and treatment of the nonhuman make *Sea of Suffering* not only a moving portrait of the physical and psychological anguish experienced by the human victims of Minamata disease but also a powerful examination of the complicated relationships among people and the nonhuman.

Green with Anxiety: *Atomic Bomb Poetry* and (Non)human Regeneration

Where Ishimure's *Sea of Suffering* explores some of the paradoxes of negotiating nonhuman suffering amid human anguish, Nagatsu's *Atomic Bomb Poetry* probes the ambiguity of negotiating nonhuman regeneration amid human suffering. Published in 2007, *Atomic Bomb Poetry* is a recent addition to the continually growing corpus of Japanese literature of the atomic bomb.[25] Nagatsu and his coeditors compiled the collection not only so that "the victims of the atomic bombings on August 6 and August 9, 1945, would never be forgotten." They also were determined that "the nuclear weapons used in Hiroshima and Nagasaki would be the first and the last to be deployed" and that "as soon as possible in the twenty-first century the planet would be made a homeland free of nuclear weapons."[26] *Atomic Bomb Poetry* includes selections by some of Japan's most celebrated writers of the atomic bomb, including Tōge Sankichi (1917–1953), Kurihara Sadako (1912–2005), and Hara Tamiki (1905–1951), as well as by a number of lesser-known individuals, including several non-Japanese; many texts were previously published elsewhere, but a significant number, solicited for this collection, appear here for the first time. *Atomic Bomb Poetry* is notable for its intratextuality, with a number of selections citing from or alluding to others in the volume. Writers are identified by their dates of birth (and, if relevant, death), places of birth and residence, and principal publications; survivors and those who visited Hiroshima and Nagasaki shortly after the bombings and were exposed to radiation are identified as such. The anthology is divided into six sections: texts written between 1945 and 1959; a section each for those of the 1960s, 1970s, 1980s, and 1990s; and a final section of texts written after the turn of the twenty-first century. Significantly, this last section contains by far the most writers and texts; in fact, the total numbers of twenty-first-century writers and texts both exceed those of all the other sections combined. This, together with the large number of texts included by writers born after 1945, points to sustained concern over Japan's and the world's future under the nuclear shadow.

The poems in *Atomic Bomb Poetry* vary considerably in length, structure, diction, and subject. Some are exceptionally fragmentary, while others read like polished prose; some focus entirely on human emotion, while others carefully record statistics. Like much Japanese literature of the atomic bomb, they movingly depict the extreme suffering of *hibakusha* (victims and survivors of the bombings) of all nationalities from the 1940s to the present day, as well as the suffering of those exposed to radiation from nuclear testing and other human-on-human violence. They do so even while lamenting the impossibility of ever really conveying in words the traumas these people experienced. But many of the poems also refuse to allow Japan to see itself solely as a victim; they criticize both the United States for developing and deploying the atomic bomb and Japan's wartime government for demanding the complete loyalty of its people and for colonizing and committing atrocities in other parts of Asia. They also denounce late twentieth- and early twenty-first-century politicians and military maneuvers. Adopting an eco-cosmopolitan position, many of the poems voice outrage at the continued worldwide proliferation of nuclear weapons. Like much Japanese literature of the atomic bomb, the poems in *Atomic Bomb Poetry* call on individuals everywhere to devote themselves to creating a more peaceful future.

In addition, although titled *Atomic Bomb Poetry,* Nagatsu's anthology in fact contains a number of prose selections. These include prefaces that address the important relationships between poetry and pacifism and a final section of four essays on topics such as the Manhattan Project, contemporary world politics, and the story behind the collection itself. More than a dozen essays are also scattered throughout the volume, ranging from very personal narrations to short-short stories and (creative) nonfiction. The subject matter itself likely would prevent readers of this collection from becoming too comfortable, but the jarring variety of materials also works powerfully to stave off passivity.

The poetry and prose in *Atomic Bomb Poetry* depict diverse interactions among people and their environments. Not surprisingly, many selections expose the devastation of nature. Inoue Kyūichirō (1909–1999), for instance, opens "Jumoku no nai machi wa sabishii: Hiroshima (1947–49)" (A city without trees is desolate: Hiroshima [1947–49]) with the following lines:

> A city without trees is desolate
> Stones and clay are wet with evening rain
> In the vacant lot behind the temporary barracks
> Green peas are blooming
> Ah, when will the city
> Have the joy of flourishing trees?[27]

Peas are blooming, but larger plants, not yet having had time to thrive, exist only in memory.

Also appearing in significant numbers in *Atomic Bomb Poetry* are texts that depict people at the mercy of devastated environments. Among the most straightforward is Kurihara Sunao's (1953–) twenty-first-century "Bakuhatsu wa mō owatta" (The explosion has finished):

> Irradiated
> air
> Irradiated
> water
> Irradiated
> milk . . .
> Every day
> Children drink 400 cc's
> of irradiated
> milk.
> I've been drinking it for seven days now.
> When
> will we die?[28]

Although the explosion itself was quickly "finished," the resulting pollution of the nonhuman continues to threaten people; the poet suggests that the threat is so powerful that rapid death is inevitable.

More subtle but perhaps over time just as destructive is the alacrity with which certain parts of nature "recover," or at least appear to "recover," from nuclear pollution. To be sure, some poems in *Atomic Bomb Poetry*—including Yamashita Shizuo's (1929–) twenty-first-century "Toita no hito wa" (Person on a shutter)—simply contrast the rapid recovery of the nonhuman with continued human struggles.[29] But an important subset of poems reveals deeper discrepancies—mixed feelings toward, first, a nonhuman environment whose regeneration masks or even erases memories of human suffering, and second, nonhuman regeneration that paradoxically enables further destruction of environments. The poems themselves are often ambiguous on these matters, challenging and unsettling the reader.

Certainly, few would advocate actively preventing regeneration of the nonhuman. At the very least, exposure to a flourishing landscape can give hope to people in despair. But it also can provoke anxiety by masking human injury. For instance, Makabe Jin's (1907–1984) "Midori osanaku" (Young green) reads,

> You likely saw.
> The seven rivers that run so clearly
> reflecting the image of every butterfly, missing not a one,
> . . . Where do they harbor the afterimages of the bloody river,
>   the valley of corpses?[30]

Hara Tamiki's poem "Hika" (Elegy), also included in *Atomic Bomb Poetry*, points to individual suffering concealed by a flourishing nonhuman:

> Green has already come to the willows by the moat
> smiling under the sky, wrapped in drizzly mist
> Water clearly stands still
> asking for an elegy in my heart
> As if all parting words were exchanged so casually
> as if all grief were wiped away so casually.[31]

And Yi Mija concludes her twenty-first-century "Hasu no hana" (Lotus flower), a poem lamenting the multiple traumas experienced by Korean survivors of the atomic bomb, with comments on an oblivious and oppressively verdant nonhuman:

> Suffocating green of life
> Toward a penetratingly clear summer sky
> Pale pink lotus flowers are blooming,
> Rhizomes growing fat in the mud
> As though nothing had happened.[32]

By obscuring trauma, a vibrant nonhuman paradoxically has the potential to propagate suffering.

The sentiments of a school principal shortly after World War II, cited in Isakawa Masomi's (1930–) "Kosumosu no hana" (Cosmos flower, 1970s), echo numerous voices in postwar Hiroshima and Nagasaki:

> For ten years even grass won't grow at the epicenter of the blast
> Despite such rumors
> already by autumn, weeds had sprouted from the rubble.
> In a desolate corner of the school's ruins
> I saw a cosmos flower. . . .
> All right, [I thought], I've somehow got to quickly rent a school building
> and start up classes again. . . .
> It's already been thirty years [since that speech]
> Hiroshima has been remarkably restored
> but there always is a war going on, somewhere in the world.
> Even though the cosmos blooms everywhere and every year.[33]

Witnessing a flower blooming a decade before he thought he would inspires the principal to resume educating the city's children. But the final lines of Isakawa's poem reveal the ambiguous consequences of rapid recovery: three decades after the blast, Hiroshima looked nearly "normal," flowers bloomed around the world, but combat was far from eliminated.[34] "Cosmos Flower" does more than lament the prevalence of war. It paradoxically suggests that Hiroshima's remaining a wasteland might have helped forestall future conflicts.

Likewise, the second half of Nakaoka Jun'ichi's (1937–) twenty-first-century "Midori ga shitatari" (Green trickles)—reflecting the eco-cosmopolitanism so prominent in *Atomic Bomb Poetry*—discusses the 1986 Chernobyl nuclear power plant disaster. The poet then remarks: "The dripping green of 'Beautiful Japan' / Completely conceals this danger-filled scene."[35] "Green Trickles" points not only to the global consequences of the explosions at Chernobyl but also to widespread responsibility for these events and for ecological recovery. Just as significant is the poem's evocation of "beautiful Japan" (*utsukushii* Nihon), appropriated from Kawabata Yasunari's (1899–1972) Nobel Prize acceptance speech.[36] Inherently ambiguous, "beauty"—particularly beauty in the wake of disaster—often can be a sign of rebirth. But regeneration of the nonhuman does not preclude future devastation. In fact, it can give a false sense of security.[37] And this often allows for the continued degradation of both people and the nonhuman.

The March 2011 triple tragedy of the Tōhoku earthquake, tsunami, and Fukushima nuclear meltdowns is likely to have a sustained impact on Japanese literary production. Japan's best-known contemporary authors—Ōe Kenzaburō and Murakami Haruki—have already published on the quake and its aftermath, and numerous figures, from popular writers such as Yoshimoto Banana to authors unknown outside of Japan, have written poems and short stories grappling with the three-way disaster. Increasing anxiety over human and nonhuman futures in Japan and worldwide makes it likely that the dangers of both nuclear weapons and nuclear power will become more central concerns of Japanese literary output. This is particularly true considering the great confusion surrounding the timetable for remediating the radiation pollution of the wide area, both terrestrial and marine, surrounding the Fukushima nuclear power plant.

From earliest times, Japanese literature has illuminated multiple aspects of Japan's natural legacies that are less readily accessible via documentary sources or even direct experience. Literature's style and substance often evoke the empathy required to understand the need for changing attitudes and behaviors vis-à-vis the nonhuman, as well as to enact actual change. Like many of the world's literatures, Japanese literature describes, reminisces, warns, celebrates, condones, and condemns aspects of human/nonhuman interactions in ways more nuanced than other discourses. Most significant, it grapples with the ambiguity that has always suffused interactions among people and their surroundings. To be sure, literature's explorations of these complexities are themselves often paradoxical. But this, perhaps, is precisely the point. Creative texts, with their often demanding and at times unforgiving multivalent discourses, not only provide conflicting perspectives on the empirical world and on the actual and ideal behaviors of human beings. More important, they also embody the many problematic ways the place of people within the planet's ecosystem(s) can be understood.

Notes

1. James Engell, "Plant Beach Grass: Managing the House to Sustain It," Phi Beta Kappa oration, Harvard University (June 2, 2009), 23.

2. Lawrence Buell, *The Future of Environmental Criticism: Environmental Crisis and Literary Imagination* (Malden, MA: Blackwell Publishing, 2005), vi.

3. This has been true since *The Epic of Gilgamesh* (second millennium BCE), an epic poem often considered the first work of world literature. See Louise Westling, *The Green Breast of the New World: Landscape, Gender, and American Fiction* (Athens: University of Georgia Press, 1996), 21; Robert Pogue Harrison, *Forests: The Shadow of Civilization* (Chicago: University of Chicago Press, 1992), 14–18.

4. What constitutes "Japanese literature" has been a matter of some debate. See Karen Thornber, *Empire of Texts in Motion: Chinese, Korean, and Taiwanese Transculturations of Japanese Literature* (Cambridge, MA: Harvard University Asia Center, Harvard-Yenching Institute, Harvard University Press, 2009), 21–22, 399–400. In the present chapter, this term refers simply to that corpus of texts written by individuals whose primary identity is Japanese, regardless of the language used or place of publication. For alternate views on Japanese literature and the environment, see Un'no Keisuke, "Ekokuriteishizumu [Ecocriticism] to

Nihon bungaku: Koronbia [Columbia] daigaku Haruo Shirane kyōju ni kiku" (Ecocriticism and Japanese Literature: Interviewing Professor Haruo Shirane of Columbia University), *Kokubungaku* 52:6 (June 2007): 126; Karatani Kōjin, *Nihon kindai bungaku no kigen* (The origins of modern Japanese literature, Tokyo: Kōdansha, 1980); Karen Colligan-Taylor, *The Emergence of Environmental Literature in Japan* (New York: Garland Publishing, 1990); Gregory Golley, *When Our Eyes No Longer See: Realism, Science, and Ecology in Japanese Modernism* (Cambridge, MA: Harvard University Asia Center, Harvard University Press, 2008).

5. Julia Adeney Thomas, *Reconfiguring Modernity: Concepts of Nature in Japanese Political Ideology* (Berkeley: University of California Press, 2001), 8.

6. For a broad definition of "ecocriticism," see Scott Slovic, *Going Away to Think: Engagement, Retreat, and Ecocritical Responsibility* (Reno: University of Nevada Press, 2008), 27.

7. Edwin Cranston, *A Waka Anthology,* vol. 1: *The Gem-Glistening Cup* (Stanford, CA: Stanford University Press, 1993), 194.

8. *Man'yōshū* (Collection of ten thousand leaves), in *Nihon koten bungaku taikei* 4 (Compendium of classical Japanese literature 4, Tokyo: Iwanami Shoten, 1957), 9–11.

9. Haruo Shirane, ed., *Traditional Japanese Literature: An Anthology, Beginnings to 1600* (New York: Columbia University Press, 2007), 64.

10. Ibid. Jomei's ability to see what ordinary mortals cannot points to his ties to the "other world" of spirits and gods. Mount Kagu is a mere 152 meters high.

11. Conrad Totman, *The Green Archipelago: Forestry in Preindustrial Japan* (Athens: Ohio University Press, 1998), 11.

12. For more on environmentality in Miyazawa's writing, see Golley, *When Our Eyes No Longer See;* Komori Yōichi, *Saishin: Miyazawa Kenji kōgi* (Lectures on Miyazawa Kenji, Tokyo: Asahi Sensho, 1996).

13. For more on other Japanese and East Asian texts and environmental degradation, see Karen Thornber, *Ecoambiguity: Environmental Crises and East Asian Literatures* (Ann Arbor: University of Michigan Press, 2012).

14. Ursula Heise, *Sense of Place and Sense of Planet: The Environmental Imagination of the Global* (New York: Oxford University Press, 2008), 10. For more on "world environmental citizenship," see Patrick Hayden, *Cosmopolitan Global Politics* (Burlington, VT: Ashgate, 2005). Eco-cosmopolitanism expands on cosmopolitanism as understood by Kwame Anthony Appiah in *Cosmopolitanism: Ethics in a World of Strangers* (New York: W. W. Norton & Co., 2006), xv. The American ecologist and environmentalist Aldo Leopold (1887–1948) articulates an early form of eco-cosmopolitanism in *A Sand County Almanac: And Sketches Here and There* (New York: Oxford University Press, 1968), 209.

15. Lawrence Buell, "Literature as Environmental(ist) Thought Experiment," in *Ecology and the Environment: Perspectives from the Humanities,* ed. Donald K. Swearer, with Susan Lloyd McGarry (Cambridge, MA: Center for the Study of World Religions, Harvard Divinity School, 2009), 21.

16. W. Eugene Smith and Aileen M. Smith, *Minamata: Words and Photos* (New York: Holt, Rinehart, and Winston, 1975). For key dates in the Minamata story, see Timothy S. George, *Minamata: Pollution and the Struggle for Democracy in Postwar Japan* (Cambridge, MA: Harvard University Asia Center, Harvard University Press, 2001), xviii–xix, 17.

17. George, *Minamata,* 155. Livia Monnet introduces Ishimure's life and writings, as well as the cultural imaginary of *Sea of Suffering,* in "'A Book for the Future': *Kugai jōdo* and

the Minamata Protest Movement," in *Paradise in the Sea of Sorrow: Our Minamata Disease,* trans. Livia Monnet (Ann Arbor: Center for Japanese Studies, University of Michigan, 2003), vii–xxxi.

18. Ishimure Michiko, *Kugai jōdo: Waga Minamatabyō* (Sea of suffering and the Pure Land: Our Minamata disease), in *Ishimure Michiko zenshū* 2 (Complete works of Ishimure Michiko 2, Tokyo: Fujiwara Shoten, 2004), 218. Confirmed in 1965, Niigata Minamata disease was caused by methyl mercury released into the Agano River by the Shōwa Electrical Company.

19. Aldo Leopold speaks of "land health" as "the capacity of the land for self-renewal." Leopold, *A Sand County Almanac,* 221. See also Gregg Mitman, "In Search of Health: Landscape and Disease in American Environmental History," *Environmental History* 10:2 (2005).

20. Ishimure, *Kugai jōdo,* 107.

21. Ibid., 112.

22. Ibid., 167–168.

23. Jared Diamond, *Collapse: How Societies Choose to Fail or Succeed* (New York: Viking, 2005).

24. See Conrad Totman's comments cited by Gregory Pflugfelder in "Preface, Confessions of a Flesh Eater: Looking below the Human Horizon," in *JAPANimals: History and Culture in Japan's Animal Life,* ed. Gregory M. Pflugfelder and Brett L. Walker (Ann Arbor: Center for Japanese Studies, University of Michigan, 2005), xv.

25. For overviews of the genre, see Karen Laura Thornber, "Atomic Bomb Writers," in *Modern Japanese Writers,* ed. Jay Rubin (New York: Charles Scribner's Sons, 2001), 49–70; John Whittier Treat, *Writing Ground Zero: Japanese Literature and the Atomic Bomb* (Chicago: University of Chicago Press, 1995).

26. Nagatsu Kōzaburō, Suzuki Hisao, and Yamamoto Toshio, "Sekaijū no heiwa o makoto ni negau hitotachi e: 'Genbakushi 181 ninshū' eigoban goaisatsu" (To the people of the world sincerely longing for peace: Foreword to the English edition of *Atomic Bomb Poetry: Collection of 181 People*), in *Against Nuclear Weapons: A Collection of Poems by 181 Poets, 1945–2007,* trans. Koriyama Naoshi et al. (Tokyo: Coal Sack Publishing Co., 2007), 3.

27. Inoue Kyūichirō, "Jumoku no nai machi wa sabishii: Hiroshima (1947–49)" (A city without trees is desolate, Hiroshima 1947–49), in *Genbakushi 181 ninshū, 1945–2007 nen* (Atomic bomb poetry: Collection of 181 people, 1945–2007), ed. Nagatsu Kōzaburō, Suzuki Hisao, and Yamamoto Toshio (Tokyo: Kōru Sakkusha, 2007), 56.

28. Kurihara Sunao, "Bakuhatsu wa mō owatta" (The explosion has finished), in *Genbakushi 181 ninshū,* 190–191.

29. Yamashita Shizuo, "Toita no hito wa" (Shutter person), in *Genbakushi 181 ninshū,* 269.

30. Makabe Jin, "Midori osanaku" (Young green), in *Genbakushi 181 ninshū,* 48. Makabe was a prolific poet, critic, and editor.

31. Hara Tamiki, "Hika" (Elegy), in *Genbakushi 181 ninshū,* 22.

32. Yi Mija, "Hasu no hana" (Lotus flower), in *Genbakushi 181 ninshū,* 150.

33. Isakawa Masomi, "Kosumosu no hana" (Cosmos flower), in *Genbakushi 181 ninshū,* 72.

34. Hiroshima and Nagasaki, in fact, looked "normal" long before the mid-1970s.

35. Nakaoka Jun'ichi, "Midori ga shitatari" (Green trickles), in *Genbakushi 181 ninshū,* 227.

36. Nakaoka's poem also anticipates former Japanese prime minister Abé Shinzō's (1954–) remarks, on assuming office in 2006, that his goal was creating a "beautiful country, Japan" (*utsukushii kuni*, Nihon). Abé Shinzō, "Dai 165 kai kokkai ni okeru Abe naikaku sōri daijin shoshin hyōmei enzetsu" (General policy speech by Prime Minister Abé to the 165th session of the Diet), http://www.kantei.go.jp/abespeech/2006/09/39syosin.html.

37. An excellent example of this phenomenon is Sakai Izumi, ed., *Genbaku shishū: Hachigatsu* (Collection of atomic bomb poems: August, Tokyo: Gōdō Shuppan, 2008).

12

Japanese Environmental Policy
Lessons from Experience and Remaining Problems

KEN'ICHI MIYAMOTO
Translated by Jeffrey E. Hanes

Following the Pacific War, Japan experienced Minamata disease and other terrible effects of pollution. Since the late 1960s, due largely to public criticism of pollution and the rise of an antipollution citizens' movement, Japan has addressed the problems of air pollution (sulfur dioxide and nitrogen dioxide) and water and soil pollution (mercury and cadmium). This positive result has impelled numerous researchers from the West to conduct surveys and research in Japan on its antipollution measures and policies. Although we cannot assert that Japan has advanced as much as the European Union from the 1990s in its environmental policies and ecological activism, among the nations of Asia—including the Republic of Korea and the People's Republic of China—Japan's environmental research and policies still exert a powerful influence. This chapter explores the historical lessons that can be drawn from Japan's environmental policy making to date as well as the key environmental policy challenges that confront Japan today.

Pollution Problems before World War II

In the process of promoting civilization on a Western model in the Meiji Era (1868–1912), Japan reproduced the environmental problems experienced earlier in Europe and the United States. Whereas England took three hundred years to develop its modern economy following the industrial revolution, Japan pushed to accomplish the same task in a few decades. Just as it reproduced the level of economic development in the West, Japan also reproduced the environmental problems of the West. During the era of primitive accumulation, the aggressive exploitation of mineral resources—such as copper at Ashio, Besshi, Hitachi, and Kosaka—resulted in toxic mining runoff; later, following Japan's industrial revolution, heavy industry in such places as Yahata, Amagasaki, and Kawasaki produced air and water pollution; and still later, urban and regional development wrought the destruction of the natural and historical landscape. Rather than occurring gradually and serially, as they had in Europe and the United States, these pollution problems followed rapidly, one upon the other, creating an overlapping pattern of environmental destruction.

Under the "Wealthy Country/Strong Military" (*fukoku-kyōhei*) policy, the Meiji government did not promulgate laws or regulations related to worker safety or environmental pollution, nor did it prioritize urban planning or decent housing and living conditions. Kitakyushu's Yahata, then the largest steel-producing city in East Asia, did not possess a single centimeter of sewer line until 1961, resulting in deficient public hygiene that overlapped other problems such as labor accidents and environmental pollution. Although the residents of places like Yahata at first considered smoke "a symbol of urban development," they soon launched an anti-pollution movement as conditions grew worse and impelled the initiation of pollution control measures. More than any other, the Ashio Copper Mine Pollution Case had a decisive impact on prewar Japan. Because there is ample scholarship on Ashio, I will not attempt to address its significance to the history of modern Japan here—except to note that toward the end of the Meiji period, the corporate and public spheres alike raised their voices again in a repeat performance of that disaster and implemented pollution control measures. By the end of the Taisho period (1912–1926), antipollution movements pushed forward by local residents established the basic principles that inform the pollution control measures of the present day. Over the next few pages, let us take a longer view of the major pollution incidents that marked the modern era.

THE WORLD'S TALLEST SMOKESTACK: THE CASE OF HITACHI MINING

Toward the end of Meiji Era, Hitachi Mining (now Hitachi Ltd.) in Ibaraki Prefecture incited a vocal protest from local farmers over air pollution. Hitachi sent one of its engineers, Kaburagi Tokuji, to talk with the leaders. Kaburagi, who had studied forest pollution at Tokyo University, began monitoring the altostratus above the Hitachi Mine—the first time such monitoring had taken place in Japan. On the basis of his findings, Hitachi erected the world's tallest smokestack, at 156 meters in height, on a mountain 325 meters high atop the mine in 1914. This smokestack dispersed sulfur dioxide (SO2) emissions and, in the process, reduced smoke pollution by 80 percent.[1]

THE FIRST SUCCESSFUL LAWSUIT BROUGHT BY FARMERS: THE CASE OF OSAKA ALKALI

Osaka Alkali (now Ishihara Sangyo Kaisha, Ltd.), the largest chemical factory in Japan at the beginning of the Taisho period, did such grave damage to local rice fields with its sulfur dioxide emissions that local landlords and farmers sued the firm. The Osaka Higher Court of Appeals initially decided the case in favor of the complainants, but the Supreme Court reversed the decision and sent the case back down to the Osaka Higher Court. In 1919, the Osaka Higher Court ruled once again in the farmers' favor in an epoch-making decision wherein Osaka Alkali admitted fault. Although the company did not build a smokestack quite as tall as Hitachi Mining's, it did erect a smokestack thirty-three meters high to disperse the acrid smoke from its chemical operations.[2]

THE WORLD'S FIRST LEGAL MEASURES REGARDING AIR POLLUTION: SUMITOMO METAL MINING CO.

Over the course of fifty years, thanks to the antipollution struggles of local farmers, Japan witnessed the world's first deployment of smoke extraction and desulfurization technologies in the so-called Shisakajima Sulfur Dioxide Incident. The struggle began in 1893 with protests by farmers in the vicinity of Sumitomo's Niihama Smelting Works in Ehime Prefecture on the island of Shikoku. The company refused to accept responsibility for the crop damage and in 1904 elected instead to move the facility offshore to the uninhabited island of Shisakajima. By 1905, four counties along the shore of the Inland Sea opposite Shisakajima reported serious damage to crops. In the shadow of a fierce protest movement by local farmers, the government intervened. Starting in 1910, antipollution measures were taken and a compensation agreement was reached between the Farmers Smoke Pollution Eradication Alliance and the Sumitomo Metal Mining Company. In 1939, after having renegotiated the antipollution measures annually, Sumitomo succeeded in perfecting an experimental smoke extraction technology pioneered in Germany. Although this brought the struggle between the two parties to a close, it is important to note that between 1910 and 1939, Sumitomo Metal Mining paid out 8.48 million yen to victims' groups—a figure larger than the budget for fiscal year 1939 for Ehime Prefecture. Rather than being distributed to individuals, the money was used for regional development. It funded the construction and management costs of several local institutions, including public high schools, four new agricultural schools, a girl's school, a livestock auction, and a marketplace for domestic animals. At the time, Sumitomo Metal declared the compensation arrangement "a weighty [corporate] burden unmatched in any other country of the world." Later, when Sumitomo Metal established Sumitomo Chemistry to produce ammonium sulfate from the waste created by their smoke extraction apparatus, the company acknowledged that it had received great benefit, "making good from bad."[3]

THE MOVEMENT TO ERADICATE SOOT AND SMOKE IN OSAKA

In Osaka, the so-called Manchester of the Orient, air pollution seriously endangered the health of residents. Under Mayor Seki Hajime, a renowned social policy thinker and former professor at the Tokyo Commercial School (now Hitotsubashi University), Osaka established one of the few laboratories of public health in the world to monitor soot and smoke emissions, with the goal of eradicating smog altogether.[4]

Up to this point, we have focused exclusively on prototypical examples of antipollution policy. During the 1910s and 1920s, the so-called Era of Taisho Democracy, public opinion ran high against pollution. Although the antipollution movement was sufficiently active at the time that corporations and local governments across Japan were impelled to implement pollution control measures, following the fall of democracy and the beginning of World War II such activity was rendered virtually nonexistent.

In the prewar period, under such laws as the National Treasure Preservation Law and the Historic Scenic Monument Preservation Law, Japan set about preserving historic shrines and temples and designating protected scenic and tourist zones. As is well known, however, the bombing of Japanese cities at the end of the war resulted in the destruction of the built environment and the ecosystem alike. Not only did Japan suffer terrible loss of human life, it also lost historical and natural landscapes.

High-Speed Growth and the Explosive Growth of Pollution after World War II

Following World War II, Japan abandoned the pollution control measures it had taken in the prewar period and began promoting a focused economic development policy of high-speed growth. This resulted in severe pollution.[5]

THE FOUR MAJOR POSTWAR POLLUTION CASES

Minamata Disease

In 1956, Minamata disease was discovered in the city of Minamata in Kumamoto Prefecture. The disease was caused by methyl mercury, a by-product of the manufacture of acetylene and acetaldehyde, which was discharged into Minamata Bay in wastewater by an electrochemical company called Chisso. This wastewater polluted fishing grounds and shellfish farms, whose products were eventually eaten by unknowing local consumers. In 1959, a research team at Kumamoto University testified that the health problems reported by local residents were traceable directly to the methyl mercury released in wastewater from the Chisso factory. Until Chisso finally discontinued the production of acetylene and acetaldehyde in 1968, however, neither the company nor the government would acknowledge this as a case of environmental pollution. Through the intervening years, Chisso discharged large amounts of methyl mercury into the Shiranui Sea. In 1973, when victims won their first trial related to Minamata disease, Chisso was held responsible for the first time. During the repeated trials that followed, the government continued to deny any responsibility. Finally, in 2005 the Japanese Supreme Court acknowledged that the government also bore responsibility. Although the epidemiological research on Minamata disease has yet to determine the exact number of victims, it is estimated that victims in Kumamoto Prefecture numbered about twenty thousand, with about ten thousand more in Kagoshima Prefecture. Of these, only two thousand have been officially designated as victims of Minamata disease; yet twelve thousand more have been awarded medical assistance by the government. With the government continuing to this day to deny fault, three thousand local residents have demanded recognition as official victims, and about half that many have taken the government to court. In 2009, the government enacted the Minamata Disease Special Measures Law for the relief of undesignated victims. But we will have to wait and see whether this offers all victims the relief they deserve.[6]

Niigata Minamata Disease

Because the government was late in introducing anti-Minamata measures, the disease also appeared in Niigata Prefecture in 1964. In 1967, a governmental research team traced the outbreak to wastewater from a Showa Denko electronics factory. The company for its part denied the accusation, attributing the pollution instead to agricultural chemicals released by an earthquake. Local victims eventually sued Showa Denko and won their case in 1971. Nonetheless, among the 2,178 estimated cases, the government designated only 692 as Minamata disease.[7]

Itai-Itai Disease

Itai-Itai disease (cadmium poisoning) resulted from tainted wastewater discharged into the Jinzū River in Toyama Prefecture from the Kamioka Mine operated by Mitsui Mining and Smelting Company, Ltd. (Mitsui Kinzoku). The wastewater polluted drinking water and rice fields, leading to serious kidney and bone marrow damage in victims. In this case, too, the corporation and the government obstructed serious investigation into the cause of the pollution. Consequently, the victims took Mitsui Mining and Smelting to court, winning their case in 1971. In the end, the government officially acknowledged only 195 victims of the disease, almost all of whom were middle-aged women who had given birth to more than one affected child.[8]

Yokkaichi Air Pollution

The incident that has had the greatest influence on postwar Japanese environmental policy is the air pollution emitted by the Yokkaichi industrial complex. This was the result of Japan's postwar policy of high-speed growth, which relied heavily on the oil supplied by the petrochemical industry for fuel and raw materials. The Yokkaichi petrochemical complex, which was the model for such development, was responsible for air pollution that triggered asthma in approximately one thousand identifiable victims in 1960. The central government, which was avidly promoting similar petrochemical development projects around the country, declined to treat the sulfur dioxide emissions as pollution and thus introduced palliative measures alone. In response, the victims sued six different companies in the petrochemical complex, winning their suit in 1972.

This trial made one thing crystal clear: that pollution-related ailments such as asthma, unlike Minamata disease, afflicted victims anywhere and everywhere (not just Yokkaichi) that sulfur dioxide or nitrogen dioxide were emitted from petrochemical products used by factories or automobiles. Not only was the government thus compelled to take measures to prevent such pollution throughout the nation, it conceded that environmental assessments should be conducted prior to the initiation of future regional development projects in order to avoid the severe pollution that had afflicted Yokkaichi.[9]

METROPOLITAN POLLUTION

Pollution worsened in big cities during the postwar period due to the sharp increase in population that accompanied urban industrialization, as well the sharp rise in automobile traffic. As shown in figure 12.1, the city of Osaka experienced 165 days of smog in 1960. In Nishi Yodogawa Ward of Osaka, the levels of sulfur dioxide exceeded 1–3 parts per million (ppm) on many days. While Osaka accounted for one of every two thousand victims of metropolitan air pollution at

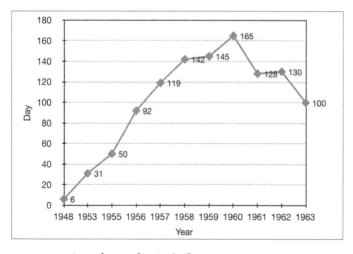

FIGURE 12.1 Annual smog days in Osaka. SOURCE: OSAKA KŌGAI TAISAKU SHITSU.

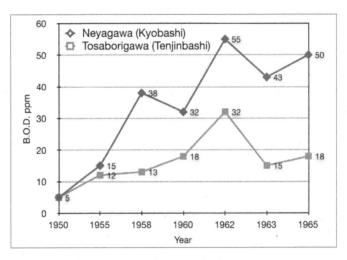

FIGURE 12.2 Change in BOD of rivers in Osaka. SOURCE: OSAKA KŌGAI TAISAKU SHITSU.

the time, similar problems were rapidly springing up across the nation. By 1988, the number of air pollution victims designated by the government reached one hundred thousand, and polluting companies were paying out approximately 100 billion yen per year in victim compensation.

The rivers of Osaka were also polluted. As shown in figure 12.2, the wastewater from industry and household use contained high levels of biochemical oxygen demand (BOD), measuring 50 ppm over the ordinary level of 5 ppm. Osaka's rivers had become drainage ditches of sewage, and the pollution and stench tormented riverside residents.

From the middle of World War II, as they pumped up groundwater and gas, factories in Osaka's coastal industrial zone began to sink. As shown in figure 12.3, cumulative subsidence in the Nishi Kujō district between 1935 and 1962 measured 280 centimeters. In 1961, when a typhoon hit the city, 110,000 homes were flooded, affecting 470,000 people. In short, by the 1960s, the major metropolises and industrial cities of Japan were in a hellish condition that, left unaddressed, would have resulted in serious damage to the health of all urban residents.[10]

DESTRUCTION OF NATURE, LANDSCAPE, AND HISTORICAL CULTURAL ASSETS

The rebuilding of war-devastated cities was largely achieved through urban planning that prioritized the construction of wide roads and tall steel-reinforced concrete buildings. Given the bland uniformity of postwar reconstruction, all urban neighborhoods were reborn as "Little Tokyos" with little individuality.

The unique landscapes of prewar Japanese cities were lost. In the coastal areas, land was reclaimed for factories and port facilities; and on the outskirts, forests and uncultivated fields were destroyed for the construction of "new town" suburbs. As shown in figure 12.4, the most beautiful landscapes in Japan, bordering the Inland Sea, were subject to increasing land reclamation.[11]

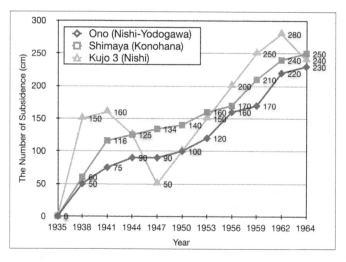

FIGURE 12.3 Change in land subsistance in Osaka City. SOURCE: OSAKA KŌGAI TAISAKU SHITSU.

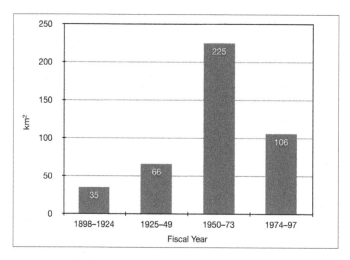

FIGURE 12.4 Shifting of reclaimed land of the Seto Island Sea. SOURCE: MINISTRY OF THE ENVIRONMENT AND MINISTRY OF LAND, INFRASTRUCTURE, TRANSPORT, AND TOURISM.

DEFICIENCIES OF POLLUTION CONTROL MEASURES

Learning from the prewar experience of pollution, a number of postwar local governments passed pollution prevention ordinances: Metropolitan Tokyo in 1949, Kanagawa Prefecture in 1951, Osaka Prefecture in 1954, and Fukuoka Prefecture in 1955. The regulatory standard set by Osaka Prefecture prescribed acceptable levels for labor accidents and occupational disease that were simply not suitable as a standard for pollution prevention. Nonetheless, it was this standard that South Korea later imported. The Fukuoka Management Association opposed the Fukuoka Prefecture ordinance, asserting that "the most important issue today is to expand and develop mining and manufacturing. If we employ this ordinance, it will become difficult to expand business. It is our serious concern that we will fail to lure companies into setting up new plants and will thus see contraction and stagnation of production. It is far too early in the game to enact restrictive ordinances such as these." Thus, in actuality, antipollution measures met with obstruction in the immediate postwar era.[12]

In 1955 and again in 1957, the Ministry of Welfare prepared legislation for the introduction of the new national Human Environment Pollution Prevention standard. But they met with the opposition of Keidanren (Japan Business Federation) and other corporate groups, who argued that it was too early to introduce such legislation and face internal divisions within the government itself. In 1958, after fishermen angered by wastewater pollution in the Edogawa Ward of Tokyo broke into the Honshu Seishi Paper Factory in protest, the government enacted two new laws: the Water Quality Law and the Industrial Wastewater Regulation Law. Ironically, neither of these laws was deemed applicable to Minamata disease.[13]

With air pollution growing worse across the nation, the government enacted the Clean Air Act in 1962. Yokkaichi was initially exempted from the new law, but under local pressure the law was applied retroactively the following year. The Clean Air Act stipulated a standard of 2,200 ppm and below for smokestack sulfur dioxide emission levels. This standard was actually higher than the 1,900 ppm discharged on average by the prewar smelting operation at Shisakajima mentioned earlier. Not only did the Clean Air Act apply a slipshod emissions standard, it also permitted companies to avoid investing in expensive new smoke extraction and desulfurization technologies by simply erecting taller smokestacks. While Hitachi Mining counted only one smokestack in the prewar period, the postwar industrial complex at Yokkaichi had nearly too many to count. Although not all smokestacks could be heightened, those that were resulted in the spread of air pollution damage to an even wider area than before.

In 1967, Japan passed the Basic Law for Environmental Pollution Control. As will be discussed later, this pioneering environmental policy legislation was introduced by a government that feared a slowdown of economic growth in the face of mounting pressure from a burgeoning antipollution movement. The fundamental objective of the law was to "devise a way of harmonizing [the twin goals] of economic development and preservation of the human environment" (Article 2). In prioritizing the goal of economic development—by which the framers meant ensuring corporate profits—the law effectively deprioritized preservation of the human environment. While this law represented the first legitimate use of legislation to set environmental standards, its impact was severely compromised by the law's flawed conceptual framework. The panel of experts called in to set sulfur dioxide emission levels proposed an average of 0.05 ppm per year, but the law instead set the level at 0.05 ppm per day. In other words, the law set an emission standard far less demanding than the experts proposed. This standard equaled the average emissions measured in the Tobata Ward of Kitakyushu and the Shinjuku district of Tokyo at the time, thus implicitly identifying the emission levels of Kitakyushu and Shinjuku as an acceptable standard. Consequently, the law did nothing to prevent the spread of air pollution.[14]

The Citizens Residential Movement and the Advancement of Environmental Policy

DISTINGUISHING FEATURES OF JAPANESE ENVIRONMENTAL POLICY MAKING

In 1985, H. Weidner, a German environmental researcher, produced a comparison of the environmental policies of Japan and Germany. He noted that Japan worked from the bottom up in establishing environmental legislation and policy, relying heavily on the influence of public opinion and popular activism, while German decisions were taken from the top down by the government and the political parties. In Japan, it is fair to say that citizens' environmental activism led directly to environmental assessments, the environmental regulatory system, environmental pollution standards, aggregate pollution regulations, aid and compensation for victims, epidemiological research, nature and landscape preservation policies, and other key antipollution measures. In addition, these citizens' movements were supported by experts, including university and laboratory researchers, lawyers, and doctors. Recognizing that the victims were being overlooked prejudicially, these experts devoted themselves to the empirical investigation of environmental damage, causal analysis, and relief for victims.[15]

DISTINGUISHING FEATURES OF POSTWAR CITIZENS' ENVIRONMENTAL ACTIVISM

The textbook on postwar antipollution activism was written by the towns of Mishima, Numazu, and Shimizu in Shizuoka Prefecture during their movement against the local petrochemical complex in 1963–1964. In order to assist Sumitomo Chemical and the Fuji Oil Company in the construction of a petrochemical complex, the central government and the Shizuoka prefectural government had designated the region a special industrial zone. In an effort to protect local industries, including agriculture, fishing, tourism, and light manufacturing, local residents initiated the long-running "No More Yokkaichi" movement. One-third of the region's voters participated in a massive antipollution demonstration, illustrating the extent of local opposition, and all three local assemblies, as well as the Shizuoka Prefectural Assembly, finally called for a halt to the development project. This was the first time that pressure from a citizens' environmental movement succeeded in halting a government-supported corporate development project, and it owed its success to three main factors.

First, unlike the prewar period when antipollution activism took the form of a confrontation between different industries—namely, the manufacturing industry versus the agricultural and fishing industries—the activists in Shizuoka mounted a citizen's movement to defend the fundamental human rights of health and human life against pollution and to preserve the cultural landscape of Mount Fuji. Up to this point, the key players in Japan's social movements were reformist political parties and labor unions. By contrast, the Mishima-Numazu Movement, formed by grassroots stakeholders, was citizen centered. Local agricultural cooperatives, fishing cooperatives, chambers of commerce and industry, and medical and pharmacists associations that had once been the mainstay of the conservative political establishment found themselves participating in public demonstrations.

Second, this citizens' movement was a scientific movement. Experts from the National Institute of Genetics, as well as local teachers from the Numazu Technical High School with expertise on air pollution, formed special research teams. With tiny budgets, they managed to conduct inventive environmental assessments and publish timely reports. In reaction, the government formed its own research committee and, mobilizing military planes from the Self-Defense Forces, conducted the first basic environmental assessment of its kind in Japan. The two assessments were totally different: the local group insisted that there was a serious pollution threat, while the government said there was none. As scientists from both of groups debated the results, it became clear that the government's survey results were full of errors and problems. Local citizens subsequently participated in more than three hundred "Lessons from Kōgai" sessions conceived to bolster their scientific understanding of the issues at stake.

Third, the movement galvanized the energy of the people by making the most of postwar democracy and its emphasis on popular rights. Rather than petitioning the central government, activists set about changing policy at the local level. The times had changed since the days of the Ashio Mining Pollution Incident of the early 1900s. In 1960s Shizuoka, the local government had no alternative but to call a halt to regional development—and the central government and industry had no choice but to comply—because the overwhelming majority of local people were in opposition. This citizens' activism was the key to success.[16]

The success at Mishima-Numazu exerted a powerful influence on other citizens' movements across Japan. Following the model of the Mishima-Numazu Movement, antipollution criticism and popular activism spread nationwide, resulting in environmental assessments, study groups, and pressure on local governments. Previously, the labor movement was central to social activism, but from this point forward citizens' movements gained political strength as a new form of social movement.

THE ENVIRONMENTAL POLICIES OF REFORM-MINDED LOCAL GOVERNMENTS

With the upsurge in citizen activism in response to pollution and urban problems—calling for environmental preservation, human welfare, and local autonomy—local representatives affiliated with the Social Democratic and the Communist parties began to make waves in urban Japan. Such leaders accounted for one-third of all local government representatives at the peak of their influence. While they opposed conservative politics, they did not advocate revolution. Instead, they strove for peace under the postwar constitution, basic human rights, and popular democracy. In opposition to the antipollution measures implemented by the central government—measures that prioritized corporate profits—leaders such as Tokyo's Governor Minobe Ryōkichi committed themselves to the goal of prioritizing the human environment. In 1979, Minobe imposed a legal obligation on businesses to prevent pollution, introducing epoch-making regulations under the Tokyo Metropolitan Environmental Pollution Control Ordinance, designed to set stringent new environmental standards. In response, the central government declared the regulations illegal and put up such obstacles to their implementation as refusing to allow the city to issue new municipal bonds. But with pollution across the nation growing more serious, international criticism toward Japan growing more severe, and scientific support for Tokyo's ordinance growing stronger, the government convened the "National Parliament on Pollution" toward the end of 1970. The primary objective was a wholesale revision of the Basic Law for Environmental Pollution Control focused on the human environment. Thirteen new laws related to environmental policy were enacted, and in 1971 Japan established the Environmental Agency.

From this time forward, until the early 1980s, reform-minded local governments implemented much stricter policies than the central government. What drew a great deal of international attention was that local governments cooperated with local residents to set up operations centers and conclude agreements devoted to pollution prevention. They issued newsletters with information on pollutants and pollution-reduction plans, playing a concrete regulatory role, and ultimately they forged more than three thousand different agreements of various sorts.[17]

POLLUTION TRIALS AND POLLUTION RELIEF

It is relatively easy to cultivate reformist governments in local settings where the majority opinion among the public is opposed to pollution. But in places such as Minamata or Yokkaichi, where corporate influence is strong, this is a difficult proposition. Because local administrations cannot always be relied on to seek reform, as in the so-called Four Major Postwar Pollution Incidents, public lawsuits are often the only way to recover human rights and demand justice. As noted above, supported by the nationwide public opinion against pollution, researchers and lawyers have volunteered their time, working pro bono, to provide support to pollution victims. In addition, the mass media has offered support, helping plaintiffs to overcome the odds against victory in pollution trials and come out as winners.

Pollution trials have exerted a powerful influence on environmental policy. In the case of Yokkaichi, in particular, a prominent precedent was set for rulings (and appropriate compensation) that assessed broad-based responsibility for injuries rather than requiring individuals to show cause and effect. The Yokkaichi decision stated that plaintiffs could be designated as air pollution victims—whether or not they could specify the source of pollution that caused their medical condition—simply by verifying that they had lived in the polluted area in question for a fixed period of time. For the first time in a pollution trial, epidemiology was used to adjudicate a decision. Beyond this, the court decided that randomly discharging a mixture of pollutants was illegal and that guilty companies had a blanket responsibility to compensate all victims whether or not the victims could trace a specific ailment to pollution caused by a specific company. The Yokkaichi decision was applied to the new legal principle of "collective illegal conduct" for polluters located in the same general area. Despite being held to a high standard of environmental regulations, the petrochemical industry continued to cause serious pollution. Accordingly, the court ruled that even in the absence of explicit violations of environmental law, in instances of egregious, pollution-related injuries companies could be prosecuted as polluters on the grounds that the legal standards themselves were deficient.[18]

Although the government was not prosecuted directly in the Four Major Postwar Pollution Cases, the verdicts revealed serious deficiencies in existing laws that required it to initiate new regulations for legal relief. Fearing that the verdicts had also worsened their social image, companies demanded that the government bureaucracy seek ways to solve Japan's pollution problems. Victims also requested help from the government bureaucracy to deal with cases that involved long trials and heavy expense. In response, the government enacted the world's first Pollution-Related Health Damage Compensation Law in 1973, utilizing precedents set for victim compensation during earlier pollution trials involving cases in Osaka, Amagasaki, and Yokkaichi. Under the new law, epidemiological studies formed the basis for assessment of injuries to victims, and the principle of collective corporate responsibility was introduced. Along with the Workers Accident Compensation Law, this new law represented an epoch-making response to victim relief from industrial disaster. Beyond providing compensation to the victims of air pollution, the new Pollution-Related Health Damage Compensation Law offered relief to the victims of Minamata disease, Itai-Itai disease, and other ailments caused by arsenic poisoning from heavy metal and chemical substances. At the same time, it set more stringent emission standards for sulfur dioxide and nitrogen dioxide.[19]

In its initial form, this new compensation law had many defects where anti-pollution policy was concerned. For example, air-polluting enterprises stopped designating new pollution victims from 1988 because they claimed to have kept the levels of sulfur dioxide under acceptable legal limits. Yet as the number of automobiles increased, of course, the number of sufferers from air pollution steadily increased as well. Amidst fears that compensation under the new law would soon be discontinued, new lawsuits were introduced in Tokyo, Kawasaki, Osaka, and Amagasaki. Because the plaintiffs prevailed in every case, the government was compelled to reexamine the compensation system. Additionally, it was discovered that large numbers of sufferers from Minamata disease and Itai-Itai disease had had their cases disallowed, apparently due to financial considerations that had impelled the government to set narrower standards of victim designation. Because problems such as these have yet to be resolved, pollution trials have continued on for years.

THE RESULTS OF ANTIPOLLUTION MEASURES

During the 1960s, companies took almost no pollution prevention measures of their own. The amount of investment in pollution prevention for fiscal year 1965 was 29.5 billion yen, accounting for 1.7 percent of the total for capital investment, and none of that at all went toward water purification. From the 1970s, under pressure of new laws and pollution prevention agreements, as well as public opinion and popular activism, the amount of investment rapidly went up. Between 1973 and 1976, as seen in figure 12.5, pollution prevention investments jumped dramatically. In 1975 these investments reached 96.45 billion yen, or 17.7 percent of the total costs of capital investment—the highest level of investment in the

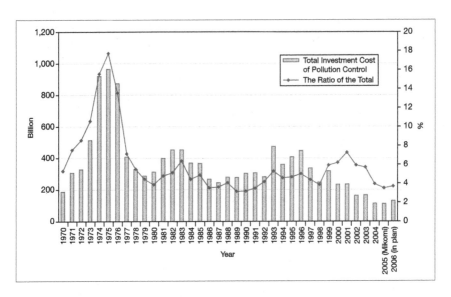

FIGURE 12.5 Investment in pollution control by the private sector. SOURCE: MINISTRY OF ECONOMY, TRADE, AND INDUSTRY.

world at the time. Of this, roughly 70 percent of the total was invested by steel, electric power, and oil companies in air pollution prevention. Since 1977, however, the amount of this investment has drastically decreased. This resulted from the rapid alteration of Japan's industrial structure, including the improvement of energy-saving technologies triggered by the sudden rise in oil prices and inroads made by the Chinese and others into the heavy chemical industry. As pollution prevention equipment was more widely distributed, it became necessary to locate trained operators as well. In 1971 the government initiated the State Examination for Pollution Control Operators. By 2005, approximately three hundred thousand candidates had passed. It was not only the "hard" aspects of pollution prevention that showed results, in other words, but the "soft" aspects as well. With the easing of pollution control restrictions from the beginning of the twenty-first century, however, the demand for trained equipment operators has decreased, and the attendant neglect of operations has led to an increase in the frequency of environmental standards violations and environmental accidents.

By the same token, the central government and local governments dramatically increased their environmental policy budgets in the 1970s. In 1973, the national budget for environmental protection was only about 76.5 million yen, and local governments had almost no budgets of their own. As shown in table 12.1, however, by 1974 the national budget for environmental policy had risen to 34.2 billion yen and that of local governments to the enormous figure of nearly

95.4 billion yen. Between 1961 and 1974, the number of managers and staffers engaged in administration of environmental policy grew forty times over, from 300 to 12,317. Thus, the improvement of pollution control measures by both the public and private sector helped Japan to work toward solving the pollution problems of the 1960s. As shown in figure 12.6, by the second half of the 1970s the environmental standard for sulfur dioxide emissions had been met; and, as seen in figure 12.7, there was at least a leveling off of the increases in nitrogen dioxide emissions. The persistence of the nitrogen dioxide pollution problem had to do with the rising

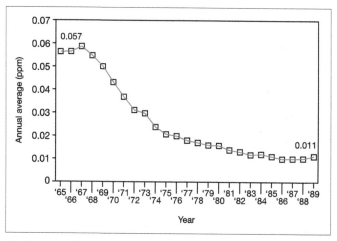

FIGURE 12.6 Changes in annual concentration of SO_2.

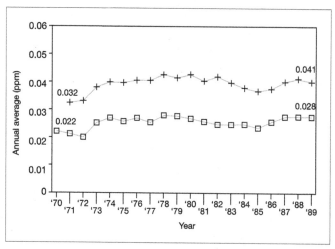

FIGURE 12.7 Changes in annual concentration of NO_2.

volume of traffic. This not the sort of problem that can be solved through the development of pollution prevention technologies, of course: it requires far-reaching economic reforms to revamp public transportation system facilities.[20]

Historical and Theoretical Lessons Concerning the Environmental Problem in Japan

What are the basic causes of the environmental problem in Japan? Here we must examine the social, political, and economic systems that lurk in the background. While the problems are clearly caused by a combination of "market defects" and "government defects," they issue ultimately from a range of different social, political, and economic factors. We can glean the following lessons from the history of pollution in prewar and postwar Japan:

1. The structure of capital formation (accumulation) in the public and private sectors: Is this capital accumulation centrally devoted to mass production and large-scale public works, or is it primarily devoted to the creation of adequately funded amenities related to expenditures on environmental preservation? (See figure 12.5 and table 12.1.)
2. Industrial structure: Do we cultivate an environment-destroying and energy-wasting industrial structure or an ecology-oriented industrial structure?
3. Regional structure: Do we promote a national land structure that seeks a unipolar concentration of economy, politics, and culture in metropolitan regions, or do we cultivate a spatial formation that seeks a balance between villages and cities that prioritizes coexistence?
4. Transport system: Do we want an automobile-centered heavy traffic society, or do we aspire to create a public transportation-centered and traffic-restricting one?
5. Lifestyle: Are we content with an American-style mass consumption–oriented way of life, or do we want live an ecologically oriented life that subsists on regional resources?
6. Waste and the circulation of material goods: Shall we maintain an extravagant system that simply throws out the waste from mass production, distribution, and consumption, or shall we embrace one that does its best to recycle waste as renewable resources?
7. Fundamental human rights: Will politicians and bureaucrats infringe upon fundamental human rights such as life, health, and social amenities, preserving the present "market defects," or shall they choose to protect the environment?

TABLE 12.1. Changes in environmental policies of local governments

	1961		1974		1986		1995	
	Prefecture	City Town Village	Prefecture	City Town Village	Prefecture	City Town Village	Prefecture	City Town Village
Environmental sector	14	16	47	765	47	562	47	845
Administrator	300		5,852	6,465	5,865	4,816	6,384	4,534
Budget (hundred million yen)	140		3,501	6,036	8,910	20,800	14,458	46,738
Budget except sewage dispose (hundred million yen)	2		3,828		8,785		17,319	
Environmental Act	6	1	47	346	47	496	47	608

Source: Data for fiscal 1961 from the Ministry of Welfare and the rest of each year from the Ministry of Environment.

8. Democracy and freedom: Shall Japan continue to tolerate the "political defects" that have limited freedom of the press, as well as freedom of thought, expression, and action, or shall it commit itself to a state built on the principle of the separation of executive, legislative, and judicial powers, in which local self-government is firmly established?

9. Civil society: Can Japan create a society where citizens are free from discrimination based on class or birth and free from corporate and community hierarchies, so that they may realize their natural rights?

10. Internationalization: Are there international organizations in Japan devoted to the preservation of the environment? And does Japan acknowledge the independence of all different peoples and cultures to seek a future of peaceful coexistence?[21]

In the era of high-speed growth, as the private sector followed a mass-production pattern of capital accumulation that restricted investment in pollution control, the public sector also promoted large-scale public works (development projects) that destroyed the environment. Japanese industrial structure at the time was centered on the heavy chemical industry. As seen in table 12.2, Japan also witnessed a unipolar pattern of urbanization, with Tokyo at the center. Figure 12.8 illustrates how Japan's transportation system was altered from a railroad-centered structure

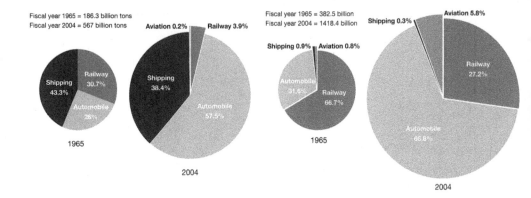

FIGURE 12.8 *Left:* changes in volume of freight transportation; *Right:* changes in volume of passenger transportation. SOURCE: NIHON KOKUSEI KAI, 2006, 407.

TABLE 12.2. Trends in population of big three urban areas

	1960		1965		1975		1985		1995	
	population	%	population	%	population	%	population	%	population	%
Big three urban area	37,380	40	39,773	40.5	53,233	47.6	58,342	48.2	61,644	49.1
Tokyo	17,864	19.1	21,017	21.4	27,024	24.2	30,273	25	32,575	25.9
Osaka	12,186	13	13,896	14.1	16,773	15	17,838	14.7	18,259	14.5
Nagoya	7,330	7.8	8,013	8.2	9,418	8.4	10,231	8.5	10,810	8.6

Note: Tokyo (The metropolis of Tokyo, Kanagawa Prefecture, Chiba Prefecture, and Saitama Prefecture). Osaka (Osaka Prefecture, Kyoto Prefecture, Hyogo Prefecture, and Nara Prefecture). Nagoya (Aichi Prefecture, Mie Prefecture, and Gifu Prefecture).

Source: "Public-Opinion Poll" the Prime Minister's Office.

to an automobile-centered one. As Japanese life shifted dramatically from humble simplicity to mass consumption, people discarded huge amounts of trash. Because Japan followed this prototypical pattern of environmentally destructive economic development, the country generated serious pollution in a very short period of time. Today, China and other nations in the Asian economic system exhibit these same developmental characteristics.

In conservative parts of Japan, where corporations dominated the development scene, pollution victims remained isolated. With the rise of citizen activism, which was brought to life by the democratic rights secured under the postwar constitution, things changed: cases of pollution were prosecuted, the private and public sectors both instituted antipollution measures, Japanese industry underwent structural change, and the country turned to problem solving. Treating the Japanese experience as a bellwether, the key to solving China's pollution problems today is certainly to establish basic human rights and democracy.

AN OVERARCHING PICTURE OF THE ENVIRONMENTAL PROBLEM

As shown in figure 12.9, pollution problems issue from changes in regional society, such as the destruction of regional ecosystems and cultures. The root causes of pollution—and more generally of global environmental problems—are the social, political, and economic systems that human societies share. Thus, the pollution problem is linked to the larger environmental problems faced by the earth as a whole.

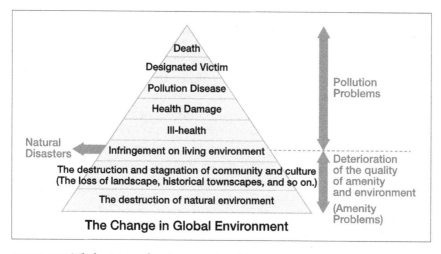

FIGURE 12.9 Whole picture of environmental problems.

SOCIAL CHARACTERISTICS OF POLLUTION AND ENVIRONMENTAL PROBLEMS

Biologically Weak Organisms

The damage from environmental destruction begins with biologically weak organisms. Environmental pollution begins with the destruction of the ecosystem, starting with organisms that are easily susceptible to environmental pollution, including plants and animals and extending to human beings. The first human victims tend to be the young, the aged, and the handicapped. Looking at the number of air pollution victims designated by the government under the Pollution-Related Health Damages Compensation Law in 1988, which came to 98,694 people, 33.9 percent were aged fourteen or younger and 28.5 percent were aged sixty or older, accounting for 62.4 percent of the total. Victims in the eighteen to sixty age range included many housewives who spent virtually all of their days and nights in the same polluted environment.

Socially Weak People

Low-income people represent the largest concentration of victims. Among the 2,647 executives of big companies located in Osaka city, only 197 (or 7 percent of the total) live within the city limits. The rest commute to work from exclusive residential districts in Hyogo, Kyoto, and Nara Prefectures. The city of Osaka is famous the world over as a commercial and industrial city, but it is also a low-income district, with the highest proportion of air pollution victims in Japan. These low-income people live in houses near factories and expressways, in locations that may be convenient but where housing, urban infrastructure, and nutrition are substandard. Accordingly, they are apt to become victims of pollution.

The two factors discussed above help explain why pollution control measures were delayed in Japan. Biologically weak people are not employed by private companies in most cases, and thus they do not contribute to the GDP. When they get ill, production in the medical and pharmaceutical sectors increases, and the GDP also rises. When biologically weak victims say nothing and entrust their lives to the free market, they continue to experience neglect. The rich, on the other hand, can solve such problems on their own—possessing the freedom to change residences when the environment worsens. Socially weak people, by contrast, don't have the option to choose. Thus it is impossible to find a solution to the pollution problem by making the victims responsible for themselves. Instead, it is necessary to create a system of social relief.

Absolute Irreversible Loss

Unlike other economic problems, environmental problems include absolute irreversible losses that cannot be compensated after the fact. There is the Pollution-Related Health Damages Compensation Law, but this does not help victims recover their lost health and lives. Virtually all pollution-related diseases contracted by victims are difficult to cure; and lost coastlands and virgin forests destroyed by regional development represent valuable natural landscapes that cannot be reclaimed. Such absolute irreversible losses include the following: (1) damage to health and death; (2) destruction of the conditions necessary to regenerate nature for the benefit of human society; and (3) destruction of irreplaceable cultural assets, landscapes, and scenery.

Where such absolute irreversible losses are concerned, compensation is not an option. Rather, it is important to halt such projects before they lead to problems or at least to alter them. As with environmental assessments, therefore, the public and private sectors have an obligation to assess the total impact of their projects before carrying them out. This alone will prevent absolute irreversible losses, such as those associated with environmental problems.

NEOLIBERALISM AND THE EBB TIDE OF ENVIRONMENTAL POLICY

In the second half of the 1980s, as economic globalization and the US-Japan alliance flourished, reformist political parties and the labor movement were dissolved, reform-minded local governments lost influence, and public environmental activism stagnated. As Japan entered the 1990s, following the collapse of the "bubble economy" people no longer demanded a social amenity–laden economy. Instead, they demanded a return to the halcyon days of rapid economic growth, and accordingly, neoliberalist policy flourished. Influenced by the Rio Summit of 1992, the government abolished the Basic Law for Environmental Pollution Control and enacted the Basic Environment Law in its place. Since then there has been a rush to initiate new legislation, and countless new environmental laws have been enacted. Unlike the 1970s when corporations were charged with responsibility for their actions, however, the new laws are not the least bit strict, instead portraying environmental preservation as a national duty. The government promotes the perception that pollution has been eradicated. Concerning global environmental problems, the government has revisited the idea that environmental preservation falls under the rubric of economic development.[22]

Remaining Problems

STOCKPILED POLLUTION

In June 2005, three people living in the vicinity of Kubota Industries, a machinery maker located in Amagasaki, were diagnosed with mesothelioma and sued the company on the grounds that it had been caused by asbestos pollution. This was the first case brought to the courts concerning asbestos-related injuries, and as such it had a great impact across Japan. Subsequently, Kubota announced that more than 120 of their employees had died and that 153 more people in the vicinity of the Kubota plant had been designated victims of the asbestos pollution. Kubota had paid out "sympathy money" (*mimaikin*), ranging from 24 to 46 million yen, as compensation to the mesothelioma victims. In February 2006, the government introduced the Asbestos Relief Law for the victims of asbestos pollution, and in 2008, lagging well behind Europe, it finally prohibited the use of asbestos in Japan. Under the Asbestos Relief Law, the government paid out

3 million yen each to mesothelioma and asbestos-related lung cancer patients who had not received aid under the Workmen's Accident Compensation Law but had been designated by a special investigative committee as victims. As of 2007, more than three thousand victims had received compensation. Local residents suffering from pulmonary asbestosis, as well as construction company laborers denied victim status under the Asbestos Relief Law, have also taken the government to court. Although the government has acknowledged that it neglected to take antipollution measures earlier on, it continues to deny legal responsibility for any asbestos-related injury to local residents. As a result, the government has not applied the Pollution-Related Health Damages Compensation Law to many local victims, offering monetary compensation only to those suffering from mesothelioma and lung cancer—and then only in small amounts. For its part, Kubota has also denied legal responsibility for the pollution and thus paid out compensation to victims exclusively in the form of "sympathy money."

Up to the 1990s, asbestos was used on a massive scale. Since buildings filled with asbestos will continue to be pulled down for the foreseeable future, the effects of asbestos damage are likely to be felt for the next fifty years. In the case of Minamata disease, it was possible to put a halt to the damage by putting a halt to the production process that created the pollution in the first place, but asbestos remains "stockpiled" in commercial products and in the human body. The symptoms of asbestos-related disease do not commonly appear for fifteen to forty-five years after exposure. Because asbestos accumulates in the body over the long term, people frequently have no memory of how they were exposed, and because many of the companies that once used asbestos have long since gone out of business, it is notoriously difficult to assign responsibility. But to the extent that we find asbestos in various stages of production, distribution, consumption, and disposal, the risk of damage remains.[23]

As seen in figure 12.10, developing countries such as Russia, China, Thailand, Brazil, and India continue to use large amounts of asbestos. If its use continues at current levels, asbestos pollution will soon represent the greatest industrial disaster in history.

PROBLEMS RELATED TO THE NATURAL ENVIRONMENT AND CULTURAL LANDSCAPES

In the area of environmental policies related to the natural environment and cultural landscapes, Japan lags more than twenty years behind Europe. During this lag period, valuable natural assets and landscapes have been lost. At present, various regions across Japan are attempting to regenerate nature, especially the water-related environment. In the Biwa Lake region, where there is a long history of residential activism, they are attempting to transform reclaimed land into a biotopic

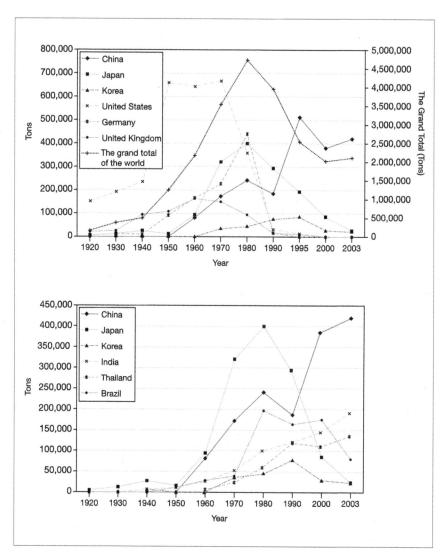

FIGURE 12.10 *Top:* asbestos consumption; *bottom:* amount of asbestos consumption.
SOURCE: US GEOLOGICAL SURVEY, WORLDWIDE ASBESTOS SUPPLY AND CONSUMPTION TRENDS FROM 1990 TO 2003.

habitat. In 2007, the City of Kyoto established a municipal ordinance to regulate the height and color of buildings, as well as restrictions on billboard advertising, to preserve the city's landscape. Even when it comes to large-scale public works projects, such as dam construction, the threat of environmental destruction has led to reconsideration. The Shinjiko Lake drainage project has been halted, and it is likely that the Isahaya Bay drainage project will be reconsidered as well.[24]

THE GLOBAL ENVIRONMENTAL PROBLEM

Although the time has arrived to implement the Kyoto Protocol, carbon dioxide emissions in Japan have actually risen 6.2 percent rather than falling toward the goal of a 6 percent reduction. Not only has the business world declared its opposition to the regulations, it has refused even to endorse the business-friendly economic methods proposed to support them, such as an environmental tax and emissions trading (the so-called cap-and-trade system). Since Japan's forests should absorb 3.8 percent of the planned 6 percent reduction in emissions, the goal to reduce greenhouse gas emissions represents only 0.6 percent of the total reduction goal. Yet even this goal has yet to be achieved. Under international political pressure, Prime Minister Fukuda was compelled to project reduction benchmarks over the long term, working forward from the carbon dioxide emissions total for 2005: a 14 percent reduction by 2020 and 50–80 percent before 2050. But if the government's energy plan to make a 14 percent cut in emissions by 2020 is to work—a cut that would represent only a 4 percent reduction from the emissions levels of 1990—according to the government's energy plan, just 2 percent of the total energy generated would come from new sources of energy, 44 percent from nuclear power, and 20 percent from coal. In earthquake-prone Japan, however, it is doubtful that the government will persuade people to build more nuclear power plants. After all, even the plan for a waste processing plant in Kōchi Prefecture was put on hold recently due to strong public opposition. The global environmental problem does not have to do only with greenhouse gas emissions caused by the use of nonrenewable fossil fuels. It also has to do with another important issue: the exhaustion of renewable resources such as foodstuffs, forests, fresh water, and soil. Indeed, the exhaustion of renewable resources is likely to lead us much faster into a global environmental crisis than the greenhouse effect.

Due to the substitution of biofuel for fossil fuel, a vicious cycle has already begun of steeply rising food prices and an impending food supply crisis. If we are to realize the goal of reducing greenhouse gas emissions, we must adopt an environmental tax and give local governments the authority to eradicate pollution. As with the pollution prevention agreements mentioned earlier, local governments and residents should require large-scale polluters to track their carbon dioxide emissions and to follow emissions reduction plans with specific targets. Otherwise, the greenhouse gas emissions problem will not be solved.[25]

Sustainable Society

FROM SUSTAINABLE DEVELOPMENT TO A SUSTAINABLE SOCIETY

At the Rio Summit in 1992, sustainable development was presented as the collective aspiration of humankind. But under this developmental rubric, the question remains: What sort of sustainable society will we build? In my view, we need to create a society that collectively meets the following five standards:

1. The maintenance of peace and most especially the prevention of nuclear war.
2. Preservation and renewal of the environment and other resources. Given that the earth is a diverse ecosystem that includes human beings, it is essential to sustain and improve the environment.
3. The conquest of extreme poverty and the elimination of social and economic injustice.
4. The establishment of democracy, domestically and internationally.
5. The realization of basic human rights, the attainment of freedom of thought and expression, and the acceptance of cultural and ethnic diversity.

In the real world we occupy, the Iraq War has yet to end, and developing countries continue to struggle with the threat of starvation and poor hygienic conditions. Since there is no "world nation" representing all human beings, it may be a pipedream to propose such a global society. Nonetheless, these are clear objectives to which we should aspire. Through the World Trade Organization, the International Monetary Fund, and the World Bank, multinational enterprises have been able to promote investment and trade liberalization; but, although political leaders have proposed the establishment of a World Environment Organization (WEO) that could put the brakes on global environmental destruction, this goal has yet to be realized. While the establishment of the WEO is critical, this will not solve all our problems instantly, which is to say that the global environment problem is something that needs to be addressed immediately. The European Union's Sustainable Cities and Towns Campaign, introduced in the 1990s, is a concrete example of a bottom-up policy that promises to bring about meaningful change.[26]

Japan has yet to develop a sustainable city plan with national scope, but there is a movement under way to regenerate the environment and to create a society that recycles its resources. For example, in the Nishi Yodogawa district of Osaka, pollution victims contributed a part of their compensation to establish the Aozora (Blue Skies) Foundation, which aims to create neighborhoods free from pollution. Sharing this idealistic sentiment with the Osaka-based foundation, pollution victims from other regions such as Kawasaki, the southern districts of Nagoya, Yokkaichi, and the Mizushima district of Kurashiki have mounted a campaign to regenerate polluted neighborhoods in their own locales.[27]

In Shiga Prefecture, where the long-running environmental movement to preserve Lake Biwako has set the precedent for local activism, the Shiga Prefectural

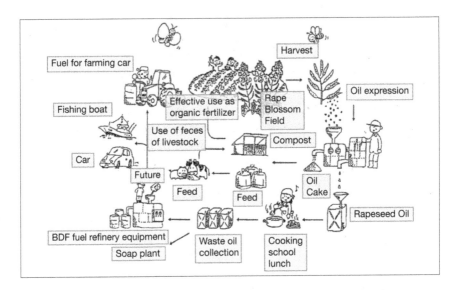

Figure labels:
- Harvest
- Fuel for farming car
- Oil expression
- Fishing boat
- Effective use as organic fertilizer
- Rape Blossom Field
- Use of feces of livestock
- Compost
- Car
- Future
- Oil Cake
- Feed
- Feed
- Rapeseed Oil
- BDF fuel refinery equipment
- Soap plant
- Waste oil collection
- Cooking school lunch

FIGURE 12.11 Circulation of rape blossom's resources.

Environmental Living Cooperative Union recently initiated the "Rapeseed Blossom Project," as seen in figure 12.11. Planted in fallow fields, the rapeseed blossoms are harvested to produce cooking oil to fry tempura in homes and schools. Later, the used oil is converted into diesel fuel. Unlike biofuels made from sugarcane and corn, this is a perfect case of recycling, as the oil is not made from a foodstuff that, removed from the market, might trigger a rise in food prices or a food shortage. Similar rapeseed blossom projects are now being carried out in two hundred different locations across Japan, as well as in South Korea. What was once a small local experiment has now become a far-reaching experiment in the creation of a "sustainable rural area."[28]

ON ENDOGENOUS DEVELOPMENT IN ASIA

For the past twenty-five years, I have been conducting collaborative research with Korean and Chinese environmental scholars. We have noted that China's pollution problems in recent years are even more serious than those that Japan experienced during the era of high-speed growth. Although the Chinese government has issued environmental laws and promoted environmental management, the situation has not improved significantly. This is because victims do not have the right to take polluters to court or to foster administrative reform. Although the realities of pollution damage have at last become clear and relevant information has been made available to the public, this is just the tip of the iceberg. China's pollution problems will not be solved until epidemiological research is conducted, a system of victim relief is established, experts are allowed to conduct their research freely, and proper adjudication of pollution cases is conducted and administrative relief assured.

Following the path of modernization traced earlier by the Western nations and Japan, with China in the lead the nations of Asia are advancing at an even faster pace. In order to achieve this rate of development, these nations rely on foreign capital and technology, taking the developmental road of so-called *exogenous development*. Not only has this generated pollution, expanded the gap between rich and poor, and widened the gap between urban areas and farm villages, it also threatens to drive the global environment to ruin.

After India gained its independence from Great Britain, M. K. Gandhi expressed his skepticism of the Western model of civilization building: "If India copies England, it is my firm conviction that she will be ruined. . . . [The state of England] is not due to any peculiar fault of the English people, but the condition is due to modern civilization. It is a civilization in name only. Under it the nations of Europe are becoming degraded and ruined day by day."[29] Gandhi's ideal for the newly independent India, by contrast to England, was for it to be self-supporting. He regarded urbanization as needless and based his social ideal on the small village. For him, the ideal society was a social network that connected self-sufficient regions.

In the 1990s, India discarded Gandhi's ideal, placing the nation on a capitalist path. Following the current trajectory of globalization, after all, wouldn't it be impossible to follow the path that Gandhi suggested? Not necessarily. As Gandhi pointed out, if India or China elects to follow the path of modernization set by the Western nations and Japan, then there are not enough earths to reach the final goal. What Gandhi meant, put in another way, is that we should not endorse exogenous development, but rather we should promote *endogenous* development. Japan has already amassed valuable experience of such endogenous development. From this moment forward, rather than devoting ourselves exclusively to the study of environmental policy, we should be telling the story of endogenous development in Japan and holding it up as a prime example of forward-looking Asian economic development.[30]

Notes

1. Seki Umenojō, *Hitachi kōzan engai mondai mukashibanashi* (The legend of the Hitachi Mine's smoke pollution problem) (Hitachi: Kyōdō Hitachi Bunka Kenkyūkai, 1963).
2. Awaji Takehisa and Nomura Yoshihiro, *Kōgai hanrei no kenkyū* (Studies of judicial precedents in antipollution cases) (Tokyo: Toshikaihatsu Kenkyūkai, 1971).
3. Hiratsuka Masatoshi, *Besshi kaikō nihyakugojūnen shiwa* (A 250-year history of Besshi Mining) (Osaka: Sumitomo Honsha, 1941); *Shisakajima engai baishō kyōgikai*

kaigiroku, 1910–37 (Minutes of the Shisakajima air pollution compensation conference, 1910–37); Isshiki Kōhei, *Ehime-ken Tōyo engai shi* (The history of air pollution in Tōyo, Ehime Prefecture) (Ehime: Shōsō-gun Engai Chōsakai, 1926).

4. Koyama Hitoshi, *Senzen Shōwa-ki Osaka no kōgai mondai shiryō* (Sources for the study of pollution problems in Showa Osaka) (Osaka: Kansai Daigaku Keizai/Seiji Kenkyūjo, 1973); Miyamoto Ken'ichi, *Osaka no kōgai/kankyō seisaku shi ni manabu* (Learning from the history of pollution/environmental policy in Osaka) (Osaka: Osaka-shi Komonjokan, 2007).

5. Miyamoto Ken'ichi and Shōji Hikaru, *Osorubeki kōgai* (Fearsome pollution) (Tokyo: Iwanami Shinsho, 1964); Miyamoto Ken'ichi and Shōji Hikaru, *Nihon no kōgai* (Pollution in Japan) (Tokyo: Iwanami Shinsho, 1975).

6. Harada Masazumi, *Minamatabyō* (Minamata disease) (Tokyo: Iwanami Shinsho, 1972); Miyamoto Ken'ichi, ed. *Kōgai toshi no saisei—Minamata* (The rebirth of pollution city—Minamata) (Tokyo: Chikuma Shobō, 1978); Tsuru Shigeto, ed., *For Truth and Justice in the Minamata Disease Case: Proceedings of the International Forum on Minamata Disease 1988* (Tokyo: Keisō Shobō, 1989); Miyamoto Ken'ichi, *Minamata Requiem* (Tokyo: Iwanami Shoten, 1994); Minamatabyō Higaisha/Bengōdan Zenkoku Renkaku Kaigi, ed. *Minamatabyō saiban zenshi* (A complete history of the Minamata trials) (Tokyo: Nihon Hyōronsha, 1998–2001).

7. Saitō Hisashi, *Niigata Minamatabyō* (Niigata Minamata Disease) (Tokyo: Mainichi Shinbunsha, 1996); Funabashi Harutoshi and Iijima Nobuko, eds., *Niigata Minamatabyō mondai* (The Niigata Minamata disease problem) (Tokyo: Tōshindo, 1999).

8. Kurachi Mitsuo, Tonegawa Haruo, and Hata Akio, eds., *Mitsui shihon to itai-itai byō* (Mitsui capital and Itai-Itai disease) (Tokyo: Ōtsuki Shoten, 1979); Itai-Itai Byō Sōsho Bengōdan, ed., *Itai-Itai byō saiban* (The Itai-Itai disease trials) (Tokyo: Sōgō Tosho, 1971–74); Nogawa Koji, ed., "Advances in the Prevention of Environmental Cadmium Pollution and Countermeasures" (Eiko Laboratory, 1999); Matsunami Jun'ichi, *Itai-itai byō no kioku* (Recollections of Itai-Itai disease) (Toyama: Katsura Shobō, 2006).

9. Yoshida Katsumi, *Yokkaichi kōgai* (Yokkaichi pollution) (Tokyo: Kashiwa Shobō, 2002); Miyamoto Ken'ichi, *Chiiki kaihastu wa korede yoi ka* (Is this the right way to approach regional development?) (Tokyo: Iwanami Shinsho, 1973); Miyamoto Ken'ichi, "Industrial Policy and the Case of Large Industrial Complexes," in Shigeto Tsuru and Helmut Weidner, eds., *Environmental Policies in Japan* (Berlin: Edition Sigma, 1989).

10. Tsuru Shigeto, ed., *Gendai shihonshugi to kōgai* (Contemporary capitalism and pollution) (Tokyo: Iwanami Shoten, 1968); Miyamoto Ken'ichi, *Osaka no kōgai/kankyō seisaku shi ni manabu* (Learning from the history of pollution/environmental policy in Osaka) (Osaka: Osaka-shi Komonjokan, 2007); Tokyo-to Kōgai Kenkyūjo, *Kōgai to Tokyo-to* (Pollution and metropolitan Tokyo) (Tokyo: Tokyo-to, 1970); Tokyo-to, *Tokyo Fights Pollution* (Tokyo: Tokyo Metropolitan Government, 1971).

11. Miyamoto Ken'ichi, *Kankyō keizaigaku shinpan* (Environmental economics: New edition) (Tokyo: Iwanami Shoten, 2007).

12. Fukuoka-ken Keieisha Kyōkai, *Fukuoka-ken kōgai bōshi jōrei ni taisuru yōbō* (The cry for pollution control regulations in Fukuoka Prefecture) (Fukuoka: Fukuoka-ken, 1955).

13. Iijima Nobuko, *Kōgai/rōsai/shokugyō byō nenpyō* (A chronology of disease related to pollution, labor accidents, and employment) (Tokyo: Kōgai Taisaku Gijutsu Dōyūkai, 1977); Iijima Nobuko, *Pollution Japan: Historical Chronology* (Tokyo: Asahi Evening News, 1979).

14. Miyamoto Ken'ichi, *Nihon no kankyō mondai* (Environmental problems in Japan) (Tokyo: Yūhikaku, new ed., 1981); Hashimoto Michio, *Shishi kankyō gyōsei* (A personal history of environmental administration) (Tokyo: Asahi Shinbun, 1988).

15. Helmut Weidner, "Die Erfolge der Japanishen Umweltpolitik," in S. Tsuru and H. Weidner, ed., *Ein Modell für Uns: Die Erfolge der Japanishen Umweltpolitik* (Berlin: Verlag Kipen Heuer & Witsch, 1985).

16. Miyamoto Ken'ichi, ed., *Numazu Jūmin undō no ayumi* (The story of the Numazu citizens' movement) (Tokyo: NHK Shuppan, 1979); Ken'ichi Miyamoto, "Environmental Problems and the Citizens' Movements in Japan," *Japan Foundation Newsletter* 11:4 (1983).

17. OECD, *OECD Environmental Performance Review Japan* (Paris: OECD, 1977); Tajiri Muneaki, *Kōgai tekihatsu saizensen* (The front line of pollution exposure) (Tokyo: Iwanami Shinsho, 1980).

18. Miyamoto Ken'ichi, "Environmental Policies in the Past Twenty Years: A Balance Sheet," in H. Nagamine, ed., *Nation Building and Regional Development* (Tokyo: Maruzen, 1981); Miyamoto Ken'ichi, *Nihon no kankyō seisaku* (Environmental policy in Japan) (Tokyo: Ōtsuki Shoten, 1987); Yokemoto Masafumi, *Kankyō higai no sekinin to hiyō futan* (Environmental damage and the burden of its costs) (Tokyo: Yūhikaku, 2007).

19. Hashimoto Michio, *Shishi kankyō gyōsei* (A personal history of environmental administration) (Tokyo: Asahi Shinbun, 1988).

20. M. Jaenicke, *Staatsversagen: Die Ohnmacht der Politik in der Industriegesellschaft* (Munich: Piper, 1986); M. Jaenicke and H. Weidner, eds., *Successful Environmental Policy: A Critical Evaluation of 24 Cases* (Berlin: Edition Sigma, 1995).

21. Miyamoto, *Kankyō keizaigaku shinpan.*

22. Miyamoto Ken'ichi, *Kankyō seisaku no kokusaika* (Globalization of environmental policies) (Tokyo: Jikkyō Shuppan, 1995); Miyamoto Ken'ichi, *Nihon shakai no kanōsei* (The possibilities for Japanese society) (Tokyo: Iwanami Shoten, 2000).

23. Barry I. Castleman, *Asbestos: Medical and Legal Aspects* (New York: Aspen, 2005); Miyamoto Ken'ichi, *Iji kanōna shakai ni mukatte* (Toward a sustainable society) (Tokyo: Iwanami Shoten, 2006); Miyamoto Ken'ichi, Morinaga Kenji, and Mori Hiroyuki, *Asbestos Disaster: Lessons from Japan's Experience* (Tokyo: Springer, 2011).

24. Nakajima Akira, *Keikan hogo no hōteki senryaku* (The legal battle to preserve natural scenery) (Kyoto: Kamogawa Shuppan, 2007); Hobo Takehiko, *Kōkyō jigyō o dō kaeru ka* (How to change public works) (Tokyo: Iwanami Shoten, 2001); Ishihara Ichiko, *Keikan ni kakeru* (Risking natural scenery) (Tokyo: Shinhyōron, 2007).

25. Miyamoto Ken'ichi, *Kankyō keizaigaku shinpan.*

26. A. Rechkemmer, ed., *UNEO—Toward an International Environment Organization: Approaches to a Sustainable Reform of Global Environmental Governance* (Baden-Baden: Nomos Verlagsgesellshaft, 2005); European Commission, Expert Group on the Urban Environment, *European Sustainable Cities: Report* (Brussels: European Commission, 1996).

27. Endō Hiroichi et. al., eds., *Kankyō saisei no machizukuri* (Neighborhood planning through environmental regeneration) (Kyoto: Mineruba Shobō, 2008).

28. Fujii Ayako, ed., *Nanohana eco kakumei* (The rape blossom eco-revolution) (Tokyo: Sōshinsha, 2004).

29. M. K. Gandhi, *Hind Swaraj*, 1909; see www.mkgandhi.org/swarajya; S. L. Bahuguna, *A Political Step Towards a Sustainable Society* (1984).

30. Tsuru Shigeto, *The Political Economy of Environment: The Case of Japan* (London: Athlone Press, 1999).

THE TRIPLE DISASTER OF 3/11 | V

13

An Envirotechnical Disaster

*Negotiating Nature, Technology,
and Politics at Fukushima*

SARA B. PRITCHARD

The Tōhoku earthquake, now called the "Great East Japan Earthquake," began rattling the island nation at 2:46 in the afternoon (JST) on that fateful spring day. The enormous magnitude 9.0 earthquake—the largest ever known to have hit Japan and also one of the five most powerful earthquakes in the entire world since modern record keeping began in the early twentieth century—shook buildings, buckled streets, and terrified the country's citizens for an astounding six minutes. A major tsunami, eventually rising to the height of a four-story building, soon began rushing headlong toward northeastern Japan, barreling down on the country's coastline at the speed of an airborne jumbo jet. Japan's many inlets and bays became particularly vulnerable as the tsunami, approaching the shore, became concentrated in the ever-narrowing landscape, pushing the foreboding wall of water even higher into contracting valleys. In one bay, the tsunami is believed to have reached 38.9 meters (127 feet). Once the tsunami made landfall, it slammed large ships into bridges and tossed cars as if they were children's toys, washing away coastal villages and highways in mere seconds. There were at least twenty thousand casualties that afternoon. But the calamity was not yet over.

The tsunami easily breached the thirteen-foot cliff on which the Fukushima Daiichi nuclear power station owned by Tokyo Electric Power Company (TEPCO) is located, flooding the basements of buildings where most of the plant's backup generators had been placed. Although the havoc-wreaking tsunami has garnered much attention, some critics have wondered if the earthquake itself caused severe damage to the facility, possibly breaking recirculation and cooling pipes and causing cracks in the reactor walls even before the wall of water hit shore. Then, a few days after the destructive earthquake and enormous tsunami, three of the six nuclear reactors at Fukushima Daiichi experienced full meltdowns—possibly even melt-throughs.[1]

Such was the triple disaster Japan suffered on that early spring day. A single word—"Fukushima"—now stands for the multifaceted complexity of the events that took place on March 11, 2011, and all that has transpired in the months ever since.[2]

Even before Fukushima, the early twenty-first century had already offered environmental historians several significant teaching moments—for better and for worse.[3] Now Japan's triple disaster provides yet another occasion for environmental historians to engage with pressing questions—questions about the construction and maintenance of energy regimes, both politically and technologically, in the modern world; the development, expansion, and implications of the atomic age for both humans and nonhumans; and the relationship between nature (including human bodies) and technological systems.[4]

Several leading scholars, including sociologist Charles Perrow and historian Thomas Parke Hughes, have studied the design and operation of large-scale, modern technological systems like those at Fukushima Daiichi.[5] Building on their insights, in this chapter I examine Fukushima as an envirotechnical disaster, a result of the convergence of natural and sociotechnical processes.[6] I argue that the concept of envirotechnical systems is a useful way to explain what happened at Fukushima that also goes beyond what Perrow and Hughes offer through their concepts of "normal accidents" and technological systems, respectively. In the final section, I employ the notion of envirotechnical regimes to particularly stress the strategic configuration of Fukushima Daiichi's envirotechnical system, highlighting the ways in which political and economic power shaped the making of the facility, both during normal operations and throughout the events that began to unfold on March 11, 2011.

Normal Accidents, Technological Systems, and Envirotechnical Analysis

In 1984, Charles Perrow published *Normal Accidents*, his now-classic study of the partial meltdown at Three Mile Island five years earlier, arguing that complex, tightly coupled systems like the nuclear reactors at Three Mile Island (and, as it turns out, the ones at Fukushima Daiichi) invariably lead to accidents.[7] In his analysis, Perrow highlighted the unpredictable dynamics of these sociotechnical systems given their size, complexity, and inextricability.[8] Journalists from the *New York Times* expressed a version of Perrow's idea two days into the Fukushima crisis when they described "a cascade of accumulating problems."[9]

Perrow asserted, however, that it is misleading, if not hazardous, to use the common term "accidents" to describe situations like that of Fukushima Daiichi because it minimizes the inherent risks of modern technological systems.[10] Such language implies that accidents are caused by technical glitches or human error, when instead they should be understood as intrinsic to those systems. In short, accidents are normal and systemic, not extraordinary and inadvertent.[11] Yet, in the aftermath of disasters such as Chernobyl, Hurricane Katrina, the blowout at BP's Deepwater Horizon drill rig, and now Fukushima, government regulators and industry officials often focus on trying to "fix" the technology in question and attempting to reduce the likelihood of future human error, rather than asking deeper, far more difficult questions about those technologies—questions such as: Whose goals do these technologies serve? What political and economic interests shape the design and use of complex technological systems? And what assumptions about the natural world and human-natural relations are embedded in these technologies?[12]

Also in the mid-1980s, Thomas Parke Hughes theorized the concept of technological systems within the context of the history of technology. In his influential book *Networks of Power* (1983), Hughes traced the development of electricity networks in the United States and Western Europe, demonstrating their establishment by a coalition of entrepreneurs, politicians, and engineers. By focusing on systems, Hughes showed how technological artifacts rarely exist in isolation. Moreover, "system builders" create not just technical infrastructure such as power lines but also the capital, political support, market demand, and values that help to enable and perpetuate that system.[13]

Hughes' understanding of technological systems was predicated in part upon an explicit conceptualization of the relationship between the environment and technology. As Hughes declared, likely echoing the language and mindset of the systems theorists he studied, "Those parts of the world that are not subject to a system's control, but that influence the system, are called the environment. A sector of the environment can be incorporated into a system by bringing it under system control. An open system is one that is subject to influences from the environment; a closed system is its own sweet beast, and the final state can be predicted from the initial condition and the internal dynamic."[14] In Hughes' view, technological systems "incorporate" the environment if and when they need, say, coal, oil, copper, or a river's flow.[15] At the same time, Hughes suggested that such factors can "influence" systems, at least "open" ones. By conceptualizing technological systems in this way, Hughes assumed and thus reproduced a clean boundary between technology and the environment. Yet Hughes held a much more uncertain view regarding nature as a technological agent, his ambivalence ultimately destabilizing such a clear-cut assumption. In his formulation, technology shapes the environment; but at certain times, the environment can also influence technology.[16]

Perrow was wrestling with these very issues on the edges of his own work. He is best known, of course, for the concept of normal accidents, but Perrow developed an ancillary concept, "eco-system accident," which was predicated on something he called an "eco-system" (not to be confused with ecosystem) in his thick tome. Perrow did not define his eco-system, but he did define "eco-system accident." As he put it, such an accident is the result of "an interaction of systems that were thought to be independent but are not because of the larger ecology." More precisely, "eco-system accidents illustrate *the tight coupling between human-made systems and natural systems*. There are few or no deliberate buffers inserted between the two systems because the designers never expected them to be connected."[17] Perrow argued, then, that historical actors (with technical experts being the foremost suspects) may have conceived of technological systems as distinct from natural systems; but he questioned this assumption, maintaining that while actors may have firmly and neatly cleaved technological and natural systems, this was actually difficult to achieve in practice. According to Perrow, eco-system accidents result precisely from the inability to realize this goal—which brings us back to Fukushima.

Given what has already taken place in Japan, not to mention what will probably develop in the years ahead, Perrow's eco-system probably resonates with us more than Hughes' technological system. Indeed, it seems increasingly tough to sustain the tidy categories as well as some of the suppositions informing Hughes' concept of technological systems. After all, Hughes expressed confidence in "system control" and seemed to advocate the realization of closed systems (those "sweet beasts"). Hughes' analytic framework may reflect, then, the modernist, technocratic ideals of his so-called expert actors.[18] Furthermore, although Hughes left room for the environmental shaping of systems, he seemed to suggest that technology can, will, and should ultimately control nature. Environmental historians, who generally relish evidence of the dynamism, complexity, and mutual shaping of nature-culture, will likely find such arguments difficult to understand, let alone defend. This is particularly true now, in the early twenty-first century, with climate change altering supposedly remote environments, technologists seeking to mimic nature, and endocrine disrupters challenging the seemingly stable category of sex.[19] Hybrids of nature-culture and nature-technology surround us. And arguably, we humans are hybrids, too.[20] Fukushima may not only confirm these insights but even come to illustrate them in ways that are powerful, disturbing, and also humbling.

Both Perrow and Hughes, though, help us begin to understand situations such as Fukushima. Perrow's work challenges reductive thinking and has allowed scholars, not to mention technologists and policy makers, to perceive the systemic vulnerabilities within complex technologies like nuclear reactors.[21] For instance, in the case of Fukushima Daiichi, high pressure inside the reactors made it difficult for emergency workers to inject necessary cooling water. Consequently, in one of the Faustian bargains made and that will continue to be demanded in

Japan, plant operators repeatedly released vapor contaminated with radioactivity to reduce the pressure within the reactors in order to avoid an even more catastrophic situation.[22] In addition, Perrow's lesser-known notion of eco-system accidents may have particular appeal to environmental historians, especially after Fukushima. Hughes, meanwhile, reminds us—citizens, technical experts, and scholars alike—to take heed of the whole. Backup generators, for example, may seem mundane technologies, especially in the so-called advanced West, but as the crisis at Fukushima Daiichi made abundantly clear, they are critical to the safe operation and shutdown of nuclear power stations during emergencies.[23]

At the same time, scholarship at the intersection of environmental history and the history of technology both extends and refines the important contributions that Perrow and Hughes offer us, as scholars and also as planetary citizens.[24] Over the past two decades, those working at the nexus of these fields have developed several historical and analytical insights. Some scholars have focused specifically on actors' ideas about nature, technology, and their relationship, sometimes tracing how these cultural attitudes then shaped interactions with the material world. Particularly crucial is actors' strategic definition of these terms; for example, hydraulic engineers naturalizing dams to help justify large-scale intervention in human and nonhuman communities.[25] Other scholars have explored how various historical actors used the environment, particularly managed and harnessed "natures," as technology to do things; Edmund Russell calls them biotechnologies.[26] Still others have argued that environmental factors shape (but do not determine) technological change, an assertion that challenges recent accounts of technical development within the history of technology that highlight the social, political, and cultural shaping of technology.[27] As a whole, "envirotech" scholarship, which has been influenced by theoretical work on hybridity, actor networks, and coproduction, seeks to explore dynamic relationships between nature and technology—physically and culturally, historically and analytically.[28]

Integrating the contributions of this literature with the insights of Perrow and Hughes better explains what took place at Fukushima and why, in at least three ways. First, envirotech scholars push us to see the environment as *always* part of technological systems, not just, as Hughes asserted, of "open" systems. The concept of *envirotechnical system* encapsulates and specifically foregrounds this dynamic imbrication of natural and technological systems.[29] As the term itself suggests, we might think of these systems as mutually articulating.[30] Yet, as Fukushima showed, their choreography is not necessarily synchronized or even synchronizable.[31] The concept of *envirotechnical* system captures this entanglement and dialectical shaping.

Nevertheless, these entanglements of environmental and technological systems do not emerge out of thin air. Rather, they arise from specific historical, cultural, and, importantly, political contexts. Thus, a related concept—*envirotechnical regime*—stresses the historical and political production of envirotechnical systems like those at the Fukushima Daiichi nuclear power plant. This concept emphasizes the specific, often strategic reblending of natural and technological systems to serve particular ends, although, as the disaster demonstrated, these configurations do not always develop exactly as the people and institutions promoting them intended. For example, radioactive elements may have been harnessed to produce energy, but, as we are now painfully aware, their properties did not easily conform to mechanistic models. Finally, envirotech perspectives also call attention to how historical actors thought about the definition, relationship, and dynamics between natural and technical systems, often quite strategically. In the wake of Fukushima, for instance, government regulators and industry officials have conveniently pointed to the earthquake and tsunami in an attempt to absolve themselves of responsibility. Together, these insights complicate and enrich Hughes' understanding of "technological systems," in the process lending more credence to Perrow's concepts of normal and eco-system accidents.

Interpreting 3/11

On one level, Fukushima Daiichi's reactors were envirotechnical by design. Radioactive elements fueled nuclear chain reactions that eventually generated electricity—the whole point of the facility.[32] Reactors "incorporated," to borrow Hughes' phrase, water to regulate cooling processes in their cores, as well as the storage ponds housing thousands of spent fuel rods.[33] From the outset, these entities were at once both natural and technological in that they were mobilized for their valuable properties and yet also managed in specific ways, from producing energy to diffusing heat. In addition, almost two decades ago, Arthur McEvoy encouraged environmental historians to consider the bodies of workers—in this case, usually short-term laborers subject to questionable labor, health, and safety standards—as part of the nature of industry.[34] While some environments were integral to the basic functioning and operation of the reactors, others were explicitly kept out. At least this was the goal. Engineers designed the facility to withstand a maximum tsunami height of 10.5 feet. Because the complex is located on a cliff thirteen feet above the Pacific Ocean, they believed that Fukushima Daiichi would be safe. But on March 11, 2011, the tsunami was almost twice the height of the facility and cliff combined.[35] Furthermore, the earthquake caused land subsidence from one to three feet in northeastern Japan, making the region even more vulnerable to the ensuing tsunami.[36]

During the actual crisis, government officials, plant managers, and workers both tightened and transformed the imbrication of the natural and the technological at the Fukushima Daiichi power plant. We can see these processes at work by examining, in turn, water, air, and the bodies of workers at the complex, although it is worth noting that these terms do not fully represent their hybrid forms at Fukushima Daiichi. Water was at the center of emergency measures during the initial phase of the crisis. As the first forty-eight hours of the disaster unfolded, our television and computer screens were filled with images of standard firefighting equipment—trucks, hoses, and diffuse spray, all of which seemed utterly dwarfed by the huge facility. The fear was that failing to restore normal cooling processes or to establish effective emergency measures to replace them—and quickly—might lead to a catastrophe. As reporters from the *New York Times* explained in rather dry language on March 13, "A partial meltdown can occur when radioactive fuel rods, which normally are covered in water, remain partially uncovered for too long. The more the fuel is exposed, the closer the reactor comes to a full meltdown."[37]

Indeed, water levels inside the reactor cores had already begun to fall. Estimates varied during the initial few days, in part because key gauges weren't working properly.[38] However, government officials and industry specialists guessed that the top four to nine feet had been exposed to air, which risked leading to a partial and possibly full meltdown of the reactor cores. To compound matters, it was not just water in the cores that incited concern. It was also the cooling ponds for spent fuel rods, recently discharged from the reactor cores and thus highly radioactive. Just two days into the disaster, experts had already expressed fears that some of these rods had become exposed to the air and begun emitting gamma radiation, the most lethal form of radiation to humans.[39] The material properties and qualities of water from the surrounding natural environment initially external to the facility were thus vital to the safe operation of a complex, ostensibly high-tech system. The emerging crisis highlighted, indeed magnified, this dependency.[40]

Part of the problem facing those trying to control the situation at Fukushima Daiichi is that nuclear reactors are never—and can never be—completely off. A nuclear chain reaction may be stopped and the reactor is, at least in theory, safely shut down. Fukushima's managers and technicians did have time to perform these protocols before the reactor cores started melting. This was a major difference from Chernobyl, which also lacked a hard containment shell. However, residual heat in the reactors remains for two reasons. First, the reactors had been operating at high temperatures (550 degrees Fahrenheit) that resist rapid dissipation. Second and more significantly, the fuel still produces heat, even once the facility has technically been turned off, due to continuing radioactivity and the release of subatomic particles and gamma rays. It may be only 6 percent of the heat produced during normal operations, but that is still plenty. Pumps must therefore keep water circulating through the reactor core and spent fuel storage ponds, and, crucially, the temperature of that water must be closely regulated by pulling warmed water to a heat exchanger and bringing in new cool water to draw off that heat. Otherwise, the "cooling" fluid will evaporate—and, unfortunately, rather quickly. Recalling Perrow, a cascade effect threatens to make a bad situation even worse: as radioactive decay continues, more heat is produced, which boils off more water, causing water levels to drop further, exposing more fuel to steam and air, which results in greater fuel damage, raising temperatures even higher, which causes even more water to evaporate, and so on. This downward spiral only increases the possibility of a meltdown. Without electrical power at Fukushima Daiichi, customary cooling processes were inoperable and thus ineffective, thereby precipitating precisely the kind of scenario described above.[41]

Several hard-learned lessons have come to light in the hindsight of 3/11 and its continuing aftermath. The properties of radioactive elements and water—and, importantly, how they interact with one another—matter during both normal operations and "normal accidents." Radioactive elements also do not—and cannot—conform to the mechanical idea, or perhaps ideal, of an on/off switch. In fact, when it comes to nuclear reactors, the common and convenient dualism of on/off is not only reductive but inadequate; as we have seen, the reality is much more complicated.

However, although the plant's cooling system and backup support had failed, operators perceived the nearby Pacific Ocean and the air surrounding Fukushima Daiichi as part of an emergency control system. Or rather, they could become part of that system, indeed vital to it. Consequently, Fukushima operators quickly developed a makeshift practice of flooding—or trying to flood—the reactors' containment vessels with seawater and let the fuel cool by boiling off that water.[42] However, as that water boiled, pressure in the vessel increased and actually became too high to inject more water. As one American official explained, forcing water into the vessel is like "trying to pour water into an inflated balloon." They therefore "have to vent the vessel to the atmosphere, and feed in more water, a procedure known as 'feed and bleed.'"[43] The key was to ensure that plant operators kept an adequate supply of water flowing into the containment vessels to make up for the "lost" water as it heated, turned into steam, and was eventually vented. Instrument problems only compounded an already difficult situation, as technicians were not sure exactly how much water remained in the reactors and therefore how much more water needed to be injected. In effect, they were "flooding blind." Furthermore, the emergency solution was not even a short-term fix. Nuclear engineers estimated that the process of injecting water could entail several thousand gallons per day, for "potentially as long as a year."[44] After all, given the radioactive elements' continuing decay (not to mention their long half-lives), the process of injecting water, followed by its warming, evaporation, and sanctioned release, would necessarily be ongoing. In retrospect, we now know that these efforts, heroic but piecemeal, did not prevent the meltdown of three reactor cores.

These emergency practices did, however, create new relationships between ecological and technological entities within and outside Fukushima Daiichi, demonstrating that the boundaries of these systems are fluid, dynamic, and negotiable. Some of the ensuing relationships were inadvertent, as certainly no one had wanted or planned the earthquake, tsunami, or reactor problems at Fukushima Daiichi (let alone all three) in the first place. Nonetheless, the tsunami had blurred the borders of the Pacific and nuclear reactors, hydraulic and atomic. But, as we have seen, other relationships were intended to solve or at least diminish the severity of the disaster precisely because plant operators and nuclear regulators perceived environmental and technological boundaries as negotiable and sought to make them even more permeable as part of their crisis management efforts. The "feed and bleed" procedure is a prime example of the ways in which borders broke down because historical actors perceived them as porous and acted accordingly. Yet, in the process, desperate officials and workers ended up unintentionally introducing new wrinkles in the "cascade of accumulating problems" at Fukushima Daiichi.

The influx of seawater from the Pacific Ocean, later laced with boric acid to prevent the fuel from reaching criticality, attempted to contain a situation that seemed to be spiraling out of control.[45] That fluid may have averted even more disaster, but at the same time, this solution ended up creating a new problem: the liquid, once savior, had now itself become dangerous, a risk object.[46] Not all of the doctored seawater injected into the reactors boiled off (and thankfully so). Consequently, what remained became contaminated with radiation as well. By late June 2011, more than one hundred thousand metric tons of "water"—in reality, a salty, noxious mixture of seawater, fresh water, and radioactive materials that exemplified the new envirotechnical system at Fukushima Daiichi—had collected in the bowels of the stricken reactors. One journalist called the brew "a radioactive *onsen* (hot bath)," an erroneous translation of the Japanese word for natural hot springs.[47] Moreover, even in June 2011 (three months after the disaster), an additional five hundred metric tons of seawater was being poured into the facility because leaks prevented normal cooling systems from being restored.

To contend with this literal and figurative overflow of contaminated liquid, TEPCO installed devices to filter radioactive residue from the infusion. The utility did so for two reasons: to reduce the volume of contaminated fluid overall and to decrease the amount of radiation so that some of that fluid could be reused on the fuel rods. After all, these rods still needed to be cooled, but without being filtered first, the infusion would leave radiation levels in the reactors too high for cleanup workers to continue their mitigation efforts. Importantly, this precaution suggests not only that human bodies were becoming envirotechnical objects but also that actors themselves perceived them as such, crucial points to which I will return.

However, a trial run with the filtering devices was aborted after less than five hours when it captured as much cesium 137 as they expected to be filtered in an entire month. In addition, the capacity of enormous tanks TEPCO delivered to store some of the excess fluid proved entirely inadequate, especially as workers continued to spray the reactors daily. Facing a Sisyphean situation, TEPCO released more than eleven thousand metric tons of the toxic brew into the Pacific in April 2011. The rationale: dumping less-contaminated water allowed limited storage facilities to be dedicated to more highly contaminated water. Only two months later, more sanctioned releases were expected.[48] If the tsunami had confounded the boundaries of the oceanic and the atomic, sea and reactors, then cleaning up Fukushima further blurred those borders.

Other boundaries were also transgressed at the nadir of the calamity: just as the water of the Pacific became an integral part of Fukushima in the attempt to manage the crisis, so too did the atmosphere surrounding the facility. Once doctored seawater was injected and began boiling, plant operators planned releases of steam to reduce the pressure in the reactors. The aim here was to ease the infusion of even more fluid, while simultaneously reducing the likelihood of a catastrophic explosion that might rupture containment shells and release much higher doses of radiation from the reactor cores and spent fuel storage ponds into the atmosphere. Radioactive contamination within the reactors meant, however, that this vapor was contaminated as well. Initially, when the fuel was intact, the steam workers released was infused by "modest" amounts of radioactive materials "in a non-troublesome form." However, as the condition within the reactors deteriorated and fuel became damaged, that steam became "dirtier."[49] Without these planned releases, the situation might well have worsened. Still, they were apparently not enough. Explosions rocked four of the reactors during the first few days, indicating that technical experts did not have as much control over the process of venting excess pressure as they had hoped. These episodes undermined confidence in the notion of system control, suggesting that large-scale, modern technological systems were more vulnerable than many believed or represented.[50]

I have focused thus far on the complex dynamics of radioactive elements, water, and air in and beyond the reactors. But we must not forget the human element—from the so-called Fukushima Fifty, a core set of workers who remained at the facility as the crisis deepened in a desperate attempt to regain control over the precipitous cascade of events, to the over eighteen thousand men who had participated in cleanup efforts by early December 2011.[51] These workers were vital to the system in a situation of crisis and its aftermath. Their labor, their physical bodies, which attempted to assess and repair, flood and vent in precariously precise proportions, were crucial to getting the new envirotechnical system of Fukushima Daiichi under control, indeed modifying it to reduce the level of risk. However, the extent of their radiation exposure is yet unknown and will probably be debated, if not hotly contested. Given their extended proximity to the nuclear power plant, these workers will likely embody, quite literally, new configurations of the natural and technological in the latest chapter of Japan's atomic age.

It is vital to note that TEPCO and nuclear regulatory officials themselves perceived these connections, both as the disaster unfolded and as the herculean cleanup efforts have begun. On March 14, four days into the crisis, TEPCO's president asked Japan's prime minister Naoto Kan to allow the utility to pull the remaining skeleton crew of workers, obviously fearing these men would be exposed to extremely high doses of radiation if they remained at Fukushima Daiichi. Kan refused and installed a trusted aide at the utility's headquarters the next morning, suggesting that the greater good required individual sacrifice.[52] The nuclear power utility thus constructed workers' bodies as a site where the atomic and biological were coming together dangerously during the disaster. Conveniently, this allowed the company to claim that it was worried about the health and safety of these nuclear heroes, a concern that they had apparently not had for workers during the facility's normal operation and maintenance.

Thousands of workers are now part of the new system at Fukushima Daiichi. However, these temporary laborers are let go from their jobs once they reach their radiation exposure limit, a practice that again suggests how actors perceive—and fear—the merging of the natural and the technological in the workers' own bodies. Structuring labor in this way is thus not only a political and economic act, but it is also an envirotechnical one. Unfortunately, these workers have a strong financial incentive to forget the dosimeters that measure their radiation exposure during a given shift to prolong employment, thus increasing their levels of exposure. Their bodies suffer the consequences.

Power and Politics at Fukushima

As an environmental historian, I have not only emphasized the nature of the "technological" system at Fukushima Daiichi but also argued that we should think of these systems as *envirotechnical* in order to capture the ongoing ways that environmental processes both shape and are shaped by technologies. Doing so helps remind us that technologies often obscure our connections to the environment, but "there are no technologies that remove us from nature."[53]

However, there is a real risk in naturalizing 3/11, paying too much attention to environmental factors and processes involved either in the normal functioning of these reactors or during the crisis. Over a decade ago, Ted Steinberg stressed the unnatural history of so-called natural disasters in his book *Acts of God*.

Unfortunately, Hurricanes Katrina and the oft-forgotten Rita and the differential effects of earthquakes in places such as Haiti and Chile have recently only reconfirmed Steinberg's insights.[54]

In fact, some Japanese citizens today are wary of analysis that stresses the role of nonhuman nature in modern technological systems, or anything resembling what Brett Walker calls "hybrid causation."[55] This was emphasized by Tyson Vaughan, a PhD student in Cornell's Department of Science and Technology Studies, who was recently discussing Walker's concept, as well as envirotechnical analysis, with several people in Japan involved in ongoing debates over mercury poisoning at Minamata Bay during the 1950s. This discussion arose in the context of Vaughan's own research on postdisaster reconstruction efforts in Japan and the United States. His interviewees included the curator of the Minamata Disease Municipal Museum, the curator of Soshisha (the Supporting Center for Minamata Disease), a Nippon Hōsō Kyōkai (Japan Broadcasting Corporation) journalist, and *kataribe* (storyteller) Miyako Kawamoto, the widow of Teruo Kawamoto, who had been the leader of one of the primary victims' advocacy groups.[56] Vaughan conveyed that all four interviewees, but particularly Miyako, were distressed by the notion of hybrid causation or seeing technologies as envirotechnical. In their view, focusing, say, on the properties of mercury or how different organisms, including humans, absorbed it at Minamata diverts attention from the corporate and government decisions that contributed to the poisoning of two thousand victims, with an untold number of others not officially recognized. In short, they fear that multicausal accounts reflecting complex understandings of historical agency that decenter people as primary causal agents threaten to diffuse, if not undermine, the responsibility and ultimate culpability of powerful groups. In this particular case, they worry that such concepts water down the assignation of responsibility to Chisso Corporation, the company that released mercury into Minamata Bay.[57]

It may be tempting for scholars to dismiss their understanding of historical causality, arguing that it is too simplistic and fails to reflect advances in scholarship. But the past very much matters to citizens of Japan today, and it informs their views of nature, technology, politics, and their relationship with one another. For one, other tragedies—perhaps most prominently, Hiroshima, Nagasaki, and Minamata—loom large in the nation's memory, particularly for those active in citizens' movements and litigation related to these crises. Given such a past, it is understandable why they may be reading Fukushima partly through the lenses of events such as Minamata. Indeed, the protracted court battle over Minamata only ended on March 22, 2011, eleven days after the situation at Fukushima Daiichi began.[58] In addition, as Maruyama Masao and Julia Adeney Thomas have argued, naturalizing state power in twentieth-century Japan has historically served to disempower critiques by citizens, ultimately crushing social movements and disabling antistate reform. Thus, because naturalization and hybridity have essentially functioned as powerful tools of the state, the response of Vaughan's interviewees to scholarly trends that develop and promote such concepts is even less surprising.[59] After Fukushima, they may be more dubious than ever about framing technological systems as envirotechnical. It seems, at least at first glance, too apolitical: pointing to environmental factors can naturalize a crisis, while technical explanations carry the false sense of objectivity, both of which evade fundamental questions of power. Importantly, such critiques and the wider political stakes they signal remind scholars of the "real world" implications of their work.

Nonetheless, I suggest that we can and should read what took place at Fukushima Daiichi as an envirotechnical disaster. Indeed, thinking envirotechnically does not necessarily obscure the critical political issues these Japanese actors stress. To the contrary, as Douglas Weiner succinctly put it in his American Society for Environmental History presidential address several years ago, "Every environmental story is a story about power."[60] Indeed, politics are central to the Fukushima of today because they are central to its history. They were inscribed into the facility from the very outset, starting with Japan's decision to develop atomic energy. Facing pressure from the antinuclear movement, industry supporters, not just in Japan, invoked the mantra of safety time and again.[61] Yet, as one former plant operator stated after the crisis at Fukushima Daiichi began to unfold, "You can take all kinds of possible situations into consideration, but something 'beyond imagination' is bound to take place, like the March 11 tsunami."[62] As he suggests, probabilistic thinking, which inherently downplays possibilities such as a 9.0 earthquake or a fourteen-meter tsunami (let alone both), dominates the nuclear industry, although it is certainly not unique. This tendency is signaled by the fact that Japan's Nuclear Safety Commission (the equivalent of the US Nuclear Regulatory Commission) did not include any measures regarding tsunami in its guidelines until 2006, long after the country's reactors were actually built.[63]

Perrow argued in an essay published several weeks after Fukushima that we should instead "consider a worst-case approach to risk: the 'possibilistic' approach," a concept articulated by sociologist Lee Clark.[64] There are, of course, powerful vested interests against adopting such an approach. For one, the ways in which notions of the nation and the nuclear have become entwined in the post-1945 world, including in Japan, helps to explain past decisions such as the nuclear industry's "safety myth" and inadequate government regulation of TEPCO.[65] In addition, economics are a powerful form of politics. One TEPCO engineer admitted that he falsified records regarding the containment vessel of reactor number 4 at the Fukushima Daiichi power plant, and design decisions may have prioritized convenience and cost over safety.[66]

Politics also significantly shaped how the natural and the technological became entangled at Fukushima Daiichi, whether before 3/11 or afterwards. The concept of envirotechnical regime foregrounds the politics of this process, including how particular groups and institutions pushed for linking nature and technology in specific ways, both in situations of normalcy and those of crisis. Let me return to three examples that I have cited in this chapter.

First, Japan established and expanded a nuclear industry on the edge of the Pacific "Ring of Fire," a perimeter known for its major earthquakes and potential for destructive tsunamis. Imperatives of reconstruction, nation building, industrialization, and modernization drove such decisions in spite of the hazardous environment in which they were being undertaken. Lesson: in the context of powerful political and economic motives, supporters of nuclear power in Japan conveniently differentiated natural and technological systems, even as these material linkages were actually being forged and strengthened on the ground.

Second, the timing of the seawater injections at Fukushima has been much debated and contested. It has been suggested that TEPCO's administration delayed flooding the reactors with water from the Pacific because doing so "amounted to sacrificing the reactors."[67] As *Wall Street Journal* reporters wrote on March 19, "TEPCO considered using seawater from the nearby coast to cool one of its six reactors at least as early as last Saturday morning, the day after the quake struck. But it didn't do so until that evening, after the prime minister ordered it following an explosion at the facility. TEPCO didn't begin using seawater at other reactors until Sunday." According to Akira Omoto, a former TEPCO executive and a member of the Japan Atomic Energy Commission, the utility "hesitated because it tried to protect its assets."[68] Lesson: seawater injections may indeed illustrate the reblending of environmental and technological systems at Fukushima Daiichi, but the context, timing, and meaning of that process matter as much as the act itself. In other words, it's not just that the oceanic and atomic were again linked through the desperate emergency protocol but that they were connected only when TEPCO, pressured by government leaders, was forced to recognize how truly disastrous the situation had become.

Finally, the Fukushima Fifty have received a great deal of attention, being heralded in the national and international media for their selfless sacrifice. But as we have seen, many more labor below the radar screen—or, perhaps more aptly, below the dosimeter. However, it is not just a question of the forgotten masses, focusing on the nuclear heroes at the nadir of the crisis while ignoring the thousands of short-term workers carrying out cleanup as the disaster fades from our memories (at least for those of us who are located thousands of miles away from Japan). Rather, as Gabrielle Hecht has powerfully shown, the political and economic context of their presence, their work, and their bodies is noteworthy.

The structure of subcontracting work in the nuclear industry—in Japan but also elsewhere—is such that these workers, often called "nuclear nomads," are basically left unprotected by environmental health and safety regulations, unaccounted for by corresponding statistics. Furthermore, most of them are men from the evacuation zone surrounding Fukushima Daiichi who are desperate for work because the disaster left them unemployed or poor day laborers who live in slums surrounding Japanese cities. This practice conveniently elevates the safety ratings of a given utility like TEPCO or that of the nuclear industry overall while reducing official statistics regarding human health exposure. Lesson: it's not just any bodies that are being exposed to increased rates of radiation in Japan, before and after Fukushima.[69] Rather, some of the poorest, most economically vulnerable people in Japan are more likely to be affected (and affected more significantly) by the merging of the biological and the atomic in the modern world.

As these examples illustrate, the political shaping of Fukushima Daiichi's technological system is unquestionably vital. It demands careful consideration by scholars and citizens alike. Yet politics alone does not explain the triple disaster. Obviously, the massive earthquake and tsunami have a bearing. As do the properties of radioactive materials, water, air, and human bodies, and the relationships among them both during normal operations and "normal accidents," purposefully and inadvertently. At the same time, as the concerns of skeptical Japanese citizens remind us, it is indeed hazardous to focus on the nature of the disaster alone, isolating it from the larger system of which it was a critical part. It is precisely the complex, dynamic, porous, and inextricable configuration of nature, technology, and politics that *together* helps us understand all that the single word "Fukushima" now signifies.[70] It was due to an earthquake, nuclear reactors, *and* delayed seawater injections; a huge tsunami, backup generators located in basements, *and* probabilistic thinking; continued radioactive decay, spent fuel rods, *and* weak government oversight of industries characterized by high-modernist technologies. As Michelle Murphy states in a much different context, "*And. . . . And. . . . And . . .*"[71]

Conclusion

In the end, Fukushima explodes, so to speak, Hughes' idealized representation of "closed" and "open" technological systems, where "closed" systems are those that have brought the environment under system control and "open" systems remain subjected to environmental influences.[72] Instead, by thinking in terms of envirotechnical systems, we can avoid the pitfalls of such tidy categories, firm borders, and static notions of both nature and technology that fall apart in places like Fukushima. Meanwhile, the concept of envirotechnical regimes draws attention to the political processes by which these systems are brought into existence and maintained. This approach therefore encourages us to consider how, why, and in what particular ways technological and natural systems articulate with one another, even when, as Perrow put it, "designers never expected them to be connected."[73] Examples abound, especially in the early twenty-first century, but Fukushima has particularly—and poignantly—brought these lessons home.

Notes

Author's note: A previous version of this chapter appeared in *Environmental History* 17:2 (2012): 219–243; published by Oxford University Press on behalf of the American Society for Environmental History and the Forest History Society. I thank the journal and its editor, Nancy Langston, for allowing an updated version to be republished here. I would also like to thank Ian Miller, Julia Adeney Thomas, Brett Walker, and two anonymous journal reviewers for their insightful comments on earlier versions of this chapter. Finally, I thank Nancy Langston for soliciting the original essay, Tyson Vaughan for his critical research contributions, and Connie Hsu Swenson for her editorial assistance.

1. The US Geologic Survey concluded that the Tōhoku earthquake was magnitude 9.0, although some newspaper accounts cited 8.9. See http://earthquake.usgs.gov/earthquakes/recenteqsww/Quakes/usc0001xgp.php (all Web sites last accessed January 26, 2012). For a historical study of earthquakes in Japan and their relationship to the nation, see Greg Clancey, *Earthquake Nation: The Cultural Politics of Japanese Seismicity, 1868–1930* (Berkeley: University of California Press, 2006). Reports of the tsunami's height also vary. In a recent *Scientific American* article, David Biello refers to fourteen meters: "Fukushima Meltdown Mitigation Aims to Prevent Radioactive Flood," *Scientific American,* June 24, 2011, http://www.scientificamerican.com/article.cfm?id=fukushima-meltdown-radioactive-flood, while Charles Perrow quotes estimates ranging from thirty to forty-six feet: "Fukushima, Risk, and Probability: Expect the Unexpected," *Bulletin of the Atomic Scientists,* April 1, 2011; and a *New York Times* journalist references fifty feet: Hiroku Tabuchi, "Company Believes 3 Reactors Melted Down in Japan," *New York Times* (hereafter *NYT*), May 24, 2011. On the speed of the tsunami, see CTV.ca News Staff, "Tsunami Speed Comparable to Clip of Jumbo Jet," CTV News, http://www.ctv.ca/CTVNews/TopStories/20110311/quake-feature-110311/. On the possibility that the earthquake caused significant structural damage before the tsunami hit, see David McNeill and Jake Adelstein, "What Happened at Fukushima?" *Asia Times Online,* August 12, 2011, http://www.atimes.com/atimes/Japan/MH12Dh01.html. In June 2011, Japan's Nuclear Emergency Response Headquarters declared that three reactors experienced full meltdowns (CNN Wire Staff, "3 Japan Nuclear Reactors Had Full Meltdown, Agency Says," June 6, 2011, http://news.blogs.cnn.com/2011/06/06/3-japan-nuclear-reactors-had-full-meltdown-agency-says/). The following day, the *Daily Yomiuri* (*Yomiuri Shimbun*), a leading Japanese newspaper, expressed concern that the reactors had actually experienced "melt-throughs," which are more severe than core meltdowns and "the worst possibility in a nuclear accident" ("'Melt-through' at Fukushima? Govt Report to IAEA Suggests Situation Worse Than Meltdown," *Yomiuri Shimbun,* June 8, 2011, http://www.yomiuri.co.jp/dy/national/T110607005367.htm).

A subsequent government report asserted, however, that Fukushima had not experienced a melt-through: "Concerning Units 1 to 3 of the Fukushima Dai-ichi NPS [Nuclear Power Station], as the situation where water injection to each RPV [Reactor Pressure Vessel] was impossible to continue for a certain period of time, the nuclear fuel in each reactor core was not covered by water but was exposed, leading to a core melt. Part of the melted fuel stayed at the bottom of the RPV." See "Report of Japanese Government to the IAEA Ministerial Conference on Nuclear Safety: The Accident at TEPCO's Fukushima Nuclear Power Stations," p. 8, http://www.kantei.go.jp/foreign/kan/topics/201106/iaea_houkokusho_e.html. For an accessible overview of what occurred at Fukushima, see "Status of the Nuclear Reactors at the Fukushima Daiichi Power Plant," *NYT*, last updated April 29, 2011, http://www.nytimes.com/interactive/2011/03/16/world/asia/reactors-status.html?ref=earth. See also *NYT* blogs during the early days of the crisis, such as http://thelede.blogs.nytimes.com/2011/03/11/, for more detailed coverage of events as they evolved.

2. Kent Anderson argues that some have started referring to the disaster as "3-11," obviously evoking the political valence of 9/11 in the United States and forging a parallel between the two crises and societies. See his essay, "A Hundred Days after Japan's Triple Disaster," *East Asia Forum,* June 20, 2011, http://www.eastasiaforum.org/2011/06/20/a-hundred-days-after-japan-s-triple-disaster/. I emphasize "ever since" because Japan's Atomic Energy Commission announced in late October 2011 that it may take more than three decades to clean up Fukushima: http://www.guardian.co.uk/world/2011/oct/31/fukushima-nuclear-plant-30-years-cleanup.

3. A number of environmental historians have engaged with recent crises and debates. On Hurricane Katrina, see Ari Kelman, "Nature Bats Last: Some Recent Works on Technology and Urban Disaster," *Technology and Culture* 47 (2006): 391–402; Ari Kelman, "Boundary Issues: Clarifying New Orleans's Murky Edges," *Journal of American History* 94 (2007): 695–703. On hydraulic fracturing in the Marcellus Shale ("hydrofracking"), see Joel A. Tarr, "There Will Be Gas," *Pittsburgh Post-Gazette,* August 2, 2009, http://www.post-gazette.com/pg/09214/987834–109.stm. On the Deepwater Horizon oil spill, see Christopher Jones, "Defining the Problem," posted to H-Energy, June 27, 2010, http://www.h-net.org/~energy/roundtables/Jones_Gulf.html; Peter Shulman, "A Catastrophic Accident of Normal Proportions," posted to H-Energy, June 27, 2010, http://www.h-net.org/~energy/roundtables/Shulman_Gulf.html; and several other responses at http://aseh.net/teaching-research/environmental-historians-respond-to-the-gulf-oil-spill/copy_of_ehresponsetoGulf OilSpill.pdf. A number of scholars of Japan from diverse disciplinary backgrounds (and nationalities) have contributed to the scrutiny of Fukushima since March 11, 2011; for over one hundred analyses, see the *Asia-Pacific Journal's* forum on the triple disaster: http://www.japanfocus.org/Japans-3.11-Earthquake-Tsunami-Atomic-Meltdown.

4. On "energy regimes, both politically and technologically," I am influenced here by Gabrielle Hecht's notion of technopolitics, which emphasizes the specifically technological means of political ends, Paul Edwards' arguments regarding the power (and often invisibility) of infrastructure, and Thomas Parke Hughes' work on the "momentum" of technological systems. See Gabrielle Hecht, *The Radiance of France: Nuclear Power and National Identity after World War II,* 2nd ed. (Cambridge, MA: MIT Press, 2009); Paul N. Edwards, "Infrastructure and Modernity: Force, Time, and Social Organization in the History of Sociotechnical Systems," in *Modernity and Technology,* ed. Thomas Misa, Philip Brey, and Andrew Feenberg (Cambridge, MA: MIT Press, 2003): 185–226; Thomas Parke Hughes, *Networks of Power: Electrification in Western Society, 1880–1930* (Baltimore: Johns Hopkins

University Press, 1983), especially 14–15 and chapter 6. On the relationship between fossil fuels and political systems, see Timothy Mitchell, "Carbon Democracy," *Economy & Society* 38:3 (2009): 399–432; a much elaborated version is his more recent *Carbon Democracy: Political Power in the Age of Oil* (New York: Verso, 2011). For a few implications of the atomic age, see Stephen Bocking, "Ecosystems, Ecologists, and the Atom: Environmental Research at Oak Ridge National Laboratory," *Journal of the History of Biology* 28 (1995): 1–47; Jacob Darwin Hamblin, *Poison in the Well: Radioactive Waste in the Oceans at the Dawn of the Nuclear Age* (New Brunswick: Rutgers University Press, 2008). For syntheses of literature at the intersection of environmental history and the history of technology, see Jeffrey K. Stine and Joel A. Tarr, "At the Intersection of Histories: Technology and the Environment," *Technology and Culture* 39 (1998): 601–640; Martin Reuss and Stephen H. Cutcliffe, eds., *The Illusory Boundary: Environment and Technology in History* (Charlottesville: University of Virginia Press, 2010), especially the introduction, the afterword, and the essay by Hugh S. Gorman and Betsy Mendelsohn, "Where Does Nature End and Culture Begin? Converging Themes in the History of Technology and Environmental History," 265–290; Sara B. Pritchard, *Confluence: The Nature of Technology and the Remaking of the Rhône* (Cambridge, MA: Harvard University Press, 2011), introduction.

5. I do not take up the question of what makes technological systems "modern" here. One classic study is Bruno Latour, *We Have Never Been Modern*, trans. Catherine Porter (Cambridge, MA: Harvard University Press, 1993). It is also possible to question the use of singular "system" (versus "systems") to describe Fukushima. As the loss of electrical power at Fukushima demonstrated, "high-tech" reactors were dependent on seemingly "low-tech" technologies such as power grids. In a recent talk, Paul Edwards highlighted the problems that occur when multiple technological systems do not articulate effectively with one another, especially in times of crisis. This issue raises concerns about not only the vulnerabilities of an individual system but also the ways in which systems are often entangled and interdependent, thereby creating new vulnerabilities from their synergies and dissonances. See Paul N. Edwards, comments at "Infrastructure(s) and the Fukushima Earthquake: A Roundtable on Emergencies, Nuclear and Otherwise," annual meeting of the Society for the History of Technology, Cleveland, OH, November 3–6, 2011.

6. I set aside here the important issue of how natural and sociotechnical factors are categorized and differentiated, both historically and analytically. Sociologists and historians of technology often use the term "sociotechnical" to stress the social and political shaping of technology, particularly as technical and technological are often placed in opposition to the social. Their larger point is to emphasize the mutual shaping of society and technology.

7. Charles Perrow, *Normal Accidents: Living with High-Risk Technologies*, 2nd ed. (Princeton, NJ: Princeton University Press, 1999). See also his more recent book *The Next Catastrophe: Reducing Our Vulnerabilities to Natural, Industrial, and Terrorist Disasters* (Princeton, NJ: Princeton University Press, 2007).

8. On the idea of sociotechnical systems, see Hughes, *Networks of Power*, 6. See also Wiebe Bijker, Thomas Hughes, and Trevor Pinch, eds., *The Social Construction of Technological Systems: New Directions in the Sociology and History of Technology* (Cambridge, MA: MIT Press, 1987).

9. David E. Sanger and Matt Wald, "Radioactive Releases in Japan Could Last Months, Experts Say," *NYT*, March 13, 2011.

10. I use the adjective "hazardous" to evoke Leo Marx's argument regarding technology as a hazardous concept. See Leo Marx, "Technology: The Emergence of a Hazardous

Concept," *Technology and Culture* 51 (2010): 561–577. He published an earlier version of this article in *Social Research* in 1997.

11. For these ideas in the context of the BP oil spill, see Shulman, "A Catastrophic Accident of Normal Proportions."

12. Discussions of "better" modeling techniques exemplify this kind of thinking—what historians of technology sometimes call a "techno-fix." For a consideration of models of nuclear reactors and the field of "atomic forensics" in light of Fukushima, see William J. Broad, "From Afar, a Vivid Picture of Japan Crisis," *NYT*, April 2, 2011. In addition, scholars in science and technology studies (STS) would critique this approach because it focuses on either technical or social issues, reifying the binary in the process. Moreover, reflecting other fundamental STS insights, how the problem gets framed shapes what solution(s) are possible and thus actionable. For thoughts on this issue regarding BP's Deepwater Horizon, see Jones, "Defining the Problem."

13. Hughes, *Networks of Power.*

14. Hughes, *Networks of Power,* 6. However, on Hughes' last point, Perrow would probably argue that internal dynamics are often far more complex than Hughes implies here. He might also question whether a given system's final state can always be predicted, although, as his book *Normal Accidents* shows, Perrow ultimately believed in the ability of analysts and policy makers to classify and predict "normal accidents." In addition, in his later work, Hughes seems to return to these questions about the relationship between technology and the environment when he proposes the notion of "ecotechnological environment," which he defines as "intersecting and overlapping natural and human-built environments" (*Human-Built World: How to Think about Technology and Culture* [Chicago: University of Chicago Press, 2004], 153). In this book, Hughes discusses several examples that illustrate the interpenetration of the natural and technological, but he does not situate his analysis within existing literature or develop the concept as an analytic tool. Hughes also elaborates that "ecotechnological" focuses on "more sustainable" relations between nature and technology. I view "ecotechnological," at least as Hughes defines it, as a subset of the envirotechnical, which can be *any* connections between the environmental and technological.

15. One can also ask if everything comes under Hughes' definition of "environment" here, from unstable commodity prices to striking workers, as both may resist "system control." For an overview of fossil fuels, see J. R. McNeill, *Something New under the Sun: An Environmental History of the Twentieth-Century World* (New York: Norton, 2000). On copper, see Timothy J. LeCain, *Mass Destruction: The Men and Giant Mines that Wired America and Scarred the Planet* (New Brunswick, NJ: Rutgers University Press, 2009). On harnessing rivers in different historical and national contexts, see Theodore Steinberg, *Nature Incorporated: Industrialization and the Waters of New England* (New York: Cambridge University Press, 1991); Richard White, *The Organic Machine* (New York: Hill and Wang, 1995); Mark Cioc, *The Rhine: An Eco-Biography, 1815–2000* (Seattle: University of Washington Press, 2002); David Blackbourn, *The Conquest of Nature: Water, Landscape, and the Making of Modern Germany* (New York: Norton, 2006); Pritchard, *Confluence.*

16. On the problem of agency, see Linda Nash, "The Agency of Nature and the Nature of Agency," *Environmental History* 10 (2005): 67–69. It is worth noting that there were probably reasons why Hughes conceptualized technological systems in this way. For one, Hughes was influenced by post–World War II systems theory. He therefore seemed to use contemporary systems thinking to inform his historical analysis of earlier systems. On systems theory, see Agatha C. Hughes and Thomas Parke Hughes, *Systems, Experts, and*

Computers: The Systems Approach in Management and Engineering, World War II and After (Cambridge, MA: MIT Press, 2000).

17. Perrow, *Normal Accidents,* 14, 296. Italics added.

18. It's worth noting that Perrow expressed confidence in system control as well. After all, his book examines and classifies accidents in the hope that analysts can deduce their fundamental characteristics and identify common patterns, thereby improving the predictive power of both experts and scholars.

19. On climate change, see Clark A. Miller and Paul N. Edwards, *Changing the Atmosphere: Expert Knowledge and Environmental Governance* (Cambridge, MA: MIT Press, 2001); Spencer R. Weart, *The Discovery of Global Warming* (Cambridge, MA: Harvard University Press, 2003); Elizabeth Kolbert, *Field Notes from a Catastrophe: Man, Nature, and Climate Change* (New York: Bloomsbury, 2006); Paul N. Edwards, *A Vast Machine: Computer Models, Climate Data, and the Politics of Global Warming* (Cambridge, MA: MIT Press, 2010). On remaking human bodies and the intersection of the body and environment, see Conevery Bolton Valenčius, *The Health of the Country: How American Settlers Understood Themselves and Their Land* (New York: Basic Books, 2002); Barbara Allen, *Uneasy Alchemy: Citizens and Experts in Louisiana's Chemical Corridor Disputes* (Cambridge, MA: MIT Press, 2003); Gregg Mitman, Michelle Murphy, and Christopher Sellers, eds., *Landscapes of Exposure: Knowledge and Illness in Modern Environments* (Chicago: University of Chicago Press, 2004); Michelle Murphy, *Sick Building Syndrome and the Problem of Uncertainty: Environmental Politics, Technoscience, and Women Workers* (Durham, NC: Duke University Press, 2006); Linda Nash, *Inescapable Ecologies: A History of Environment, Disease, and Knowledge* (Berkeley: University of California Press, 2006); Gregg Mitman, *Breathing Space: How Allergies Shape Our Lives and Landscapes* (New Haven, CT: Yale University Press, 2007); Jody A. Roberts and Nancy Langston, "Toxic Bodies/Toxic Environments: An Interdisciplinary Forum," *Environmental History* 13 (2008): 629–703 and the related articles in this special issue; Sarah A. Vogel, "The Politics of Plastics: The Making and Unmaking of Bisphenol A 'Safety,'" *American Journal of Public Health* 99 (2009): 559–566; Nancy Langston, *Toxic Bodies: Hormone Disruptors and the Legacy of DES* (New Haven, CT: Yale University Press, 2010); Joy Parr, *Sensing Changes: Technologies, Environments, and the Everyday, 1953–2003* (Vancouver: University of British Columbia Press, 2010); Brett Walker, *Toxic Archipelago: A History of Industrial Disease in Japan* (Seattle: University of Washington Press, 2011).

20. On hybrid landscapes, see White, *Organic Machine;* Mark Fiege, *Irrigated Eden: The Making of an Agricultural Landscape in the American West* (Seattle: University of Washington Press, 1999); Richard White, "From Wilderness to Hybrid Landscapes: The Cultural Turn in Environmental History," *Historian* 66 (2004): 557–564. "Nature-culture" is from Latour, *We Have Never Been Modern,* 7. A related concept, "naturecultures," is from Donna J. Haraway, *The Companion Species Manifesto: Dogs, People, and Significant Otherness* (Chicago: Prickly Paradigm Press, 2003), 1; Donna J. Haraway, *When Species Meet* (Minneapolis: University of Minnesota Press, 2008), 16.

21. On vulnerability, see Wiebe E. Bijker, "Globalization and Vulnerability: Challenges and Opportunities for SHOT around Its Fiftieth Anniversary," *Technology and Culture* 50 (2009): 600–612.

22. Hiroko Tabuchi and Matthew L. Wald, "Japanese Scramble to Avert Meltdowns as Nuclear Crisis Deepens after Quake," *NYT,* March 12, 2011; Sanger and Wald, "Radioactive Releases." The phrase "Faustian bargain" is from Christine L. Marran, "Contamination: From Minamata to Fukushima," http://www.japanfocus.org/-Christine-Marran/3526.

23. Tabuchi and Wald, "Japanese Scramble." The tsunami apparently flooded emergency diesel generators. Battery power provided a second backup, but those batteries died fairly quickly. On the staying power of "old" technologies, see David Edgerton, *The Shock of the Old: Technology and Global History since 1900* (New York: Oxford University Press, 2007).

24. For useful historiographical overviews, see Stine and Tarr, "At the Intersection of Histories"; Reuss and Cutcliffe, eds., *Illusory Boundary*, introduction and afterword; Gorman and Mendelsohn, "Where Does Nature End and Culture Begin?" in *Illusory Boundary*.

25. It is worth noting that these kinds of arguments illustrate the problematic boundary between the cultural and the material within environmental history. In addition, although a number of envirotech scholars have discussed the porous boundaries between environmental and technological entities (regardless of whether or not actors believed this was the case), it is critical for historians to differentiate between actors' and analysts' moves. Based on my own research, actors' claims provide a rich source to investigate in its own right. I discuss several examples of actors' strategic conflation and separation of nature and technology in *Confluence*.

26. Of course, managed and harnessed natures suggest how humans have interacted with and transformed "nonhuman" nature, thus further challenging the notion of a supposedly pristine nature without human influence. See Edmund Russell, "The Garden in the Machine: Toward an Evolutionary History of Technology," in *Industrializing Organisms: Introducing Evolutionary History,* ed. Philip Scranton and Susan R. Schrepfer (New York: Routledge, 2004). See also specific examples in William Boyd, "Making Meat: Science, Technology, and American Poultry Production," *Technology and Culture* 42 (2001): 631–664; Robert Gardner, "Constructing a Technological Forest: Nature, Culture, and Tree-Planting in the Nebraska Sand Hills," *Environmental History* 14 (2009): 275–297; Ann Norton Greene, *Horses at Work: Harnessing Power in Industrial America* (Cambridge, MA: Harvard University Press, 2008); and many of the essays in Scranton and Schrepfer, eds., *Industrializing Organisms,* and Reuss and Cutcliffe, eds., *Illusory Boundary.*

27. At times historical actors may have made this argument; for example, in my research, I have found that technical experts invoked environmental factors to support a particular "technical" design feature of a project. These factors may well have shaped the technology, but they may have also have been used to naturalize the ultimate "technical" choice and thereby obscure political, economic, and other considerations in shaping that decision. It is beyond the scope of this chapter to detail historiographical trends within the history of technology. I will simply note here that although there are certainly analytical tensions between the history of technology (and science studies more broadly) and environmental history, largely centering on the inseparability of nature and knowing nature, the former's arguments regarding coproduction, materiality, and affordances and the latter's commitment to the "agency" of nature indicate productive synergies between the fields.

28. For critiques of dichotomies and the articulation of cyborg, "naturecultures," and companion species, see the works of Donna Haraway, especially "A Cyborg Manifesto: Science, Technology, and Socialist-Feminism in the Late Twentieth Century," in *Simians, Cyborgs, and Women: The Reinvention of Nature* (New York: Routledge, 1991), 149–181; *Companion Species Manifesto;* and *When Species Meet.* For an overview of actor network theory, see Bruno Latour, *Reassembling the Social: An Introduction to Actor-Network Theory* (New York: Oxford University Press, 2005). See also Michel Callon, "Society in the Making: The Study of Technology as a Tool for Sociological Analysis," and John Law, "Technology and Heterogeneous Engineering," both in *Social Construction of Technological Systems.*

On mutual or coproduction, see Ronald R. Kline, *Consumers in the Country: Technology and Social Change in Rural America* (Baltimore: Johns Hopkins University Press, 2000); Sheila Jasanoff, ed., *States of Knowledge: The Co-Production of Science and the Social Order* (New York: Routledge, 2004).

29. Perrow's "eco-system" clearly seeks to emphasize the coupling of natural systems (abbreviated as "eco") and human-made systems (represented by "system"), although his play on the word "ecosystem" may end up somewhat obscuring the human component. In contrast, the "technical" in envirotechnical makes this explicit. I am grateful for the NSF-sponsored "Envirotech" workshop at the University of Maryland in 2006 for providing a stimulating environment in which to wrestle with these and related issues. I developed the concepts of envirotechnical systems and regimes in response to conversations at that workshop, presented them at the 2007 Society for the History of Technology meeting, and extended them in *Confluence,* especially the introduction. See also Hughes, *Human-Built World;* LeCain, *Mass Destruction;* Gardner, "Constructing a Technological Forest"; Reuss and Cutcliffe, eds., *Illusory Boundary;* Mark Finlay, "Far beyond Tractors: Envirotech and the Intersections of Technology, Agriculture, and the Environment," *Technology and Culture* 51:2 (2010): 480–485. Let me also clarify that I opt for "envirotechnical system," rather than working within Hughes' notion of "open" systems, for several reasons. Hughes defined "open" and "closed" systems relationally, indicating that "closed" systems exist and "open" systems can eventually be "closed." He therefore expressed confidence in the ability of humans and technologies to attain "system control," as well as the notion that some systems are (and can be) entirely outside environmental influence. In contrast, the idea of an envirotechnical system works from the assumption that environmental factors and processes are always there (thus, by definition, there are no closed systems); however, these factors may be dynamic, and the specific "environment" that is relevant is also historically specific. Why not just refer to such phenomena as "nature" and "technology"? Put simply, it reproduces the binary and distinction, rather than emphasizing hybridity and mutual constitution. STS scholars have used a number of terms such as "nature-culture," "sociotechnical," and "technopolitics" to instead highlight the inextricability of categories and materialities that are often opposed, thereby underscoring their "*bothness.*" Envirotechnical systems and related concepts attempt to do this for nature and technology. In other words, it's not that environmental systems become technological or that technological systems become natural; they are *both* environmental and technological.

30. Again, this can be investigated both historically and analytically.

31. As mentioned in note 5, Edwards highlighted the fact that historians of technology rarely pay attention to the dynamics between or among systems, instead generally concentrating on the history and production of a single system. In his talk, Edwards focused on technological systems articulating with other technological systems. For instance, in the case of Fukushima, we are now aware of the consequences of electricity technologies not meshing with nuclear reactor technologies. Given what happened at Fukushima, one might push Edwards' argument further, to widen our notion of "systems" beyond technological ones and consider the ways that, say, hydrologic or atmospheric systems articulated or did not articulate with the systems of reactors.

32. During the crisis, some discussion focused on whether or not the reactors at Fukushima ran on a mixed fuel known as "MOX," or mixed oxide, which includes reclaimed plutonium. If so, released steam could be more toxic than some other radioactive elements. See Sanger and Wald, "Radioactive Releases."

33. For an overview, see Sanger and Wald, "Radioactive Releases."

34. Arthur F. McEvoy, "Working Environments: An Ecological Approach to Industrial Health and Safety," *Technology and Culture* 36 (1995): S145–172. On the hidden history of the subcontracting system centered on short-term employment in the nuclear industry, including but not limited to Japan, see Gabrielle Hecht, "Nuclear Nomads: A Look at the Subcontracted Heroes," *Bulletin of the Atomic Scientists,* January 9, 2012. I say "usually" because "since the late 1980s," states Hecht, "some 90 percent of nuclear power plant workers in the country [Japan] have been subcontracted."

35. Perrow, "Fukushima, Risk, and Probability."

36. Geospatial Information Authority of Japan, "Land Subsidence Caused by 2011 Tōhoku Earthquake and Tsunami," April 14, 2011, http://www.gsi.go.jp/sokuchikijun/sokuchikijun40003.html.

37. Hiroko Tabuchi and Matthew L. Wald, "Second Explosion at Reactor as Technicians Try to Contain Damage," *NYT,* March 13, 2011.

38. Meanwhile, as Japanese specialists were analyzing what was taking place at Fukushima, experts in "atomic forensics," or modeling atomic simulations abroad, were developing their own analyses of the situation. See Broad, "From Afar."

39. Sanger and Wald, "Radioactive Releases"; Sonja Schmid, "Both Better and Worse than Chernobyl," *London Review of Books,* March 17, 2011. On gamma radiation, see Joy Parr, *Sensing Changes: Technologies, Environments, and the Everyday, 1953–2003* (Vancouver: University of British Columbia Press, 2010), 66–67. In May 2011, TEPCO workers were finally able to get close enough to reactor number 1 to fix a water gauge; once working, it showed that the water level in the reactor was much lower than expected, even with the massive infusion of seawater. In fact, "one of the most startling findings announced Thursday was that water levels in the reactor vessel, which houses the fuel rods, appeared to be about three feet below where the bottom of the fuel rods would normally stand" (quotation from Hiroko Tabuchi and Matthew L. Wald, "Japanese Reactor Damage Is Worse than Expected," *NYT,* May 12, 2011).

40. Edgerton, *Shock of the Old.*

41. This description is based primarily on Sanger and Wald, "Radioactive Releases."

42. Emergency measures were undertaken "quickly," but critics believe it was not fast enough. As I discuss below, seawater injections were probably delayed because of the economic costs of the decision: flooding the reactors with salt water essentially meant scrapping them for good. TEPCO therefore had a strong financial incentive to try other emergency measures first, while the government did not push the company to proceed with flooding until the severity of the crisis was apparent.

43. Quotations from Sanger and Wald, "Radioactive Releases."

44. Description of this process is drawn from Tabuchi and Wald, "Second Explosion"; Tabuchi and Wald, "Japanese Scramble"; Sanger and Wald, "Radioactive Releases"; Henry Fountain, "A Look at the Mechanics of a Partial Meltdown," *NYT,* March 13, 2011.

45. Peter Behr, "Desperate Attempts to Save 3 Fukushima Reactors from Meltdown," *NYT,* March 14, 2011. At the same time, there was concern that delays in water injections worsened the situation at Fukushima. I discuss this point briefly below, but see also Norimitsu Onishi and Martin Fackler, "In Nuclear Crisis, Crippling Mistrust," *NYT,* June 12, 2011.

46. Stephen Hilgartner, "The Social Construction of Risk Objects: Or, How to Pry Open Networks of Risk," in James F. Short and Lee Clark, eds., *Organizations, Uncertainties, and Risk* (Boulder, CO: Westview Press, 1992).

47. Quotation from Biello, "Fukushima Meltdown." Biello's naturalization of the toxic liquid is particularly unfortunate, given that government and corporate interests have worked to focus attention on the earthquake and tsunami alone. Nonetheless, in view of the long-standing importance of bathing rituals and hot springs in Japanese culture, including Shinto religious traditions, the extensive contaminated fluids within and now beyond Fukushima are likely freighted with meaning, from offending animistic spirits to possibly being hell on earth. Interestingly, however, the boundaries between "baths" and "natural" hot springs may be increasingly unclear in Japan, as these springs are often highly managed and cultivated landscapes, which would further complicate interpretations of Fukushima's fluids as a toxic *onsen*. I thank John S. Harding for his critical insights here.

48. Biello, "Fukushima Meltdown"; Andrew Monahan, "Tokyo Electric Power Delays Dumping Water at Fukushima Daiichi Plant," *Wall Street Journal*, April 11, 2011; Marran, "Contamination."

49. Sanger and Wald, "Radioactive Releases."

50. On the explosions, see Behr, "Desperate Attempts," and especially Onishi and Fackler, "In Nuclear Crisis, Crippling Mistrust." On vulnerability, see Bijker, "Globalization and Vulnerability."

51. Details regarding Fukushima workers are from Hecht, "Nuclear Nomads."

52. Some analysts have argued that closer government supervision altered the way TEPCO managed the crisis from that point forward. See Onishi and Fackler, "In Nuclear Crisis."

53. Richard White, "Are You an Environmentalist or Do You Work for a Living? Work and Nature," in *Uncommon Ground: Rethinking the Human Place in Nature,* ed. William Cronon (New York: Norton, 1995): 182.

54. Ted Steinberg, *Acts of God: The Unnatural History of Natural Disaster in America* (New York: Oxford University Press, 2000).

55. Walker, *Toxic Archipelago,* especially 16–20.

56. For more information about the Minamata Disease Municipal Museum, see http://www.minamata195651.jp/guide_en.html. On Soshisha, see http://soshisha.org/english/index_e.htm. For an overview of Teruo Kawamoto and his efforts, see http://www.nytimes.com/1999/02/22/world/teruo-kawamoto-victims-advocate-in-mercury-outbreak.html. I am grateful to Tyson Vaughan for sharing this research story with me and allowing me to include it here. The response of these actors pushed me to consider more thoughtfully the political implications of envirotechnical analysis and inspired much of the discussion in this section. For more on Minamata, see Timothy S. George, *Minamata: Pollution and the Struggle for Democracy in Postwar Japan* (Cambridge, MA: Harvard University Asia Center, 2002); Walker, *Toxic Archipelago,* especially chapter 5. For parallels between Minamata and Fukushima, see Marran, "Contamination."

57. The larger point here is that actors may strategically construct agency to suit their political (and perhaps legal) interests. This brief example suggests how historians can explore actors' conceptions of historical agency and causality in addition to developing their own theoretical approaches. For another illustration, this one focusing on the causes of hydrologic change in the Rhône valley amid postwar modernization efforts, see Pritchard, *Confluence,* chapter 5. For analyzing technological determinism as an actor's move, see Gabrielle Hecht and Michael Thad Allen, eds., *Technologies of Power; Essays in Honor of Thomas Parke Hughes and Agatha Chipley Hughes* (Cambridge, MA: MIT Press, 2001), introduction.

58. On the end of the Minamata court case, see Marran, "Contamination."

59. Julia Adeney Thomas, *Reconfiguring Nature: Concepts of Nature in Japanese Political Ideology* (Berkeley: University of California Press, 2002). I also thank her for helping me historicize and contextualize Vaughan's research story.

60. Douglas R. Weiner, "A Death-Defying Attempt to Articulate a Coherent Definition of Environmental History," *Environmental History* 10 (2005): 404–420.

61. Jacob Darwin Hamblin, "Fukushima and the Motifs of Nuclear History," *Environmental History* 17:2 (2012): 285–299.

62. Quotation from "Nuclear Crisis: How It Happened, Safety Vows Forgotten, 'Safety Myth' Created," *Yomiuri Shimbun,* June 15, 2011.

63. Perrow, "Fukushima, Risk, and Probability"; Onishi and Fackler, "In Nuclear Crisis."

64. Perrow, "Fukushima, Risk, and Probability."

65. However, on the contested notion and definition of "nuclearity," see Gabrielle Hecht, "The Power of Nuclear Things," *Technology and Culture* 51 (2010): 1–30. On links between the nation and nuclear power in the French context, materially and culturally, historically and theoretically, see Hecht, *Radiance of France.*

66. On falsified records and the (convenient) design of the spent fuel storage ponds, see Perrow, "Fukushima, Risk, and Probability."

67. Quotation from Behr, "Desperate Attempts."

68. Quotations from Norihiko Shirouzu, Phred Dvorak, Yuka Hayashi, and Andrew Morse, "Bid to 'Protect Assets' Slowed Reactor Fight," *Wall Street Journal,* March 19, 2011. See also Ken Bradsher, Keith Belson, and Matthew L. Wald, "Executives May Have Lost Valuable Time at Damaged Nuclear Plant," *NYT,* March 21, 2011. For discussion of another aspect of the injection debate—specifically the conflict between TEPCO executives and the plant manager of reactor number 1—see Onishi and Fackler, "In Nuclear Crisis."

69. Christine Marran emphasizes the ways that radioactivity can cross national and other political borders in "Contamination." I certainly don't question her argument. However, it's also worth paying attention to the ways in which radiation exposure can affect all humans yet still have differential impacts on certain bodies.

70. Timothy Mitchell, *Rule of Experts: Egypt, Techno-Politics, Modernity* (Berkeley: University of California Press, 2002), especially chapter 1; Paul Sutter, comment on J. R. McNeill's *Mosquito Empires: Ecology and War in the Greater Caribbean, 1620–1914,* annual meeting of the American Society for Environmental History, Tucson, AZ, April 13–15, 2011; on hybrid causation specifically, see Walker, *Toxic Archipelago.*

71. Murphy, *Sick Building Syndrome,* 180.

72. Hughes, *Networks of Power,* 6.

73. Perrow, *Normal Accidents,* 296.

14

Postcrisis Japanese Nuclear Policy
From Top-down Directives to Bottom-up Activism

DANIEL P. ALDRICH

The earthquake, tsunami, and resulting nuclear power plant meltdown beginning on March 11, 2011, not only destroyed Fukushima's coastline and more than twenty thousand human lives, it altered the course of Japan's energy policy. Throughout the postwar period, there has been a complex interplay between two camps over atomic energy. On one side the Japanese central government, local officials, and the nuclear power industry have advocated energy autarky for an island nation without much gas, oil, or coal through heavy use of nuclear power. On the other side, Japanese citizens have worried about the threat of nuclear accidents to their health and livelihoods and have been concerned about government manipulation of public opinion on the topic. This chapter outlines the fifty-year history of this interplay between top-down directives and grassroots activism, suggesting that the triple disaster of 3/11 may topple the pronuclear iron triangle of government officials, local politicians, and business interests.

In the wake of the crisis, citizens are taking scientific measurements, organizing large-scale protests, and articulating new energy and health priorities. But two questions remain unanswered: first, whether Japanese people and businesses are willing to bear the costs and suffer the externalities of nonnuclear sources of energy in the future, and second, whether the alternative sources of energy will result in less harm to the environment. These questions of political will and technological possibility lie at the heart of understanding the Fukushima disaster and its consequences for Japan's economic and ecological viability.

Japan's "Nuclear Allergy" and Top-down Directives

Following the devastation at the end of World War II, the Japanese population developed a social condition known as *kaku arerugi* (nuclear allergy). The atomic bombings created a strong antinuclear weapons sentiment in Japan, as did the *Lucky Dragon* incident less than a decade later. In March 1954, twenty-three fishermen aboard the *Daigo Fukuryū Maru* (*Lucky Dragon Number 5*) passed through the fallout created by a Pacific Ocean test of the American hydrogen bomb. Soon after returning to Japan, Aikichi Kuboyama, the radio operator, succumbed to acute radiation contamination and became the first victim of the hydrogen bomb. Newspapers covered the incident and monitored his deteriorating health, detailing the all-too-familiar effects of radiation in front-page stories that captured the public's attention. Motivated by this tragedy, residents of the Suginami Ward in Tokyo began a petition drive to ban hydrogen bombs, and by August of 1955 they had secured more than 30 million signatures. Put another way, roughly one-third of the people of Japan expressed their support for a nuclear weapons ban. Many respondents envisioned nuclear power as equally unwanted. The two longest-standing antinuclear organizations in Japan, Gensuikyo and Gensuikin, emerged from these events and continue to hold rallies and disseminate information on nuclear issues.[1]

The widespread fear of radiation and distrust of nuclear power among Japanese civilians following the bombings at Hiroshima and Nagasaki have deterred Japan from pursuing nuclear weapons. Some explain it as a function of the nation's postwar pacifist norms, while others say it is the outcome of institutional design.[2] At the same time, however, Japan has built one of the most advanced commercial nuclear power frameworks in the world. While the United States and France abandoned experimental technologies such as fast breeder reactors, mixed oxide (MOX) fuel, and plans for a closed fuel cycle,[3] Japanese decision makers stuck with these schemes as crucial for achieving indigenous, self-contained energy production.[4] That goal remains in place today. Even the crisis and meltdown at the nuclear power plant in Fukushima and public protests have not elicited an open, formal dialogue on Japan's long-term energy production goals.

Some scholars have argued that Japan's nuclear power program is the outcome solely of market forces, a lack of access points for antinuclear groups, or a top-down political culture.[5] While these approaches partially explain the current situation, the government has carefully designed and refined a broad repertoire of policy instruments to further its nuclear power goals. In the same year as the *Lucky Dragon* incident, the young politician Yasuhiro Nakasone (who eventually became prime minister) proposed that the central government allocate money to nuclear research. The Japanese legislature passed the Atomic Energy Basic Law and developed Japan's own Atomic Energy Commission to mirror institutional developments in the United States. Soon afterward, however, Japan departed from America's primarily market-based approach to energy policy (although the 1957 Price-Anderson Act remains a clear example of the US government amortizing the industry's risks). Rather than allowing private energy utilities throughout the nation to handle the issues of siting and public acceptance on their own, the Japanese government developed an extensive array of policy instruments and soft social control techniques designed to bring public opinion in line with national energy goals. Authorities and regulators overcame opposition and concerns among the broader population and in specific demographic groups, such as coastal fishermen and students, through focused policy instruments intent on manipulating public support.

The government provided a number of different types of support to the Tokyo Electric Power Company (TEPCO) and other regional power monopolies in the early years of nuclear power; one form of help involved logistical and financial support in mapping out potential host communities throughout Japan. Government bureaucrats assisted the utilities both in the physical charting of potential locations—to ensure that they met certain technocratic criteria, such as having access to cooling water, proximity to existing power grid lines, support from relatively aseismic rock, and so forth—and in mapping the social characteristics of nearby communities. Internal documents from the Japan Atomic Industrial Forum (JAIF) industry group showed that planners of the late 1960s and early 1970s were very cognizant of the dangers posed by well-organized horizontal associations, especially fishermen's cooperatives (*gyogyō rōdō kumiai*). Analyses of the siting of nuclear power plants in Japan demonstrate that planners placed these projects in rural communities that were less coordinated and more fragmented and hence less likely to successfully mount antinuclear campaigns.[6] To overcome any remaining opposition in such localities, the government often offered jobs and assistance to fishermen to ensure that the nuclear power plant would not be seen as curtailing their livelihoods.

Initially, the government agency known as MITI (the Ministry of International Trade and Industry, or Tsūshō Sangyō Shō,[7] which became METI in 2001—the Ministry of Economy, Trade, and Industry) had only a handful of techniques to induce public support for nuclear energy. Some communities rallied against planned nuclear complexes in their backyard—fishermen at the Tokaimura nuclear complex, for example, expressed their opposition through boat rallies and marches, and others stopped a planned teaching reactor at Kansai University, located in a densely populated urban area near Uji City—but large-scale opposition had not yet developed in the 1960s and early 1970s. By the late 1970s, however, several national antinuclear umbrella organizations sprang up and began to organize protests across the country. The oil shocks of the 1970s pushed Japan's energy bureaucracy into high gear, as the nominal price of oil skyrocketed and the market price quadrupled from $3 to $12 a barrel.

The high and unstable price of oil—critical for Japan's petrochemical industries as well as a host of other fields, including automobiles and oil refining—created pressure for Japanese planners to achieve a new goal: "energy security." The government hoped that between hydroelectric dams and nuclear power plants, Japan would be able to wean itself off oil from the Middle East. This would require the consent of the citizens of Japan on a large scale. As a result of this new push, the system that allocated benefits to actual and potential nuclear power plant host communities became so complex that the central government created a new agency, the ANRE (Agency for Natural Resources and Energy, or Shigen Enerugi Chō). Over the course of the next decade, more spin-offs were created, including the Japan Atomic Energy Relations Organization, the Japan Industrial Location Center (Nihon Ricchi Sentā), and the Center for the Development of Power Supply Regions. The personnel and budgets of these agencies were focused primarily on the placement of new nuclear power plants throughout the country. Policy instruments for improving nuclear power's image included pep talks from central government bureaucrats, the development of science curricula for school-aged children, Nuclear Power Day, and annual fairs where local fishermen and farmers could sell their products.

ANRE bureaucrats listened closely to the concerns of these demographic groups, who often feared "nuclear blight"—the inability to sell their fishing and agricultural products because of possible radioactivity—more than they feared health risks or environmental damage. In response, the various government agencies set up an annual, large-scale exhibition outside Tokyo called the "Electricity Hometown Fair," where fishermen and farmers from nuclear power plant host communities would be ensured a profit thanks to the hundreds of thousands of tourists and consumers who descended on the convention center, Makuhari Messe, outside Tokyo. Similarly, local government officials began to worry about recall elections, which had ended the political careers of several pronuclear mayors. To address their concerns, the central government organized workshops that educated local elected officials about what had worked—and what had failed—in past attempts to boost nuclear plants in various localities around the country. Mayors and governors who supported atomic reactors in their areas would find themselves invited to the prime minister's residence in Tokyo for a public recognition ceremony honoring their assistance with meeting national energy goals. These hortatory tools sought to create pronuclear agents at the local level who would help rally support for nuclear power plants and overcome any opposition.[8]

The government provided up to $20 million a year to acquiescent communities through the Three Power Source Development Laws (known by the abbreviation Dengen Sanpō). What had initially been a series of ad hoc measures designed to win public support for nuclear power complexes became a tremendously well-funded policy instrument that funneled hidden taxes on electricity use into a pooled account. Bureaucrats then distributed these funds to host communities throughout rural coastal Japan. Through this institutionalized redistributive system and a variety of other measures designed to convince local residents that nuclear power was both safe and necessary, the Japanese government created many host community volunteers among the depopulating towns and villages. For these small communities, such as Futaba in Fukushima and Tomari in Hokkaido, the promise of a nuclear power plant meant potential jobs, millions of dollars in grants and loans, new infrastructure, and the prospect of survival. Commentators have argued that the flow of money into often older, impoverished rural communities has created a "culture of dependence" and a "cycle of addiction."[9]

The breadth of policy instruments for manipulating public opinion, while effective, has not guaranteed success at siting. Research has shown that of the roughly ninety-five attempts to site nuclear power plants over the postwar period, only fifty-four were actually completed. With well-organized and informed opposition groups operating since the early 1980s, including the Citizens' Nuclear Information Center (CNIC, or Genshiryoku Shiryō Jōhō Shitsu) and the antinuclear newspaper *Hangenpatsu Shinbun,* many communities fought back in highly publicized battles. The accidents at Three Mile Island and Chernobyl worried many Japanese residents, but authorities reassured them that these would not be possible in Japan, given its strong engineering credentials, in-depth safety controls, and highly educated and motivated staff. The government also enlarged the range of projects to which the Dengen Sanpō funds could be applied, lengthened the period for which they would be available, and increased the pool of funding provided to local communities. Overall, despite ongoing opposition, the government and regional energy monopolies saw few reasons to worry about the future. One white paper envisioned the construction of an additional seventeen nuclear power plants in Japan by 2024, which would increase the amount of electricity generated by nuclear power from one-third to roughly one-half. These optimistic visions of nuclear power's future, however, were not to be realized.

The Final Straw? The Ongoing 3/11 Disaster

By the late 1990s, siting planners encountered serious bottlenecks in the system of constructing new nuclear power plants. The time between the proposal of the plant and its activation stretched from less than a decade in the early 1970s to more than three decades by the late 1990s.[10] Citizen opposition to nuclear power because of potential health effects, the lack of a long-term storage facility for nuclear waste, and potential proliferation concerns grew steadily. The CNIC and the *Hangenpatsu Shimbun* publicized ongoing fights against siting attempts and provided advice to would-be opposition groups. Across the industrialized democracies, residents began to demand more from their governments, moving beyond basic materialist concerns to focus on the environment, sustainability, and health.[11] In addition, a series of large- and small-scale accidents and cover-ups in the industry, including three fatalities at a nuclear facility in Tokaimura, chipped away at public support for the industry in the mid-1990s.

On December 8, 1995, the experimental sodium-cooled fast breeder reactor known as the Monju experienced a huge sodium leak. The resulting fire was hot enough to melt various steel structures in the chamber. The Japanese agency in charge of the Monju, however, decided to suppress details of the accident and to doctor a publicly released videotape of the leak and its aftermath. Local residents successfully fought attempts to restart the experimental reactor until the summer of 2005, when the Supreme Court ruled in favor of restarting. Some four years after the Monju fire, Japan experienced its worst nuclear accident to date. On September 30, 1999, when three workers at the nuclear fuel cycle company JCO in Tokaimura were preparing fuel for one of Japan's experimental fast breeder reactors, they set off a criticality (that is, an uncontrolled chain reaction) that exposed them to tremendously high levels of radiation. Two of the three died from extreme radiation exposure, and local residents in the nearby town were told to remain indoors to avoid contamination.

These were not the only events that began to break apart public support and faith in the industry. Revelations that TEPCO had covered up numerous accidents, leaks, and cracks since the 1980s also came to light. Engineers came forward in the early 2000s to reveal that at least thirty serious incidents had been hidden by company management. In response, several upper-management executives lost their jobs, and the central government ordered the shutdown of TEPCO's seventeen nuclear reactors in 2002. These events further undermined the industry's credibility. The recent (and ongoing) accident at the Fukushima nuclear complex may be the straw that breaks the camel's back.

On March 11, 2011, a 9.0-magnitude earthquake struck off Japan's northeastern coast, which caused much damage but very few fatalities. Recent data show that less than 6 percent of the deaths were caused by the collapse of buildings.[12] Far more destructive was the tsunami set off by the earthquake, which had waves as high as fifty feet in some places. The tsunami swamped existing seawalls and devastated communities, causing at least twenty thousand deaths, primarily in Iwate, Miyagi, and Fukushima prefectures. Estimates of the damage exceed $220 billion. The highly touted backup systems at the Fukushima Daiichi nuclear complex operated by TEPCO—namely, the diesel generators and batteries—went offline soon after the earthquake and tsunami, although investigators have yet to pin down which event was primarily responsible for the failure.

As a result, although the reactors automatically shut down, residual heat caused fuel meltdowns in three of the six reactors at the site. Temperatures rose tremendously in the first day after the tsunami, soaring above 2,000 degrees Fahrenheit and melting the Zircaloy tubes containing the fuel pellets in the reactors. Engineers sought to reduce the growing pressure inside the containment units by deliberately venting the reactors to the atmosphere (thus releasing radioactive elements into the air), and they tried to cool the reactors and ensure that the spent fuel rods would remain underwater by pumping in hundreds of thousands of gallons of seawater. This procedure, which engineers refer to as a "feed and bleed," resulted in approximately one hundred thousand tons of contaminated water accumulating in the basements of the reactors, flowing into the ground and water table nearby, and being dumped into the ocean.[13] Adding to the chaos, hydrogen explosions blew the tops off three of the buildings containing the reactors, the result of Zircaloy and water interacting.

Japanese authorities eventually categorized the incident as a 7 ("major accident") on the International Nuclear Event Scale (INES) due to the amount of radiation released; the 1986 Chernobyl disaster is the only other atomic accident to date in this category. Then prime minister Naoto Kan initially set up a twelve-mile evacuation zone around the Fukushima Daiichi plant and moved to expand the radius of the evacuation over the next two weeks. As of October 2011, more than seventy-five thousand residents of the area were unable to return to their homes in Fukushima Prefecture because of high levels of radioactivity. Foreign governments, including the United States, strongly encouraged their citizens in Japan to evacuate the immediate area (and, in some cases, the country) when details of the accident began to circulate. Since the accident began, a number of agricultural companies were forced to stop exporting food from the area due to radioactive contamination of tea, beef, rice, and citrus products. Many Japanese parents have shown increasing anger over reassurances from the central government that their children are safe, despite blood and urine tests showing high levels of exposure, even in areas far removed from the Fukushima area, such as northern Tokyo, Yokohama, and Saitama.

As the Japanese government struggled to deal with the rising death toll from the tsunami, the slow release of information about the accident from TEPCO, and rising citizen distrust, governments around the world have begun to reevaluate their own commitments to nuclear power. The event's political fallout has spread well beyond Japan's borders. Italy, Germany, and Switzerland, among other industrialized nations, have used the Fukushima nuclear crisis as a focal point for shifting policy away from nuclear power toward less potentially catastrophic sources.

To add fuel to the fire, managers at the Kyūshū Electric Power Company were discovered to have tampered with a public opinion poll posted on June 26, 2011. The poll focused on the restart of the nearby Saga nuclear power complex and was initiated at the suggestion of the Saga prefectural governor, Yasushi Furukawa.[14]

The scandal, known as the *yarase mairu* (staged mail) scandal, involved employees at the utility sending 140 supportive comments to the station, which were enough to tip the balance of opinion in favor of restarting.[15] When the media first reported the problem, the company denied doing anything wrong, but it has since apologized for its actions.

Public opinion polls done by the Roper Center for Public Opinion Research in early August 2011 of some one thousand residents across Japan reported that nearly 60 percent of the respondents had either little or no confidence in the safety of Japan's nuclear power plants. Gaffes from government ministers have not improved matters. Yoshio Hachiro, who was at the time the new trade minister, called the village near the Fukushima Daiichi complex a "town of death," and then had to apologize after tremendous criticism. He soon stepped down from the post.[16] Prime Minister Yoshihiko Noda has apologized to Fukushima governor Yuhei Sato for the government's "inadequate response" to the disaster. After years of manipulation and incentives from the central government, the recent actions of the regional monopoly to alter public opinion have motivated many citizens to mobilize in the wake of the crisis.[17]

Molding the Future

Along with altering the decision-making calculus on nuclear power for Japan and other nations, the events of March 11 opened a window for bottom-up initiatives and bold actions, and they provide hope that the "business as usual" mentality will be upended. Only twelve of Japan's fifty-four reactors were in use as of November 2011, and restarting and reintegrating them into the national power supply will require tremendous public relations work. Japan's major financial newspaper, the *Nikkei Shimbun,* published a series of surveys showing that many corporations plan to relocate their manufacturing to offshore locations—including India, China, and Malaysia—if the Japanese government cannot create a plan to ensure stability in the electricity supply over the next three years. One Japanese business analyst argued that "if we completely abandon nuclear power generation . . . I think most industries would lose competitiveness and go out of Japan."[18] Many observers have underscored the fact that corporations dislike uncertainty, and uncertainty about disruptions in Japan's power supply (or a spike in costs for electricity) has made many Japanese firms deeply anxious. Given the economic difficulties the nation has faced over the past two decades, these new economic threats are being taken very seriously. Some private firms, such as the energy utility KEPCO (Kansai Electric Power Company), have stepped forward with new plans for safer alternative energy sources, including a new ten-thousand-kilowatt solar facility in Osaka Prefecture. Tohoku Electric Power Company has stated its intent to double the capacity of its wind farms by 2020.[19] Popular entrepreneur Masayoshi Son, creator of SoftBank, pledged an investment of a billion yen in the new Japan Renewable Energy Foundation, which is centered on solar energy.

Beyond economic concerns from the business community, several new initiatives show how Japan's civil society has been energized by this tremendous tragedy. The new Safecast project embodies an innovative focus on "citizen science"—that is, the participation of everyday residents as volunteers in data collection, technical measurement, and analysis in fields such as ecology, biodiversity, and astronomy.[20] Participants in such collaborative projects work together, often using Web-based platforms and affordable instrumentation to achieve results that lone researchers in highly funded laboratories would not be able to accomplish.

The full map available on the Safecast Web site (http://blog.safecast.org) is made up of more than six hundred thousand data points collected by volunteers—not TEPCO engineers, central government bureaucrats, or subcontractors from the nuclear industry. Instead, Japanese citizens and foreign residents who own Geiger counters have traveled throughout Japan (including areas in Fukushima), measured radiation levels, and electronically uploaded the collected data to the Safecast project's central Web site. Volunteers have turned the data into a map that illustrates the amount of detected radiation in each spot. In doing so, Safecast has created a public repository of data generated through transparent methodology in real time. This trumps the data released by the government and TEPCO, whose collection methodology has been opaque and whose reporting has been slow. At a time when many survivors of the tsunami have fled their homes in Fukushima seeking what they see as safer shelter in Tokyo, this kind of data sheds light in an otherwise dark time. Japanese bureaucrats have taken notice of the surge in citizen science. Minister of Education and Science Masaharu Nakagawa told reporters, "Citizen's groups have played a very important role in examining their neighbors closely. I really appreciate their contribution, as it's most important to eliminate as many hot spots as possible."[21]

Citizen activism became increasingly visible at recent public meetings hosted by officials from the central government. These meetings have typically been "rituals of assent,"[22] where bureaucrats make statements and the audience says little in response. Many people in nuclear plant host communities reported that government-sponsored attendees have regularly lectured them on the necessity and safety of nuclear power plants since the 1990s. Following Fukushima, many citizens have been unwilling to accept statements from the government or industry at face value.

A new video of Fukushima citizens challenging grim-faced bureaucrats has garnered nearly a quarter of a million views so far.[23] The video shows a number of clearly angry citizens facing down bureaucrats with statements such as,

"People in Fukushima have a right to avoid radiation exposure and live healthy lives, don't they?" Residents forced from their homes in Fukushima have similarly shouted down government representatives as they attempted to justify laborious, sixty-page applications for government assistance. Some yelled, "We don't know who we can trust! Can we actually go back home? And, if not, can you guarantee our livelihoods?"[24] In the past, polls such as the World Values Survey have shown that Japanese residents are not likely to participate in large-scale demonstrations; the Fukushima disaster has brought out a new type of activism.

A recent *Wall Street Journal* article quoted Tokyo resident Taichi Hirano, who said that while he used to shy away from protest rallies, his feelings have changed: "I wanted to go somewhere where I could say loudly that I was scared and not be ashamed."[25] He now uses social media platforms such as Twitter to seek out other participants for marches in the capital. Organizers across the country carried out a Sayonara Nuclear Power Rally in Tokyo's Meiji Park in mid-September, which drew roughly forty thousand participants. Holding placards—and chanting "End nuclear power!"—the large crowd listened to talks from celebrities such as popular author Kenzaburo Oe and musician Ryuichi Sakamoto.[26] These coordinated antinuclear protests are significant not only because they are relatively rare and indicate new levels of activism, but also because the very act of participation in public protest deepens Japan's democracy and enhances the presence of often unrepresented demographics, such as urban workers and youth, in the public sphere.[27]

The government's decision to move away from top-down, technocratic decision-making processes demonstrates that public pressure is altering decades of business-as-usual politics. While the pre-Fukushima strategy for national energy involved siting up to fifteen more nuclear power plants over the next few decades, with the goal of increasing nuclear power's share of production to 50 percent, plans have clearly taken a new direction. The government has taken an important step in promising to separate nuclear regulators from nuclear promoters. Previously, MITI (now METI) was charged with the unsustainable task of both ensuring that the industry cut no corners and encouraging firms to create new plants with government subsidies to host communities. A new institution will take over the Nuclear and Industrial Safety Agency (NISA) and will absorb radiation monitoring activities carried out by bureaucrats within the Ministry for Education, Culture, Sports, Science, and Technology (often known as MEXT). To avoid criticism that the same bureaucrats will simply be reshuffled into the new agency, the government has claimed it will draw on the Ministry of Environment to staff it.

Former prime minister Naoto Kan spoke of moving Japan away from nuclear power, and while many companies may be skeptical of the government's ability to fill in the gap with renewable energy sources, the public is convinced that Japan needs a new energy policy. Local mayors and governors, who in the past could be counted on to support restarts of nuclear power in their communities, seem unwilling to move forward even half a year after the accident. Prime Minister Noda has called plans for building new reactors "unrealistic," though he also recognizes the tremendous financial costs it will entail.[28] Further, Noda and the Democratic Party of Japan have sought alternative cost estimates for maintaining Japan's extensive nuclear program, beyond those provided by the "iron triangle" of firms, bureaucrats, and politicians deeply committed to the industry. Initial reports indicate that these alternative estimates are far higher than the costs typically stated, which might strengthen government support of solar, geothermal, and wind power.[29] However, while there are now political and social challenges to the iron triangle of the nuclear industry, no public discussion has taken place on the subject of changing the elaborate Dengen Sanpō system or eliminating subsidies to rural host communities. Only time will tell if this large-scale catastrophe will break the cycle of addiction created by more than thirty years of redistribution to the periphery of Japan.

Japan's tragedy has taken lives, destroyed homes and communities, and slowed an already underperforming economy. Decommissioning the Fukushima reactors may take four decades and cost upward of $30 billion, and the Japanese government has talked seriously about nationalizing the ailing TEPCO, already having injected more than $13 billion into the private firm in early 2012 to keep it afloat. The disaster has accelerated the depopulation problem in Tohoku coastal towns, causing a decade's worth of natural population loss in less than a year as residents relocate inland. Debris from the area has created a floating island of garbage that may reach the shores of Canada and North America by the beginning of 2013. But beyond these huge costs and long-term problems, the crisis has also activated a civil society that for decades has been seen as weak and nonparticipatory.

Citizens who in the past said little in opposition to the government's failings have stepped forward to engage in community-based science, challenge the information and explanations given to them by government officials and other authorities, and protest existing policies. Rather than remaining passive in the face of opaque institutions and calm reassurances, they have moved to create and analyze their own data and to draw their own conclusions. Seeking to end six decades of state domination of the field of nuclear power, citizens have sought to make their voices heard in the political arena and to dent the iron triangle of atomic policy. Members of the private sector have joined with them in pushing for a new energy policy that takes their concerns and the holistic costs of nuclear energy more seriously. At the crossroads of energy and politics, Japanese citizens have the chance to take the path they make themselves and to determine their own future.

Notes

Author's note: An earlier form of this article appeared in the journal *AsiaPacific Issues* 103 (January 2012): 1–11. I thank the East-West Center for permission to include that material in this chapter.

1. For details on the split between the two organizations, see Hitoshi Yoshioka, *Genshiryoku no shakaishi* (The social history of nuclear power) (Tokyo: Asahi Shinbunsha, 1999).

2. University of Southern California professor Jacques Hymans has written extensively about the long-term institutional stability in Japan's nuclear power regime, which has kept that nation from pursuing nuclear weapons. Some of his writings are available at http://dornsife.usc.edu/cf/faculty-and-staff/faculty.cfm?pid=1020019.

3. See Gabrielle Hecht, *The Radiance of France: Nuclear Power and National Identity after World War II* (Cambridge, MA: MIT Press, 1998) and John L. Campbell, *Collapse of an Industry* (Ithaca, NY: Cornell University Press, 1988), for a discussion of national-level energy plans in these countries.

4. Susan Pickett, "Japan's Nuclear Energy Policy," *Energy Policy* 30 (2002): 1337–1355.

5. See Linda Cohen, Mathew McCubbins, and Frances Rosenbluth, "The Politics of Nuclear Power in Japan and the United States," in Peter Cowhey and Mathew McCubbins, eds., *Structure and Policy in Japan and the United States* (Cambridge: Cambridge University Press, 1995), 177–202; Karen Nakamura, "Resistance and Co-optation: The Japanese Federation of the Deaf and Its Relations with State Power," *Social Science Japan Journal* 5:1 (2002): 17–35; and Chie Nakane, *Tateshakai no rikigaku* (The workings of vertical society) (Tokyo: Kodansha 1978), for such perspectives.

6. Daniel P. Aldrich, "Location, Location, Location: Selecting Sites for Controversial Facilities," *Singapore Economic Review* 53:1 (2008): 145–172.

7. MITI was popularized in the West in Chalmers Johnson, *MITI and the Japanese Miracle* (Stanford, CA: Stanford University Press, 1982).

8. See Daniel P. Aldrich, *Site Fights: Divisive Facilities and Civil Society in Japan and the West* (Ithaca, NY: Cornell University Press, 2008 and 2010), for details on these programs.

9. These are quotes from Martin Fackler and Norimitsu Onishi, "Utility Reform Eluding Japan after Nuclear Plant Disaster," *New York Times,* May 31, 2011; and from Kōichi Hasegawa, *Constructing Civil Society in Japan: Voices of Environmental Movements* (Melbourne, Australia: TransPacific Press, 2004), 26.

10. See S. Hayden Lesbirel, *NIMBY Politics in Japan: Energy Siting and the Management of Environmental Conflict* (Ithaca, NY: Cornell University Press, 1998), for more information.

11. Ronald Inglehart is well known for his work on postmaterialist consciousness; see his article, "Changing Values among Western Publics from 1970 to 2006," *West European Politics* 31:1 (2008): 130–146.

12. Social scientists under the sponsorship of the Earthquake Engineering Research Institute provided a detailed report of their field visit to the Tohoku region, which is available online at http://www.eqclearinghouse.org/2011-03-11-sendai/files/2011/03/Japan-SocSci-Rpt-hirez-rev.pdf.

13. New studies by researchers such as Takuya Kobayashi have shown that the amount of radiation in the sea is at least three times higher than initial estimates released by TEPCO. See the *Yomiuri Shimbun* report on this topic at http://www.yomiuri.co.jp/dy/national/T110909005415.htm.

14. "Worker Exposed Deception/Whistleblower Informed JCP of Kyushu Electric's Plans," *Yomiuri Shimbun,* July 9, 2011. http://www.yomiuri.co.jp/dy/national/T110708005861.htm.

15. Chester Dawson, "Scandal Taints Japan Nuclear Sector," *Wall Street Journal,* August 13, 2011. http://online.wsj.com/article/SB10001424053111904823804576499942442007306.html.

16. *Japan Times,* September 10, 2011.

17. The government's attempts to solve difficult social problems with financial incentives is quite parallel to its use of money as a panacea in the ongoing struggle over United States military base relocation in the Okinawan island chain. See Alex Cooley and K. Marten, "Base Motives: The Political Economy of Okinawa's Antimilitarism," *Armed Forces & Society* 32:4 (2006): 566–583; see also Hayashi Kiminori, Ōshima Ken'ichi, and Yokemoto Masafumi, "Overcoming American Military Base Pollution in Asia," *Asia-Pacific Journal* 28-2-09, July 13, 2009.

18. Linda Sieg, "Energy: Can Japan Afford Not to Be Nuclear?" *Business Day,* July 27, 2011.

19. Risa Maeda, "Tohoku Electric Aims to Triple Wind Power by 2020," Reuters news agency, September 30, 2011.

20. Arfon Smith, Chris Lintott, and the Citizen Science Alliance, "Web-scale Citizen Science: From Galaxy Zoo to the Zooniverse" (proceedings of the Royal Society discussion meeting "Web Science: A New Frontier," London, September 29–30, 2010); Janis L. Dickinson, Benjamin Zuckerberg, and David N. Bonter, "Citizen Science as an Ecological Research Tool: Challenges and Benefits," *Annual Review of Ecology, Evolution, and Systematics* 41 (December 2010): 149–172; Vincent Devictor, Robert Whittaker, and Coralie Beltrame, "Beyond Scarcity: Citizen Science Programmes as Useful Tools for Conservation Biogeography," *Diversity and Distribution* 16:3 (May 2010): 354–362.

21. Yuka Hayashi, "Japanese Seek Out 'Hot Spots,'" *Wall Street Journal,* October 19, 2011.

22. See Hugh Gusterson, "How Not to Construct a Radioactive Waste Incinerator," *Science, Technology, and Human Values* 25:3 (summer 2000): 332–351, for a description of how an antifacility movement used similar tactics when confronting scientists from the Livermore Laboratory.

23. The footage is available at http://www.youtube.com/watch?v=rVuGwc9dlhQ (accessed November 29, 2011).

24. Yoko Kubota, "Fukushima Victims: Homeless, Desperate, and Angry," Reuters new agency, October 18, 2011.

25. Daisuke Wakabayashi, Yuka Hayashi, Gordon Fairclough, Kana Inagaki, and Phred Dvorak, "Japan's Way Back," *Wall Street Journal,* section C12, September 11, 2011.

26. "Fukushima Protesters Urge Japan to Abandon Nuclear Power," Associated Press news agency, September 19, 2011. http://www.guardian.co.uk/world/2011/sep/19/fukushima-protesters-japan-nuclear-power.

27. Mary Alice Haddad, "From Undemocratic to Democratic Civil Society: Japan's Volunteer Fire Departments," *Journal of Asian Studies* 69:1 (February 1, 2010): 33–56; Haddad, "A New State-in-Society Approach to Democratization with Examples from Japan," *Democratization* 17:10 (October 2010): 997–1023.

28. Hiroko Tabuchi, "Japan Leader to Keep Nuclear Phase-Out," *New York Times,* September 2, 2011.

29. *Asahi Shimbun,* September 14 and 16, 2011.

15

Using Japan to Think Globally

The Natural Subject of History and Its Hopes

JULIA ADENEY THOMAS

Today "the global" in its many manifestations is shouldering aside local and national histories, dismissing them as inadequate to understanding our planetary context. Nowhere is the necessity of a global grasp more keenly felt than in environmental history where scholarship on the earth as a whole abounds. Climate change affects different parts of the earth differently but disregards national borders and encourages scholars to do likewise. Big history and deep history work on such large canvases that nations barely figure. These trends raise the question of why we focus on Japan in this volume, and here in the final chapter I want to make the case for our national study. In order to do so, I will first sketch some of the critical problems raised by global environmental history, particularly whether the human species tout court can serve (as some propose) as the proper subject of history, and secondarily how, if the practice of history demands a future, we can find hope in the face of catastrophic climate change.[1] Japan, I will argue, sheds light on these globally generated conundrums less as a limited case study than as a theoretical and practical resource. In relation to the environment, as the chapters in this book demonstrate, Japan is not a peculiarity as much as a participant in the global problematic.

From the new global perspective, the environment often trumps the economic, social, political, and cultural stories of earlier world histories proclaiming their foci merely epiphenomenal. For example, historian of China Kenneth Pomeranz argues that the great divergence between European and East Asian economic development rested principally on Europe's access to native coal and American natural resources rather than on Europe's long-term commercial progress, distinctive social and political formations, or some underlying cultural hunger for invention and discovery. As his history and others like it demonstrate, our increasingly sophisticated understanding of the true material bases of life—the water, air, soil, and temperatures in which our species and others have thrived—gives precedence to natural resources, climate, biology, geography, demographics, and physical factors over older objects of historical investigation.[2] With this research, we are moving toward the "new materialism" that Italian Marxist Sebastiano Timpanaro (1923–2000) advocated years ago, a materialism that goes beyond the immensely productive critiques of capitalism's global effects to grapple with the ultimate limits on productivity, social formation, and human life itself.[3] As this new materialism comes to the fore, some historians have insisted that capitalism alone cannot be held responsible for environmental degradation. Pomeranz, for instance, argues that "if one measures industrialization not by the market value of output but by the quantities of land and people that become involved—probably more relevant criteria for environmental historians—then non-capitalist (or at most semicapitalist) regimes have presided over most of the spread of industrialization."[4] Decentering the transformation from precapitalism to capitalism and focusing instead on the continuities between the early modern and modern "developmentalist project," as Pomeranz calls it, changes the global story, helping us to see the commonalities between Asia and Europe. Some of the chapters in this volume—such as Jakobina Arch's work on Wakayama whaling and Philip Brown's investigation of major flood control projects in Niigata—confirm the continuity of the developmentalist project whether the economic regime is guided by the prescripts of neo-Confucianism or the capitalist logic of accumulation and labor exploitation. In this sense, the new materialism of environmental history is reshaping older global stories and challenging the distinction between premodern and modern, noncapitalist developmentalism and capitalism, and Asia and the West.

However, the new materialism offers even more radical provocations than the revision of old historical narratives. As our analysis moves away from the means of exploitation (though they remain important) to the ecological foundation of exploitation, two crucial transformations in our understanding emerge: one is a shift of attention from mindful human agency to the aggregate activity of the entire human species, and the other is a recognition of the unwitting rupture in the continuity of human experience caused by contemporary climate collapse, what Edmund Burke III has called "the unprecedented break in human relations with nature and the environment."[5] In other words, the invigorating scholarly pursuit of a "new materialism" in the environmental sense comes at a cost to the complacencies about historical agency and continuity that have comfortably defined historical practice—complacencies that have included the importance of the nation as a central actor and setting for action. Not only must we examine the ecological foundations of the past but we must also consider the ecological foundations of historical practice itself, because in eroding the conditions that permitted human hegemony on the planet, climate change is also eroding the foundations of historical understanding that produced notions of agency and meaningful narrative.

The material foundation of historical practice, as of so many human endeavors, was the relative stability of the Holocene's long stretch beginning about ten to twelve thousand years ago. Compared with the global turbulence beginning to encompass us due to climate change, those were the good old days or, rather, the good old millennia. With the "globally averaged temperature swinging in the narrowest of ranges, between fifty-eight and sixty Fahrenheit," we were living in the "sweetest of sweet spots," as climate activist Bill McKibben puts it.[6] This environmental beneficence, capped by our seeming mastery of nature from the nineteenth century onward, made possible historians' ideas of humanity (especially human agency) and of time (especially forms of narrative continuity). One could even say that the rise of the discipline neatly parallels the species' extraordinary ecological dominance over the past two or three centuries.

However, agency and narrative, the discipline's traditional modes of representation, are becoming less plausible under the pressure of global climate change. It is not just that historians are expanding our archive to include objects, events, and nontextual sources far outside the traditional archives. Rather, the need to rethink disciplinary practices extends to our fundamental concepts and modes of representation. As historian Dipesh Chakrabarty persuasively argues in "The Climate of History: Four Theses," "What scientists have said about climate change challenges . . . the ideas about the human that usually sustain the discipline of history."[7] As Chakrabarty suggests, we need to be as radical in rethinking our practices as our new circumstances demand. I will circle back to his important arguments several times in the course of my discussion.

Climate science tells us that we stand at the beginning of a fundamentally new era: both "we" and "era" are no longer what they were. Consider first the "human." As my coeditor Brett Walker demonstrates in *Toxic Archipelago*, the human species has transformed its own physical makeup by introducing into our bodies inorganic, human-made chemical compounds never before in existence.[8] We have yet to take the measure of this unwitting reengineering project, though the most dramatic cases of toxicity already prove that these chemical compounds can destroy the "human" in all its senses, mind as well as body. These effects, understood historically, not only change the nature of the individual as agent, but also put the collectivity in question. Neither singly nor in toto are we any longer essentially organic in the way we once were.[9] Nor are our current interactions with the environment essentially only biological. Instead, our species has today become a geophysical agent to an unprecedented degree. Although we have always altered our physical environments locally, never have we altered the entire planet's so radically, changing it not only biologically but chemically and physically. In so doing, Chakrabarty argues, we have precipitated a "collapse of the age-old humanist distinction between natural history and human history."[10] Geophysical agency rests not with individuals, communities, classes, nations, ideas, or any of the other entities that have propelled our histories but with the entirety of what was once a biologically defined category, the category of the human species.

This conceptual shift in agency to the species defined geophysically as well as biologically raises another difficulty: the temporal frame of concern to historians. To understand the species in its overall emergence necessitates recourse to a *longue durée* much longer than that imagined by the Annales School and reaching back, in some studies, to the origins of the universe.[11] But just as our past is becoming longer, our future is becoming shorter. While history is being stretched backward to the literal origins of time, we confront a radical break in the continuity of conditions that has given history its raison d'être—that is, its ability, in looking backward, to provide imaginaries for the future. The "horizons of expectation" of which Reinhart Koselleck spoke are now clouded.[12] Human beings have entered, as Ian Miller notes in his introduction, the era defined by chemist Paul J. Crutzen and marine scientist Eugene F. Stoermer as the "Anthropocene."[13] We cannot yet know the precise predicament that the forecast 10.1 billion of us will face by 2050, but the stresses on daily life, on economic activities, on social formations, and on ideas of justice and decency will not be just quantitatively greater but qualitatively as well.[14] There *is* something, John McNeill argues, "new under the sun" in the contemporary situation.[15]

The new circumstances of the Anthropocene are forecast to be so different that the political, moral, social, and cultural understanding gained from most studies of the past may no longer be of any import. Accordingly, new global studies must do more than show us that history, in ignoring environmental factors, has largely misapprehended how we got to where we are. They must also actively recover cultural and political resources that will help meet the challenge of climate collapse and provide a humanistic and sustainable story about how we might go forward. Otherwise history is reduced to mere antiquarianism. In sum, in challenging our understanding of what has happened, the new global environmental awareness challenges our previous modes of representing what happened, dethroning traditional ideas about the subject of history and its hopes. We find ourselves radically redefined as actors on a radically altered stage.

It is precisely in considering these global issues that a return to Japan makes sense. Even beyond the intrinsic interest of this volume's essays charting Japan's participation in the "developmentalist project" of resource exploitation and the consequent regrets, our book, in calling attention to this particular place, provides a space for knowledge, some it cautionary and some of it hopeful. There are at least two quite profound ways in which Japan speaks to the global conundrums described above. First, the work of Japanese philosopher Tanabe Hajime (1885–1962) on the concept of species (*shu*) cautions us (over and beyond Chakrabarty's own cautions) about the political, social, and intellectual costs of adapting this scientific concept to the purposes of history. By comparing Tanabe's early iteration of "species" as historical agent to contemporary efforts, we gain a salutary vantage on the natural subject of historical inquiry: "species" as a category of historical thought is politically dangerous. Second, the contemporary situation in Japan has led to some innovative thinking about the practical challenges of environmental sustainability. With its static economy and declining population, Japan is often held up as the poster child of decline. But decline is not the only possible narrative here. Real though current problems are, they forecast doom only if one assumes that current neoliberal systems of production and finance are immutable and that the human population and levels of consumption should increase forever. These are common, often implicit assumptions, although neither is environmentally viable. More realistically, if we take seriously both the need to live within our ecological means and the predictions, recently disputed, that the human population will begin to stabilize after peaking around 2070, Japan looks less like a disaster in its "decline" and more like a model for the future.[16] Today, a few Japanese governmental entities and some nongovernmental bodies and individuals are considering how Japan might constitute itself as a postcapitalist, protoecological nation, how its declining population might rest more lightly on the land, leaving room for other species and for replenishing renewable natural resources. Precedents for this alternative relationship with the natural world can be excavated from the country's archives as well. Only through intensive engagement with past and present possibilities in particular nations can alternatives to neoliberal modernity be recuperated for global consideration. For these two very different reasons (among many others to which we could attest), "the nation," and Japan in particular, is still a worthy object of interest to the environmental historian.

Species as the Global Historical Subject

Let me make two obvious assertions grounded in current scientific findings: human activity has produced global climate change, and global climate change is radically altering the conditions of human life everywhere on the planet.[17] As many environmental historians have argued, if we begin with these propositions, it follows that the human species as a whole is the proper subject of history since it is the activity of the species as a whole that has caused dramatic environmental changes and the species as a whole that will suffer from these changes. This is one reason why national histories seem to some passé. Yet, "species" is a fraught term. On a moral level, it erases the differences between the rich and the poor, those most responsible for the production of greenhouse gases and those least at fault. On a philosophical level, it raises of panoply of conceptual difficulties. A term normally associated with biology, when transferred to historical analysis it has produced a number of difficulties in contemporary scholarship. In exploring these difficulties, we can usefully return to older ideas of "species," including the work of Japanese philosopher Tanabe Hajime. Interestingly and tellingly, the problems raised by his deployment of the concept, just as with contemporary species thinking, involve crisis, negation, and the inability to achieve his desired end—an engaged understanding of the modern condition and the possibilities within it. In describing Tanabe's work, I want to highlight this trio of crisis, negation, and failure in light of Chakrabarty's analysis of how "species" operates as a concept today in global environmental history.

The crisis that Tanabe faced was both moral and philosophical. During the 1930s, Tanabe supported the Japanese Empire's military domination of northeast China, Korea, Taiwan, Okinawa, Micronesia, and Sakhalin, and yet his philosophical goal was an attempt to elucidate the philosophical grounds for freedom. Between 1932 and 1938, in the series of essays eventually collected as *Shu no ronri* (The Logic of Species), Tanabe sought to provide the intellectual grounds for free agency, not in opposition to imperial Japan but *within* the imperial state and its colonial dominions. This attempt, as Mark Driscoll has elucidated, fails, and it is important to see how and why an effort that rests largely on the concept of "species" or *shu* should collapse. It was not simply that imperialism was a bad idea and thus all ideological support for it must ipso facto be flawed, but that the concept of species as historical subject in itself produces difficulties.

As the Japanese Empire spread, Tanabe rejected the idea of a harmonious organic state for a state of dynamic struggle. Tanabe's biologically informed political vision, like the concept of an organic nation-state, claimed the imprimateur of scientific certainty but stressed nature's structural contradictions rather than its organic harmonies. He proposed a "complex process of negation, othering, and mediation" between the individual (*ko*), the species or group (*shu*), and the universal or totality (*rui*).[18] Ideally in Tanabe's system, neither *ko* nor *shu* nor *rui* would have positive predicates but would instead emerge through dynamic antagonism with one another. As negations, each element would be reliant upon yet in tension with the others. The resulting undecidability and antifoundationalist quality was meant to produce freedom and allow for difference without sublimation. There was to be no consonant whole, no hierarchy of coalescence as there was with the concept of an "organic society" proposed by scholars such as Oka Asajirō (1868–1944), a prominent zoologist, seeking to unify late Meiji society, or the wartime advocates of *kokutai* (the family-state).[19] However, Tanabe failed to articulate this negative freedom because he ultimately assigned positive characteristics,

298   JULIA ADENEY THOMAS

particularly Japaneseness and maleness (Tanabe's "necromaternalistic symptom," as Driscoll terms it) to species. Ultimately, "species" refers not to some unessentialized collectivity or even to the entirety of human beings but to ethnic groups, with Japanese ethnicity decidedly foremost and Japanese males the only operative, free subject. The facile move to a world where Japanese men rightly rule over all others forecloses the freedoms that Tanabe pretends to seek. As Driscoll persuasively argues, "Although Tanabe explicitly delineated anti-foundational possibilities for human agency against the encroachments of State power by pointing to singular moments of undecidability and freedom, he betrays his philosophical commitment to these moments by positivizing them with the predicates of ethnic Japaneseness and masculine gender."[20] Tanabe's process of negation cannot be sustained over time. For *shu,* the central term of the *ko-shu-rui* configuration, Tanabe chooses the same *kanji* used for the biological concept of species. Although he tries to squirm away from biology—from his perspective, self-consciousness (*jikaku*) is not a biological condition—it is telling that he retains the term despite its organic overtones. It is even possible to argue that although he claims that "species" has nothing to do with biological classification, he incorporates sub rosa what he overtly denies by adopting this particular term and that his choice is at least partly to blame for his failure to conjure a negative form of freedom.[21] Through *shu,* a "natural" category is reintroduced. This slippage allows the Japanese race or, rather, Japanese men to take on the armor of natural science to secure their distinctiveness and dominion over lesser *shu* and all women. In my reading, though not in Driscoll's, the use of *shu* helps enable the return to the biologically inflected categories of ethnicity and maleness that Tanabe had, at least superficially, rejected. The subject, in being at least partly naturalized, can no longer be defined as emerging through the process of pure negation.

Tanabe's failure to find in *shu* the desired basis for freedom resonates with problems surrounding species thinking in global history today. First, his concept of species, like our contemporary ones, emerges at a moment of crisis, and there seems to be a strong connection between considering species as a historical subject and intimations of disaster. Historian of Islam Faisal Devji, for instance, argues that the human race emerged as the subject of global history only when its existence was threatened, first by nuclear weapons and now, even more, by virulent pandemics and climate change. In this negative condition on the brink of annihilation, "humanity has ceased to be the abstraction and ideal it once was."[22] Chakrabarty also sees the idea of the human collectivity as something that "arises from a shared sense of a catastrophe."[23] What this suggests is that thinking about the species as historical subject is tied to concern about its impending doom; in other words, the species emerges as a historical subject just as its future seems particularly precarious.

The second point of resonance between Tanabe and recent thinking about the environment—particularly that of Chakrabarty—is that "species" serves as a negation. Tanabe values it as a moment of radical discontinuity posited against the individual and against the whole, but unwittingly, as Driscoll has shown, he cannot sustain it; instead, "species" acquires positive attributes that undermine Tanabe's goal of freedom. While Chakrabarty also sees "species" as negation, he recognizes that we can only retain its negativity by limiting its duration. Echoing Walter Benjamin, Chakrabarty argues that "Species may indeed be the name of the placeholder for an emergent, new universal history of humans that flashes up in the moment of danger that is climate change,"[24] but this flash of recognition can be, for Chakrabarty as for Benjamin, only momentary, resulting in what Chakrabarty calls provisionally a "negative universal history."[25] As Chakrabarty acknowledges and as Tanabe unintentionally reveals, one of the problems of species thinking is that since it emerges as negation, it is unsustainable over time. To think with it, to activate it as a positive entity, is to give it "universal" characteristics that are never universal whether they are the particularities of Japanese ethnonationalism and masculinity as in Tanabe's case or, as in other cases, Enlightenment reason and rational self-interest or neoliberal desires. In short, we cannot as historians really think about "the species" in any sustained and meaningful way; in considering the past from our own particular moment, we must always return to the particularities of culture and place. Indeed, as Hannah Arendt insisted, "Nobody can be a citizen of the world as he is the citizen of his country."[26]

The third point of commonality is the failure of species thinking to produce the desired ends—be they Tanabe's freedom or Chakrabarty's historical understanding—precisely because something produced through negation provides no basis for positive attributes. Whereas Tanabe shows, without realizing it, how difficult it is for "species" to retain the condition of negativity requisite to his idea of freedom, Chakrabarty argues explicitly that species thinking cannot produce the empathy required by the historical enterprise. According to Chakrabarty, although our contemporary crisis in "pointing to a figure of the universal" suggests that "species" should be the new global subject of history, this new "us" "escapes our capacity to experience the world."[27] Since it is the unimaginable antithesis of true human connection, "we can never *understand* this universal."[28] By "understand" here, Chakrabarty means more than an intellectual grasp. Obviously, we can comprehend the problems that have arisen due to the demands of our species on natural resources; indeed, this is precisely what biologists and climate scientists are doing all the time. Instead, what Chakrabarty means by "understand" in this context is a particular form of historical comprehension predicated on the facility to sympathetically and cognitively identify with historical agents, in part through the procedures laid out by R. G. Collingwood. Already in moving to species or even conjuring it in the Benjaminian flash of insight that Chakrabarty invokes, we have undermined the definition of "human" that made us historical by Collingwood's account: that "man is regarded as the only animal that thinks, or thinks clearly enough, to render his actions expressions of his thoughts."[29] "Species" as such does not think. Its effects are cumulative, not willed or even imagined. The growing hole in the ozone layer, contaminated water, unbreathable air, and violent weather are in this sense not even historical events. Returning to Tanabe's work underscores the problem of "species" that Chakrabarty recognizes.

Some of the chapters in this volume suggest an alternative way of negotiating the subject of global environmental history precisely through a focus on Japan. For instance, instead of apprehending the human species, Andrew Bernstein's essay "Weathering Fuji" and Christine Marran's "Animal Histories: Stranger in a Tokyo Canal" portray a series of negotiations between people, other species, and landscapes that gesture toward the planetary. Both authors grapple with a problem that neither Tanabe nor Chakrabarty acknowledge, which is that the concept of the human species necessarily implies the existence of other species in a physical topography, raising the question of why historical subjectivity should be resolutely human. Bernstein's concept of "bodyscapes" melds mountains with gendered human forms; the figuration of the lost seal, Tama-chan, analyzed by Marran is at once human and nonhuman. In Bernstein's work, the universal observations of scientific research are arrived at through complex negotiations between husband and wife, individual and nation, and the careful measurement of temperature and wind velocity every few hours on Mount Fuji. It is only through sampling particular temperatures and suffering the winds of a precise locale that knowledge applicable to the whole planet can emerge. The universal requires the national. In Marran's essay, understanding the universal of the natural world begins with Japanese individuals attempting to grasp the existential and environmental losses signified by a disoriented seal in a murky urban river or by the disappearance of Murakami's fictional elephant. In both essays, we see how the universal is arrived at not by comprehending it in its entirety but approaching it instead through specificities, minutiae, and brief encounters. In both cases, the imbrication of human and nonhuman, the organic and the nonorganic begins locally and nationally before it becomes global.

In Berstein's bodyscapes and Marran's signifying creatures, we see the emergence of complex subjectivities within local and national networks that produce global history from the ground up, as it were. Instead of a unified, universal history with a singular subject, "the global" emerges in this process through multiple, minor, rooted negotiations among many life forms and their physical and cultural landscapes. The subject of global history is not "the species" but the systems of interactions that produce globality, of which national formations are one.[30]

Hope and Historical Resources

Some environmental historians banally define history as "everything that's ever happened in the past." For this one-thing-after-another approach, adding new actors, environmental changes and conditions, adding all events from the Big Bang to the banking collapse is unproblematic. But consider this: if history were mere chronicle, merely one thing after another, the only question it could answer is when something happened, not whether it was important, why it happened, who made it happen, or what it meant. More crucially, if history were mere chronicle, it could not mobilize new possibilities; it would provide no political or moral insight to help guide our steps into the future. It would be inert.

But history defined as praxis insists that the past provides resources for imagining a variety of political and social configurations, ones that might, depending on our values, undermine the status quo by defamiliarizing it or resuscitate lost modes of social interaction. In order to function in this way, history rests on the presumption of an intelligible continuity to the human condition as well as the possibility of breaking that continuity through an act of political and social will. Whatever one's politics or perspective, it is assumed that the past serves as prologue. Today, as the planet suddenly and dramatically warms due to greenhouse gases, the story of human hopes and fears may need to be renarrated to deal with levels of implacable dearth and constraints on our options that we have never confronted during the Holocene era. Dipesh Chakrabarty sums up this position, arguing, "The discipline of history exists on the assumption that our past, present, and future are connected by a certain continuity of human experience. But, for environmental historians concerned with history as praxis, our current predicament in threatening our future alters our relationship with the past. We normally envisage the future with the help of the same faculty that allows us to picture the past."[31] While the end of natural abundance augers poorly for history as praxis in Chakrabarty's terms, for history as chronicle, it means little. The seamless chronicle continues, come what may, and nothing can deflect it from the relentless march of facts energized by no particular vantage nor any set of values. The chronicler sits amid the stinking debris of a dead land, content that he performs his duties by noting occurrences.

The distinction I make here between chronicle and practice draws on Hayden White's work distinguishing between "chronicle"—the "one thing after another" approach—and "story"—the crafted narrative that historians attempt to achieve. White describes this distinction as follows: "Historical *stories* trace the sequences of events that lead from inaugurations to (provisional) terminations of social and cultural processes in a way that *chronicles* are not required to do. Chronicles are, strictly speaking, open-ended. In principle they have no *inaugurations;*

they simply 'begin' when the chronicler starts recording events. And they have no culminations or resolutions; they can go on indefinitely."[32] Many environmental historians have resorted to chronicle, sometimes unconsciously, without realizing how their practice eviscerates history's political and moral relevance.

For instance, environmental historian and geographer I. G. Simmons begins his *Global Environmental History* with Paleolithic cave "art," the image of an owl dating from about thirty thousand years ago, and announces at the end of the book, "In history-writing it might well be desirable that some level of cut-off horizon has been reached. Yet quite obviously we are leaving this story in mid-flow and there is no indication that the year 2000 marked any special stage in the entwined histories of humanity and nature. There is, then, no Conclusion."[33] Such open-ended chronicling of events as found in Simmons requires no critical assessments about why things happened nor whether they were good or bad and thus suggests no horizon of future expectations. Time's relentlessness and the march of occurrences alone are guaranteed. In contrast to chronicle, it is precisely a story's resolution, however provisional, that gives it the moral and political charge that compels engagement with both past and future. For this reason, chronicle is not a fundamentally *productive* way of thinking about the past and is, as White indicates, merely the first order of conceptualization, replaced in historiography by crafted narratives that provide not just a sequence of information but evidenced arguments about why things happened, what they mean, and where we might go in the future.

The global environmental crisis, since it is a crisis of a new type and in proportions larger than any we have ever witnessed, presents a precarious break with the past: the species emerges as an ungraspable agent and the knowledge we have painfully attained may not apply. The challenge is to narrate our way through E. O. Wilson's environmental "bottleneck" to a livable future, not simply to chronicle the activities of the past that led to this crisis. We need to draw on past experience to imagine the economies, values, and political forms that might exist in a sustainable world, even though the climate of the new "Eaarth," as McKibben calls it, will be substantially different from the one we have known.

Japan, demographically and in other ways, provides a laboratory for thinking about the global future in relation to the national past. In *Shock of Gray*, Ted C. Fishman says, "In 2005, Japan became the first modern, industrial nation to shrink in population for reasons unrelated to war or disease. Fujimasa Iwao of the National Graduate Institute for Policy Studies, a think tank that serves the central government, predicts that by 2050 Japan will have 41 million fewer inhabitants, in effect dialing back Japan's population to its level before 1950."[34] This startling vision of a shrinking, aging nation does not haunt Japan alone. Demographers anticipate the number of children per mother to continue to decline worldwide. "As a result," says Bill McKibben, "the world's population won't double even once more; as early as 2070, by the latest predictions, the number of human beings may actually begin to fall."[35] Japan is merely the forerunner. "All of the industrial countries, and then most of the world will eventually follow Japan," argues Fishman: "Japan matters because it is one of a handful of countries leading the way, and showing the world the consequences of contracting demographics, a shortage of young people and a growing population of elderly."[36] While in some quarters this prognosis has caused despair and in others the mindless advocacy of yet more "efficient" markets to produce growth, there are sectors where the environmental opportunities of population decline are embraced.

Japanese agriculture is one arena where the proper response to global trends is much in dispute. Today, Japan has a very low rate of food self-sufficiency, producing only about 41 percent of what the population needs to survive.[37] Many regret this situation, including the Ministry of Agriculture, Forestry, and Fisheries (MAFF), which seeks a "stable supply of food for the future" given "the significant changes in the global food situation."[38] The MAFF is right to point to "significant changes." Due to the 2008 food crisis, one-sixth of the world's human population was "at risk of hunger" according to Martin Parry, one of the cochairs of the Intergovernmental Panel on Climate Change. In 2009, that number topped 1 billion.[39] In wealthy countries like Japan, this crisis currently seems far away, but in the next decade food costs are predicted to rise by as much as 40 percent, and shortages may not be far behind.[40] To avoid this crisis, MAFF officials want to encourage greater production by persuading talented people to become farmers.

The problem with the MAFF solution, according to Yukie Yoshikawa, senior research fellow at the Edwin O. Reischauer Center for East Asian Studies at Johns Hopkins University, is that Japan's "farm size is so small that it is almost impossible to make a living by farming" and therefore that talented people are unlikely to choose this line of work.[41] Yoshikawa points out, "While today in Japan 10 *ha* or more is said to be the optimal farmland size for full-time agriculture, only 0.7% of Japanese farmers have land this size. The vast majority—92%—have 3 *ha* or less; this has not changed much since the 1947 Land Reform which created a structure in which 99% of Japanese farmers owned land of this size, one considered optimal for farmers at the time." The reason that optimal farm size has changed, according to Yoshikawa, is that "due to technological improvements leading to rising cost[s] in agricultural tools and machines, more revenue, or land, is required to cover costs. But while the minimum size of farmland to make [a] living has increased by more than 300% in 60 years, the farmland per farm household has not expanded."[42] What Yoshikawa never questions is his notion of "improvements," even though, by his own admission, these carbon-based modes of farming are the source of the increased costs. Instead, his proposed solution is to consolidate farms by transforming the real estate market so that farmers are more willing to sell their land to other farmers rather than to developers, who often pay much more. The larger farms would allow for more carbon-based "economies of scale." Yoshikawa's proposal and those of Japan's political parties adhere unquestioningly to the assumption that mechanized agriculture is "good," making economies of scale "necessary," even though the 300 percent rise in expenditure actually seems to have forced farmers from the land and resulted in diminished output. In these responses, we see that the ideological commitment to capitalist expansion has itself become naturalized, a "second nature whose collapse would be more dramatic than that of the physical environment," as historian and art critic Sven Lütticken has suggested.[43]

Nongovernmental groups within Japan are questioning such market-based solutions on three grounds. First, mechanized agriculture is not only currently more expensive than it was, but its costs will rise exorbitantly in the coming years since it relies on fossil fuels. Second, mechanized agriculture's monocropping and use of chemicals is an ecological bane, harming a range of species and debilitating the soil. Third, mechanized agriculture does not always provide greater yields per hectare than more traditional modes of farming, although it is widely assumed to do so. Plant pathologist Masanobu Fukuoka (1913–2008) achieved harvests matching and even exceeding those obtained through mechanized means on his own farm in Shikoku using an environmentally sustainable approach. Eschewing insecticides, weed killers, and chemical fertilizers, Fukuoka worked to balance plants and plant predators through such means as spreading straw. Beginning in the mid-1970s with *The One-Straw Revolution,* he published a series of books advocating natural farming while practicing the agrarian arts himself well into his eighties.[44] Other groups have since taken up the challenge, urging alternative farming methods. Through such means, the nutritional needs of the Japanese population could be met especially as the population declines, the Japanese archipelago could begin to detoxify, and opportunities for meaningful employment could be created. The MAFF's hope of luring the currently underemployed workforce back to the farm might be realized by creating conditions where individual creativity and initiative matter.

Presented as a matter of policy, the rebirth of sustainable agriculture has its attractions, and yet I would argue that reasonable policies and sensible economics alone are insufficient to alter Japanese society—and societies in general—to meet the contemporary environmental threat. A transformed future requires a compelling national past, and this is where environmental history as a self-reflective, critical practice rather than as chronicle can be summoned to produce the cautionary knowledge and the energizing hope that might help make sustainable agriculture not a countercultural anomaly but central to national self-understanding. Noncapitalist agrarian movements with a range of ideological valances have a long history in Japan, stretching back into the Tokugawa period.[45] For instance,

Andō Shōeki (1703–1762) and Ninomiya Sontoku (1787–1856) took seriously the neo-Confucian respect for agriculture in their advocacy of independent rural communities. By the 1920s and 1930s, the promotion of agricultural interests against industrialization (*nōhonshugi*) propelled both left-leaning rural movements including that of Yokoi Tokiyoshi and right-wing alliances between militarists and the landlord class.[46] Looking at this history shows that alternative forms of agriculture are not simply matters of different farming methods but of different social formations, some of them more attractive politically, emotionally, ethically, and intellectually than others. Recovering the full complexity of lifeworlds at odds with the dominant neoliberal one can authenticate them as genuine possibilities because this history reveals the fullness of lived experiences and their place in the national genealogy. In other words, sustainable modes of living discarded during the "developmentalist project," the former "dead-ends" of history, can be rerouted as thoroughfares of future possibility. The break in continuity that they represent on a small scale may provide a model for coping with the radical break being produced by climate collapse today.

Agriculture is of course not the only arena where alternative lifeworlds are crafted. A similar case can be made for the history of industry, as Takehiro Watanabe shows in his analysis of Sumitomo's corporate environmentalism and as Timothy George so vividly conveys with the horrors of labor at the Toroku chemical mines. The research of Ken'ichi Miyamoto chronicles modern Japan's environmental disasters while also demonstrating that local, democratic political action can stem catastrophe and turn narratives of decline into parables of possibility. On a broad scale, then, the assets of the past, such as Japan's social and cultural cohesion, high levels of education, and its rich, contentious political history can be leveraged against ecological destruction. Particularly after the disasters of 3/11 and the meltdown of the Fukushima nuclear reactors, as detailed in this volume by Sara Pritchard and Daniel Aldrich, seeking these points of leverage is more vital than ever. In the fullness of history lies hope, however frail, however imperfect.

Conclusion

As historians enter the torrid age of the Anthropocene, do we have something distinctive to offer as opposed to the other disciplines of the humanities, social sciences, and sciences? With an archive newly stocked with animals, water, and geological forces, with a fresh conception of the agents of history, and with a renewed commitment to the tendentious art of narrative, what, even then, is the purport of our practice? Climate scientists David Archer and Stefan Rahmstorf have argued that we have the means for preventing total environmental collapse if we immediately cut carbon and methane production and cease pumping killer chemicals into our air, water, and soil.[47] Rationally, it makes sense to adopt this course of action. But rational presentist knowledge is insufficient for political will and emotional commitment. Our histories show that human beings are creatures for whom meaning, value, habit, consolation, and hope are crucial, and these modalities in their specifities can only be elaborated through particular cultures over time. They cannot be manufactured whole cloth on the basis of rational imperatives. What historical research might do, and what our volume attempts, is to mobilize past events as imaginaries to help provide the energy necessary to embrace rational solutions. As Dipesh Chakrabarty has rightly reminded us, "The possibility of knowledge is the possibility of hope." Even though it may be phantasmagorical to conjure the species tout court as the global subject and difficult to construct a useable past as we enter an unprecedented age of violent storms, poisonous water, and diminished abundance, in more pedestrian yet meaningful ways we can imagine local and national subjects and look there for the "space for utopianism" that Chakrabarty calls for. Since the continuity of humanity, such that it can be sustained, will always also be locked within specifities of time and space, the practice of history can rightly situate itself upon occasion in the modest realm of national history as it looks toward the planetary.

Notes

1. Reinhart Koselleck has provided the seminal vocabulary for discussions of the relationship between history and the future. See Koselleck, *Futures Past: On the Semantics of Historical Time*, trans. Keith Tribe (New York: Columbia University Press, 1985), and, more recently, "AHR Forum: Histories of the Future," featuring four essays on the subject, *American Historical Review* 117 (December 2012): 1402–1485. For a scientific consideration of the future, see Curt Stager, *Deep Future: The Next 100,000 Years of Life on Earth* (New York: St. Martin's Press, 2011).

2. The effort to combine world history and environmental history is taking place in many venues. Of particular interest are Edmund Burke III and Kenneth Pomeranz, eds., *The Environment and World History* (Berkeley: University of California Press, 2009), and "Transnational Environments: Rethinking the Political Economy of Nature in a Global Age," *Radical History Review* 107 (April 2010).

3. I discuss the contributions of Sebastiano Timpanaro's *On Materialism* (London: Verso, 1980; originally published in Italian in 1970) briefly in *Reconfiguring Modernity: Concepts of Nature in Japanese Political Ideology* (Berkeley: University of California Press, 2001) and at greater length in my preface "Atarashii busshitsu shugi" (The New Materialism) to the Japanese translation of *Reconfiguring Modernity, Kindai no saikochiku: Nihon seiji ideorogii ni okeru shizen no gainen* (Tokyo: Hosei University Press, 2008). Older Marxist explorations of the way that "materialism" might be expanded to encompass the environment also include André Gorz, *Ecology as Politics* (Boston: South End Press, 1980 [original French publication 1975]), and *Capitalism, Socialism, Ecology* (London: Verso, 1994, original 1991). For more recent work on the theme of materialism and politics, see Diana Coole

and Samantha Frost, eds. *New Materialisms: Ontology, Agency, and Politics* (Durham, NC: Duke University Press, 2010), especially Jason Edwards, "The Materialism of Historical Materialism;" Jane Bennett, *Vibrant Matter: A Political Ecology of Things* (Durham, NC: Duke University Press, 2010); and Mick Smith, *Against Ecological Sovereignty: Ethics, Biopolitics, and Saving the Natural World* (Minneapolis: University of Minnesota Press, 2011).

4. Kenneth Pomeranz, "Introduction: World History and Environmental History," in Edmund Burke III and Kenneth Pomeranz, eds., *The Environment and World History* (Berkeley: University of California Press, 2009), 8. For this argument, see also Robert B. Marks, "Commercialization without Capitalism: Processes of Environmental Change in South China, 1550–1850," *Environmental History* 1:1 (January 1996): 56–82.

5. Edmund Burke III, "The Big Story: Human History, Energy Regimes, and the Environment," in Burke and Pomeranz, *Environment and World History*, 33. David W. Orr uses the phrase "climate collapse" instead of "climate change," and here I have not attempted to draw a distinction between them. Orr, *Down to the Wire: Confronting Climate Collapse* (Oxford: Oxford University Press, 2009).

6. Bill McKibben, *Eaarth: Making a Life on a Tough New Planet* (New York: Time Books, Henry Holt and Company, 2010), 1.

7. Chakrabarty, "The Climate of History: Four Theses," *Critical Inquiry* 35 (winter 2009), 198.

8. Brett L. Walker, *Toxic Archipelago: A History of Industrial Disease in Japan* (Seattle: University of Washington Press, 2010).

9. Daniel Lord Smail's discussion of the evolution of the human brain in relation to Western historical traditions concerns *organic* transformations brought on by agriculture. See Smail, *On Deep History and the Brain* (Berkeley: University of California Press, 2008). Work on the way *nonorganic* chemicals are penetrating our bodies and brains includes Jody A. Roberts and Nancy Langston, "Toxic Bodies/Toxic Environments: An Interdisciplinary Forum," *Environmental History* 13 (2008): 629–703; Sarah A. Vogel, "The Politics of Plastics: The Making and Unmaking of Bisphenol A 'Safety,'" *American Journal of Public Health* 99 (2009): 559–566; Nancy Langston, *Toxic Bodies: Hormone Disruptors and the Legacy of DES* (New Haven, CT: Yale University Press, 2010); Michelle Murphy, *Sick Building Syndrome and the Problem of Uncertainty: Environmental Politics, Technoscience, and Women Workers* (Durham, NC: Duke University Press, 2006); Arthur F. McEvoy, "Working Environments: An Ecological Approach to Industrial Health and Safety," *Technology and Culture* 36 (1995): 145–172; Theo Colborn, Dianne Dumanoski, and John Peter Meyers, *Our Stolen Future: Are We Threatening Our Fertility, Intelligence, and Survival?—A Scientific Detective Story* (New York: Dutton Publishers, 1996) which is updated on their Web site: http://www.ourstolenfuture.org/aboutOSF.htm; Elizabeth Grossman, *Chasing Molecules: Poison Products, Human Health, and the Promise of Green Chemistry* (Washington, DC: Shearwater Books, Island Press, 2011); and Mark Shapiro, *Exposed: The Toxic Chemistry of Everyday Products and What's at Stake for American Power* (White River Junction, VT: Chelsea Green Publishing, 2009).

10. Chakrabarty, "The Climate of History," 201.

11. See, for instance, Cynthia Stokes Brown, *Big History: From the Big Bang to the Present* (New York: New Press, 2008), and David Christian, *Maps of Time: An Introduction to Big History* (Berkeley: University of California Press, 2005).

12. Koselleck, *Futures Past*, esp. 270–275.

13. Paul J. Crutzen and Eugene F. Stoermer, "The Anthropocene," *IGBP [International Geosphere-Biosphere Programme] Newsletter* 41 (2007).

14. When I completed the first draft of this paper, the forecast population was 9.3 billion, a figure I drew from Ted C. Fishman, *Shock of Gray* (New York: Scribner, 2010), 147. A year later it was 10.1 billion, as reported in Justin Gillis and Celia W. Dugger, "U.N. Forecasts 10.1 Billion People by Century's End," *New York Times* (3 May 2011).

15. John McNeill, *Something New under the Sun: An Environmental History of the Twentieth Century* (New York: W. W. Norton, 2000).

16. Erica Klarreich, "Population Set to Decline," *Nature*, August 2, 2001. Others are also thinking in positive terms about Japan's shrinking population. See Peter Matanle and Yasuyuki Sato, "Coming Soon to a City Near You! Learning to Live 'Beyond Growth' in Japan's Shrinking Regions," *Social Science Japan Journal* 13:2 (published online April 15, 2010), 187–210, accessed December 9, 2010. Peter Matanle kindly shared with me his unpublished lecture "Towards a Feasible Utopia for Japan—Or Is This How a Country Dies? Reconsidering the Tōhoku Tsunami and Fukushima Nuclear Disaster."

17. See, for instance, David Archer and Stefan Rahmstorf, *The Climate Crisis: An Introductory Guide* (Cambridge: Cambridge University Press, 2010); Naomi Oreskes, "The Scientific Consensus on Climate Change: How Do We Know We're Not Wrong?" in *Climate Change: What It Means for Us, Our Children, and Our Children's Children*," ed. Joseph F. C. Dimento and Pamela Doughman (Cambridge, MA: MIT Press, 2007); and, McKibben, *Eaarth*. With specific reference to population, see William N. Ryerson, "Population: The Multiplier of Everything Else," in Richard Heinberg and Daniel Lerch, *The Post Carbon Reader: Managing the 21st Century's Sustainability Crisis* (Santa Rosa, CA: Watershed Media, 2010).

18. Mark Driscoll, "Destination and Clan-Destination in the Political Philosophy of Tanabe Hajime," in Livia Monnet, ed., *Approches critiques de la pensée japonaise du xxe siècle* (Critical readings in twentieth-century Japanese thought) (Montreal: Les Presses de l'Université de Montréal, 2001), 176.

19. Oka Asajirō, "Jinrui no shōrai" (The future of humankind), *Chūō kōron* 42:11 (1909): 4–33. I discuss Oka in "Naturalizing Nationhood: Ideology and Practice in Early Twentieth-Century Japan," in Sharon A. Minichiello, ed., *Japan's Competing Modernities: Issues in Culture and Democracy, 1900–1930* (Honolulu: University of Hawai'i Press, 1998). See also Greg Sullivan, "Tricks of Transference: Oka Asajirō (1868–1944) on Laissez-faire Capitalism," *Science in Context* 23 (2010).

20. Driscoll, "Destination and Clan-Destination," 163.

21. The term is translated, idiosyncratically, by James Heisig as "the specific." I find this translation unhelpful both in obscuring the resonances of Tanabe's argument with its manifest connection to the Japanese concept of biological "species" and in obscuring the scientific resonances within European nineteenth-century philosophies that are central to Tanabe's argument. James W. Heisig, "Tanabe's Logic of the Specific and Nationalism," in James W. Heisig and John C. Maraldo, eds., *Rude Awakenings: Zen, the Kyoto School, and the Question of Nationalism* (Honolulu: University of Hawai'i Press, 1994).

22. Faisal Devji, "The Language of Muslim Universality," *Diogenes* 57: 2 (May 2010): 36.

23. Chakrabarty, "The Climate of History," 221.

24. Ibid.

25. Ibid., 222.

26. Quoted in Stefan-Ludwig Hoffmann, "Koselleck, Arendt, and the Anthropology of Historical Experience," *History and Theory* 49 (May 2010), 228.

27. Chakrabarty, "The Climate of History," 222.

28. Ibid.

29. R. G. Collingwood, *The Idea of History* (Oxford: Oxford University Press, 1946), 216.

30. Charles Bright and Michael Geyer, "Benchmarks of Globalization: The Global Condition, 1850–2010," in Douglas Northrop, ed., *A Companion to World History* (Chichester, Sussex, UK: Wiley-Blackwell, 2012).

31. Chakrabarty, "The Climate of History," 197.

32. Hayden White, *Metahistory: The Historical Imagination in Nineteenth-Century Europe* (Baltimore: Johns Hopkins University Press, 1973), 6.

33. I. G. Simmons, *Global Environmental History* (Chicago: University of Chicago Press, 2008), 219.

34. Ted C. Fishman, *Shock of Gray*, 145.

35. Bill McKibben, *Enough: Staying Human in an Engineered Age* (New York: Henry Holt, 2003), 116.

36. Fishman, *Shock of Gray*, 149.

37. Yukie Yoshikawa, "Can Japanese Agriculture Overcome Dependence and Decline?" *Asia-Pacific Journal*, 26-3-10 (June 28, 2010). Web site accessed June 29, 2010.

38. "Topical subjects during the year 2008," Japanese Ministry of Agriculture, Forestry, and Fisheries, (MAFF). Web site: http://www.maff.go.jp/e/annual_report/2008/pdf/e_topic.pdf. Accessed 10 July 2010.

39. McKibben, *Eaarth*, 24.

40. Katie Allen, "Food Prices Set to Rise to 40% over Next Decade, UN Report Warns," *Guardian* online, June 15, 2010. Web site accessed June 15, 2010.

41. Yoshikawa, "Can Japanese Agriculture Overcome," 3.

42. Ibid.

43. Sven Lütticken, "Unnatural History," *New Left Review* 45 (May/June 2007), 117.

44. Masanobu Fukuoka, *The One-Straw Revolution: An Introduction to Natural Farming* (New York: New York Review of Books, 1978).

45. One could say the same for other initiatives, such as the growing support for pure preservation, environmental justice, and community building (*machizukuri*) in relation to parks detailed in Thomas Havens, *Parkscapes: Green Spaces in Modern Japan* (Honolulu: University of Hawai'i Press, 2011).

46. See, for instance, my discussion in *Reconfiguring Modernity*, 196–197.

47. See Archer and Rahmstorf, *The Climate Crisis*, especially chapter 10, "Climate Policy."

CONTRIBUTORS

Daniel P. Aldrich is an associate professor of political science at Purdue University who has been a visiting scholar at the University of Tokyo's Law Faculty in Japan, an advanced research fellow at Harvard University's Program on US–Japan Relations, a visiting researcher at Centre Américain, Sciences Po in Paris, France, and a visiting professor at the Tata Institute for Disaster Management in Mumbai, India. Daniel has authored two books (*Site Fights*, 2008; and *Building Resilience*, 2012), along with more than forty peer-reviewed articles, book chapters, reviews, and op-eds. He is a board member of the journals *Asian Politics & Policy* and *Risk, Hazards & Crisis in Public Policy* and a Mansfield CGP fellow.

Jakobina Arch is a PhD candidate in history and East Asian languages at Harvard University. She was originally trained as a biologist, with an MSc in biology studying cetacean behavior.

Andrew Bernstein is an associate professor of history and East Asian studies at Lewis and Clark College, Portland, Oregon. He is the author of *Modern Passings: Death Rites, Politics, and Social Change in Imperial Japan* (2006) and is currently writing a "biography" of Mount Fuji that traces the historical development of the volcano as a site both physical and imagined.

Philip C. Brown, a professor of history at Ohio State University, is a specialist in early modern and modern Japanese history. His most recent book is *Cultivating Commons: Joint Ownership of Arable Land in Early Modern Japan* (2011). He is currently researching changing responses to flood and landslide risk in nineteenth- and twentieth-century Japan. He is the author of numerous articles published in the *Journal of Asian Studies, Social Science History, Journal of Japanese Studies, Monumenta Nipponica,* and other venues.

Timothy S. George is a professor of history at the University of Rhode Island, where he teaches courses on modern Japan, modern China, East Asia, and Southeast Asia. He has also taught courses at Harvard University on modern Japan, East Asian environmental history, and democracy in East Asia. His publications include *Minamata: Pollution and the Struggle for Democracy in Postwar Japan* (2001), and he is cotranslator of Harada Masazumi's *Minamata Disease* (2004) and of Saitō Hisashi's *Niigata Minamata Disease* (2009).

Jeffrey E. Hanes teaches modern Japanese history at the University of Oregon. He is also director of UO's Center for Asian and Pacific Studies and director of its Title VI East Asia National Resource Center. He is a longtime student of Professor Miyamoto Ken'ichi's, and he has translated several of his mentor's seminal essays into English.

David L. Howell is a professor of Japanese history at Harvard University. He is the author of *Geographies of Identity in Nineteenth-Century Japan* (2005) and *Capitalism from Within: Economy, Society, and the State in a Japanese Fishery* (1995), as well as numerous articles on the social and economic history of Tokugawa and Meiji Japan. His current research focuses on social disorder and the fear of foreign invasion in the early nineteenth century.

Federico Marcon is an assistant professor of history at Princeton University.

Christine L. Marran is an associate professor of Japanese literature and cultural studies at the University of Minnesota. The author of various articles on the environment and human-animal relations in Japanese culture, she is currently writing a book on literary authors of environmental pollution while sailing Minnesota's lakes.

Ian Jared Miller teaches modern Japanese history at Harvard University. His first book, *The Nature of the Beasts* (2013), explores the strange nature and peculiar culture of the Tokyo Imperial Zoo at Ueno, East Asia's first zoological garden. It is forthcoming from University of California Press. He is currently writing an environmental history of energy and everyday life in twentieth-century Tokyo.

Ken'ichi Miyamoto is a professor emeritus of Osaka City University and Shiga University. He has published extensively on public finance and environmental economics. Recent books include *On Social Overhead Capital (Shakai shihon ron), Urban Economics (Toshi keizai ron), Environmental Economics (Kankyō keizaigaku)* and, in English, *Asbestos Disaster: Lessons from Japan's Experience* (edited with K. Morinaga and H. Mori).

Micah Muscolino is an associate professor of history at Georgetown University. He is the author of *Fishing Wars and Environmental Change in Late Imperial and Modern China* (2009).

Sara B. Pritchard is an assistant professor in the Department of Science and Technology Studies at Cornell University who specializes in environmental history and the history of technology. She is the author of *Confluence: The Nature of Technology and the Remaking of the Rhône* (2011).

Julia Adeney Thomas writes about nature, politics, historiography, and photography in Japan and comparatively. Her interest in how we grapple with the natural world has led to work on the Korean DMZ, a comparison of Maruyama Masao's ideas with those of Frankfurt School philosophers, a manifesto on the future of environmental history for Munich's Rachel Carson Centre, and her book, *Reconfiguring Modernity: Concepts of Nature in Japanese Political Ideology,* which received the 2002 John K. Fairbank Prize in East Asian History from the American Historical Association. Trained at Princeton,

Oxford, and Chicago, she has taught at the University of Illinois–Chicago and the University of Wisconsin–Madison, and she currently teaches at the University of Notre Dame, where she is an associate professor of history.

Karen Thornber is a professor of comparative literature and a professor of East Asian languages and civilizations at Harvard University. She is the author of *Empire of Texts in Motion: Chinese, Korean, and Taiwanese Transculturations of Japanese Literature* (2009), which won both the John Whitney Hall Book Prize of the Association for Asian Studies for the best English-language book on any contemporary or historical topic related to Japan in any field of the humanities or social sciences, and the Anna Balakian Prize from the International Comparative Literature Association for the best book in the world in the field of comparative literature published in the last three years by a scholar under age forty. Karen also is author of *Ecoambiguity: Environmental Crises and East Asian Literatures* (2012), the first book in any language on East Asian literatures and environmental degradation. Her two current book projects, for which she is now studying Hindi and Urdu, are *Translating Global Health and World Literatures* and *Cultures of Empire and In(ter)dependence.*

William M. Tsutsui is a professor of history and dean of Dedman College of Humanities and Sciences at Southern Methodist University. A specialist in the business, environmental, and cultural history of twentieth-century Japan, he holds degrees from Harvard, Oxford, and Princeton Universities. He is the author or editor of eight books, including *Manufacturing Ideology: Scientific Management in Twentieth-Century Japan* (1998) and *Godzilla on My Mind: Fifty Years of the King of Monsters* (2004). He received the 2000 John Whitney Hall Prize of the Association for Asian Studies and the 2005 William Rockhill Nelson Award for Literary Excellence.

Brett L. Walker is Regents Professor at Montana State University, Bozeman. He is author of *The Conquest of Ainu Lands: Ecology and Culture in Japanese Expansion, 1590–1800* (2001), *The Lost Wolves of Japan* (2005), and *Toxic Archipelago: A History of Industrial Disease in Japan* (2010), which earned the George Perkins Marsh Prize from the American Society of Environmental History.

Takehiro Watanabe is an assistant professor of anthropology at Sophia University in Tokyo. He is completing an ethnography of the environmental and economic legacies left by the Besshi Mine in southern Japan. He has also conducted research on resource extraction in the Andes mountain range and the Amazon rain forest.

INDEX

climate change, global, 246, 294–295, 297–298

Collingwood, R. G., 300–301

commodification of nature, 201–203

"constructionist state," 90

copper poisoning cases. *See* sulfur dioxide pollution cases (Sumitomo)

Cove, The (documentary; Psihoyos), 1, 7–14, 181

crabbing, 24, 30

crested ibis, Japanese (*toki*), 196, *197*

crisis, negation, and failure, 298–301

Cronon, William, 13, 16n8

Crutzen, Paul J., 3–4, 5–6, 296

Dengen Sanpō (Three Power Source Development Laws), 283–284, 290

Derrida, Jacques, 183–184

Devji, Faisal, 299

Diaoyu (Senkaku) Islands, 33

Dokdo (Takeshima), 33, 178, 179

dolphins, 7–14, 181

Driscoll, Mark, 298, 299

earthquakes, ix–x, 108, 255, 285

Echigo Plain. *See* riparian engineering on the Echigo Plain

eco-cosmopolitanism, 210, 211, 214

economic development vs. environmental preservation, 231

eco-system accidents, 257–258, 259

Edwards, Paul, 271n4, 272n5, 276n31

Ehime Prefecture. *See* sulfur dioxide pollution cases (Sumitomo)

"Elephant Vanishes, The" (Murakami), 181–184

Ellis, Richard, 45

Endō Tetsuya, 11

endogenous development, 248–249

engineering, civil. *See* riparian engineering on the Echigo Plain

enlightenment, geographical, 158

environmental consciousness, 177–178

environmental history: border crossings and, 117; both nature and culture in, 16n8; chronicle vs. praxis and, 302–303; global awareness and, 293–296; human-nature divide and, 154; new materialism of, 294–295; species concept (*shu*) and, 297–301; terrestrial bias in, 21

envirotechnical systems and regimes, 259–260, 269–270, 276n29

erosion and deposition processes, 91–94, *92, 93*

European Union Sustainable Cities and Towns Campaign, 247

extinct species, 196, *197*

fertilizer. *See* shit (night soil)

fisheries, 23–26, 35n15, 57–67, 62

Fishman, Ted C., 303, 304

flood control. *See* riparian engineering on the Echigo Plain

foreign-born residents, 178–179

Foucault, Michel, 202

frontier transformations, 115

Fuji: anthropomorphic images of, 163–164, 172n55; naturalized vs. institutionalized images of, *156*, 156–158, *157*; winter blankness of, 152, 170n4; worship of, 154

Fuji annai (Nonaka Itaru), 168

Fuji meteorology and bodyscape: bodyscape concept, 152–155; Chiyoko's role, 161–163; Fuji mandalas and, 156–158, *157*; human body, toll on, 153, 163–164; Itaru's exploratory climbs and meteorological practice, 159–161; Meiji emperor and, 154–155; published accounts, 165–169; report to Meteorological Association, 164–165; rescue mission and medical report, 164–165; storytelling and, 169; *Taiyō* portrait and yin-yang iconography, 155–158, *156*, 162; visitors from Gunji Shigetada expedition, 163, 164

Fukuoka Prefecture, 230

Fukushima nuclear disaster: description of, ix, 255, 285–286; envirotechnical interpretation of, 260–265; envirotechnical regimes and, 269–270; in literature, 217–218; normal accidents, technological systems, and envirotechnical systems, 256–260; power and politics and, 265–269; public opinion, policy, and, 286–290

Law of the Sea Convention, 34
Lefebvre, Henri, 50n6
Leopold, Aldo, 220n19
Liebig, Justus von, 142
Lindo, Isaac A., 102–103, 105
Linnaeus, Carl, 199, 202
Lippit, Akira Mizuta, 183
Lucky Dragon incident, 281

Mackenthun, Gesa, 23
Mahan, Alfred, 22, 26
Makabe Jin, 216
Mancke, Elizabeth, 35n6
Man'yōshū (Collection of ten thousand
    leaves), 208–209
Marx, Karl, 189
materialism, new, 294–295
Matsudaira Norisato, 192
Matsugasaki Diversion Channel, 100
Matsuo Taseko, 172n43
McEvoy, Arthur, 55n62, 260
McKibben, Bill, 4, 131, 295, 303–304
McNeill, J. R., 21, 115
meibutsu ("names of things"), 201, 204n12
Meiji emperor and nationalized bodyscape,
    154–155
Meiji modernization, 6, 40–43, 56, 74–76,
    121–123, 171n26
Melville, Herman, 1, 3, 14
merchant marine, Japanese, 27
mercury. *See* Minamata disease
mesothelioma, 243
Meteorological Association (Kishō Gakkai),
    162, 164–165
meteorology. *See* Fuji meteorology and
    bodyscape
"Midori ga shitatari" (Nakaoka), 217
"Midori osanaku" (Makabe), 216
Mill, John Stuart, 189
Minamata disease, 10–11, 116, 211–213,
    225–226, 235, 266
Minamoto Toritomo, 118
Minamoto Toshitsune, 118
Ministry of Agriculture and Commerce, 79,
    82–83
Ministry of Agriculture, Forestry, and
    Fisheries (MAFF), 304–305

Minobe Ryōkichi, 233
Mitsui Mining and Smelting, 226
Miura Moriharu, 164–165
Miyazaki Hayao, 180
Miyazaki Shinpei, 180
Miyazaki Yasusada, 137–138
Moby Dick (Melville), 1, 3, 14
modes of production, changing, 115
Moeran, Brian, 43, 45
Monju fire (1995), 285
mori (forest realm), 200–201
Morinaga Milk, 131n6
Morita San'ya, 116, 119–121
Mount Fuji. *See* Fuji meteorology and
    bodyscape
Murakami Haruki, 182–184, 217–218
Murata Tamotsu, 28–29
Musolino, Micah, 26
Mutō Kinkichi, 73, 80

Nagatsu Kōzaburō, 209–210, 213–218
Nakaoka Jun'ichi, 217, 221n36
Nakasone Yasuhiro, 281
Nash, Linda, 12, 125, 154
national interest (*kokueki*), 46, 53n43
National Parliament on Pollution, 233
natural history. *See honzōgaku* surveys
    under Tokugawa Yoshimune
nature: division of people and, 6–7, 154;
    lack of Japanese concept of, before
    nineteenth century, 204n12;
    secularization of, 200–201;
    specimens as species and
    commodification of, 201–203;
    yama and *mori* (mountains and
    forest) as separate realm, 200–201
negotiations, 74, 75, 81–85
neo-Confucianism, 191, 205n34, 306
neoliberalism, 243
night soil. *See* shit (night soil)
Niigata City. *See* riparian engineering
    on the Echigo Plain
Niigata earthquake (1964), 108
Niigata Prefecture, 226
Niihama Refinery pollution case, 73,
    76–78, 224
nitrogen dioxide, 227, 235, *237*, 237–238

Nitta Jirō, 163, 168–169

Niwa Shōhaku, 190–199, 204n9

Noda Yoshihiko, 287, 290

Nōgyō zensho (The agricultural compendium) (Miyazaki), 137–138

Nonaka Chiyoko: death of, 168; "Fuyō nikki" (diary), 153, 155, 165–166, 169; Meteorological Association and, 162; in portraits, 155–158, *156*, 166–168, *167;* role in expedition, 161–163; on weak woman's body, 152, 161, 162. *See also* Fuji meteorology and bodyscape

Nonaka Itaru. *See* Fuji meteorology and bodyscape

Normal Accidents (Perrow), 256–260, 273n14

Norō Genjō, 190, 199

nuclear technology: *Atomic Bomb Poetry* (Nagatsu et al.), 209–210, 213–218; Chernobyl disaster, 217, 261; Hiroshima and Nagasaki, 213–217, 281; *Lucky Dragon* incident, 281; Monju fire, 285; nuclear "allergy" and top-down policy, 280–284; public opinion and bottom-up activism, 286–290; Three Mile Island, 256. *See also* Fukushima nuclear disaster

O'Barry, Richard, 7, 9, 11, 12

oceanography, 27–28

oceans and empire. *See* pelagic imperialism, Japanese

Ochiai Naobumi, 166–168, 173n75

Office for Japanese Pharmacology, 192–193

Okada Yutaka, 79

Okōtsu Diversion Channel, 100–107

Okubo Toshimichi, 102–104

Okunoshima ("Poison Gas Island"), 129

Ōkura Nagatsune, 141, 147

Onomichi Talks (1909), 81

Oriental Whaling Ltd. (Tōyō Hogei KK), 49

orientalism, environmental, 6–7, 8, 90, 110

Osaka, 114n48, 145, 146, 224–225, *227*, 227–228, 230, 247

Osaka Alkali, 223–224

Osaka Office of Mines, 77, 79

Ōura Kanetake, 78, 81

Pana Wave, 178, 180

pelagic imperialism, Japanese: decline after Pearl Harbor, 31–32; fisheries development and expansion, 23–26; legacies of, 32–34; merchant shipping and undersea cables and, 27; national rivalries and power on the seas, 26–27; ocean as socially constructed space, 32; oceanography and, 27–28; rhetoric and literature of imperialism, 28–31; terrestrial bias and, 21–23

Perrow, Charles, 256–260, 262, 267, 273n14, 274n18, 276n29

Perry, Matthew C., 1–5, 8, 13–14, 15n1, 90, 100

poetry and literature: *Atomic Bomb Poetry* (Nagatsu et al.), 209–210, 213–218; Fuji expedition and, 162, 166; Japanese "love of nature" and, 208; *Man'yōshū* (Collection of ten thousand leaves), 208–209; role of, 207–208, 218; *Sea of Suffering* (Ishimure), 209–210, 211–213

policy, environmental: Asian endogenous development and, 248–249; budgeting, investment, and improvement of control measures, 235–238; citizens' movements, 231–233; court cases and pollution relief, 234–235; growth and pollution after World War II, 225–231; historical and theoretical lessons from, 238–241; local reform-minded policies, 233–234; neoliberalism and, 243; nuclear policy, 281–284, 287–290; pollution problems before World War II, 222–225; problems remaining, 243–246; social characteristics and, 241–243; sustainable society and, 246–249; whole picture of environmental problems, 241, *241*

pollution diseases, recognized, 116–117

Pollution Investigation Association of Shūsō County, 78

Pollution-Related Health Damage Compensation Law (1973), 235, 242, 244

Pomeranz, Kenneth, 293, 294

population changes, human, 225–231, 303–304

species (*shu*), 201–203, 297–301
Steinberg, Philip, 32, 57
Stoermer, Eugene F., 296
subsidence, 108–109, 228, *229*
suburbanization, 228–229
sulfur dioxide, 223–224, 227, 231, 235, 237, *237*
sulfur dioxide pollution cases (Sumitomo): Air Pollution Compensation Talks (1910–1939), 74, 81–85; antipollution measures and, 224; Ashio Mine, campaign against, 74; background, 73–76; as natural-resources conflicts, 85; Niihama Refinery incident and scientific skepticism, 73, 76–78; Shisakajima Refinery incident and science as political capital, 73, 78–81; social meaning of sulfur dioxide, 75–76
Sumitomo, 129–130. *See also* sulfur dioxide pollution cases (Sumitomo)
Sun Yat-sen, 65
surveys of species. See *honzōgaku* surveys under Tokugawa Yoshimune
sustainability, 246–249, 302–306
Suzuki Hisao, 209
systems, 256–260, 269, 273n16, 276n29, 276n31

"Taiheiyō kōshinkyoku" (The Pacific March) (Fuse), 28
Taiji dolphin fishery, 8–14
Taiji Gorōsaku, 45–46, 53n32
Taiji whaling disaster (1878), 39, 47. *See also* whaling
Taisho Democracy, Era of, 225
Taiyō, 155–158, *156,* 165
Takahashi Yoshitaka, 62
Takane no yuki (Ochiai), 166–168, *167*
Takeshima (Dokdo), 33, 178, 179
"Tamachan" (bearded seal), 175–181, 301
Tanabe Hajime, 297, 298–301
Tanaka Shōzō, 73, 124
technological systems, 257–260, 273n16, 276n31
telegraph cables, undersea, 27
3/11. *See* Fukushima nuclear disaster
Three Lagoons (Sangata), 99
time, 5–6, 154–155, 160, 204n17, 296

Timpanaro, Sebastiano, 294
Tōhoku earthquake and tsunami, ix–x, 111, 217–218, 255, 285
"Toita no hito wa" (Yamashita), 215–216
Tokugawa Yoshimune, 190, 191–193, 198–201, 203
Tokyo, 146, 175–181, 230
Tokyo Electric Power Company. *See* Fukushima nuclear disaster
Tokyo Fisheries Institute (Suisan kōshūjo), 58, 62
Tokyo Metropolitan Environmental Pollution Control Ordinance, 233
Toroku arsenic mine: arsenopyrite processing, 125–126; border crossings and, 115–117; discovery and opening as silver mine, 115–116; early human history in Toroku, 117–118; effects on crops, 124–125; effects on workers, 126–129; frontier transformations, changing modes of production, and, 115; lawsuit, 130; Meiji agricultural modernizations, 121–123; Morita San'ya and, 116, 119–121; Satō Dōgen legend, 118–119; suspensions and closure of, 129; Wagōkai cooperative, 123–125, 130; worker photographs, *127, 128*
Toroku furnace song, 116, 120
Totman, Conrad, 16n14, 205n36
tragedy of the commons, 51n21
True Pure Land Sect of Buddhism (Jōdo Shinshū), 123
tsunami (2011), ix–x, 111, 255, 260, 263, 280, 285
Tsuruno Kumi, 115, 126–130, *129*
Tsuruno Masaichi, 115, 126–130

Uemura Saheiji, 190, 199
umi no hi (Marine Day), 37n46
umi no kinenbi (Marine Memorial Day), 29–30
urine, 141, 144–145, 147–148

Vaughan, Tyson, 266

Wada Yorimoto, 47
Wada Yoroku, 47

Wada Yūji, 159, 162, 164, 165–166, 173n76, 173n78
Wagōkai cooperative, 123–125, 130
Walker, Brett L., 10, 53n29, 266, 295
Walthall, Anne, 172n43
Wang Wentai, 61–65
"Wealthy Country/Strong Military" (fukoku-kyōhei) policy, 223
Weber, Max, 205n37
whale products, 2, 42
whale shows, 8–9
whaling: coastal vs. offshore, 41–42; corporate shift in, 48–50; cow-calf pairs and, 45–46; economic pressures and foreign techniques, 46–48; expansion of, 25; Meiji modernization vs. Western technology and, 40–43; Perry and, 1–2, 3; right, gray, and humpback populations, 43–45, 52n22, 52n24; Taiji disaster (1878), 39, 47; "traditional" Japanese culture and, 9, 14; use of all parts, 42; Wada and Taiji whaling groups, 47–48, 54n48; Western industry, 41
White, Hayden, 15n8, 302–303
White, Richard, 55n62, 63, 117
Wigen, Kären, 34n5, 35n6, 158

wolf, Japanese (ōkami), 196, 197
women's bodies, "weakness" of, 152, 161, 162, 172n43
World Environmental Organization (WEO), 247
Worster, Donald, 115

yama (mountain realm), 200–201
yamabushi mountain priests, 120
Yamamoto Toshio, 209
Yamashita Shizuo, 215–216
Yamashita Shōto, 45–46
Yanagita Kunio, 29, 205n31
Yasuda Ken, 194–195, 198
yellow croaker fishery, 26, 31, 65
Yi Mija, 216
yin-yang iconography, 156–158, 157, 162, 172n41
Yokkaichi industrial complex, 226–227, 232, 234
Yokohama, 146, 175–181
Yokota dike failure, 104, 104–105
Yonemoto, Marcia, 41
Yoshikawa, Yukie, 304–305

Zhang Jian, 59–60